THE URBAN SOUTH
AND THE COMING OF THE
CIVIL WAR

The

URBAN SOUTH

and the COMING of the

CIVIL WAR

FRANK TOWERS

University of Virginia Press
Charlottesville and London

University of Virginia Press
© 2004 by the Rector and Visitors of the University of Virginia
All rights reserved
Printed in the United States of America on acid-free paper
First published 2004

1 3 5 7 9 8 6 4 2

Library of Congress Cataloging-in-Publication Data

Towers, Frank.
   The urban South and the coming of the Civil War / Frank Towers.
      p.   cm.
   Includes bibliographical references and index.
   ISBN 0-8139-2297-6 (cloth : alk. paper)
      1. Southern States—Politics and government—1775–1865.   2. Secession—
Southern States.   3. Southern States—Social conditions—19th century.
4. City and town life—Southern States—History—19th century.   5. Working
class—Southern States—Political activity—History—19th century.
6. Southern States—Race relations—Political aspects.   7. Baltimore (Md.)—
Politics and government—19th century.   8. Saint Louis (Mo.)—Politics and
government—19th century.   9. New Orleans (La.)—Politics and government—
19th century.   10. United States—History—Civil War, 1861–1865—Causes.
I. Title.
   F213.T68   2004
   973.7'13—dc22   2004009576

FOR TOM TOWERS

Contents

Acknowledgments

The initial ideas behind *The Urban South and the Coming of the Civil War* originated a long time ago. I became interested in the American South because, having grown up in Rhode Island in the 1970s and 1980s, the South seemed like the region whose history differed the most from the modern America that I knew. In looking to the South for the past's "other America," its cities stood out as anomalies inside of an anomaly. Cities nurtured the patterns of work, culture, and politics upon which modern American society was built. However, Southern cities developed these ways of life in a region that not only dedicated itself to slavery, but also went to war in 1861 against the modernizing North. This book explores the puzzle of slave-state cities and their significance for the coming of the Civil War.

My interest in this topic and in history in general would have gone undeveloped had it not been for my teachers. The most influential have been Joyce Appleby, who taught me in my first graduate seminar, and Michael P. Johnson, my doctoral adviser. Joyce Appleby convinced me to stay in graduate school. Mike Johnson persuaded me to study Baltimore. Beyond having made these fundamental contributions, Professors Appleby and Johnson have my deep gratitude for sticking by me during the long process of getting this book in print. They are examples of the kind of historian I aspire to be.

In producing this book, I have incurred innumerable debts. Although I cannot thank every individual who helped me, I would like to acknowledge some of those who made this book much better than it would otherwise be.

Thanks to the staffs of the Maryland Historical Society; Maryland State Archives; Baltimore's Jewish Historical Society; the National Archives in Washington, D.C.; the Southern Historical Collection at the University of North Carolina, Chapel Hill; the Missouri Historical Society in St. Louis; the Hill Memorial Library at Louisiana State University; the New Orleans Public Library; and the Hagley Museum and

Library, Wilmington, Delaware. Becky Gunby at the Baltimore City Archives (BCA) deserves special thanks for making the BCA's valuable records accessible and for making research at the BCA so enjoyable.

I received research funds from the Pennsylvania State System of Higher Education, Faculty Professional Development Fund; the College of Arts and Sciences, Clarion University of Pennsylvania; the Faculty of Economics, Administrative, and Social Sciences at Bilkent University in Ankara, Turkey; and Colorado State University's Career Enhancement fund.

The structure and argument of the book as well as the quality of my writing improved greatly because of feedback from colleagues who read the manuscript in its many draft stages. My thanks go to Tyler Anbinder, Eric Arnesen, Eugene Berwanger, Robert J. Brugger, Russell Johnson, John Quist, T. Stephen Whitman, and the anonymous readers at the University of Virginia Press. In the final stage of manuscript preparation, Tom Towers gave valuable advice on writing style. The most important critic in this process has been Jewel Spangler, who read, and has had read out loud to her, more of this manuscript than anyone else. Her patience and insight have vastly improved this book.

Dick Holway at the University of Virginia Press saw this project through its long road to completion. Piril Atabay logged Baltimore's secession voters into a database. John M. Sacher guided me to sources for the politics of New Orleans and, in an act of incredible generosity, gave me his photocopied notes on Louisiana Know-Nothings. Kevin Murphy, Maribel Dietz, Jordan Kellman, Arthur Towers, and Anna Ginsberg made research money go farther by providing room and board when I traveled to archives. George Towers created the map. Michael G. Lacy gave invaluable assistance with table 5. He and James Huston strengthened the quantitative analysis of this book. Pat May, Seth Rockman, and T. Stephen Whitman helped me find and better understand sources for Baltimore history.

I would also like to thank colleagues not mentioned above whose friendship has made history an enjoyable pursuit. They are Bill Billingsley, Brian Dunn, Slobodan Ilic, Elizabeth Bright Jones, Jim Lindsay, Lana McClune, Scott Moore, John Rosa, Thaddeus Sunseri, and Billy Turbitt. The same sentiment holds for my colleagues in the history departments of Clarion University, Bilkent University, and Colorado State University. Although Aksin Somel had nothing to do with the book, I really appreciated working for two years with him. He is another great example of what a historian should be.

ACKNOWLEDGMENTS

The book is dedicated to my father, Tom Towers. He got me started thinking about history, academics, and a lot of other stuff. My brothers, George and Art, have also been great supporters. All four of us honor the memory of Patricia Henkes Towers. The best parts of this effort reflect her influence. The example set by Eleanor Koether has also guided me. Finally, I express gratitude for Jewel Spangler, my wife. As joyous as that phrase sounds to me, I still can't believe it's true. We are together, the book is done, and life is a whole lot better.

Portions of chapter 5 appeared as "Secession in an Urban Context: Municipal Reform and the Coming of the Civil War in Baltimore," in *From Mobtown to Charm City: New Perspectives on Baltimore's Past,* edited by Jessica I. Elfenbein, John R. Breihan, and Thomas L. Hollowak (Baltimore: Maryland Historical Society Press, 2002).

THE URBAN SOUTH
AND THE COMING OF THE
CIVIL WAR

Introduction

This book examines the interaction between urbanization and the sectional politics of the 1850s in the slave South. More specifically, it analyzes the growing power of working-class voters in slave-state cities, particularly the three largest, Baltimore, St. Louis, and New Orleans, and its consequences for Southern secession.

At the outset it should be made clear what this study does and does not say about the causes of the Civil War. It does not contend that the politics of Baltimore, St. Louis, and New Orleans caused the South to secede from the Union and thereby brought on the Civil War. Sectional differences related to slavery caused the war, and Southern whites who supported secession were primarily concerned with the threat that Northern abolitionist and free-soil advocates posed to slavery.

While this study does not advance a global reinterpretation of the causes of the Civil War, it does argue that Baltimore, New Orleans, and St. Louis influenced the course of Southern secession in two important ways. These cities constituted obstacles to Southern white unity and served as examples that secessionists cited to show the corruption of contemporary politics. That white workers in Baltimore, St. Louis, and New Orleans used politics to advance ideas and issues unique to their condition as free laborers in a slave society comprises one of the two main arguments of this book. The second thesis is that politics in the largest cities of the South provided a focal point for secessionists to articulate their concerns about the tension between the democratic principle of majority rule and the hierarchical society that racial slavery supported.

These two contributions to the coming of the Civil War resulted from the ways that demographic and economic growth affected politics in the largest cities of the South. By the 1850s, Baltimore, St. Louis, and New Orleans had tens of thousands of wage earners, and in each city the majority of white men worked for wages. White wage labor was not a new phenomenon in Southern society, but the concentration in one

1

Relative sizes of the South's ten largest cities in 1860. The sizes of the symbols are proportional to city populations; the key shows sample populations and their corresponding symbols. (Source for city populations: Joseph C. G. Kennedy, *Population of the United States in 1860* [Washington, 1864]. Map by George Towers.)

place of thousands of white wage earners who lacked property yet possessed the vote was new. Inside the South's largest cities, white workingmen developed a slave-state variant of the free-labor politics that the Republican Party used to gain prominence in the North. Like workingmen in the free states, wage earners in Southern cities struggled with what one historian describes as the "uneasy tension" between competing definitions of free labor, "one that characterized the laborer as small producer and the other that cast him as freely contracting wage earner."[1] Pressured by economic changes that had undermined their living standards, skilled labor simultaneously pursued strategies that would shore up their status as independent household heads, the social condition of the small producer, and adjusted to the reality that they would work for wages for most of their lives.

Because they represented the largest ethnic/occupational bloc in the urban electorate, native white mechanics were able to push municipal government to legislate in their interests. In the 1850s, politicians won the votes of American-born white labor by expanding employment on public works, hiring working-class partisans into party and government bureaucracies, tacitly supporting strikes, and facilitating efforts to push African Americans and immigrants out of trades that white natives coveted.

This Southern brand of free-labor politics had a complicated relationship to the politics of slavery. Neither Southern city politicians nor the workers who voted for them opposed slavery. In fact, white workers in Southern cities not only supported slavery, they also tried to curtail the few privileges that free blacks enjoyed. However, the urban political agenda did give priority to the interests of manual wage earners and therefore contradicted the prevailing views of white Southerners who "had condemned free labor as a disguised form of the general servitude of work."[2]

This rebuke to attitudes that associated manual labor with social degradation was one of several ways that working-class politics in the largest Southern cities challenged the state and regional power of rural planters. The new labor-friendly urban administrations troubled the planters who dominated state legislatures because white workingmen pursued actions like strikes and legislation to shorten the workday that questioned the rights of property owners. Worse yet from the perspective of enthusiasts for states' rights, urban workers sought to strengthen city municipal government—the entity that helped with strikes, patronage, and public works—and ally it with the federal government in order to counterbalance the influence of hostile Southern state legislatures. In 1861, working-class supporters of the late-antebellum administrations of Baltimore and St. Louis played vital roles in keeping their respective states in the Union, and in New Orleans the same group demonstrated for the Union in 1861 and then flocked to the federal banner when the Confederacy lost the city in 1862.

In addition to showing how white workers in the largest Southern cities used elections and government to enhance the power of free laborers in a slave society, examining the connections between urbanization and secession brings out new dimensions of the movement for Southern independence. Fire-eaters, a term for supporters of the South's secession, saw both a practical threat and an ideological principle at stake in the politics of Baltimore, St. Louis, and New Orleans, and their concerns about these cities helped to shape the arguments made for disunion. By the late 1850s, the Democratic Party, which had become increasingly sympathetic to the interests of slaveholders and had won the majority of elections in the South, dominated the state legislatures of Maryland, Missouri, and Louisiana, yet an opposition party governed the largest city in each of these states. Should, as many fire-eaters correctly predicted, the Republican Party, with its opposition to the expansion of slavery, win the presidency in 1860, these big cities, places with thousands of voters and thousands of potential soldiers, offered perfect bridgeheads for Republicans seeking to spread their power into the slave states. In the late 1850s, Southern nationalists in the Democratic Party tried mightily to put men friendly to their interests in control of big-city governments. Failing that, Democrats sought to turn over to state legislatures as many powers of municipal government as they could.

Beyond the practical problem of harboring their political enemies, big cities posed a philosophical problem for Southern nationalists who sought to insure the safety of slavery without abandoning America's democratic-republican political tradition. Since the Revolution, conservative friends of American independence had worried that democracy's principle of majority rule could result in majority tyranny because the poor would use the franchise to punish privileged minorities. Over the course of the nineteenth century, population growth and the democratization of state and local government increased the power of ordinary voters, few of whom owned slaves. While planters in the rural South had succeeded in articulating their common interests with non-slaveholding white voters and thereby prevented significant political opposition to their leadership, they had less in common and less to say to the propertyless white men in Southern cities who lacked the ties to agriculture and to patriarchal household relationships that outweighed class differences among whites in the countryside. Secessionists worried that slavery, something they regarded as the cornerstone of Southern society, could not survive in a republic subject to the kind of turbulent working-class politics that opened cities to the horrors of mob rule.

In sum, the South's urban route to the Civil War, a story that has been neglected in the vast body of scholarship on the sectional crisis, produced a struggle between social groups (urban workers versus rural planters allied to urban businessmen) and models for democracy (a free-labor vision of government and parties as agents for positive social change versus a proslaveholder, elitist model in which government defended established social relationships without input from the turbulent masses and their political parties). This clash of groups and ambitions was one of several divisions internal to Southern society that hastened the onset of the Civil War.

Since the colonial era, rural Americans had attached their fear that big cities threatened the well-being of state and society to other political and social conflicts raging around them. However, prior to the middle decades of the nineteenth century, such worries poorly fit the reality that few Americans lived in cities and that America's handful of urban places were so small as to hardly warrant being designated as cities.

In 1690, Boston claimed top rank among cities in British North America with a mere six thousand inhabitants. Two years later, in his campaign against witchcraft in nearby Salem, the Reverend Samuel Parris attacked those who "prefer farms and merchandise above [God] and his ordinances," and he praised Jesus for having been born in the "poor, mean, and contemptible village" of Bethlehem, rather than the "famous, opulent, or wealthy city" of Jerusalem.[3] At the close of the American Revolution, the largest city in the new nation, Philadelphia, housed twenty-five thousand people, and in 1790, only 3 percent of Americans lived in towns of more than eight thousand. Although the city remained an abstraction for most Americans, they continued to view it as a real danger. Thomas Jefferson's well-known tribute to American farmers as "the chosen people of God" included his equally famous warning that "the mobs of great cities add just so much to the support of pure government as sores do to the strength of the human body." Such concerns also found expression in mass politics. In 1794, western Pennsylvania farmers, rebelling against federal tax policies, threatened to raze Pittsburgh, a village of 376 people, which they called a latter-day "Sodom" that "should be burned."[4]

Drawing on this inheritance of anti-urbanism, nineteenth-century Americans frequently attacked the city as a contributor to whatever problem they faced. In the 1850s, as the nation struggled over slavery's future, Americans added criticism of cities onto their concerns about a political system that could not resolve the sectional crisis. The loudest complaints about cities came from Southerners who supported slavery's expansion. They argued that big cities harbored disorderly groups, most notably politically enfranchised wage workers, who had twisted American democracy to advance their selfish interests and in doing so threatened institutions cherished by Southerners, not only slavery but also the patriarchal family and the culture of honor that organized rural life.

These fears were well warranted. Unlike earlier eras when the small size of cities belied their danger to the rural majority, in the late-antebellum decades worries about the big city reflected a real change in urban life that had consequences for all Americans. Between 1830 and 1860, the urban population increased faster (between 62% and 92% per decade) than at any other time in the nation's history. In 1840 only New York and Philadelphia had more than 150,000 people. By 1860 America possessed eight such cities, and they existed in every region, including the stereotypically rural South.[5]

The threshold of about 150,000 residents signified a city large enough to foster new forms of social life that smaller, more homogeneous settlement had discouraged in America. New York City was the first to cross this line, late in the 1820s, and when it did, urban life changed dramatically. In politics, power at the ward level passed from the mercantile elite and into the hands of ordinary men who were supported by the burgeoning wage-earning electorate. Economically, New York stood at the "center of a manufacturing complex that reached as far south as Delaware." The city's new industrial economy replaced the traditional skills and face-to-face authority relationships of the craft workshop with a more impersonal, wage-driven system that emphasized speed and quantity and created jobs for thousands escaping impoverished farms in America and Europe. As members of crowds that gathered in a variety of public settings and as readers of a profusion of printed material in forms ranging in complexity from newspapers to street signs, New Yorkers related to one another as comparative strangers rather than as familiar neighbors living in a fixed community. This new urban sense of self put greater emphasis on autonomy and created new problems for those interested in maintaining public order.[6]

While some celebrated these possibilities, others thought that overgrown New York undermined the foundations of republican government because its people had done away with traditional systems of authority and association. "I look upon the size of certain American cities, and especially on the nature of their population," Alexis de Tocqueville said in reaction to riots in 1830s New York and Philadelphia, "as a real danger which threatens the future security of the democratic republics of the New World." At that moment, mob violence was the most alarming example of how large cities gave the turbulent masses what Tocqueville considered to be too much power.[7]

Tocqueville's concerns would echo across America in the 1850s as big cities spread beyond the mid-Atlantic. However, historians' focus on conflict over slavery's expansion has led scholars to neglect how late-antebellum urbanization interacted with the coming of the Civil War. This study examines this lesser-known urban crisis and considers its implications for the better-known sectional one as both played out in the slave South, the most unlikely region to have hosted big cities and their fractious politics.

In Baltimore, St. Louis, and New Orleans—all of which had more than 150,000 people in 1860—the increase in size of the white working class gave propertyless white men unattached to agriculture a degree of political power unprecedented in Southern history. When white workers used that power to promote new parties that defied the regional authority of proslavery Democrats, they put the South's largest cities on a collision course with their section's political leaders. During the early 1850s, wage-earning voters persuaded city government to support strikes, job-creating public works, and prohibitions on foreign competition with American labor. In the second half of the decade, workingmen consolidated this newfound power by supporting new parties that not only took issue with the interests of local businessmen but also challenged anti-urban planters who dominated their respective state governments.

This working-class activism alarmed planter-politicians who were contemplating Southern secession as a means to protect slavery from the North's electoral majority. In the big cities, the battle between friends and enemies of workingmen's politics engendered a debate over how much power the majority should wield and, in light of the changing electorate, how much power city government should have. Southern nationalists joined municipal foes of the new opposition parties in arguing that big-city politics had succumbed to mob rule. Secessionists cited events in Baltimore, St. Louis, and New Orleans to give immediacy to their case that excessive and irresponsible political partisanship had corrupted American democracy. Not only had demagogues manipulated party politics so as to turn Northern voters against the South, secessionists argued, but mayors and congressmen representing slave-state big cities were doing the same thing. Fire-eaters treated Baltimore, St. Louis, and New Orleans as outriders of an impending majoritarian attack on Southern society.

Slave-state big cities shaped the coming of the Civil War by creating a distinctive brand of Southern free-labor dissent from the planter-influenced politics that dominated the region and by stirring secessionists to articulate their cause as a struggle against mob rule. To advance these two arguments about urbanization and secession, attention is focused primarily on Baltimore, Maryland, the South's largest city in 1860 and the site of a controversial struggle waged by white workers and allied city dwellers against the regional dominance of slaveholding planters. Events in Baltimore are framed in the context of Southern history and sectionalism, and Baltimore is compared to other urban centers in the slave states.

Of all the cities in the slave states, Baltimore was both the biggest problem for slaveholders and the most visible example of trends that were under way in other metropolitan centers. In 1860, Baltimore held the top rank in several demographic categories. It had the most people (212,000) of any Southern city and the third most of any in the nation. More African Americans (27,898) lived in Baltimore than in any other American city, and Baltimore was home to the nation's largest free black community. Of all Southern cities, Baltimore had the most native-born whites and the largest number of eligible voters. Economically, it was the South's most significant industrial producer. Not only Baltimore's overall size but also the fact that it had the most enfranchised industrial white workers and the most nonenslaved African Americans make it an important site for understanding the politics of the South as it headed toward disunion.

Moreover, Baltimore exemplified trends common to the urban South. Immigrants and free blacks went to Baltimore just as they did to other Southern urban centers. Factories and mass production pressured Baltimore craft workers in the same manner that they squeezed artisan budgets in Richmond, St. Louis, and even the fire-eaters' hometown of Charleston. Baltimore's ruling American Party, also called Know-Nothings because the party emerged out of secret societies that required members to profess ignorance about the organization when asked, earned notoriety for its election riots and pursuit of the spoils of office, but it was not atypical. The American Party won office across the urban South amid similar charges of violence and corruption. An April 1861 riot between Baltimore Southern sympathizers, on one side, and federal troops and local Unionists, on the other, produced the first blood of the Civil War. That day was the most violent in a sporadic series of battles between Southerners in 1861 and 1862. Urbanites in St. Louis and New Orleans as well as farmers in Appalachia and the Missouri backcountry experienced their own versions of this partisan fighting.

In the 1850s, Baltimoreans were unaware that they lived in a state that would not join the Confederacy and that would thereafter be written out of Southern history. They saw themselves as Southerners, and residents of slave states farther south viewed Baltimore, for better or worse, as a Southern city. Merchants across the South shipped goods to and from Baltimore, and the city figured as one of the assets that Southern nationalists listed in a future slaveholding republic.

This book does not move in strict chronological order. It begins by analyzing how the fire-eaters—the strident supporters of Southern secession—connected problems of urbanization to the sectional crisis. I then turn to events in the cities themselves. What happened inside the cities confirmed the fire-eaters' fear that urbanization promoted the power of free labor in Southern politics. At the same time, the location of Baltimore, St. Louis, and New Orleans within the slave states shaped politics in ways that were distinctively Southern.

My opening chapter reexamines familiar material like James Henry Hammond's "mudsill" speech of 1858 to reveal the concerns that fire-eaters had over the explosive growth of cities in the late-antebellum South. Southern nationalists supported those aspects of urbanization that complemented plantation slavery—for instance, the development of commercial markets for farm products—but they opposed what they regarded as the evils of modern cities, such as class conflict and mob violence. Rather than test whether or not Baltimore was a typical Southern city, this study asks why Southerners thought large cities, even ones that allowed slavery, were "un-Southern" and explores the impact of the Southern metropolis on the region's drift toward disunion.

Chapter 2 shifts the focus to the cities themselves. It considers the long-term social and economic causes of a crisis in urban politics in the 1850s. An alliance between skilled workingmen and wealthy businessmen, the two most powerful economic interests represented in city politics, fell apart during the 1850s as a consequence of urban growth. In the early national era, an ethic of urban paternalism, one suggestive of the idealized master-slave relationship, governed social life in Southern cities. Skilled workingmen, many of whom ran their own businesses, sought to promote their city's economic fortunes in cooperation with the merchants, financiers, and nascent industrialists who comprised the business elite. These groups used bound-labor relationships, ranging from slavery to apprenticeship, to manage the services of manual workers. That model for authority declined as growth transformed small cities into large ones and replaced systems of personal authority with the more impersonal wage-labor contract. Pressured by immigration and mass production, craft workers lashed out at the very poor, whose growing numbers brought down wages and working conditions, and at the very rich, who encouraged immigration and the erosion of job skills in order to secure more profit for themselves. For their part, merchants and manufacturers welcomed new sources of income but discountenanced the new militancy of their employees. Militancy expressed itself in strikes and calls for legislative remedies to long hours and low pay. Meanwhile, African Americans, women workers, and European immigrants fought against vestiges of urban paternalism in their scramble for advantage in the flexible job market that big cities offered.

Party realignment paralleled the transformation of the urban workplace. Chapter 3 analyzes how the big cities diverged politically from the rest of the South as the Jacksonian era's system of Whig versus Democratic Party competition gave way to a less stable electoral contest between Democrats, Republicans, and the American Party. If for no other reason than resentment of rural domination, voters in the South's big cities tended to oppose the party that controlled state government. As the Democrats solidified their power in Southern legislatures, the American Party emerged as the champion of city voters. Although much of the South retained two-party politics until secession, the Know-Nothings fared poorly in most places after 1856 but hung on in Baltimore and New Orleans, and even more worrisome for slaveholders, free-soil Republicans made St. Louis one of their very few slave-state outposts.

Along with supporting party labels that quickly faded in the rest of the South, voters and officeholders in the big cities clung to a style of Jacksonian-era partisanship that had fallen into disfavor elsewhere in their region. At its most intense, party activists in the 1830s and 1840s had treated their partisan affiliation as a primary marker of their social identity, and the rituals of party rose to the level of a civil religion for the most dedicated. It is important to recognize that Jacksonian partisanship did not characterize all forms of antebellum party competition. In the early republic, parties existed, but loyalty to them was weak and most politicians claimed to stand above party when it came time to make important decisions. In the late-antebellum slave states, Democrats and a variety of opposition parties (including some simply called The Opposition) continued to contest elections outside of the lower South, but on each side leaders renounced loyalty to party as the principle reason for casting a ballot for a specific candidate. Even though party competition persisted, partisanship had declined as a basis for political action.

This decline in partisanship began early in the 1850s when critics revived the decades-old argument that partisanship put party interests above the public good. In response, politicians presented devotion to their organization as evidence of "personal integrity, self-sacrifice," and loyalty to the national interest, which they identified with their own party.[8] This antiparty style presented unique challenges to metropolitan politicians in the South, who engaged the new mass of anonymous wage-earning voters by doling out patronage, dissembling in stump speeches, and tacitly supporting polling-place mobs. Most Southerners regarded these tactics as corrupt, and although patronage, oratory hyperbole, and mobbing were practiced in other places, their use by metropolitan Know-Nothings fed Democratic charges that anti-Southern, unprincipled power seekers led the American Party. In response, Know-Nothings presented themselves as statesmen possessed of strong morals and exceptional cleverness who could use questionable methods for honorable purposes. This self-image appealed to the ethic of honor shared by their fellow Southerners, even as it offered a more flexible definition of Southern manhood, one that allowed for occasional deception and for alliances with social inferiors and outsiders to their region.

Chapter 4 looks at how free labor intensified this trend in Southern city politics in the latter half of the 1850s. Between 1855 and 1859, the urban opposition parties consolidated their power by winning over white working-class voters. That process stimulated violent attack by workers against the municipal business elite and their allies in state and local government. As municipal politicians drifted farther from the control of national parties and state leaders, working-class activists who had heretofore exercised little influence over local government gained more prominence. The most disturbing of these activists were members of street gangs, a fixture of antebellum big cities, that habituated taverns and indulged in criminality. Gangs served as a conduit between wage earners who had little experience in elections and government and formal political parties that needed labor's votes. Gangs also spearheaded the most controversial aspect of machine politics, election rioting, and used their sway with party leaders to acquire jobs on city police forces. The open challenge to the social order that gangs presented fed regional leaders' concern about the safety of slavery and persuaded them that the votes of free labor in slave-state cities could easily become allied to the Republicans of the North, who made "free soil, free labor, and free men" their rallying cry. However, compared with its Northern counterpart, Southern free-labor politics were more racist, more proslavery, and more organized around political partisanship.

I then move to the secession crisis and the onset of the Civil War. Because of secession's complexity, chapter 5 focuses exclusively on Baltimore. There, a self-styled Reform coalition emerged in the late 1850s to challenge the Know-Nothings. Reformers drew on antiparty rhetoric to create common ideological ground for groups who hated Know-Nothings but otherwise had little in common. Businessmen alarmed by labor militancy, moral reformers disturbed by Know-Nothing street gangs, and immigrants beleaguered by nativism could all agree that the American Party had to go and that in its place statesmen committed to antiparty ideals should rule. However, enduring Know-Nothing popularity in the city forced reformers to seek help outside Baltimore, and that search showed that partisanship could not be avoided. Reformers turned to proslavery Democratic planters in the Maryland legislature who, in 1860, gladly intervened in city politics to assist in the overthrow of Baltimore's American regime. Coming to power in the midst of Lincoln's election, the new Reform administration confronted the secession crisis simultaneous with its campaign to purge city government of Know-Nothing influence. Partisan friendship toward Confederate sympathizers in the state Democratic Party and hostility toward workers in the city American Party, who backed the federal Union, inclined Reformers to adopt the secessionist views of their rural sponsors. In Baltimore, the prior struggle between municipal parties played a vital role in shaping sectional allegiance.

I conclude by exploring the story of secession and the early Civil War in the rest of the urban South. Baltimore's history bears many similarities to the secession crisis in St. Louis and New Orleans, but it diverged from the pattern of events in smaller cities like Louisville, Mobile, Richmond, and Savannah that followed a nonpartisan path. In 1861, partisan politics (again, a style of political behavior that emphasized loyalty to party that is not to be confused with all forms of party competition) intensified in the big cities, even as it waned elsewhere in the slave states. The relative quiescence of small cities highlighted the danger that Baltimore, St. Louis, and New Orleans posed for Southern political unity.

Cities were one of several sites for a South-versus-South-style conflict that William Freehling has recently described.[9] My final chapter also compares the big cities to Appalachia, perhaps the best-known battlefield for the war of brother against brother and an area that did not share the urban style of intense political partisanship. The descent into lawlessness experienced in some parts of the Southern mountains shows how the lack of a party structure for managing conflict helped make divisions over disunion bloodier and more chaotic than in the big cities. Moreover, in the mountains, propertyless whites remained politically powerless at war's end, whereas the white working-class of the big cities used the war to further the political agenda that they had drafted in the 1850s.

Along with size, politics made the big cities unique. Many Southern states retained two-party competition until 1860, but Baltimore, St. Louis, and New Orleans held onto and intensified Jacksonian-style partisan combat at a time when the rest of the South was moving away from it. Instead of helping urbanites to keep their cool during the storm of sectionalism, something that more moderate party competition facilitated for a time in the upper and border South, the partisanship generated by big city elections deepened antagonisms that metropolitan voters felt for one another. The bitter late-antebellum party battle strengthened the resolve and created organizational structures that residents of big cities used to rally for and against secession in 1861.

The problem of free labor in slave-state politics stood at the center of this conflict. Having been comparatively silent in Southern elections and government before the 1850s, in the last antebellum decade propertyless white workers demonstrated their ability to shape politics at the municipal level. Southerners in town and country worried how much power workers would achieve and what kind of agenda they would pursue.

Inside the cities, workers advanced a slave-state brand of free-labor politics that sought to shore up their status as masters of households, a claim that craft workers had traditionally used to distinguish themselves from other manual laborers. To further this project, white workingmen waged political war against the very poor and the very rich, who they believed threatened their privileges. This campaign extolled the virtues of free labor, but it did not make fighting slavery a priority. Workingmen active in the urban opposition parties wanted the state to promote their immediate interest in gaining good jobs. Making antislavery part of that project would provoke insurmountable opposition from their fellow Southern whites. Yet even though they downplayed free soilism, workers in the South's big cities challenged planter domination of the South by advancing their own power and that of city government in state and regional politics.

Outside of the cities, planters feared that strong municipal governments influenced by workingmen would undermine the political order that protected slavery and the larger social system that slavery supported. For proslavery enthusiasts, stopping the new political machines of the cities went along with defending the power of the South against Northern free soilers and abolitionists. In a democracy where most voters owned no slaves, the slaveholding minority worried that they would be sacrificed to the will of the majority. They regarded the ascendancy of free labor in large slave-state cities as both a symptom of how American democracy had become unsafe for a society built on racial slavery and as a practical problem in that the big cities would become, as St. Louis already had by 1861, bridgeheads for a Republican Party invasion of the South. In February 1861, a secessionist editor stated the point more bluntly. "Slavery," he wrote, "cannot share a government with democracy." [10]

The politics of Baltimore, New Orleans, and St. Louis helped Southern nationalists present secession as a referendum on American democracy, rather than as a referendum on slavery. Aware that rural poor whites had occasionally protested against slaveholder privileges, planter-politicians understood that nonslaveholders would shy away from disunion if its only goal appeared to be protecting the right of the wealthy to own large numbers of slaves. Among several ways that secessionists sought to broaden to their appeal, secessionists' claim that they fought against mob rule helped disunionists define Southern identity in ways that would limit the power of free labor. Politics, more than anything else, led Southerners to perceive their largest cities as somehow alien to their region.

Much can be gained from treating Baltimore and the other two urban giants as focal points of the late-antebellum South's struggle over what direction modernizing changes would take. Much is lost if they are dismissed as irrelevant eccentricities in an otherwise monolithic, rural, slave society.

One

The Specter of Mob Rule
Secessionists and the
Southern Metropolis

In 1858, James Henry Hammond, a U.S. senator from South Carolina, delivered his famous "mudsill" speech as a defiant rejoinder to Northern criticisms of slavery. "In all social systems," Hammond argued, "there must be a class to do the menial duties, to perform the drudgery of life. . . . It constitutes the very mud-sill of society and of political government; and you might as well attempt to build a house in the air, as to build either the one or the other, except on this mud-sill." Hammond's premise, one common to proslavery thought, drew a sharp line between those engaged in the most arduous forms of manual labor, a group he claimed required "a low order of intellect and but little skill," and those who managed this labor and who, by their exemption from daily physical toil, "lead progress, civilization, and refinement."[1]

Had Hammond stopped with this assertion that manual laborers must be kept down in order for society to progress, millions of Southern whites who owned no slaves and who farmed with their own hands would have rebuked him, but Hammond went on to say that "our slaves are black of another and inferior race." He meant that the South's restriction of the hardest manual labor to African-American slaves ensured a rough equality among whites because this restriction prevented any of them from becoming degraded and dependent hirelings. For poor Southern whites, the appeal of such an argument rested on the contrast between their situation and what Hammond asserted was the condition of poor whites in the free-labor society of the North. "The difference between us," Hammond told Northern senators, "is that our slaves are well compensated. . . . Yours are hired by the day, not cared for, and scantily compensated, which may be proved in the most painful manner in any of your large towns." Hammond's logic was clear: if one assumed that manual laborers would always be at the mercy of their bosses, then it was best to restrict the worst forms of manual labor to slaves of another race. To do otherwise sowed resentment among whites who, as Northern workers, Hammond told his audience, "feel galled by their degradation."

In its critique of free-wage labor, the mud-sill argument moved from a defense of slavery as a bulwark of white social equality to an attack on the kind of democracy that the North's urbanizing industrial society promoted. Hammond asserted that slavery had made the South safe for democracy by enslaving most unskilled manual laborers and barring them from voting and officeholding: "Our slaves do not vote. We give them no political power." Withholding suffrage from the class most aggrieved by existing social arrangements prevented politics from becoming a vehicle for redressing such inequalities. In the North, where manual workers shared the racial status of the rich and possessed the franchise, Hammond foresaw a day when free labor would use its political power to plunge society into class war. Northern workingmen, Hammond said, "do vote, and, being the majority, they are the depositaries of all your political power. If they knew the secret, that the ballot-box is stronger than 'an army with banners,' and could combine, where would you be? Your society would be reconstructed, your government overthrown, your property divided." Free labor had made democracy unsafe for property and civic order by enabling the impoverished majority to rule as a tyrannical mob, a possibility, Hammond told Northerners, that had already come to pass "in any of your large towns."

This chapter explores how Southern nationalists like Hammond viewed urbanization. As the mud-sill speech showed, defending slavery was at the center of secessionist thought and fire-eaters identified cities and urban workers as forces that had turned the North into slavery's enemy. In reference to their own section, champions of secession worried that cities spearheaded change that would destabilize Southern society and thereby bring about the fall of slavery.

Since the American Revolution, Southern politicians had argued that black slavery and white freedom were inextricably linked. According to this outlook, racial slavery, reinforced by a gender hierarchy that denied women political and economic equality with men, separated unskilled manual laborers from the owners of productive property and thereby restricted political participation to white, male household heads that ideally were financially and socially independent. At home, Southern white men governed their dependents as would a wise and benevolent father. That experience instilled in household heads the "virtue" (a concept in American political thought that denoted selfless commitment to the greater good) and independence (construed as an assertive defense of one's rights) that would enable them to participate as responsible, equal citizens in governing the larger society.[2]

Without racial slavery, secessionists argued, political participation would have to be extended to unskilled workingmen lacking in education, reliant on employers for starvation wages, and driven by jealous passions arising out of their inferior position in the market economy. Expressing the views of Hammond in another way, Virginia secessionist Edmund Ruffin wrote that "most fortunately for the preservation of the political freedom and safety of all of the ruling class, known as the citizens by the Constitution, the lowest, and necessarily the most ignorant and degraded class in the South, are not, as in the North, citizens and voters, but are negro slaves, who have no political rights." He contrasted the exclusionary democracy of the South with the free-labor society of the North that gave political rights to the poor. The "natural evils" of this system were evident in "large cities," where, Ruffin asserted,

> there is collected an enormously predominating number of ignorant, needy, and unprincipled men—when a very large proportion of the population of these cities is composed of newly arrived foreigners often vicious and turbulent, and necessarily unacquainted with the principles of free government, and unused to freedom in any form— I say it is certain under such circumstances as these, that the body of the people will be directed, governed, and in effect enslaved by a few master-minds—and these minds generally acting solely for the promotion of base self-interest and personal aggrandizement.[3]

Another Virginia secessionist noted that "in the chief cities, mobs dispute the right of private citizens to consult their own taste in a play actor; they set fire to convents of helpless females, and they tear down the house of God because it shelters the wretched [immigrant] from their brutal fury." Whereas in the rural South the "relations of parent and child, of husband and wife, of master and slave, and the right of property which all go to make up the great cornerstone of the social edifice" created a political consensus such that "government rests its authority not upon force but upon universal consent; there is no despotic public opinion to stifle freedom of thought; no King Numbers to flatter; no rapacious majority can use the forms of law to gratify its ravenings for plunder."[4] Secessionists argued that by extending the suffrage to rootless and propertyless wage earners, democracy in the North had been cut loose from the moorings of the patriarchal household. This brand of democracy, the kind that fire-eaters associated with the North's free-labor enthusiasts, would inevitably lead to tyranny by a majoritarian mob that would use the state to redress inequalities of property and status.

Southerners who claimed that this nightmare of mob rule could become reality cited historical examples from the fall of classical republics to the French Revolution to the slave revolt in San Domingo. Seeking evidence from their own times, the South's proslavery polemicists pointed to the violent, class-driven politics of American cities to show how what one called an "indiscriminate democracy" could result in tyrannical majority rule.[5] Fire-eaters claimed that an unprincipled Northern majority would soon take hold of the federal government and use it to exploit the South for the North's advantage and, for this reason, the South should quit the Union. Secessionists warned that unless the South acted quickly, the North's electoral majority would be augmented by the South's own free-labor mobs that concentrated in its largest cities—Baltimore, New Orleans, and St. Louis—places so distinct from the rest of the slave states that they might be termed the Southern metropolis.

Although scholars have written on antebellum Southern urban history, the existence of an industrializing urban South inhabited by nonslaveholding whites, immigrant workers, and free blacks remains an inconvenient and mostly overlooked anomaly for the popular understanding of the Civil War as the climax of a long-brewing conflict between two sections that were so different as to suggest a struggle between Northern and Southern civilizations. Antecedents of this popular understanding predate the Civil War. In the 1850s, secessionists promoted a version of this clash-of-civilizations image in order to persuade their fellow Southerners, particularly poor ones who did not own slaves, that the South was distinct from the North and superior to it. Key to this superiority, Southern nationalists argued, was the equality that Southern whites enjoyed as a result of African slavery. Prior to becoming the Confederacy's vice president, Georgia's Alexander Stephens said that "with us, all of the white race, however high or low, rich or poor, are equal in the eye of the law. Not so with the negro. Subordination is his place." Reading big cities out of Southern society bolstered the case for slavery as a bulwark of white equality because it enabled Southern nationalists to claim that their section lacked the kind of class hierarchy among whites that was evident in Northern cities. Proslavery enthusiasts seeking to convince nonslaveholding whites that slavery blocked their downward slide to hireling status demonized cities as the locus of white labor's misery and claimed that the South had not been infected with the ills of urban life.[6]

However, secessionists did not oppose all social changes associated with the expansion of markets and manufacturing that characterized the modern West. Like later nationalist movements that struggled against what they conceived of as a hegemonic industrial power, proponents of a Southern confederacy wanted to incorporate into their society beneficial aspects of modern change and shear off its harmful features.[7] In reference to urbanization, secessionists promoted the building of Southern cities to expand market services for plantation agriculture, but they sought to exclude from the process the kind of industrial-based urban economy that had promoted excessive growth and class conflict in the North and in England. The antiurbanism of Southern nationalists therefore focused on a specific kind of city, one torn by class conflict associated with the industrial revolution. In February 1860, Virginian John C. Rutherfoord cited urban industrialism as a problem that could be avoided by quitting the Union. "Let us leave to Old England and New England their hives of suffering humanity, their Manchesters and Lowells, their Chartist mobs and 'labor strikes,' their social evils, in the present, and their alarming social problems, in the future."[8]

Fire-eaters who hoped to make the South economically self-sufficient explained that the economics of plantation slavery had spared Southern cities from this kind of class conflict. According to J. D. B. DeBow, an advocate of Southern urbanization and secession, "the cities, towns and villages of the South, are but so many agencies for converting the product of other labor obtained from abroad. . . . In the absence of every other source of wealth at the South, its mercantile interests are so interwoven with those of slave labor as to be almost identical. What is true of the merchant is true of the clerk, the drayman, or the laborer he employs." Slavery produced the export crops that enabled urban Southerners to concentrate on commerce and avoid industrial wage labor. DeBow warned that if slavery fell, the South would experience "the competition between native and foreign labor in the Northern states, [that] has already begotten rivalry and heartburning, and riots; and led to the formation of political parties there which have been marked by a degree of hostility and proscription to which the present age has not afforded another parallel." Supporters of Southern independence welcomed the material progress that cities promoted, but they strongly objected to the class conflict that they associated with urban industry and the enfranchisement of wage labor.[9]

DeBow's argument that, in his section, town and country shared mutual interests bears up under scrutiny if one excludes from consideration the South's most populous cities. In Virginia, the largest slave state in 1860, Southern town boosters benefited from Northern trade, but they nonetheless believed that they would remain colonized dependents of New York City financiers unless they developed an independent commercial network within the South. Some Old Dominion planters worried about the cities' heterogeneous and politically unreliable working class, but many agreed with DeBow that the South needed its own commercial centers in order to be economically self-sustaining. The urban businessmen who agreed with these planters supported slavery and wanted to keep poor whites politically loyal to elite rule. In late-antebellum Richmond, whose thirty-eight thousand people made it Virginia's biggest city and the South's seventh largest, the number of slaves grew steadily as industrialists like John C. Anderson, head of the famed Tredegar Iron Works, found uses for their labor. On occasion, enfranchised white workers challenged the business elite's authority, but they did not rally en masse for the Union, and much less for emancipation. In fact, white labor militants sometimes called for greater controls on slaves and free blacks, with whom they competed in industrial workplaces.

Rural versus urban disputes encompassed many issues ranging from railroad building to legislative apportionment, but Virginia's urban places showed no greater unanimity on the question of secession than did its countryside. Seven states in the lower South quit the Union after Abraham Lincoln, an Illinois Republican opposed to slavery's expansion, won the 1860 presidential election with an exclusively Northern majority. In February 1861, Virginians elected delegates to a special convention that would consider their state's entry into the new Southern Confederacy. Virginia towns heavily involved in northern commerce (Wheeling, Norfolk, and Lynchburg) elected Unionists, while those reliant on Southern trade (e.g., Petersburg) voted for secession, and the rest, most notably Richmond, split their tickets. The firing on Fort Sumter on April 12, 1861, and Lincoln's call for seventy-five thousand volunteers to defend federal property in the seceding states convinced most urban leaders to reject a shaky future under the Republicans in favor of a partnership with the planter class. Based on Virginia's example, the South experienced a process of urban development similar to the North's, but Southerners found ways to make urbanism complement, rather than undermine, their drive for sectional advantage.[10]

The pattern exemplified in Richmond roughly characterized the four other midsized Southern cities—Charleston, Mobile, Savannah, and Memphis—places with populations between twenty thousand and forty thousand in 1860.[11] While the experiences of these urban centers differed—for example, Charleston was among the few American cities to lose population in the 1850s, whereas Memphis grew by a phenomenal 155 percent—each had a mixture of immigrants, free blacks, and slaves; and in each city native-born whites comprised either a minority or a bare majority of the population. These cities traded with their agricultural hinterland to the detriment of manufacturing.

Prior to 1860, the Whig Party, which faded after its disastrous showing in the 1852 presidential election, and then the American Party, also called Know-Nothings because of their origins as a secret society, governed the midsized cities despite the growing dominance of the Democratic Party in the South. Except for Charleston, which elected a Southern and States' Rights mayor in 1855, they supported the Union provided that slavery remain protected. Working-class voters at times defied the leadership of Whig merchants, but they failed to unseat them, and workers often cooperated with Whig and American Party businessmen in pushing for municipal reform and expanded urban power vis-à-vis state government. Most residents of the midsized cities agreed with A. A. Echols of Savannah, who had been a Unionist until Lincoln's election "consummated the folly of Northern delusion in striking the deathblow to the best government on Earth." By then the Unionist political leaders of each city had either declared their support for secession or had been replaced by Southern nationalists.[12]

DeBow's argument for Southern cities as regionally distinctive makes the most sense of the commercial towns and small cities where trade related to the agricultural export sector dominated the economy and industry played a minor role. However, the biggest Southern cities clearly did not fit this description, and while slavery's defenders disapproved of the occasional factory strike or opposition party victory in the midsized cities, their anxieties about the political consequences of Southern urbanization focused on the major metropolitan centers of Baltimore, New Orleans, and St. Louis. DeBow recognized their danger in his critique of class conflict in Northern cities when he cautioned that "at the South we have known none of this, except in two or three of the larger cities, where relations of slavery and freedom scarcely exist at all." [13]

Rather than representing exceptions to the pattern of Southern urbanization, as DeBow suggested, Baltimore, New Orleans, and St. Louis were at the forefront of trends making all Southern cities more like urban places in the North and in western Europe and less like the rural communities of the Southern countryside. Ethnic diversity and manufacturing in some form had always characterized American cities, but never on such a scale. Keeping pace with the unprecedented national urban growth rate, during the 1850s the South's ten most populous cities increased their size nearly twice as fast as the entire region. Their ethnic composition also veered from the regional norm. The proportion of whites in Southern city populations rose from 76 percent to 84 percent, while the regionwide proportion of whites barely changed, rising from 64 percent to 66 percent; conversely, the numbers of slaves and free blacks fell in the cities, but rose in the countryside. [14]

These trends were even more pronounced in Baltimore, New Orleans, and St. Louis, which had grown faster than the next seven cities. In 1860, 90 percent of their people were white, and only 3 percent were slaves. More industrial workers (17,054) lived in Baltimore than dwelled among the entire populations of eleven of the fifteen slave states. New Orleans housed more than half of Louisiana's free blacks, and the city's proportion of free blacks (12 percent) was eight times greater than the share of free blacks in the seven states of the lower South. Immigrants, two-thirds of St. Louis's population, were omnipresent in the city, but hardly visible elsewhere in Missouri, where they were only 6 percent of the population, or the rest of the South, where they made up 4 percent. In the North, the five urban centers containing population in excess of 150,000 were situated in states with several midsized cities of more than 20,000. The northern pattern made urbanity seem less alien to those living outside of the central cities. By contrast, the second largest settlement in Maryland, Louisiana, and Missouri, had fewer than 9,000 people, making the big city unlike any other place in its state or section. Growth had turned the South's largest cities into glaring multicultural and industrial contrasts to the homogeneity of rural life. [15]

Although the differences between big cities and the Southern countryside took many forms, perhaps the most troubling for rural Southerners was the divergence of urban work relationships from the paternalistic labor system that, at least in the ideal, characterized plantation slavery. In the early Republic, an ethic of corporatism, a hierarchical model of community cooperation, governed urban life. While it was not identical to the master-slave relationship of the plantation, the urban elite practiced a form of paternalism that was compatible with the mores of the rural gentry. Leadership emanated from a business elite of financiers, industrialists, and merchants who received deference from those below them in the civic order. Although not the equals of the business elite, craft workers enjoyed modest prosperity and exercised power over apprentices, slaves, and hired hands. Most numerous in the city were those workers in the bottom ranks of the economy, a group that historians following contemporary usage have classified as the "lower sort." As servants and casual unskilled labor, this propertyless lower sort looked to patrons in the upper ranks to provide jobs and social advantage.[16]

By 1860, the workforces of the South's largest cities contained tens of thousands of transient newcomers from disparate cultures. Patrons had greater difficulty than in the past in establishing lasting personal ties with this new mass of manual laborers. The breakdown of personalized systems of authority had the strongest impact on the South's big three cities, where the number of wage earners was two and three times as great as in midsized Richmond and Savannah, respectively. Commenting on this process, a traveler observed that "there is, in New Orleans, from the renewal of one half of its inhabitants every few years, and the constant influx of strangers, strictly speaking no exclusive clique or aristocracy, to give tone to society and establish a standard of propriety and respectability."[17]

Demographic increase gave this new working-class the potential to influence statewide politics in ways that the lower sort of the early Republic cities could not. In the early 1800s, Southern cities were not only smaller, and therefore less influential in state elections, but also their working class included a larger proportion of slaves and people who had little access to the suffrage, such as free blacks, recent immigrants, and native white women. On the eve of the Civil War, the sheer size of Baltimore, New Orleans, and St. Louis gave their voters, the majority of whom were wage earners, extraordinary power in statewide elections. In 1860, an average of 7 percent of the eligible voters in a given Southern state lived in its largest city. However, in Maryland and Louisiana the largest city accounted for 35 percent of all voters, a rate higher than any free state, including New York, and in Missouri the largest city accounted for 14 percent, a larger ratio than in all but four Northern states.

As these figures indicate, demography made the politics of the three largest slave-state cities differ from what occurred in smaller urban centers. Baltimore, New Orleans, and St. Louis had many more workers who could vote, a smaller ratio of blacks to whites that gave working-class voters more impact on elections, and a German majority in their immigrant populations, as opposed to the Irish majority that prevailed in smaller cities, a phenomenon that made big-city politics more na-tivist and more Unionist. Germans held skilled jobs in greater propor-tion than the Irish, and Germans had more difficulty assimilating into Anglo-American culture because of language. They therefore provided a more visible target for nativist attacks on immigrants as competitors for desirable jobs and as corrupters of American institutions. On the other hand, Germans generally demonstrated stronger support for the federal Union and emancipation than did the Irish, whose votes Democrats cultivated. When the secession crisis pushed nativism into the background, German and American workers joined together to support the Union. Quantitative differences in population and econ-omy translated into a qualitatively different form of class-and-ethnic politics that made enfranchised workers in Baltimore, New Orleans, and St. Louis some of the South's staunchest supporters of nativism and the federal Union.

Prior to the secession crisis, big-city voters had already defied the regionally dominant and militantly proslavery Democratic Party by de-feating it in favor of the anti-immigrant American Party at elections marked by violence at the polls. The Know-Nothings built their major-ity on the votes of native-born white workers, a group that held better-paying, skilled jobs and was overrepresented among enfranchised workers because the law barred black voting and because naturalization requirements diminished immigrant electoral power. American-born white labor backed the Know-Nothings because they promised to pro-vide jobs in public works for the unemployed, combat immigrant influ-ence in work and politics, and helped disrupt patron-client relation-ships that employers had used to keep wages low and labor docile. By expanding government spending and patronage and by encouraging working-class street gangs to intimidate Democratic voters on election day, urban Know-Nothings in the slave states experimented with prac-tices of machine politics that swept American cities later in the century.

Nascent political machines emerged in the North as well, but they had more impact on the coming of the Civil War in the South because slave-state urbanites had more difficulty separating municipal battles from the sectional conflict. In the North, few residents of town or country advocated disunion, and city politics rarely threatened the sectional unity of the free states. In the South, municipal politicians hesitated to criticize slavery, but they advanced issues, such as expanding urban representation in state government or condoning strikes, that planters viewed as wedges for a broader campaign against their power as slaveholders and political leaders. Workers in the three largest cities of the South hosted a slave-state version of free-labor Unionism, one that had even less concern for African-American advancement than did the free-labor views of many Northern Republicans, but which nonetheless challenged the regional power of slaveholders. The cities became embroiled in sectional controversy because their politics threatened Southern unity and because union and secession each had urban supporters who often brought sectional issues to bear on municipal conflicts.

Although scholars have paid comparatively little attention to it, this saga of machine politics in the urban South adds an important dimension to understanding the role played by the South's nonslaveholding white majority in the secession crisis. For years, Southern politicians had found ways to smooth tensions between voters who owned slaves and ones who did not. Usually, political leaders emphasized the things besides slave ownership that whites had in common, such as agriculture and a shared regional identity. Political conflict in the South's big cities presented these leaders with the more difficult task of accommodating white industrial labor and its style of mass politics to the concerns of voters oriented toward slave-based agriculture and the more deferential pattern of rural politics. By drawing attention to the problems that widespread wage labor created for democracy, the South's big cities helped connect concern over slavery's future—the core issue of the sectional conflict—to other aspects of nineteenth-century social change that had put slaveholders on the defensive.

As one of several arguments for secession, fire-eaters claimed that Northern democracy was headed toward mob rule and that the South must separate itself from the Union before a tyrannical free-labor majority subjugated it. To give their case immediacy, Southern nationalists argued that party politics as practiced in Baltimore, New Orleans, and St. Louis represented a corruption of democracy that would soon spread to other slave-state cities, should the South remain tied to the industrializing North. Secessionists, in sum, used big cities to frame their cause as a referendum on American democracy, rather than as a referendum on slavery, because Southerners who linked the politics of slave-state cities with the politics of the North could perceive both politics as unwanted consequences of antebellum social change.

Fire-eaters like James Henry Hammond argued that the very poor could not be trusted with the franchise because they would use the vote to turn government into an instrument of class war against the rich. Propagandists for secession held that such a situation had already come to pass in the North, but that slavery, which denied the vote to those at the bottom of the social order, had spared the South from the tumult of class politics. In February 1861, Leonidas Spratt, editor of the *Charleston Mercury,* identified the enfranchisement of poor men as the chief evil of the free states and the defining difference between the sections. In the North, Spratt wrote, "the pauper laborer has the power to rise and appropriate by law the goods protected by the state . . . and thus the ship of state turns bottom upwards. In the [South] there is no pauper labor with the power of rising; the Ship has the ballast of a disfranchised class: there is no possibility of political upheaval." For these reasons, Spratt felt confident that the new Confederacy "will sail erect and onward for an indefinitely distant period."[18] Secessionists concluded that Southern democracy as they understood it (i.e., a democracy built on the foundation of slavery) could not survive continued growth in the political power of propertyless wage earners like those who had so recently turned politics upside down in the South's big cities.

This conclusion about fire-eaters' concern with urbanization and democracy sheds new light on an aspect of secession that has generated a long debate among historians. Although on the eve of the Civil War only one Southern white family out of every four owned slaves, the breakaway Confederacy made the defense of slavery its organizing principle. Contemporaries as well as later historians wondered how a revolution waged in the name of slavery could draw the majority of its support from nonslaveholders. In 1861, William H. Trescott, a leading South Carolina disunionist, expressed concerns felt by many slaveholders about the politics of the nonslaveholding majority in both sections:

> The march of fanaticism has not been checked but gathers strength each day, and in its course this Government will be overturned and the South will be found without preparation to resist what fate may be in store for her. . . . And if we are to judge by the past, when matters have reached that position, think you that 360,000 Slaveholders will

dictate terms for 3,000,000 of non-slaveholders at the South? I fear not. I mistrust our own people more than I fear all of the efforts of the Abolitionists.[19]

Trescott's comments can be read either as evidence of his belief that Southerners, Trescott's "own people," were united in their support of slavery but fainthearted when it came to standing up to Northern politicians or as an indication of his "mistrust" not only of nonslave-holders' support for secession but of their support for slavery itself.

Following these two interpretations, historians have considered Trescott and his compatriots either as the leaders of a solid white South that acted, as a contemporary put it, from "a spontaneous outburst of human feelings which . . . caused every heart to thrill with the same emotions" or as a smaller class of wealthy planters, demonized by Republicans as the "Slave Power," that sought to consolidate their own authority within the South by securing its independence.[20] Recent studies harmonize these opposing interpretations by concluding that planters seceded to promote their political and economic power as slaveholders, whereas nonslaveholding whites, encouraged by planters, backed secession in order to protect material interests bound up in white supremacy. As an ideology of power, white supremacy found expression in personal ethics in the rituals of honor and in politics through Herrenvolk democracy, or "the equal superiority of all who belong to the Herrenvolk (master race) over all who do not." In a typical formulation of this argument, James M. McPherson writes that "secessionists invoked Herrenvolk democracy to remind yeomen of their racial stake in defending slavery."[21]

Among its contributions, the racial-stake argument accounts for the stages of secession in which the seven states with the highest slave concentrations quit the Union in the winter of 1860–61; the four immediate neighbors of this group delayed secession until the spring and summer of 1861; and the four northernmost slave states, the ones with the fewest slaveholders, remained in the Union. Although some had more slaves than others, in no Southern state did slaveholders outnumber nonslaveholding whites, and it is in its ability to show how proximity to slaveholders shaped the allegiances of nonslaveholding whites that the racial-stake argument opens up the relationship between society and politics in the antebellum South.

While there is much to commend this interpretive model, it tends to reduce all ideological arguments for secession with the ones that best fit the social-power relationships that typified the plantation districts of the lower South, where scholars have been most persuasive in arguing for white supremacy's secessionist appeal. This tendency presents two problems in applying the racial-stake argument to the rest of the nine-teenth-century South. First, antebellum political culture discouraged interest-based arguments; secondly, some secessionists had little objec-tive stake in the material benefits of slavery.

To more fully understand the first of these points it is useful to note that political discourse in the Civil War era operated within the broad republican framework inherited from the Revolution. Key to republi-canism was the belief that government should pursue a unitary public good without reference to social divisions among fully enfranchised cit-izens, a group that by 1860 included all native-born and naturalized adult white men. Instead of using terms related to social identity like race, class, and gender, republicanism's keywords, *liberty, power,* and *virtue,* offered little room for interest-group arguments that to be ef-fective needed a rhetoric that emphasized social difference.[22] While they acted to uphold and enhance their privileges as men, slaveholders, and whites, planter-politicians nonetheless presented secession primar-ily and forthrightly as a defense of good government and the welfare of all Southerners and only secondarily and furtively as a way to enhance the raw power of white men. Recognizing republicanism's influence helps to explain why protagonists in the sectional conflict spent so much energy discussing political corruption and partisanship.

The social diversity of the late-antebellum South presents another difficulty for the racial-stake interpretation of secession. The argument that disunion's popularity corresponded with large slave populations begs the question of why secession not only won out in the upper South but also why the Confederate military drew nearly one hundred thou-sand volunteers from the border states. These soldiers represented 15 percent of all adult white men living in the border South, and few of them owned slaves. While secession drew fewer supporters outside of plantation districts, it nonetheless won more followers near the sec-tional border than would be expected had nonslaveholding Southern whites acted strictly on an interest-based logic.

The outspoken secessionist minorities of Baltimore and St. Louis are instructive on this point. In 1860 and 1861, Southern sympathizers in Baltimore and St. Louis won elections and rioted against federal troops. Louisville, Kentucky, an industrializing Ohio River port with sixty-eight thousand people, only 7 percent of whom were slaves, also backed the Union, but unlike Baltimore or St. Louis, Louisville had no cadre of militant would-be Confederates willing to attempt a violent takeover of the city.[23] Sharing Louisville's location in the slave-scarce border South and even more heavily invested in industry, Baltimore and St. Louis were improbable sites for secessionist rioters to make their stand. Just as the lower South imposed constraints on the politics and society of New Orleans, the border South shaped Baltimore and St. Louis by bringing them nearer to the North and providing them with local allies in nonslaveholding farming districts of the border South. Nevertheless, the intensely partisan and often violent politics of Baltimore and St. Louis prepared their residents for the secession crisis in ways not shared by other border Southerners. Sworn enemies of the Unionist Know-Nothings, big-city Democrats sympathetic to planters in their own states and to ones further south saw danger in an alliance between federal troops and Baltimore Know-Nothings or St. Louis Republicans. These urban Democrats drew on their local party organization and the tactics of urban political violence to stand for secession despite many obstacles that foredoomed their efforts. Ironically, oversized Baltimore and St. Louis bred more secessionists than could smaller, politically unified cities like Louisville.

The same pattern characterized New Orleans, whose location at the mouth of the Mississippi challenges those who would dismiss big cities as exclusively border-South outposts of free-labor society and politics. In New Orleans, the 1850s battle over machine politics created the organization and experience that Crescent City Unionists needed to rally against a determined secessionist majority, making its Unionist diehards exceptions to the lower-South rule of secessionist consensus. Although the balance of power varied according to subregion, the big cities differed from smaller ones by serving as organizing bases for both secession and union.

The imprecise fit between some Southerners' objective racial stake in secession and their subjective political choice brings to light cultural and social dynamics associated with urbanization that encouraged protagonists in the sectional conflict to tack arguments about democracy's appropriate form onto a struggle caused by slavery. In nineteenth-century America, the biggest cities led a double life. On the one hand, they served as marketplaces for their respective rural hinterlands and bore traces of that local identity; on the other hand, metropolitan centers with populations approaching two hundred thousand belonged to an urban economic and social network that operated independently of any city's rural backyard. Baltimore, New Orleans, and St. Louis imported as many goods and admitted as many migrants from other cities as they did from neighboring farm districts. Cities stood apart from their hinterlands by way of their overcrowded, heterogeneous public space and their economic mix of industry, administration, service, and commerce. This "novel environment," says one historian, represented "the most striking outward symbol of the industrial world." Residents of large cities shared a cosmopolitan urbanity that transcended regional and national boundaries. According to an 1850s European traveler, "it is not apparent that St. Louis is the major city of a slave state. . . . [L]ife here looks wilder and more strident, as if expended faster." That some scholars have viewed the transnational urbanity of Baltimore, New Orleans, and St. Louis as grounds for excluding them from consideration as Southern places highlights the unique status that these cities held in the slave states.[24]

The sense of separateness between the Southern metropolis and its rural hinterland made for a big-city-versus-country conflict that differed from more familiar struggles between upcountry yeoman and tidewater planters. Yeomen and planters did not always get along, but they could agree that big cities were unwanted developments within their region. Similarly, inside the metropolis, capital and labor often came into conflict, but both groups cooperated in promoting the interests of the city against the countryside. The largest Southern cities brought a unique set of combatants to the secession crisis and created an image for rural Southerners of what a future in the Union might hold.

In nineteenth-century America and Europe, cities represented the most visible examples of the changes wrought by industrialism. Supporters of the new order thought cities embodied liberal progress, while traditionalists abhorred them as the catch basin for modern ills.[25] What was a cultural debate in the North and Europe became a political issue in the South because the idealized image of rural life that traditionalists extolled provided common ideological ground for uniting planters with nonslaveholding voters. Planter-politicians who associated themselves with the virtues common to farmers skillfully turned criticism of well-off slaveholders into criticism of the countryside and, by extension, criticism of the South. When big-city voters protested the power of slaveholders, if not the legitimacy of slavery, planters invoked anti-urbanism to discredit their foes as un-Southern. This argument put fundamental social identities, like the Southern ideal of manhood, to work against politicians who advocated for the cities.

The linkage of pastoralism and slavery encouraged Southern nationalists to interpret political problems in their big cities as part of the same trend that brought the Republican Party to power in the North; and in reference to both cases, secession expressed the sharp decline in white Southerners' confidence in American democracy. When confronted with Northern challenges to slavery's spread in the 1820s and 1850, most Southern voters had opted to stay in the Union because they believed that it provided better protection for slavery and a better overall future than did the breakaway republic envisioned by secessionists. Capping a decade of sectional discord in national politics, the election of 1860 shook moderate Southerners' faith in slavery's security within the Union because the numerically superior North showed it could elect a president whom Southerners hated. For secessionists, Lincoln's election dramatized the political consequences of antebellum social change. They viewed urbanization, industry, and the burgeoning working-class electorate as forces that had subverted the founding generation's goal of creating a democratic republic that protected the liberty of all citizens. Secessionists thought that majority rule, an integral part of American democracy, had come to rest decisively with voters utterly lacking in civic virtue or social independence. Power-mad demagogues, they argued, had exploited the electorate's fallen state to aggrandize themselves at the expense of Southern rights and liberty.

When they discussed Baltimore, St. Louis, and New Orleans, proslavery Democrats attacked these cities as outposts of mob rule and abolition. Alarmed by violence at Baltimore's polls during the 1856 elections, DeBow suspected that Republicans would soon take control of the city. He said that "Baltimore must be counted not for us but against us. We must deal with her as with the other Northern cities, all sectional enemies who are assailing our domestic peace and property and our perpetuity as a free and equal confederacy of states. . . . Our enemies in the slave States are the most dangerous." Edward Belt, a Maryland Democrat from a tobacco-growing county, described an 1858 scheme by Maryland Know-Nothings to give cities and towns a greater share of legislative seats as "red republican." Asking his rural brethren, "if our representation be stricken down, where is our Slavery interest?" Belt conjured up the demon of Baltimore's municipal "corporation sitting on the throne of power, the emblems of Maryland lying at its feet . . . holding in its right hand the scourge that is all powerful even under existing laws, and just grasping with its left the legislative power itself; so that in the future *its* will may be the Law!"[26]

A Missouri farmer reading about urban election riots said that "the mobocracy is getting altogether too fashionable in St. Louis. Society seems to have relapsed." In 1856, rural Missouri Democrat William Napton believed that St. Louis "has already evinced an unmistakable hostility to slavery," and he feared the institution would wither in his state under "the influence of her own metropolis." As the Civil War unfolded, Edmund Ruffin wrote that "Baltimore has long been under the rule of law-breakers—of organized rioters, robbers, and murderers," and he called St. Louis "that abolition city." "If also it can be laid in ashes," he said, "it will be well-deserved."[27]

Louisiana's superintendent of elections criticized the New Orleans Know-Nothing regime for "the nightly scenes of bloodshed, intimidations, murders, and assassinations, by a band of lawless men in disguise . . . and from the wrongs, injuries, and outrages inflicted upon the helpless citizens." A Vicksburg slave trader told a friend that he would visit New Orleans "provided the Know-Nothings do not kill me for an honest Democrat." Shortly after Louisiana's secession, William Rushton, a New Orleans physician and enthusiastic Confederate, explained how majority rule had ruined city politics. According to his interviewer, Rushton was "strongly convinced of the impossibility of carrying on government, or conducting municipal affairs, until universal suffrage is put down. He gave many instances of the terrorism, violence, and assassinations which prevail during election times in New Orleans."[28] When discussing their region's largest cities, Southern nationalists connected general concerns about urban disorder to political threats to slavery and the Democratic Party.

Secessionists leveled similar criticism against the North; in fact, they had difficulty distinguishing their main battle against the North from their secondary struggle against the insurgent municipal regimes of Baltimore, St. Louis, and New Orleans. The claim that whites living apart from slavery had a predisposition toward mob rule also informed secessionist criticism of Northern voters and the Republican Party. In 1859, Louisiana's governor declared that "the Republican [Party] appears to foster the idea that . . . the majority of the voices in the whole United States, considered as one nation ought to rule. This last idea would be so fatal to the South if carried out that nearly all Southern men are now with the Democratic Party."[29]

In 1860, South Carolina planter-politician Laurence Keitt warned that "the concentration of absolute power in the hands of the North, will develop the wildest democracy ever seen on this earth—unless it should have been matched in Paris in 1789. . . . What of social security or financial prosperity can withstand northern Republican license?"[30] That year, a U.S. senator from Texas, Louis T. Wigfall, argued that "the ballot box, really, the majority being against us, is an instrument and means of oppression."[31] In the spring of 1861, Charlestonian Benjamin F. Evans concluded that Northerners had "lost all idea of states rights and constitutions and laws and only require the will of the majority [and] what the majority wants is supremacy."[32] Although secessionists could extol the virtues of democracy within the plantation districts, politics elsewhere made them wary of a democracy without guarantees for minority rights.

The anxiety that Southerners felt about democracy reflected a nationwide shift in attitudes toward party politics. Although distrust of political parties, a sentiment inherent in republicanism, continued after the Revolution, in the 1830s and 1840s most voters accepted parties as instruments of popular will that reinforced the legitimacy and responsiveness of government. By the 1850s, antipartyism intensified in both sections, and the divisive issues of slavery and nativism replaced economic questions related to banking, tariffs, and internal improvements.[33] For all of its hyperbole, the debate between Whigs and Democrats over economic development had kept political partisanship within orderly boundaries. In the 1850s, the moral charge surrounding slavery and nativism fed polarizing rhetoric that cast one's own side as virtuous and the opposition as corrupt and illegitimate. These changes increased voter skepticism of established party leaders and customary political procedures. In this throw-the-bums-out climate of reform opinion, voters least acclimated to the old party system, often workingmen politicized by ethnic and sectional issues, welcomed drastic change. This spirit eroded party loyalty and encouraged disruptive tactics like election rioting.

The emergence of the Know-Nothings in the South's big cities produced anomalous ideological formulations that contributed to secessionist unease over conventional party politics. Baltimore's American Party simultaneously campaigned for the votes of evangelical temperance reformers and rowdy working-class gangs identified with taverns and licentiousness. Roman Catholics helped lead the New Orleans Know-Nothings even as the national party railed against Vatican plots against American freedom. Know-Nothing polling-place mobs redefined proslavery symbols when they accused Democrats of failing to vote a "white man's ticket," a nativist definition of whiteness that excluded the foreign-born. Once the Civil War began, Know-Nothing workers made allies of the free blacks, immigrants, and antislavery Republicans that they had attacked during the 1850s. A laborer's 1855 letter to his father illustrates how Know-Nothing workers could link divisive ideas to disruptive behavior.

> If you had drove a milk waggon in St. Louis as long as I have I believe that you would hate the Irish about as bad as you now do Slavery especially when the City Officers, Mayor down, were about all of that class. . . . It has been the Boast of the Catholics that a Papal Flagg should float over the Polls, if that is attempted the scenes of last August [the date of an election riot], will be no comparison to those we shall have tomorrow.[34]

Urban South Know-Nothings turned the rhetoric of white supremacy on its head, resorted to destabilizing tactics like political violence, and showed remarkable flexibility in forging and breaking political alliances. From the perspective of slaveholders, especially those in states of the lower South that had effectively done away with two-party competition, these actions made parties that engaged the enfranchised wage-earning masses look like a threat to the established social order, even if Southern urban politicians never criticized slavery.

Agreeing with their brethren in the lower South, planters in Maryland, Louisiana, and Missouri regarded their big cities as enemy camps that at best sought to gain more legislative power and at worst plotted to abolish slavery. Slaveholders in states with smaller, rapidly growing cities pondered what would happen if their own metropolis, overrun as it was with foreigners, free blacks, and wage laborers, controlled one-third of the votes cast at any election. Charleston's Leonidas Spratt spelled out this potential for free labor in smaller cities to grow to the point where it threatened slavery in black-majority states like South Carolina, where, Spratt said, "it were to be supposed that here . . . the system of slave society would be permanent and pure."

> But even here [Spratt continued] the process of disintegration has commenced. . . . Within ten years past as many as ten thousand slaves have been drawn away from Charleston by the attractive prices of the West, and laborers from abroad have come to take their places. These laborers have every disposition to work above the slave . . . . And when . . . [white laborers] shall come in greater numbers to the South they will . . . question the right of masters to employ their slaves in any works that they may wish for; they will invoke the aid of legislation;

they will use the elective franchise to that end; they may acquire the power to determine municipal elections; they will inexorably use it; and thus this town of Charleston, at the very heart of slavery, may become a fortress of democratic power against it.[35]

Like other fire-eaters, Spratt made the case for secession as a preventive measure against social changes that would destroy slavery and Southern democracy. Although secession might not halt the economic forces that drove urbanization, it could stifle the political problems that antebellum social change presented to a slaveholders' democracy by severing the tie with mobocracy of the North and turning the slave states' urban voters—outriders of the North's free-labor majority—into a harmless, tiny minority in a polity dominated by country farmers who supported slavery even if they themselves owned no slaves.

The architects of secession argued that slavery and the way of life that went with it could not survive undiluted majority rule in a nation dominated by nonslaveholders. Southern nationalists had long warned that the day would come when the North could elect as president a sectional candidate. Even if that candidate promised to leave slavery alone where it existed, as Lincoln did, he would still use the powers of the federal government to block slavery's growth and then build an anti-slavery party among the South's nonslaveholding whites. Southern cities worried secessionists because urban, white wage earners looked like the first targets of such a campaign. To paraphrase Hammond's case against the North, ardent defenders of slavery wanted to prevent the class that did "the menial duties" and "performed the drudgery of life" from becoming "the majority" and "depositary of all . . . political power" in the South. If the South's enfranchised white working class "knew the secret, that the ballot-box is stronger than 'an army with banners,' and could combine, where would [the South] be?" Without secession, Southern society might be reconstructed, its government overthrown, and its property divided.

Free labor had coexisted with slave labor in the South for generations, and it was not the presence of wage laborers as such that troubled Southern nationalists. Instead, men like Hammond, Ruffin, and Spratt worried about a new kind of free-labor politics that had resulted from the erosion of common interests and identities shared between country slaveholders and urban workingmen. Baltimore and the South's other large cities began their move away from the norms of Southern life when economic and demographic growth disrupted a style of antebellum management of labor that was grounded in patron-client relationships. That ethic of personal authority (termed herein, urban paternalism) resembled the idealized master-slave relationship extolled by Southern planters. By the 1850s, coercive labor controls associated with urban paternalism could no longer suppress labor unrest that inhered in cities with tens of thousands of transient wage earners toiling in an economy subject to frequent slumps and intense competition for jobs. As a result, the slave South started to wonder what it had in common with its largest cities. To better understand the urban South's road to civil war, it is necessary to shift attention to long-term social change inside the cities.

Two

From Urban Paternalism to Free Labor
The Reconfiguration of the Social Order,
1800–1860

Between 1800 and 1860, Baltimore, New Orleans, and St. Louis grew from small commercial centers into much larger cities that mixed commerce and industry. As these cities grew, older systems for managing labor, which in turn affected the arrangement of power in municipal government, no longer suited their needs. At the dawn of the century, work was contracted, performed, and compensated through one-on-one relationships that mixed personal loyalty and coercive controls and that were modeled on a system of household governance that characterized not only slavery but also most other work and family relationships in late-eighteenth-century America.[1] On the eve of the Civil War, the more impersonal wage-labor contract had become the dominant relationship between labor and capital in the largest Southern cities. This chapter explores how an ordering of slave-state city workplaces around urban paternalism gave way to one oriented toward free labor and examines the new social conflicts that accompanied this change.

The term *urban paternalism* is used herein to designate a repertoire of traditional practices that governed work in Southern cities during the early nineteenth century. The methods of urban paternalism included slavery, apprenticeship, low pay, restrictive work rules, and ideological appeals to master-servant obedience. In general, the management strategies encompassed by urban paternalism encouraged employers and employees to conceive of their relationship as that of a powerful patron who dispensed favors to a subordinate client who reciprocated with loyal service. Because these hierarchical relationships applied mostly to the poorest and least-skilled workers who also tended to be African Americans, white females, or immigrants, they reinforced the fissures of gender, culture, and occupation that elevated native-born white craftsmen above others who performed manual labor.

By the 1850s, growth in the size of the overall workforce and of the average workplace magnified the importance of cash wages as an incentive for productivity and made the threat of dismissal rather than physical punishment the preferred remedy for poor performance. However, the gradual pace of economic change eroded the urban paternalist workplace order without entirely eliminating it. Businessmen, skilled mechanics, and unskilled labor—the three broad occupational groups that made up the midcentury urban workforce—sometimes used the patron-client tradition of urban paternalism, when it would advance their condition, but they turned against it if doing so better served their interests.

Skilled native-born craftsmen underwent the greatest change in status of the ethnic/occupational classes affected by urban growth. In the late eighteenth and early nineteenth centuries, the labor aristocracy of self-employed craftsmen and skilled journeyman enjoyed high living standards, a culture of spirited individualism, and access to political and civic leadership. Craft workers celebrated as a bulwark of their liberty artisan traditions inaccessible to the unskilled, and craftsmen who ran small shops or bossed subcontracted gangs of workers perceived themselves as independent partly because they controlled the labor of others. Although the artisans of the early Republic sometimes clashed with merchants and other businessmen, they frequently collaborated with other property owners in pursuing economic growth, and they saw themselves as independent household heads who stood on a par with the other "free men" of the new nation.[2]

By the time of the Civil War, economic growth ruptured this tenuous alliance between skilled workingmen and wealthy businessmen. During the nation's first industrial recession in the 1850s, American-born mechanics saw their living standards decline, and in some work sites they encountered paternalist labor discipline that had heretofore not applied to them. Pressured by immigration and mass production, craft workers lashed out at merchants and manufacturers who had encouraged immigration and the erosion of job skills in order to secure more profit. Native-born mechanics also took action against the growing number of unskilled laborers whose competition brought down wages and working conditions.

Meanwhile, merchants and a new class of prosperous industrialists no longer shared the economic goals of artisan labor; nor did anyone pretend that well-off businessmen stood on a plane of social equality with manual workers practicing skilled trades. The business elite of financiers, manufacturers, and merchants pursued economies of scale that enlarged their workforces and blurred the line between skilled and unskilled labor. Although they welcomed the enhanced profits of the industrializing economy, employers also worried about the new work-force's instability as manifested in strikes, high labor turnover, and conflict between different groups of workers. In the face of these challenges, the business elite tried as best it could to use vestiges of urban paternalism to contain potential conflict.

At the bottom of the new urban economic order were the casual workers who flooded big cities like Baltimore to fill jobs in factories, docks, and private homes. As it had in 1800, the "lower sort" of the Civil War era included large numbers of African Americans, women workers, and European immigrants. These unskilled laborers appealed to the patron-client tradition of urban paternalism to enlist employers in struggles against native-born mechanics who sought their jobs, but they also used their ability to quit an employer or strike for higher wages—violations of the patronage ethic—when doing so broadened their freedom of action.

In sum, economic growth reconfigured the relationship between the ethnic and occupational classes that inhabited city workplaces. Most of the workers in 1850s Baltimore, New Orleans, and St. Louis, were free laborers both in the sense of their relationship to capital—they sold their labor for a wage—and in their self-image—they resented relationships that bound them to employers and limited their ability to seek the main chance. Although remnants of patronage and coercion could be found in slave-state big cities, growth had introduced workplace conflicts that could no longer be managed by paternalist models that the cities of the early Republic had shared with the workplaces of the rural South. The new urban struggle between workers and capitalists brought to the slave states a brand of class conflict from which they had been spared—one that Southerners had theretofore considered as a problem for the American Northeast and England.

Baltimore was the largest city in the late-eighteenth-century South, and it would remain the largest in the region throughout the antebellum era. A detailed look at change in Baltimore's workplace order sheds light on the larger process experienced by cities across the South. In early Republic Southern cities, commerce and industry thrived, but the scale of the work process remained small enough to manage by traditional systems of household authority. By 1800, Baltimore, by the investment of surplus profits from the wheat trade in processing mills, had become America's primary flour producer, and a demographic boom generated by wheat-related and other jobs brought the population to 26,514.[3]

The trade boom had encouraged the development of two types of manufacturing in and around early Republic Baltimore. In the 1810s, cheap export goods like flour and glass flowed from suburban factory villages located in Baltimore County along rivers feeding into Baltimore City, a separate political jurisdiction created in 1797. These mills were heavily capitalized and relied on female and child labor. For example, in 1820, Baltimore County's makers of cotton yarn spent 81 percent of their capital on machinery and hired four children for every adult male. This system had not yet penetrated the more densely populated municipality of Baltimore, where adult artisan production for local consumers prevailed. Between 1770 and 1820, more than half of Baltimore City's white men practiced skilled trades. Most worked in shops that employed ten or fewer hands. In 1820, Baltimore City's coach makers, a representative local trade, spent less than half of their capital on tools and stock, and they gave more than three-fourths of their jobs to adult men who earned twice as much as millhands. In early nineteenth-century Baltimore City, skills had more value in manufacturing than did machines.[4]

Despite differences in organization, employers in both county and city drew on familiar methods of household governance to manage industrial labor. Like capitalists in other American mill villages, Baltimore County industrialists avoided hiring skilled workingmen and thereby excluded traditions of craft autonomy from their establishments. Whole families, unattached children, and single women tended machines, and young shopkeepers and inventors oversaw their labor. Horatio Gambrill, owner of the largest Baltimore County factories, promoted industrious habits and company loyalty by building employee schools, churches, and housing. He increased workers' reliance on this paternal largesse by holding down wages. As late as 1847, when city laborers earned a dollar a day, female millhands took home between $6 and $16 per month after Gambrill had deducted board from their pay. Gambrill and mill owners like him reinforced discipline on the factory floor by utilizing aspects of traditional household government like promoting themselves as the benefactors of their employees and paying workers in kind, rather than cash.[5]

A smaller-scale version of household authority governed manufacturing within the city limits. The coercive controls that shop masters exercised over apprentices and slaves reinforced the boundary of wealth that separated free craftsmen from the other manual laborers in their shops. Master craftsmen held legal authority over apprentices similar to the power that parents exercised over children. Compensated with room, board, education, and, occasionally, small wages, apprentices lived under their master's authority until their indenture contract expired, usually on their twenty-first birthday. Even apprentices who became prosperous artisans later in life complained about the coercive powers of their former masters. John H. W. Hawkins, a successful master hatter in 1830s Baltimore, began his career in the city in an apprenticeship that lasted from 1811 to 1818. Hawkins remembered that at his master's shop "the apprentices . . . were required to be in bed at 9 o'clock, and the hour for instruction in the school room was rigidly observed. Industry was the law of the establishment, and no drones were retained for a moment." Hawkins viewed his master as a benevolent but strict "man of iron will." At the end of his indenture, Hawkins believed that he had been "emancipated . . . from an irksome servitude," and he planned thereafter "to seek his fortune, independent of other's aid." Apprenticeship, a stage that most artisans lived through, made paternalistic labor management an everyday part of the early Republic's manufacturing economy.[6]

In the early 1800s, slaves, who toiled under the harshest form of coerced labor, worked alongside apprentices and journeymen in Baltimore craft shops. Artisans comprised 28 percent of Baltimore slave owners in 1800, and slaves—10 percent of the city's people—predominated in shipbuilding and brickmaking. Manufacturers able to afford the high initial investment in slaves profited if product demand remained steady.[7]

Master craftsmen, the people at the top of this urban manufacturing hierarchy, acted like other independent businessmen and saw themselves as such. Artisan proprietors diversified their investments by buying real estate, and they cultivated friendships with merchants who bought from them and bankrolled their enterprises. This alliance found expression in politics. Early Baltimore City government acted largely as an agent of property owners and merchants. To serve these constituents, the municipal corporation inspected commodities at the port, operated public markets, and maintained streets and the harbor. In the state legislature, merchants and artisans lobbied for economic aid and enhanced urban representation. No matter that they worked with their hands, early national artisans shared cultural and political affiliations with merchants, and they joined in boosting economic expansion even if in the long run it eroded craft vitality.[8]

Baltimore's workplace order gradually changed after the end of the

War of 1812 as new trade patterns impeded the city's competition with other ports. After 1815, England resumed its position as the principal importer of American grain and increased its exports of manufactured goods. Northeastern merchants exploited credit advantages and a shorter route to Europe to secure the bulk of exchange with the British Isles and to capture the lion's share of commerce with the agricultural northwest. Cotton, the South's primary cash crop and the largest source of antebellum export revenue, traveled through New Orleans and New York, bypassing Baltimore. Established credit institutions enabled New York and Philadelphia to better fund the race for interior trade and to develop local industries faster than could Baltimore.[9] To combat these trends, Baltimore merchants maximized their comparative advantages in less-valuable commodities like tobacco, wheat, coffee, and guano, and they invested in railroads and industry as alternatives to water-born commerce. The latter measures enhanced the profitability of factories and new technology at the expense of craft traditions and slavery and brought the suburban factory system within the boundaries of the municipal corporation.

Baltimore staked its bid for the trade of the West on the Baltimore and Ohio Railroad (B&O), chartered in 1828 with state and municipal government underwriting half of its capital stock. The B&O's demand for iron and machinery created new industrial neighborhoods in the southeast suburb of Canton, developed by local merchants and New York investors, and on the west side, where the B&O built its thousand-employee Mount Clare depot and machine shops. Better transportation enabled suburban flour mills to convert to more lucrative production of ship sails and cheap textiles. In 1838, Baltimore City's first clothing factory opened, and by the 1850s the finished clothing trade was the city's largest manufacturing employer. Hallmarks of the textile factories such as simplification of tasks, consolidation of production, and mechanization, spread to iron, chemicals, and sawed timber. The change in production made for higher volume, lower prices, and more emphasis on export markets.[10]

By the 1850s, large-scale industry had become dominant within the city, even though Baltimore craft producers continued working in hundreds of small shops patronized by local consumers. The value of industrial output rose by 50 percent during the 1840s, and investment in manufacturing doubled with ready-made clothing, iron making, and food processing driving the boom. The adoption of steam power allowed industrialists to build nearer to urban wharves and rail depots. In

1850, Baltimore housed 110 steam-powered manufacturing establishments, with approximately 4,300 workers. The share of the city's industrial workers employed in these factories rose from 29 percent to 36 percent during the 1850s. These heavily capitalized businesses profited by making economies of scale. In 1860, 18 percent of manufacturing employees labored in shops of ten or fewer workers, while 54 percent toiled in ones with fifty or more. The latter encompassed the city's four most profitable industries, whose combined revenue more than doubled that of the next six. In 1860, the size of Baltimore's industrial workforce ranked first in the South and sixth in the nation.[11]

Demographic growth accompanied industrial expansion. Baltimore's population doubled from 102,000 in 1840 to 212,000 in 1860. Prior to the 1840s, most newcomers originated in Baltimore's rural hinterland, but in the last two antebellum decades, 170,000 Europeans, mostly Germans and Irish, arrived at the port, and although enough moved on to leave native-born whites in the majority by 1860, foreign-born immigrants comprised one-quarter of the city's population.

Immigration and industrialization bolstered preexisting hierarchies of wealth and cultural background that corresponded to occupation. In 1850, commerce, construction, and industry, fields with relatively few semiskilled and unskilled workers, employed 59 percent of all Baltimore adults and common labor, service, and transport—sectors with large majorities of low-skilled jobs—employed 31 percent. Native-born white men predominated in the former areas, comprising 57 percent of manufacturers and two-thirds of building and commercial workers, whereas African Americans, women, and immigrants outnumbered them in semiskilled and unskilled jobs in labor, service, and transport. Despite a loose resemblance between this pattern of segmentation and the early 1800s, the changing ratio of employees to shops points to large-scale production as the leader in a process of growth that diminished the value of manual skills.[12]

The antebellum expansion of industry and population went the farthest in Baltimore, but the same trends transformed St. Louis and New Orleans, the major cities of the western slave states. In St. Louis and New Orleans, growth created a diverse economy, an ethnically heterogeneous workforce, and a free-labor system of employment that relied much more on wages than it did on coercive relationships like slavery.

Prior to the 1820s, St. Louis was a frontier town that lived off the fur trade and supplying the military. After recovering from the panic of 1819, St. Louis emerged as the principal transshipment point on the upper Mississippi. Although they started later than Baltimore's leading commercial families, St. Louis merchants eyed the new opportunities in manufacturing and, after 1840, they underwrote a host of new ventures that profited from the growth of trade and the labor force. Between 1840 and 1860, St. Louis's population skyrocketed from 16,469 to 160,773. In 1860, flour milling and food processing, industries developed with surplus merchant capital, led the manufacturing sector with iron making and machine making growing in significance. St. Louis had nothing to rival Mount Clare, but it did boast several factories with more than one hundred workers. Compared with Baltimore, a greater share of St. Louis's industrial laborers, who numbered roughly 12,000 in 1860, found jobs in the smaller clothing, shoe, and cigar making shops that helped give St. Louis the nation's tenth largest industrial workforce on the eve of the Civil War.[13]

Farther south, New Orleans had the longest history as a site for government and commerce, yet it trailed far behind the other metropolitan centers in developing manufacturing. Trade via the Mississippi offered so much bounty that merchants focused their energies almost exclusively on boosting commerce. In 1860, New Orleans had the smallest manufacturing workforce (5,162 industrial workers in a total population of 168,675) of any American city with more than one hundred thousand people. Nevertheless, on the eve of the Civil War, New Orleans housed approximately forty-one thousand free manual workers, more than the total population of most Southern cities. This group split almost evenly between skilled and unskilled labor, with the former category's wages doubling the latter's. Low industrial investment and a large urban consumer market meant that most skilled work occurred in artisan shops, while the majority of unskilled jobs were in the hauling of cargo and in service. Michael Daffy, a young Irish immigrant, gave a typical account of such casual work in New Orleans. "I am a laboring man. Sometimes I work on the Levee, sometimes in the cotton yard, sometime steamboating." American-born whites, many of them migrants from the upper South and northeast, made up half of the skilled workers, and immigrants, particularly the Irish, predominated in common labor.[14]

Economic expansion affected Southern city workers in different ways that accorded to their legal and occupational status. Degrees of wealth and workplace power ran along a continuum from the absolute servitude experienced by African-American slaves to the expansive freedom enjoyed by native-born white craftsmen. A survey of differing ways that blacks, immigrants, and native-born white artisans experienced freedom and coercion in late-antebellum workplaces illustrates how the wage-labor economy combined new freedoms with restrictive aspects of employer paternalism and artisan privilege that had been handed down from the early Republic.

The persistence of coerced labor and patron-client relationships made Baltimore, St. Louis, and New Orleans unique sites for the development of free labor in Civil War era America. On the one hand, the presence of tens of thousands of wage laborers differentiated the big cities from other Southern places. On the other hand, the fact that these free laborers toiled alongside slaves distinguished Baltimore, St Louis, and New Orleans from the industrial cities of the free states. Although in decline in the big cities, the presence of slavery and its acceptance by the vast majority of white Southern city dwellers gave other types of workplace coercion more legitimacy than was possible in the North, where traditional forms of household governance had come under a more vigorous and broad-ranging attack.[15]

To understand how slavery could be in decline yet still influence urban work and culture, it helps to concentrate on Baltimore, which not only had the most people of any Southern metropolis, but also had the most African Americans. By 1860, slaves had dwindled to 2 percent of Baltimore's population as a result of the Chesapeake region's faltering tobacco economy and a pattern of gradual emancipation that had unique benefits for urban masters but that eroded the viability of slavery within the city. Most late-antebellum Baltimore slaves were women, and most of them worked as domestic servants. Baltimore's 4,515 black servants, free and slave, made up more than one-fourth of African-American workers, and in the manuscript census they were 61 percent of black women listing an occupation, a pattern common to the urban South. Domestic service put the weakest players in the urban economy under direct supervision of the strongest and nurtured a paternalistic self-image on the part of employers.[16]

Serena Johnson, an enslaved domestic servant, is a case in point. She arrived in Baltimore as a six-year-old in 1829 when Henry Rieman, a prosperous German-American merchant, took her from her family by purchasing her from a rural master. Initially a playmate for Rieman's daughters, as Johnson grew into a full-fledged housekeeper her masters projected onto her the familiar slave-owner stereotypes of their chattels as childish and loyal. Rieman's daughter described Johnson as "an unconscionable little monkey" who stole toys and broke valuables. She also said that Johnson "loved all the children, was beloved by all, respected and trusted by her master and mistress." Johnson, who stayed with the family after emancipation in 1865, left her savings to Rieman's daughters and asked to be buried at the foot of her master's grave with the epitaph "Faithful servant of Henry Rieman." Johnson's life showed how the situation of enslaved domestics suppressed African-American autonomy and encouraged masters to view blacks as social inferiors whose labor was best governed through traditional household management.[17]

This cultural effect of slavery persisted into the 1850s; however, in 1860, slaveholders comprised a mere 1 percent of Baltimore whites, and the majority of whites who used African-American labor did so through coercive controls that applied to free blacks. Some slaveholders adapted to economic change by leasing their slaves to urban employers (for example, Frederick Douglass, the Baltimore slave best known to historians, was hired out to a shipbuilder in the 1830s) but by midcentury most urban masters had either sold their chattels south or manumitted them.

African Americans remained vital to the city's economy as nonenslaved household servants and common laborers. As the slave population decreased, between 1820 and 1850 the number of free blacks shot up dramatically, making Baltimore's free black population the largest in American cities. Economic expansion created some opportunities for Baltimore's free African Americans: in 1850, one-fifth of the city's African-American men held skilled jobs, with their numbers strongest in brickmaking, ship caulking, and barbering. Nonetheless, the overwhelming majority of free black Baltimoreans congregated on the lower rungs of the occupational ladder, and as a result they held a paltry $17 per capita in property in the 1850 census, compared with $286 for whites.[18] Unlike Northern cities, where African Americans made up a small share of the total wage workforce, free blacks in Baltimore and New Orleans dominated some unskilled trades, and, although less numerous, they mattered to St. Louis's economy. As both the poorest class of free laborers and the group most closely tied to the condition of slaves, free black workers predominated in the lowest paying jobs that Southern cities had to offer.

Slaves had become marginal in St. Louis as in Baltimore, but the city's free black population also failed to grow. As a share of St. Louis's population, African Americans, free and slave, fell from 25 percent in 1830 to 2 percent in 1860. Nonetheless, St. Louis's economy profited from slave sales and from the leasing of slaves to employers such as steamboat captains, who needed continuous labor for long stretches.

what does this sent. have to do w/ anything

Harshly treated by this system, William Wells Brown, a slave hired out in the 1840s, said that "no part of our slaveholding country is more noted for the barbarity of its inhabitants than St. Louis." As for St. Louis's free people of color, a handful of relatively rich families ran small businesses and sponsored schools and churches, but most worked in unskilled and semiskilled trades in almost the same proportions as in Baltimore.[19]

Located in the lower South, New Orleans had the highest ratio of African Americans in its population (23 percent in 1850) and the most complex community of color of the South's three largest cities. Despite numerical decline in the preceding decades, in 1860 more than ten thousand slaves lived in New Orleans, and slave hiring flourished. Because African Americans made up a larger share of New Orleans's total population, free blacks held more skilled jobs in the Crescent City than they did in St. Louis and Baltimore, where pressure from white newcomers drove free blacks from some trades. Construction employed most of New Orleans skilled free black workers, but some practiced crafts like shoemaking that, in cities nearer the sectional border, whites monopolized.

These advantages translated into greater wealth. New Orleans free blacks owned roughly fifteen times as much property as their Baltimore counterparts. At the top of this group stood the *gens de coleur*, wealthy Francophones who traced their origins to the West Indies and intermarriage with Europeans and who enjoyed greater legal rights, such as the ability to sue in courts, than did free blacks in other states. The French presence along with stronger cultural survivals from West Africa helped to set the Crescent City's African-American community apart from the rest of the urban South.[20]

When applied to nonenslaved African Americans, the adjective *free* obscures the numerous legal and cultural constraints that maintained white supremacy over blacks who were not slaves. The web of coercion that surrounded free blacks constituted another category of urban paternalism, and one that remained in full effect in the 1850s. Discriminatory laws limited African-American opportunities for rising out of low-paying jobs and contributed to the paucity of wealthy Southern blacks. In Baltimore, restrictions on black political rights—bans on voting, testifying against whites, public assembly, and travel—made government hostile to free blacks. Police arrested free African Americans out of proportion to their share of the population, sentenced them to longer terms than white criminals, and after 1858 sold them into slavery. To discourage black social prominence, city government segre-

poor structure & general ize then comp / verso

gated public space and joined downstate slave owners in supporting the Maryland Colonization Society, which deported free blacks to Liberia. Lobbied by influential whites, government barred African Americans from nonmanual professions (e.g., they could not form interracial business partnerships, do clerking, or command a ship), but it rejected proposals for color bars in blue-collar trades like hack driving. By the 1850s, the state required free African Americans who broke employment contracts to perform labor without pay and sent indigent black adults to workhouses and apprenticed their children. In a sample of 177 indentures filed in 1851 and 1857, blacks doubled their proportion of Baltimore's inhabitants and more than three-fourths learned trades like servant or laborer that offered little upward mobility. In the 1840s and 1850s, legislatures across the South circumscribed the already narrow liberty of free blacks in order to strengthen slavery. Antebellum racial laws isolated free blacks from other workers and could be used by employers as a buffer against labor turnover and collective action.[21]

This system of quasi freedom made friendly relationships with wealthy white patrons vital for African-American job seekers. Many cities promoted clientage with registration and sponsorship laws. For example, St. Louis's license system apprenticed all free African-American children. The law also required every black adult to find a white sponsor who would post a bond for his or her good behavior.[22]

In Baltimore, the city where free blacks were most numerous (25,680 in 1860), industrial workplace patronage found its best expression in ship caulking. Caulking, Baltimore's eighth most common black occupation, exemplified how free blacks managed to dominate some trades in slave-state cities. Prior to job-busting race riots in the late 1850s, almost no whites worked as caulkers, and in 1860 African Americans still accounted for three-fourths of Baltimore's 181 caulkers. The Caulkers Association, a black trade union, mutual benefits provider, and literary society, maintained the African-American presence in caulking by negotiating an exclusive employment arrangement with a white shipbuilders' guild that included prominent politicians. Black caulkers enforced the agreement by striking nonparticipating shipyards and sabotaging their boats.

For the shipbuilders' guild, restricting hiring to the Caulkers Association ensured a reliable and skilled workforce: most of the black caulkers were trained by and related to early Republic African-American shipyard workers. The agreement also helped guild builders to discourage newcomers who tried to set up shop in Baltimore. Employers relied on the Caulkers Association to boycott the yards of such upstart shipbuilders. A reporter's observation that "the black caulkers have been used to bring refractory members to terms" reflected the cooperation that stung nonguild builders. Like other Southern blacks who made the transition from slavery to quasi freedom, Baltimore caulkers maintained predominance in a good-paying craft (wages averaged $1.75 per day), and thereby turned one aspect of urban paternalism to their advantage. Yet this position of relative privilege had its price. Because free black caulkers relied on elite patronage for employment, they were expected to aid their wealthy patrons when circumstances required.[23]

In 1858, a gang of white workers used violence to drive the Caulkers Association from shipyards in south Baltimore. Although rare, such attempts to force blacks out of specific trades or work sites dated back to the 1830s. These efforts belonged to a broader pattern of white demand for black jobs that accompanied the whitening of Southern city populations that began in the mid-1830s. Between 1840 and 1860, the ten largest slave-state cities added 444,000 whites and lost 682 blacks. Consequently, the share of blacks in their collective population fell from one-third to one-sixth. As in other aspects of slave state urbanization, Baltimore, St. Louis, and New Orleans led the trend, taking in 331,550 whites and losing 10,659 African Americans. This shift affected politics, economy, and culture. More white workers meant more eligible voters, a workforce with greater legal rights, and a mix of ethnicities more like New York and Philadelphia than Charleston or Mobile.[24]

Confronted by the growth of the white workforce, white employers in Baltimore and elsewhere searched for ways to shore up urban paternalist controls on their workers. They viewed black labor as a counterweight to the power of politically enfranchised white wage earners. In Maryland, this outlook informed conservative opposition to reenslaving free blacks, a movement that swept the South after abolitionist John Brown raided Harpers Ferry, Virginia in 1859. That year, C. W. Jacobs, a Maryland legislator representing a downstate county engaged in plantation agriculture, put forward a referendum that would have enslaved or banished the state's large free black population. Jacobs's bill failed, with overwhelming opposition coming from Baltimore. Local opponents included influential white employers and politicians who otherwise supported slavery—men like Reverdy Johnson, the former U.S. attorney general and the lawyer for F. A. Sanford in the Dred Scott case. One such white conservative, Baltimore editor Frank Key Howard, whose grandfathers were Francis Scott Key and a former Maryland governor, argued that quasi freedom benefited employers and warned that if Jacobs's bill became law, "a class [will] pour in to take the place vacated by the negroes, who hate and are jealous of slaveholders." White employers who agreed with Howard wanted to sustain the nonenslaved African-American workforce rather than eliminate it because they not only profited from the lower wages paid to free blacks, but they also believed that black clients could be used as leverage to counteract the militancy of white workers.[25]

In this context, free blacks sought white allies to stave off even harsher measures like reenslavement or colonization, and those alliances reinforced patron-client relationships at the workplace. James Thomas, an emancipated slave who became one of St. Louis's wealthiest free blacks, remembered the value of patronage. "The free Negro was tolerated around the gentleman's home as his Barber, and frequently served as good fellow to wait the table. . . . He always had a friend in case of need if regarded worthy."[26]

Of all the varieties of urban paternalism, the condition of free blacks most clearly borrowed from the countryside's master-slave model of authority. However, the patron-client ethic and the coercive controls that supported it also applied to segments of the white workforce. They were especially evident in the lives of low-income immigrants. By mid-century, municipal governments found that boarding indigent persons with responsible families, a practice common in the smaller towns of the eighteenth century, could no longer address the problems of providing for paupers, a group that numbered in the thousands and that included many foreign-born strangers. The publicly funded poorhouse took the place of the homes of civic-minded patriarchs as the institution that supported those too poor to provide for themselves. Although government institutions like the poorhouse undermined the overall authority of household heads by supplanting one of their traditional duties, their rules were modeled on the older system of household government that treated paupers as dependents in need of supervision from their social betters.[27]

In Baltimore, poor relief involved city government through the Alms House, which had been established in 1773 as a refuge for the disabled and infirm. In the 1850s, vagrancy laws consigned to the Alms House poor people who did not meet the traditional categories of infirmity and illness. In 1852, the Alms House averaged between six hundred and seven hundred residents per month, with immigrants comprising almost one-half of those committed for vagrancy. Two years later, the state required destitute parents to "show cause . . . why such minor[s] should not be sent to the almshouse . . . and bound out to some useful art, trade or occupation." In 1858, city government opened the Home of the Friendless, a female orphanage and poorhouse that pushed girls into apprenticeships. Baltimore's poor also relied on the Alms House hospital, which admitted fifteen thousand people annually. As population growth overwhelmed private charity, city government stepped in to provide for the poor, but in doing so municipal officials sought to retain the patronage relationship between the very wealthy and the very poor.[28]

Municipal poor relief in St. Louis and New Orleans operated the same way. In St. Louis, charity and taxes supported a public hospital and a workhouse. City officials gave cash relief to applicants endorsed by prominent citizens. In the 1850s, immigrants made up three-fourths of the workhouse inmates and received most of the poor-relief grants. In New Orleans, Charity Hospital, a Roman Catholic institution supported by public funds, provided health care and poor relief for penniless immigrants. A few antebellum philanthropists even proposed colonizing indigent Europeans in the West, not unlike removal plans for Indians and African Americans.[29]

Like government, private immigrant aid and poor relief offered assistance in ways that kept recipients under the watchful eye of civic leaders. Staffed by politicians and businessmen, Baltimore's Poor Association required relief applicants to give proof of their sober and industrious habits. Baltimore's Hibernian Society, directed by established Protestant Irish commercial families, ran a school for immigrants and dispensed more than $1,000 a year to indigent Irish newcomers. To encourage thriftiness, the society limited cash assistance to three months. As in Baltimore, in St. Louis and New Orleans national churches and immigrant-aid societies led by second and third generation families dispensed aid to newcomers. Disparities in wealth inherent in private charities encouraged relief seekers to present themselves to philanthropists as deferential clients. "I hope my prayer to you make you not angry, and you would be kind and excuse me," opened one such request to a Baltimore jurist from a suburban pastor. "My poor Germans [would] like much to have a little bell in her steeple and I pray you in her names you would be so kind and help us, beloved rich gentleman! God will bless you for such benefaction."[30]

White casual laborers likely to seek charity often found that the conditions of their work limited their ability to defy their bosses. Michael

Riley, an Irish gardener employed by Baltimore flour miller Moses Merryman, exemplified this situation. Merryman put Riley to a variety of tasks at his suburban estate and provided room and board as a supplement to Riley's meager half-dollar daily pay. Riley, who lived at the estate but was often without work due to seasonal demand at the mill, received more than one-third of his yearly $40 income in food and household goods. Merryman also did favors for Riley, like hiring his son for odd jobs and supplying medicine to ill family members. For Riley, who was expected to be at the estate around the clock, losing a job meant losing a home and all support.[31]

Records from Baltimore's municipal port warden show the importance of personal influence in a more structured casual-labor environment and illustrate how unskilled immigrants—as the black caulkers had done—could put patronage to their own uses. The port warden maintained public wharves and ran dredging scows that kept the harbor channel navigable and free of noxious sewage. So that dredging could begin at daybreak, the 1850s superintendent, William Costigan, a veteran municipal employee and political activist, required crews to sleep on the scow six nights a week during the busy summer months. He routinely fired men for drinking or lingering in town on the weekend and made special efforts to steadily employ talented hands. On crew lists from 1853 to 1858, firemen, deckhands, and scowmen averaged ten months on the job, while skilled and managerial workers—wheelmen, navigators, engineers, and captains—typically stayed on for twenty-seven months. When weather prevented dredging, Costigan gave the jobs of deckhand and watchman to his blacksmiths and engineers so as to keep these valuable men with him and avoid expensive contracts with independent blacksmiths unaccustomed to his authority.[32]

Like a good patron, Costigan rewarded unskilled immigrants who adapted to his managerial demands. Hired as a deckhand in 1858, German-born Jackson Iglenfritz showed ability and advanced to blacksmithing and dredging. Costigan may have favored Iglenfritz because he could pay him less; in 1860, Iglenfritz worked as a blacksmith but continued to earn a deckhand's $1.15 daily wage. For Iglenfritz, the chance to enter a skilled trade offset low pay, and eventually Costigan promoted him to the rank of engineer and doubled his wages.[33]

Iglenfritz's case suggests how the new complexity of business organization undermined traditional promotion systems within skilled trades. The increasing size of bureaucratic organizations like city government transferred hiring decisions from independent craftsmen who often recruited members of their own kin group to salaried managers more concerned with costs and efficiency than with craft solidarity. For craft workers, a group that employers like Gambrill, Merryman, and Costigan avoided, paternalism shaped work relations for apprentices, but adult artisans prided themselves on their independence and sneered at the constraints on hirelings like Riley and Iglenfritz. Crafts resistant to deskilling and mechanization provided a haven for small-scale producers who retained control over working conditions and enjoyed social prestige traditionally accorded to artisans. The most successful of these mechanics could achieve great wealth and wield public power, and many remained convinced that their interests intertwined with those of merchants and manufacturers. Endowed with a degree of workplace autonomy that slaves, free blacks, and penniless immigrants seldom experienced, white artisans comprised the most powerful manual workers in the South's cities.

Amid the change in industrial organization, manual skills remained at a premium in some fields. For example, Joshua Vansant used hat making, a subfield of the clothing industry resistant to mass production, to launch a prominent public career. In 1818, Vansant left his family's farm on Maryland's Eastern Shore for an apprenticeship to a Baltimore hatter. Upon completing his service, Vansant worked twelve years as a journeyman, a time when he claimed never to be "out of work or out of money." In 1833, Vansant led journeymen hatters in a strike against wage cuts. Three years later, he opened a shop and became an employer in his own right. His prominence in the strike and participation in debating societies caught the attention of Democratic Party leaders, who helped him start a political career that included service as city postmaster, congressman, and mayor. In 1850, Vansant owned $1,500 in property, five times the average for adult Baltimoreans. He was the most successful of a number of hatters who used their craft to accumulate wealth and move up and out of the workshop.[34]

Construction workers also exploited the advantages accruing to skill to make money and gain public influence. Prior to the 1850s, most property owners contracted builders by the task according to customary rates, a practice that gave specialists more control over their work. Exemplifying building's opportunities, master carpenter Jacob Small Jr. was elected mayor in the late 1820s, superintended a B&O depot, and owned slaves and real estate. Employer criticism mattered little to confident artisans like Small. When church officials complained about the height of a belfry he was making, Small replied, "You think it's too low, do you? Wait, wait, maybe when you see the bill, maybe, you will find it high enough." Assertive like Small, William Otter, an itinerant plasterer who lived in 1830s Baltimore, led a gang of "jolly fellows" that delighted in violent pranks against vulnerable targets like apprentices and African Americans. In the 1840s, he ran a business in Emmitsburg, Maryland, and ran successfully for mayor. Not all mechanics were so rude. The Logan brothers, Baltimore house carpenters, abstained from drink and spent their leisure time in church and educational lyceums, and one became a Methodist minister. The ability to accumulate property and play leading roles in public associations, rather than a uniform moral tone, distinguished artisans in trades resistant to deskilling from casual labor.[35]

The careers of artisans like Vansant and Small reflected cooperation between skilled white workingmen and merchants and financiers that extended to politics. The system of urban paternalism that governed work experience and that created status and opportunities for skilled workingmen had a cognate in municipal politics, where the business elite exercised the most influence over government, but craft producers also wielded power and found reasons to forge alliances with merchants and professionals in the Jacksonian era's political parties. Historians have noted the ways that Whigs and Democrats at the federal level dampened sectional conflict by bringing voters from different regions together in national parties. Similarly, the parties quieted class conflict in urban politics because each drew support from the top and middle economic ranks, while neither afforded influence to the lower sort, a dynamic reinforced by racial and gender restrictions on the suffrage and the concentration of eligible voters in good jobs.

In Baltimore, the era of institutionalized, mass political parties began in the 1830s with the reformulation of the Democratic-Republicans into a Jackson party and a Whig opposition. Maryland's 1824 presidential balloting carried forward a voting pattern established in Thomas Jefferson's time, Andrew Jackson polling strongest in western Maryland and Baltimore, areas of Democratic-Republican strength, while John Quincy Adams, popular with former Federalists, won the slaveholding counties in the south and Eastern Shore. After Jackson won the presidency in 1828, his supporters took control of the Maryland legislature, or General Assembly, as it was called. An anti-Jackson movement then formed in reaction against the president's laissez-faire economic policies. In 1830, the opposition captured the assembly, and in 1834 a formal Whig Party organized in support of rechartering the

Second Bank of the United States (BUS), the kind of public-private joint venture that underlay economic development schemes like the B&O.[36]

With the new parties in place, Jackson's Democrats proceeded to dominate Baltimore politics for the next two decades, but Whigs had enough urban support to supplement their strength in Maryland's slaveholding agricultural counties and thereby maintain a secure hold on state government. Democrats won in Baltimore by representing an alternative to the dominance of rural Whigs and by addressing the concerns of middling craftsmen and small proprietors, groups they touted as the "bone and sinew" of their party. Their appeal to wage earners combined national stands with local opposition to regulating mechanic trades, an attack on Whig-imposed state taxes as harmful to poorer voters, and calls for greater urban representation in the state assembly.[37]

Rather than criticize Democrats for their overtures to labor, Baltimore Whigs tried to shake the mantle of a patrician party and won some support from skilled workers. Whig leaders like John Pendleton Kennedy, a lawyer and factory owner, told workingmen that local industry would benefit from party economic policies like internal improvements, tariffs, and a central bank. This argument had some success. In 1834, craftsmen contributed nearly half of the 680 signatures on a Whig memorial urging support for the BUS. Four-fifths of the remaining petitioners held nonmanual occupations. Whigs in Baltimore like Whigs across the nation drew support from the middle and upper classes.[38]

Despite its intensity, Whig and Democratic competition did not translate into a sharp cleavage in the social basis of their support; the parties agreed on issues broadly endorsed by likely voters and uniformly opposed measures like emancipation, woman's suffrage, and factory wage and safety legislation that, although popular with some city dwellers, lacked a sizeable constituency in the electorate. Similarly, in St. Louis and New Orleans, Democrats polled well among workingmen who endorsed Jackson's common-man appeal and viewed Whig planters and urban reformers with suspicion. Nevertheless Whigs scored some upsets in each city.[39]

The restriction of political participation to a privileged subset of urban society underlay this major party consensus, and understanding who voted and governed clarifies the links between what contemporaries viewed as the natural social markers of race and gender with the more abstract hierarchies of work and politics. In 1850, Baltimore's eligible voters were a well-off elite in comparison with the rest of the city because the concentration of wealth and high-status occupations among white male citizens age twenty-one and older—the criterion for the franchise—meant that the electorate overrepresented the native-born and the wealthy. According to a contemporary, "one out of eight in the whole population is entitled to vote." Immigrants comprised 32 percent of adult Baltimoreans, but a five-year wait for naturalization cut their share of the eligible voters to 23 percent. One-third of eligible voters practiced a nonmanual trade, as opposed to one-fifth of all workers. Skilled craftsmen made up the plurality of adult Baltimoreans and eligible voters, but the representation of unskilled and semiskilled manual workers, nearly one-third of the workforce, fell to one-fifth of the electorate as a result of franchise rules. A potential voter was more than twice as likely as the average adult to own property, and 50 percent more likely to do so than the typical white man.[40]

Baltimore's mix of African-American and immigrant minorities employed in an industrial setting distinguished its voting pool from those of Northern industrializing cities and smaller Southern ports. The overlapping categories of unskilled workers and immigrants exercised more political power in Northern cities than they did in Baltimore because cities in the North had a higher ratio of immigrants, two-fifths as opposed to one fourth, and Baltimore had a greater share of disenfranchised African Americans (15 percent) than the urban North (3 percent).[41] Conversely, in Charleston, Richmond, Savannah, and Mobile, African Americans were two-fifths to more than one-half of the population, and few native-born whites worked for wages. In smaller Southern cities, concentration of disenfranchised blacks and transient foreigners in manual labor limited workers' political power.[42]

Demographically and politically, Baltimore had the most in common with New Orleans, which was not as industrial but offered enough jobs through its port economy to attract working-class voters in numbers capable of rivaling the political voice of businessmen. Baltimore and New Orleans had greater shares of native-born skilled workers in their electorates than most other American cities. Nevertheless, in these cities' electorates, white-collar professionals outnumbered by two-to-one enfranchised low-skilled workers, the voters with the most objective grievances against the emerging industrial order.[43]

The conditions of political participation made government one of several venues outside the workplace where the business elite could assert their social leadership and reinforce their economic authority. Although artisans could derail a campaign that ran roughshod over their interests, the political power of the upper class increased at successive levels of participation in these cities, as it did in most of urban America. Poll books from the late 1830s and a list of voters from 1858 constitute the best available records on who actually voted in Baltimore, and they show that nonmanual workers, a minority of the entire city, cast a majority of the ballots, while semiskilled and unskilled laborers voted at roughly half the rate of their representation in the electorate. In a consecutive run of voting data from 1837 to 1840, less than one-half the voters at an election turned out for the next one, and men in higher-status occupations were most likely to vote repeatedly. While long-term residence and heading a family also correlated strongly with eligibility and voting, wealth and occupation best predicted whether an enfranchised individual would actually cast a ballot. Participation by eligible Baltimore voters averaged 50 to 60 percent in state and national contests, but the highest turnouts failed to surpass 15 percent of all city dwellers: most Baltimoreans did not vote, and those that did tended to belong to wealthier, native-born families with deep roots in the city, a pattern typical of the system of Whig-versus-Democrat competition across the country.[44]

Already underrepresented in the electorate and at the polling booth, even fewer wage earners and immigrants held a government or party office. Scholars have found no dramatic differences in the wealth, occupations, and ethnicity of Baltimore Democrat and Whig leaders for the 1830s and 1840s. Merchants and professionals dominated the highest offices in both parties, particularly those at the state and federal level, and the average wealth of party leaders was well above the city-wide mean, but skilled workers and petty proprietors held many more offices than they did prior to the 1830s. Artisans made up 40 percent of party leaders, with somewhat greater representation among Democrats than Whigs. On the other hand, unskilled workers almost never won nominations. Although both parties included prominent immigrants on their tickets, the native-born, mostly Marylanders and Protestants, comprised more than 90 percent of their leaders. Artisans and shopkeepers held real power, but wealthy men dominated both parties and left little room for the poorest eligible voters.[45]

In Jacksonian politics, craft workers wielded political influence by partnering with businessmen who dominated the top spots in politics and the economy. On occasion, skilled labor and the business elite clashed—most notably in Baltimore in the Bank of Maryland Riot of

1835, when artisan mobs destroyed the property of bank directors and allied politicians whom rioters believed had cheated small depositors. Nevertheless, cooperation between the two groups was far more common. Stable two-party competition and the hierarchy of the workplace reinforced each other because each set of relationships helped to persuade skilled workers, a much larger chunk of the population than the business elite, that they benefited from the established urban social order and should maintain it.

By the 1850s, economic and demographic change that had been building in the prior decades reconfigured the social order of Jacksonian-era Southern cities. Immigration's downward pressure on wages and the spread of large-scale industry diminished the profits and prestige of the small workshop and narrowed the chances for native-born mechanics to succeed in the manner of Vansant and Small. During the decade, Baltimore's native-born whites lost their majority in industrial and skilled jobs, and in fields that had traditionally employed American-born mechanics, like railroading and iron work, employers experimented with coercive controls and pay-cutting strategies reminiscent of labor management at textile factories and flour mills. This economic restructuring transformed urban paternalism from a source of cooperation between skilled workers and the business elite into a point of friction between the two groups as native-born artisans came to perceive businessmen and their unskilled working-class clients as twin agents of their straightened circumstances.

In the mid-1850s, American cities experienced what one historian has termed a "hidden depression," a contraction in jobs and income that bypassed the countryside.[46] This downturn hit Baltimore in 1853 when the B&O's westward expansion, which had funded machine building and home construction, halted after the railroad completed its link to Wheeling, Virginia. Slack demand for rails and machine parts sent ripple effects throughout Baltimore's industrial west side. The problem worsened the next year when the national industrial economy entered a recession from which it only briefly recovered before the panic of 1857 did more damage. Investors shifted capital to low-wage industries such as clothes, food processing, and cigar making, fields that had immigrant majorities in their workforces. Structural change in the 1850s brought to reality artisan fears that mass production and population growth would threaten their standing atop the hierarchy of urban manual labor.

As measured by the population census, employment opportunities changed subtly during the 1850s. Manufacturing jobs and unskilled service work experienced modest growth, rising respectively from 33 and 9 percent of all listed occupations in 1850 to 36 and 13 percent in 1860. Meanwhile, employment in transportation and construction, sectors with a range of job skills, declined in significance. Because many new industrial jobs required fewer skills and paid less, these shifts in employment marked a deskilling of the workforce. This was a job market fitted to European arrivals, the most rapidly growing segment of the city population, and they pursued work in competition with groups at both ends of the manual labor hierarchy.

European immigration put pressure on jobs held by preexisting class-and-ethnic groups at the bottom and top of the urban workforce. While the city grew by one-quarter in the 1850s, African-American numbers were static, consequently their share of city residents dropped from 17 percent to 13 percent, and their access to semiskilled work came under pressure from new arrivals. The poorest German and Irish newcomers congregated in cheap housing near the waterfront and pressed for jobs held by blacks in cargo handling. Between 1850 and 1860, the number of immigrants employed in hauling trades in dockside wards increased by 43 percent, while the number of blacks dropped 16 percent. The Irish led the way by acquiring sixty new jobs, more than the total of fifty-four lost by blacks. Immigrant gains in hauling stemmed from their already sizable share (38 percent) of those jobs in 1850; the absence of a black monopoly, or any union organization; and the labor demands of longshoring, which valued strong men ready to work over years of experience, a benefit to recent arrivals. In 1858, a different set of competitors, native-born whites, used violence to take work from black caulkers. African Americans driven out of transport and construction crowded into already predominantly black service jobs that magnified their dependence on wealthy white patrons.[47]

Although scholars have paid less attention to it, the proportion of native-born whites in Baltimore also declined in the 1850s. The small shift of American-born whites in the overall population—this category fell from 63 percent to 62 percent—masked their loss of majority status among working-age residents, where white natives fell from 52 percent to 46 percent.

The growing immigrant working population pushed its way into manufacturing at the expense of the American-born. Unskilled immigrants found the most work in industries where mass-production techniques and the division of labor had the greatest impact. In Baltimore as in many cities, the apparel trades were at the center of these changes. After 1830, cheaply made men's clothes rose in prominence because they sold in greater volume, employed more hands, and were amenable to the practice of sweating (i.e., outsourcing supplies to women and children who, working at home, produced sewn and trimmed pieces at cut-rate prices). Commenting on sweating's abuses, an 1857 report stated that seamstresses "on making application for work at many places are obliged to deposit the value of the goods entrusted to them in cash, and after a week of unremitting labor at almost starving prices . . . are charged with destroying the garments, and while they are refused payment because of the alleged damage the deposit money is withheld from them to make up the loss."[48]

In the 1850s, tailors and clothiers exploited the sweating system, while factories using newly available sewing machines concentrated production under one roof and employed between eight hundred and twelve hundred hands per establishment. Because it offered low-paying, entry-level jobs—daily wages averaged fifty cents—men's apparel employed immigrants who either had experience as tailors or could not access more restricted crafts. This was especially true for German newcomers, of whom one in four worked in men's clothing. In 1860, the clothing trades employed one-third of all Baltimore industrial workers and four-fifths of the women working in industry. Furthermore, immigrants comprised a majority of textile hands. Apparel made fortunes for investors like Johns Hopkins and immigrant merchant-manufacturers like the Friedenwald-Wiesenfeld family, but few cutters or sewers advanced up and out of manual labor.[49]

Along with taking new positions in garment making, immigrants also made substantial inroads into less dynamic industries previously dominated by native-born whites. In 1850, white natives outnumbered foreigners in all job sectors. In 1860, they had fallen behind immigrants in the transport sector and in all forms of unskilled work, particularly common labor and service, and they were on the verge of second-place status in manufacturing. Although Baltimore's industrial sector grew by 10 percent in the 1850s, metal and woodworking, mainstays of American mechanics, saw their share of industrial employment shrink overall. Census data show that immigrants grabbed the few new jobs that these trades offered. In metalworking, the share of jobs held by white natives fell from 64 percent to 57 percent, while the proportion of immigrants rose from 33 percent to 41 percent.

Immigration and industrial change had the same kind of impact on

St. Louis and New Orleans. In each city, unskilled European labor made gains at the expense of American-born blacks and whites. In St. Louis, a city with an immigrant majority, not only did Irish and German newcomers dominate transport and service but Germans, one-third of St. Louis's people, held one-half of all skilled jobs in 1850, and ten years later they controlled 70 percent.[50] In the 1850s, foreign-born New Orleanians increased by one-fourth—an Irish majority was followed by Germans and a sizeable French contingent—even though the number of American-born whites in the city grew faster. By 1860, Germans in New Orleans had made some of the same inroads into the workforce as they had in Baltimore and St. Louis. They were a majority in the semiskilled trade of draying and in the better-paying iron industry.[51]

In the last two antebellum decades, the three largest slave-state cities experienced enormous growth coupled with an erosion of skilled work for native-born mechanics. This structural change and its implications for regional politics alarmed secessionists, not only for what came to pass in Baltimore, New Orleans, and St. Louis but also because similar transformations occurred in midsized Southern cities with populations of twenty thousand to seventy thousand. A survey of economic growth in these midsized cities shows that in 1860 places like Richmond and Charleston were still small enough to allow urban paternalism to function. However, observers recognized that the changing economies of these smaller cities would eventually develop a multi-ethnic, wage-labor workforce like Baltimore's that could not be managed by traditional patterns of workplace authority.

A railroad boom that sought to connect southeastern ports with southwestern plantations helped the South's urban population to grow twice as fast as that of the countryside. As in Baltimore, St. Louis, and New Orleans, European immigration drove demographic increase in the smaller cities. The foreign-born share of all slave-state city dwellers rose from 35 percent in 1850 to 39 percent in 1860, nearly matching their demographic ratio in the urban North. By 1860, immigrants comprised the majority of unskilled workers in the urban South and rivaled or surpassed American-born whites in skilled work. However, the smaller cities had a larger percentage of African Americans, free and slave, in their populations, and despite inroads by white immigrants, blacks held a greater share of manual jobs than they did in Baltimore, New Orleans, and St. Louis. The greater importance of slavery in the economies of smaller cities diminished the size of their white work-

forces. As in the big cities, white labor in smaller urban centers protested the effects of immigration and industry, but the smaller scale of
their demonstrations kept labor militancy within boundaries that local
businessmen could manage.[52]

In the smaller cities, industry mattered most in Louisville and Richmond. In the two decades before the Civil War, Louisville's population
tripled to reach sixty-eight thousand, largely the result of foreign immigration. In 1860, Louisville's industrial workforce, which had a foreign-born majority, ranked third in the South, behind Baltimore and
St. Louis. Similar to those cities, important Louisville industries like
clothing and machinery underwent a transition from small shops to factories that contributed to a widening income gap between nonmanual
professionals and industrial labor.[53]

Booming mills, iron foundries, and tobacco-processing plants propelled a rise of 88 percent in Richmond's population between 1840 and
1860. White population growth, native and foreign, outpaced African-
American numerical increase. Richmond's Irish newcomers pushed
blacks out of unskilled trades, particularly domestic service, and whites
took up most new skilled positions in the iron foundries. Nevertheless,
with 11,700 slaves and more than 2,600 free blacks in a total population
of 38,000, Richmond relied more heavily on slave hiring and free-
black labor in its industrial sector than did Louisville or the largest
slave-state cities.[54]

While industry mattered less to other Southern cities with populations between 20,000 and 70,000 persons, manufacturing and foreign
immigration were on the rise in Memphis, Charleston, Mobile, and
Savannah. Memphis, Tennessee, a small town of 1,799 in 1840, grew
faster in the next twenty years than other any American city: it claimed
22,623 inhabitants by the time of the Civil War. Even though cotton exports generated the lion's share of profits for city merchants, in 1860
Memphis churned out more than $4 million in industrial goods. Irish,
followed by Germans, constituted the fastest-growing segments of the
city's population. By 1860, their increase had reduced native-born
whites to a bare majority and shrank the proportion of African Americans, most of them slaves, from 28 percent to 17 percent. Immigrants,
especially the Irish, predominated in jobs at docks and depots and in
the new shipyards, iron foundries, and bagging mills.[55]

Resembling Richmond's industrial growth minus tobacco processing, Charleston, South Carolina, home of the fire-eaters, had a strong
component of iron making and machine making in its economy. Hired-

out slaves worked alongside whites in many establishments, and urban merchants allied to planters financed large-scale factory production. Immigration affected Charleston as profoundly as it did other cities. Irish and German arrivals changed the city's racial majority from black to white, taking new industrial jobs and pushing African Americans out of low-skilled work.[56]

By 1860, Savannah had become the major Atlantic port for cotton from the lower South, and it led Georgia in industrial production by processing lumber, rice, and cotton. Savannah's population doubled in the last two antebellum decades to reach twenty-two thousand. Immigrants rose from one-tenth of city residents to one-fifth, while the proportion of African Americans fell from nearly one-half to just under two-fifths. Irish, by far the largest foreign-born group in Savannah, hauled and carted the city's commerce for low wages. In the 1850s, white labor militancy manifested itself in strikes by railroad workers and longshoremen and in demands that blacks be banned from lucrative trades.[57] Mobile, Alabama, relied almost exclusively on cotton exports, but in the 1850s it, too, saw slave numbers contract, manufactures emerge, and immigration skyrocket.[58]

When one steps back from looking at the specific differences between big Southern cities and small ones, an overall pattern of change comes into view. While industry and immigration had the most obvious impact on Baltimore, St. Louis, and New Orleans, the changes that turned workers in the big three slave-state cities into enemies of Southern nationalists were unmistakably under way in the rest of the urban South. Immigration and industrial consolidation changed the way that the various actors in the urban workplace identified their place in society and their relationships to other groups present on the job. In the 1850s, skilled labor and owners of large businesses, the groups that benefited the most from urban paternalism, found that the traditional patron-client model of labor management poorly fit the new realities of the midcentury urban economy. For skilled workers, the search for a way to articulate their interests reflected the reality that they were now the hirelings of wealthy industrialists, rather than shop masters and journeymen proprietors-in-the-making.

Late in the 1850s, slave-state white labor turned insurgent political parties into vehicles for redressing their workplace grievances. That action joined Southern electoral politics to the on-the-job politics of urban free labor and propelled the cities into the middle of the sectional crisis. However, this confrontation in elections and government oc-

curred after the struggle between urban labor and Southern capital had
already begun. To understand how free-labor politics emerged in
Southern cities, then, it is necessary to look closely at the workplaces
where the urban paternalist accommodation between businessmen and
skilled workers first came undone.

Attention again returns to Baltimore, the Southern city at the forefront of economic change. Iron making, Baltimore's second largest field
of industrial employment, witnessed one of the sharpest confrontations
between skilled labor and employers pursuing industrial consolidation.
In 1850, more than two-thirds of Baltimore's ironworkers toiled in one
of the eight foundries that employed more than fifty workers. These
large establishments had pushed aside smaller blacksmiths, the least
successful of whom had closed their shops and gone to work in the
foundries. Rather than introduce expensive machines, late-antebellum
iron masters divided tasks to squeeze wages and extra time from employees. To combat worker resistance, foundry operators curtailed traditional on-the-job freedoms and increased the number of unskilled
hands that could be easily replaced.[59]

Ross Winans, an early B&O engineer and inventor who employed
six hundred workers in a foundry near the B&O's Mount Clare shops,
exemplified these innovations. Winans divided production among several departments, relying on salaried foremen to manage labor that he
paid directly, rather than the independent blacksmiths whom other
iron masters contracted for the output of their station and who in turn
disbursed wages to helpers. Many of Winans's employees had prior experience in smaller shops, and two-thirds were Maryland-born whites.
The rest hailed from Wales, England, and Germany. Few of these men
worked for Winans for long stretches. In a sample of twelve monthly
payrolls from the finishing department, from April 1847 to June 1850,
only 7 of 288 employees worked every month, while one-time employees represented 44 percent of the total. Fluctuating demand for iron
made for high turnover in the foundries and enhanced the value of supervision from foremen and a few trusted mechanics.[60]

Despite these innovations, Winans and other iron makers retained
aspects of paternalistic management of labor (e.g., apprenticeship) that
aided in supervising workers and securing low-cost labor. In 1858, apprentices made up 43 percent of the employees in Winans's tin-making
shops. Winans's apprentices got no cash until age seventeen; they then
earned $1.50 per week, with annual raises of .50 until their contract ex-
pired on their twenty-first birthday. This wage was $8 to $18 less per

month than what Winans paid unbound employees in the finishing shops. Along with savings, Winans enjoyed contractual powers over indentured labor characteristic of the early Republic. In 1853, he threatened to arrest a runaway apprentice and told his father to "call at my offices and inform me of the cause of his absence from work. I shall expect him to serve out his time fully as agreed upon."[61]

Apprenticeship fit into Winans's belief that strong personal guidance from employers made a shop successful. Winans also extolled self-interest, "the liability of man to encroach upon the rights of others," as part of God's decision to accord differential talents to humanity. Like proslavery apologists, Winans harmonized paternalism and individualism by positing that a bond united workers, the "inferior class," with employers in a hierarchically ordered community that shared common goals. This paternalist vision manifested itself in philanthropy. In the late 1850s, his son Thomas opened a soup kitchen for the poor that at its peak gave away food to four thousand individuals per day, and in the 1870s Ross Winans built more than one hundred four-story worker homes adjacent to Mount Clare.[62]

On occasion, Winans's employees bought into his vision by rallying to their patron's aid, just as the black caulkers had done when the shipbuilders' guild needed to shut down a competitor. For example, forty-eight mechanics petitioned municipal government to enforce a B&O engine-building contract with Winans, a benefit to labor and management. However, when Winans and his workers disagreed, mechanics refused to act like grateful clients. In 1853, four thousand ironworkers went on strike for a 15 percent wage hike. The railroads and several iron makers quickly agreed to raise pay, but until April 1 around two thousand remained on strike at foundries that would not budge. Winans, one of the holdout employers, forgot about mutual bonds between labor and management and argued that raises should be awarded on individual merit. His lawyers declared the strike an "illegal combination . . . at war with the universally acknowledged rights of individuals" that denied an employer "the free exercise of his own will in the regulation of his labor." In the strike's only violence, pickets attacked men returning to Winans's foundry at the old wage. This attack resonated with fiery labor rhetoric. "In this land of liberty," it was declared at one strike rally, "where the humblest son of toil works . . . it is his privilege to say that he will or will not work for certain wages. Deny him this and you degrade him to the toiling slaves of despotism." Drawing on the tradition of artisan self-assertion in politics, strikers presented themselves as independent producers in danger of becoming the kind of compliant hirelings that Winans sought.[63] The strike also displayed ethnic conflict among workers. The turnout was led by the Order of United American Mechanics, a nativist trade union that banned foreign members. Striking Germans acted through a separate ethnic association. Nativists blamed immigrants when some men returned to work without a raise.[64]

The 1853 strike showed how skilled workers and management fought to define the new industrial work relationship. Nowhere was this contest of wills better illustrated than at the B&O, Baltimore's largest private employer. John Work Garrett, an influential board member and president in his own right after 1858, took a more ruthless, less communal, approach to employee management than paternalists like Winans. B&O workers fought Garrett's rules, but after repeated management triumphs some employees decided to act like loyal clients rather than defiant free agents.

Similar to other early railroads, in the 1830s the B&O hired work out to master craftsmen, but in 1846 the railroad reorganized into departments run by salaried managers in order to address their growing scale of operation. Tighter controls over labor, like the creation of a company police force, accompanied the switch from contractors to foremen. Typifying the new attitude toward labor, in November 1855 the B&O issued a set of work rules at Mount Clare designed to "form a corps of skillful, steady and faithful men, who will . . . promote and guard the interests of the Company." The shop superintendent handled personnel, supplies, and job orders. He was assisted by a master machinist and head carpenter, who watched employees with an eye to "strict economy in the expenditure of labor and materials." Shop foremen barred visitors and levied fines for missing work, losing tools, smoking, drinking, reading, and conversation "except in relation to work at hand." These rules, which were becoming an industry standard, gave supervisors more power to stop behavior that slowed work or lost supplies.[65]

Having won the presidency by fighting to raise profits and give private stockholders more dividends, Garrett showed little interest in providing paternalistic care for his labor force. Instead, he zealously searched out employee inefficiency. Garrett chastised the head of transportation for the negligence of a coal shoveler and fired workers for petty offenses ranging from gambling to bringing bad publicity to the B&O by testifying in murder cases. Following earlier efforts to break up regional factions of Irish trackmen, he rooted out networks of family and friends whose ties could thwart company imperatives. When a foreman defended a man dismissed for drunkenness on the grounds that he had worked long hours in wet conditions, Garrett fumed that the supervisor "should have better judgment. Another evidence of 'neighborhood' feeling of the second class agents." Appeals to mutual loyalty and employer compassion made little headway with Garrett.[66]

B&O workers fought back against this management system in 1857 in protest of new theft-prevention rules. Copying other railroads, company directors ordered freight cars sealed with tape upon loading and required conductors to provide a receipt for each car. If inspectors found a car with a broken seal, the conductor "shall be responsible for any loss from said cars and shall be immediately discharged from the service." Furious at being made liable for losses no matter their culpability, conductors walked off their jobs in what became known as the Seal Strike, the B&O's largest prewar labor conflict. To enforce the strike, conductors blockaded tracks west of the city. The conflict escalated when B&O executives persuaded Maryland's governor to deploy militia on outbound trains. Soldiers broke the barricades and exchanged gunfire with the blockaders, but could not prevent strikers from derailing other trains.[67]

At this juncture, Ross Winans, who believed in mutual bonds between management and labor, convinced strikers to give up in exchange for new antitheft rules. Ignoring this overture, B&O executives kept the sealed-car rule in place and fired "every man who has thus refused obedience to orders, and combined to prevent others from their execution. It is . . . a matter of high principle, involving the absolute discipline of its service." The company rewarded strikebreakers with an extra month's pay and remembered their loyalty for years to come. Although tested by the Seal Strike, "obedience to orders" and "absolute discipline" remained watchwords of B&O management.[68]

Garrett's hard line had an impact on employee behavior and attitudes. After he slashed wages and laid-off staff in 1859, aggrieved workers sought reprisals against middle management rather than risk another strike. Someone at Mount Clare (a writer who was anonymous except for the pseudonym "Equality and Justice") told Garrett that a superintendent had used company materials and labor in his private repair shop. Linking this indictment to the job cuts, the writer asked, "As all the working men have been put off at this place, the question arises and is often discussed, what is to be done with this idle gang of thieves?"

A twenty-year veteran employee fired to make way for a supervisor's brother-in-law denounced his superior as an "aristocratic upstart" guilty of "unprincipled tyrannical oppression" and accused him of embezzlement. Complaints about supervisors ironically demonstrated Garrett's success in winning obedience. Instead of directly criticizing Garrett, employees appealed to him as a patron to take revenge on managers who had carried out his orders to reduce costs.[69]

The conflict between labor and capital detailed in Baltimore characterized the South's two other metropolitan giants. More than ten thousand wage earners in St. Louis lost their jobs in the panic of 1857, and massive rallies forced city government to fund new public works projects. In 1853, New Orleans workers created a loose trade federation. One of its constituents was the Screwman's Benevolent Association, a multi-ethnic union of white New Orleans cargo handlers. The association struck repeatedly during the 1850s in an effort to keep wages up. In the late 1850s, Richard Trevellick, a prominent postwar labor leader, led New Orleans shipyard workers' movement for a nine-hour day. Similar to Baltimore, racial conflict between workers factored into the struggles on New Orleans docks. White stevedores tried to drive African Americans from waterfront employment, and in 1852, in retaliation, black workers agreed to replace striking Irish steamboat hands. In the 1850s, work on the docks, the center of wage labor in the city, could not be organized by familiar management methods. The multifaceted conflicts that divided manual labor occasionally erupted in violence, and all sides pushed to redraw the lines of employment in their favor.[70]

The chaotic struggle on the New Orleans levee partly reflected the heterogeneity of its workforce, but the militancy manifested by dockworkers extended to well-organized trades whose practitioners had traditionally identified their interests with those of their employers. Typographers were among the best-organized craft workers in the Old South, with local unions in several cities, including New Orleans. As late as 1852, the printers' union in New Orleans espoused the view of Jacksonian craftsmen that they should "protect and advance . . . the interests and welfare of our employers, as well as those of ourselves; that upon their prosperity and success depends our own welfare." A new hostility between printers and publishers mafishanseeanifested itself three years later when union members walked out at newspapers that imported New York printers at lower wages. In 1857, the union came under suspicion for killing a foreman they described as "arbitrary, dictatorial, and over-bearing to his fellow workmen," and a year later the printers again struck publishers who broke their wage scale.[71]

The labor conflicts of the 1850s expressed the dissatisfaction of both businessmen and mechanics with the Southern city's traditional patron-client ethic of workplace authority. Winans, Garrett, and other manu-facturers who had adapted economies of scale still relied on coercive practices like apprenticeship and hard-nosed supervision by foremen to instill obedience in their workforces. However, they found that the mutuality implied in paternalism—benevolence from the boss and loyal service from the worker—had lost its value. In 1853, Winans denied workers' demand for more pay and in 1857 his appeal to the railroad-ers' fraternity failed to resolve the Seal Strike. Garrett dispensed with Winans's philanthropic style and complained about supervisors who let loyalty to their subordinates interfere with company rules. Moreover, no businessman approved of the violent strikes and fiery rhetoric about slavery and despotism used by white machinists and conductors. Coer-cion, urban paternalism's hard side, rose in importance for employers confronting labor militancy, and their mutual interests with skilled workers faded into memory.

For skilled white labor, the new economy undermined their self-image as small masters who shared with businessmen in the profits of growth and in the overlapping privileges of race, wealth, and gender. They were now men in the middle fighting to maintain a level of social independence threatened by local capitalists and unskilled laborers from other cultures, an identity more in tune with the emerging defini-tion of free labor in the North. The paternalist ethic still governed do-mestic service and some casual labor arrangements, especially ones in which workers lacked political rights and valuable skills, but it had never characterized the way that antebellum white workingmen thought of their own relationship to employers. In the preceding generation, arti-sans celebrated their independence from masters in all aspects of their lives. By midcentury, the line between the wealthy and workers had sharpened, while the division between middling-class craftsmen and the impoverished lower sort had blurred. Unlike their fathers, the sons of Jacksonian tradesmen competed for manufacturing jobs with immi-grants unschooled in American artisan-republican traditions, and the jobs they sought afforded less control over the work process and little social prestige.

This change affected urban politics. In the 1850s, the political goals of the Jacksonian labor movement lost their relevance for urban workers. Fixed prices and mechanic lien laws, rallying points for labor activists of the prior generation, appeared irrelevant not only to German seamstresses and Irish dockworkers, but also to American-born white artisans. Instead of issues that spoke to the fading image of the craft worker as small businessman, enfranchised workingmen now focused on questions related to their status as permanent wage earners in a highly competitive labor market.

In the 1850s, the urban South's American mechanics launched initiatives focused on work and immigration that engaged the sectional conflict—but not through slavery, the issue that fueled labor political activism in the North. Native white workers wanted to enlist the state in a campaign against the business elite's power and against immigrant pressure on jobs and living standards. In order to have local government aid strikes, provide relief jobs, and combat immigration, American mechanics needed government to become stronger and larger. Pursuit of that goal promoted a prototype of machine politics that relied on labor's vote and was less beholden to state-level party operatives. The prospect of invigorated city administrations supported by free labor raised the specter of mob rule to slaveholders in state government, and slaveholders' intervention on behalf of the beleaguered business elite entangled the cities in the larger crisis of the Union.

However, it would take more than labor's impulse for big government to bring machine politics to life. Professional politicians, few of whom possessed mechanic backgrounds, would have to contemplate an end to the system of party competition that had trained them. For these political leaders, the Whigs and Democrats had not only upheld the urban social order, they had also maintained a balance in national government between antagonistic sections. Unfortunately for this political equilibrium, the relationship between the sections underwent a crisis during the 1850s that in tandem with new struggles in big city workplaces realigned the politics of the urban South.

Free laborers made their presence felt in the party realignment of 1846–55, but their voice would not be dominant in any one party until the late 1850s. The alienation of skilled labor from business occurred in urban workplaces before it manifested itself in city politics. The delayed emergence of class conflict into city politics occurred because the world of elections and government operated independently from other social arrangements. The crisis of urban paternalism along with conflict related to slavery, religion, and ethnicity all impacted politics, but these abstract forces operated through officeholders and voters who thought more about party and government than other social concerns when it came time to vote or pass a law. To understand how the parties that had managed the municipal polity for a generation fell apart, we now turn away from bosses, workers, and the shop floor to focus on politicians, voters, and legislative halls.

Three

Reform and Slavery
The Realignment of Jacksonian Parties,
1846–1855

Between 1846 and 1855, slave-state city politics underwent profound change. Old parties fell, new issues emerged, and established political practice came into disrepute. In the middle of the 1850s, the Jacksonian era's system of Whig-versus-Democrat competition gave way to a new struggle between the Democrats and the American Party. Although Democrats remained competitive, the American Party, which contemporaries also called the Know-Nothings, won control of government in 1854 and 1855 in many Southern cities. They succeeded by accommodating city dwellers' demand for reform without upsetting their section's consensus that slavery must be preserved.

In the urban South, the initial phase of party realignment resulted in a reconstruction of Jacksonian party politics that adapted the familiar practices of the old parties to meet the demands of reformers and mobilized voters around a new configuration of class, ethnic, and sectional allegiances. This chapter argues that the first years of the American Party's ascendancy in the urban South represented a victory for veteran politicians who wanted to reform, rather than overthrow, the system of Jacksonian party competition that had preserved the Union and slavery for a generation.

The collapse of the urban paternalist system of workplace authority paralleled the collapse of Jacksonian-era political parties, but one process did not cause the other. The politicians and voters who carried out this change were also involved in the transformation of the urban economy, but when they went to the polls or gathered in legislative halls, political actors responded to multivalent pressures on elections and government. Urban class relations influenced their behavior, yet it was only one among several factors that led voters and officeholders to abandon the Jacksonian system of party competition.

Political change in the cities belonged to a national process of party realignment. Conflict over sectionalism, immigration, and government corruption had allowed new parties to capitalize on a general public unease with conventional politics as practiced by the Whigs and Democrats. This unease focused more on partisanship, a commitment to party that could override other loyalties, than on the mere existence of parties as such. Voter perceptions of corruption in high places led them to reject old partisan loyalties, and many of those demanding reform took up the cause of the new American Party.

Party leaders faced a tough job in the early 1850s. They had to forge an electoral majority from a voting public that was divided along several lines. In the urban South, American Party leaders used the anticorruption theme to unite three constituencies discontented with the Whigs and Democrats. Reform appealed to businessmen who saw political democratization as a means for enacting state aid to internal improvements that rural legislators often opposed. Reform rhetoric also infused evangelical Protestant demands for moral legislation that would check what they viewed as the corrupting influence of Roman Catholic immigrants. White skilled labor comprised a third group attracted to political reform. Whig and Democratic inattention to pressure on wages and skills fueled complaints that business monopolies had bought out the parties. Lobbyists for internal improvements, temperance advocates, and strike leaders often worked at cross-purposes, but American Party politicians helped them to find common ground by linking their specific concerns to a broader cultural anxiety that the republic's virtue had been corrupted.

The politicians who organized the Know-Nothings promised to clean up corruption, but they preserved the organizational style of the Jacksonian era and kept power away from the advocates for antipartisan reform who had no affiliation with the old parties. The presence of veteran politicos in the Know-Nothing leadership fueled criticism that the American Party was old wine in new bottles; that is, its leaders were party insiders pretending to be nonpartisan outsiders, or what a Baltimore Democrat called "worn-out, broken down political hucksters," who practiced the very kind of corruption that they criticized.[1] New issues (reform of government and culture) and a new coalition of voters (workers, evangelicals, and businessmen) belied the charge that the Know-Nothings had merely slapped a new label on an old party. On the other hand, continuity in leadership and the refusal of America Party officeholders to let grassroots activists share in decision making left space for critics of the political status quo to attack the Know-Nothings as hypocritical wire-pullers of the worst sort.

In the first phase of party realignment, veteran politicians tried to maintain stable electoral competition and govern responsibly, while still accommodating the demand for reform. Men trained in politics by the Whigs and Democrats trusted parties to prevent volatile conflicts over issues like slavery from tearing government apart. After a wave of major-party defeats in the early 1850s, few longtime officeholders believed the old parties would survive unchanged, but even fewer of them wanted to allow a radical overhaul of politics that might result in civil war.

Leaders of the mid-1850s parties had good reason to see conventional party politics as a key support of the federal Union. Controversy over slavery had always threatened to divide the nation, and for decades politicians had searched for ways to compromise the competing interests of North and South. In 1820, talk of splitting the Union over the issue threatened to become reality when some Northern congressmen opposed the spread of slavery into the new state of Missouri. Compromise prevailed with the admission of Maine, a free state, to balance Missouri's representation in the U.S. Senate and an agreement on the future of slavery in the Louisiana Purchase. Afterward, some politicians pointed to the absence of strong party discipline during the Missouri crisis as a contributing cause to the controversy. New York's Martin Van Buren, a strong supporter of Tennessean Andrew Jackson's presidential hopes, led those who argued that a revival of loyalty to national parties would help voters to act on interests that crossed sectional lines.[2] Although the Union faced several tests in the 1830s, most notably over South Carolina's attempt to nullify federal law, the Whigs and Democrats prevented sectionalism from splitting their organizations into Northern and Southern factions.

In the 1830s and early 1840s, top statesmen like Democrats Van Buren and Jackson and Whig leader Henry Clay used partisan competition to increase popular participation in ways that reinforced the political system's legitimacy. On the one hand, voters perceived parties as instruments of popular will that focused government on public needs. On the other, parties were autonomous bureaucratic institutions that no single social group (for example, slaveholders or abolitionists) could control, and in that capacity they blunted the people's energy away from courses destructive of government.

In 1844, that balancing act faced its greatest test to date when Tennessee's James K. Polk emerged as the presidential nominee of Democrats who wanted to annex the independent republic of Texas. Van Buren, the initial favorite for the Democratic nomination, and Clay, the Whig standard bearer, opposed annexation. Polk won the presidency, and Texas joined the Union the following year. The United States inherited Texas's boundary dispute with Mexico, and in 1846 war broke out between the two nations.[3] By 1848, the United States had soundly defeated Mexico and acquired the land of the present-day U.S. Southwest as its reward. Because Southern whites wanted to spread slavery to the Southwest and the majority of Northern voters rejected such a move, the victory over Mexico had the unintended consequence of renewing conflict over slavery in ways that would end in civil war. One essential step on that road to disunion was the dismantling of voter loyalty to the unambiguously pro-Union and proslavery Whig and Democratic parties. The unraveling of the Jacksonian parties involved much more than the battle over slavery's status in western territory, but the renewal of sectional conflict played a central role in this process. The era of Whig-versus-Democratic competition began to break down when officeholders failed to address slavery's expansion in ways that satisfied all elements of their party.

A general pattern characterized the collapse of Jacksonian parties in the urban South, but each city had unique qualities. As elsewhere herein, priority is given to Baltimore because of its significance as the largest Southern city and because it had one of the strongest Know-Nothing movements in the slave states. In Maryland, disputes over slavery's status in the West contributed to the downfall of the state's longstanding Whig majority. In 1846, John Pendleton Kennedy, a leading Baltimore Whig, won the speakership of Maryland's lower house (the House of Delegates) and urged caution in warring with Mexico. Kennedy's stand cost him proslavery support because some saw his opposition to the war as opposition to slavery's expansion. In 1847, Maryland Democrats used Kennedy's stand on the war to defeat him in a congressional election.[4]

The national politics of slavery could also work against Southern Democrats. In 1846, David Wilmot, a Democratic congressman from Pennsylvania, proposed a ban on slavery in any land formerly held by Mexico. The measure embodied the principle of "free soil"—that is, keeping slavery out of a given territory. This policy gained adherents in the North as the sectional conflict intensified. In 1846, early in this process, Wilmot's free-soil plan (sometimes known as the Wilmot Proviso) failed to pass, but the controversy associated with it made Southerners who were interested in expanding slavery mistrust allegiance to either of the national parties.[5] Angered at the actions of free-soilers like Wilmot, in 1850 William Lowndes Yancey, Alabama's notorious Southern nationalist, repudiated the Democrats, his lifelong party. Yancey told Southerners that they must choose between "secession or submission. If you submit, behave like submissionists. Be quiet and peaceable, subservient to the will of your masters. If you resist at all, resist effectually and manfully." Secessionists like Yancey tied criticism of national parties to the ideals of Southern honor, claiming that by allying with Northerners, Whigs and Democrats forced Southerners to compromise their principles and their manhood.[6]

In this atmosphere of proslavery suspicion of political parties, Maryland's Reverdy Johnson, a Baltimore lawyer, Whig senator, and war supporter, convinced the Whig state convention to endorse Zachary Taylor for president in 1848. Taylor was a pro-expansion Mexican War hero from the South who could win votes from independent-minded Southern Democrats. The Kennedy wing backed party stalwart Henry Clay, a frequent aspirant for the presidency who had opposed Texas annexation in 1844. Clay's supporters objected to territorial gains that J. Morrison Harris, a rising Baltimore Whig leader, feared would "further jeopard the interests of the country by evolving issues threatening the integrity of the Union itself." Johnson fired back that "the Southern States owe it to themselves, one and all of them, to stand on their own equality and, exclusively at their own time and without the interference of others, to meddle in their own way with this peculiar institution."[7]

Taylor's supporters pointed to their nominee's career as a general rather than politician as proof that his character surpassed that of party insiders who put their organization's interest ahead of the nation's. A Maryland Taylor convention resolved that "we have met . . . without regard to party distinctions. . . . Gen. Taylor is the only man who can unite the moderate men of all parties." Although dominant at the state level, Whigs were a minority in Baltimore, and it may have been Taylor's nonpartisanship that helped him win 49 percent of the city's vote, the highest Whig municipal total of the decade, and a sign that Democrats could not take their urban support for granted.[8]

Party infighting over slavery increased after Taylor won the presidency. Officeholders in both parties who represented Maryland slaveholding counties in the south and the Eastern Shore stepped up their demands that slavery be permitted in California, which was speeding toward statehood to accommodate the population boom that accompanied the gold rush of 1849. Maryland's proslavery activists responded to arguments put forward by South Carolina's John C. Calhoun, the nation's leading advocate of slaveholders' rights. Calhoun had called a

Southern Rights convention in Nashville, where he planned to organize a new sectional party that would be free from interference from the Northern interests represented among Whigs and Democrats.[9]

Maryland's governor, Philip F. Thomas, an Eastern Shore Democrat, urged the legislature to send delegates to the Southern Rights convention. Just as slavery expansion had divided the Whigs, such talk from a Democratic governor was at odds with the priorities of his party brethren in the city. In his annual message of 1850, Baltimore's Mayor Elijah Stansbury, a Democrat and a brickmaker turned merchant, ignored Governor Thomas's sectional concerns while advocating Whig-like improvements to roads, the harbor, public health, and schools. In his campaign, Thomas called canal and railroad projects "Utopian schemes." Showing the gap between urban and rural Democrats, a country politician told Thomas that such projects were "corroding and festering sore[s] on the body politic."[10]

All Maryland public officials opposed the Wilmot Proviso, but Kennedy, who said that Whigs were "friends of the Union . . . [who] know nothing and can conceive nothing outside of it," led the legislature's Whig majority in refusing to attend the Nashville convention. Kennedy's views represented the faction of his party committed to preserving the Union even if it cost slaveholders some advantages in the West. He had the support of a prominent Eastern Shore Whig and U.S. senator, James A. Pearce. Pearce had worked hard to pass the compromise of 1850, a series of enactments designed to resolve the main sectional issues stemming from the Mexican War.[11]

Not all Whigs in southern Maryland agreed on the compromise, however. Thomas Pratt, a Whig senator from Prince George's County in the south, almost upset the compromise by proposing that one of its key elements, the Fugitive Slave Law, compensate owners of runaways.[12] That amendment would have enraged Northerners who already thought the law gave too much to slaveholders. In their reaction to the national controversy over slavery, Marylanders began to rethink their attachment to the major parties. Sectional conflict brought rural voters together behind whichever candidate promised to protect slavery's future, while it weakened intraparty bonds between town and country.

No city's experience exactly replicated that of another, but party realignment in Maryland, where urban dissatisfaction with state leaders created opportunities for independent candidates, bore similarities to political change in Missouri and Louisiana, homes of the South's two other big cities. In each state, the debate over slavery in federal territories heightened tensions between rural and urban supporters in each major party. In Missouri, fallout from the Mexican War divided the Democratic Party, which had dominated state government since the 1830s and in the 1840s had emerged as the majority party in St. Louis. Planter-politicians from Missouri River slaveholding counties forced a confrontation with their former ally Thomas Hart Benton, a Democratic U.S. senator from St. Louis who in the 1840s decided to oppose the spread of slavery. In 1850, the proslavery state legislature instructed Benton to support Southern stands on the compromise. Benton refused, and in retaliation his Democratic enemies helped a slavery-expansionist Whig take his seat in the U.S. Senate.[13]

"The Democracy here is in a snarl." That observation from a St. Louis Democrat on the local impact of Benton's ouster reflected the disarray in his party that enabled Whig Luther Kennett to win the mayoralty in 1850. However, similar divisions afflicted the Whigs. The cooperation between proslavery Democrats and Kennett, a member of a slave-owning family, troubled the St. Louis Whig base of transplanted New England merchants who doubted that slavery expansionists would enact banking and transportation projects necessary for urban commercial growth. In 1845, Kennett backed the American Republican Party, a nativist forerunner of the Know-Nothings, and in 1850 he courted voters alarmed by the flood of European immigrants. This policy risked electoral defeat since the immigrant population, 43 percent of the city in 1850, continued to rise. Kennett also benefited from the anger some wage-earning Democrats felt at the dictatorial tactics of their party's rural leaders. However, workers had little enthusiasm for Whig business leaders. In the long run, circumstances in St. Louis would thwart any party that equivocated on slavery, nativism, and labor conflict.[14]

Slavery and ethnicity had an equally significant impact on Louisiana's politics. After the 1803 incorporation of the French colony into the United States, Anglo-Americans settled the wheat and cotton growing regions of what would become the new state's northwest. They entered into a long contest for political power with French Creoles who grew cotton and sugar in the southern parishes that lined the Mississippi River. In the early 1800s, ethnic rivalry dominated politics, and personality mattered more than party. The 1820s presidential elections altered this pattern by increasing popular interest and by bonding state officials to national candidates. In the 1830s, partisanship spread to state and local elections. Democrats fared somewhat better than Whigs because Democrats vigorously championed popular government. Whigs won several statewide elections, however, by building a coalition of Creole planters and New Orleans businessmen, many of them Anglo migrants from the northeast United States. Both groups favored Whig support for a sugar tariff, infrastructure improvements, and expanded credit. Anglo-American small farmers and cotton planters supported the Democratic Party for its free trade policies and because Roman Catholic Creoles appeared to be a type of entrenched "aristocracy" of money and family that Jacksonians excoriated in other aspects of American politics.[15]

New Orleans inverted these ethnic allegiances. City Democrats contested the local Whig majority by cultivating the support of Irish, German, and French immigrants, who along with American-born white mechanics resented Whig employers. Notwithstanding Democratic hostility to the Creoles and their strident support for slavery, the party's claim that "Democracy is the equality of all before the law, and the liberty of each to pursue his own happiness in his own way" struck a chord with immigrants like the New Orleans Bavarian who said that "a person really lives free here . . . it is true there are many slaves here, but they are all Negroes, who know no better than to be slaves."[16]

The Mexican War opened the door for Democrats to dominate Louisiana by attracting Whig slavery expansionists to their party. In 1844, Whig planters squirmed at Clay's opposition to acquiring neighboring Texas, and in 1848 they plumped for Zachary Taylor because he could attract Southern votes. In the late 1840s, Whigs lost the governor's office and a U.S. Senate seat. In 1850, Louisiana's Democratic governor, Joseph A. Walker, a northwestern planter, joined Maryland's governor in criticizing the federal compromise and endorsing the Southern Rights convention.[17]

As the new decade began, intraparty quarrels sparked by the national debate over slavery had exposed voters in the urban South to sustained criticism of their party by some of its own officeholders. Activists outside the major parties now had an opportunity to be heard by voters restive with established leaders. In Baltimore, where Democrats were the established party, antiparty activism sprang up among wage workers, a group traditionally supportive of Democrats. During the 1850 campaign season, advocates of a law to limit the workday to ten hours convened in Baltimore to call attention to their issue. Arguing that business monopolies and political parties controlled government and ignored labor's concerns, the convention asked the legislature to "do justice to the real producers of wealth, the workers of the State of Maryland . . . contending not only against prejudice and ignorance, but against corporate and monied influences." Although the Democratic candidate for governor supported the ten-hour law and the Whig nominee opposed it, the convention's leaders, few of whom had ever held political office, "disavow[ed] all party bias" on the grounds that "a man who previous to an election announces himself either an ultra Democrat or a rampant Whig, affords no security against the seductive appliances of power, whether political or corporate."[18] By identifying their cause with the broader, antipartisan interest in government reform, labor lobbyists established common ground with other political outsiders seeking to overhaul party politics.

This antipartisan stance resonated with labor's alienation from Baltimore's Democratic Party leadership. Already feeling snubbed by Mayor Stansbury's overtures to business, workers drew little comfort from Stansbury's call for more orphanages and poorhouses where vagrants who were "strong and healthy are to be made to work."[19] By the early 1850s, Democratic stalwarts from the Jacksonian labor movement—men like Stansbury and Joshua Vansant, both of whom had been courted by an independent Workingman's ticket in 1833, and Francis Gallagher, a union leader and legislator instrumental in outlawing debtor's prison—had moved up and out of manual labor. Their social distance from wage earners and their inattention to labor issues gave rivals an opportunity to champion the cause of workers, the so-called "bone and sinew" of the Democrat Party.

The 1850 mayoral election gave an early sign of disaffection from the Democratic Party in the new industrial neighborhoods of west Baltimore that had sprung up around the machine shops of the Baltimore and Ohio Railroad (B&O) and related iron foundries. Westside Democrats preferred John Wesley Watkins, a militia commander and brickmaker, to the eventual party nominee, J. Marbury Turner, a Fell's Point butcher whose father was a noted politician. Ethnic tensions related to the concentration of immigrants on the east side and white natives in the west sparked a campaign brawl between Democratic fire companies. The New Markets, led by an Irish Catholic, Franklin "Patty" Naff, fought the nativist Watchman company, later an ally of the Know-Nothings. Turner highlighted his benevolence toward the Irish, while Whig John H. T. Jerome proposed reenacting a lapsed 1838 law that curbed alleged immigrant vote fraud.

Ethnic and class discontent helped Jerome, but instead of high-lighting these issues he chose to emphasize his nonpartisan credentials. Jerome was a politically inexperienced businessman who promised to "promote the welfare and the interests of all classes of society, without reference to any party or to any clique." Despite Democrat victories in most other city races, Jerome won because of discontent in Democratic bastions in the south and west (wards 15 and 17 to 20), where skilled workers comprised 58 percent of the eligible voters. Jerome outpolled Turner by 179 ballots in these wards, even though Democratic city council candidates won them by 871 votes. Nonpartisan reform at the state level and a local faction fight that correlated with the grievances of native-born workers persuaded some Democrats to vote for a man only lightly associated with the Whigs. Aware of this trend, the *Baltimore American* newspaper admitted that "it would not be proper to claim [Jerome's] election as a party triumph."[20]

Jerome proved an exception to the rule of Whig disarray in 1850. Whig efforts to find a common policy voice suffered from infighting over nominations and patronage, the very type of squabble that critics cited as evidence of major party corruption. In 1850, Baltimore's Reverdy Johnson and southern Maryland's Thomas Pratt steered the gubernatorial nomination to William Clarke, a downstate planter, over objections from the Baltimore Whigs, who then abandoned Clarke in the general election. Henry Winter Davis, a party supporter who had recently moved from Virginia to pursue his legal career, said that "the Whig gentlemen of Baltimore and their retainers staid at their desks by the thousands, voted for Lowe by the hundreds, and not a few gave their money for the defeat of the Whig candidate."

Angry at Clarke's failure, Johnson worked to block Kennedy's appointment as secretary of the interior under Millard Fillmore, Taylor's successor. As Taylor's attorney general, Johnson had directed federal jobs to his allies at the expense of Kennedy supporters. The latter group retaliated by defeating Johnson's choice for collector of the Port of Baltimore, a lucrative post that influenced one hundred subordinate hires in the U.S. Customs Service. However, the new collector, George Proctor Kane, a second-generation Irish merchant, angered Whig job seekers by refusing to sack fifty workers whom Kane deemed essential to the port's operation yet who lacked a tie to either party. To Whig loyalists, these men were less deserving than devoted partisans. The quarrel lasted into 1852, when the city Whig convention asked Fillmore to fire Kane. In return, Fillmore wanted unanimous endorsement of his reelection, but local disunity prevented such a consensus. By the mid-1850s, the patronage battle, along with other issues, pushed Johnson and Kane into the Democratic Party.[21]

The zealotry of sectional extremists, on the one hand, and petty bickering over offices, on the other, led younger Baltimore Whigs to express doubts about the established party system. Z. Collins Lee, who would later switch to the Democrats, complained of "the excesses of fanaticism and mad ambitions of public men."[22] Lee referred to an antiparty strand of republican ideology that many Whigs emphasized. They worried that the pursuit of office and an unseemly sensitivity to mass opinion interfered with a politician's ability to govern wisely.[23]

Some Whigs, like Jerome, capitalized on the antipartisan mood, but as in Louisiana, Maryland Democrats did better than Whigs at identifying themselves with democratizing reform. Redrawing the Maryland constitution had combined with municipal issues to stir the enthusiasm for nonpartisan reform that hurt established Whig candidates because their party had opposed constitutional reform. In line with democratizing movements in other states, Maryland reformers, whose strongest supporters lived in the northern and western counties, wanted to equalize representation, cut spending, and open appointive offices to election. Existing apportionment rules allotted a mere 6 percent of the state assembly seats to Baltimore, although the city accounted for 29 percent of Maryland's people. In 1850, a referendum calling for a constitutional convention passed statewide and received overwhelming support in Baltimore.

Excepting the mayoral upset, Democrats fared well in 1850. They were helped by their gubernatorial candidate, Enoch Lewis Lowe, a Catholic lawyer, who endorsed issues desired by city dwellers like constitutional reform and a ten-hour workday. Lowe's attentiveness to reform helped him win a majority in Baltimore, but he also had to contend with the rural planters, whose votes he needed. To appeal to slaveholders, Lowe vowed to cut spending and vigorously enforce the Fugitive Slave Law. By backing constitutional reform and supporting slaveholders' interests, Lowe brought together the diverse constituencies of the Democrats and easily defeated a divided Whig Party that had steadily lost support in the slaveholding counties of the south and east.[24]

However, the real work of constitutional reform tested the budding alliance between Baltimore Democrats and renegade Whigs from the slaveholding counties. At the 1851 convention, plantation-district leg-

islators objected to the principle of majority rule embodied in constitutional changes that doubled Baltimore's representation in the state
assembly to one-eighth of all seats and turned judgeships and other appointed posts into elected offices. "Government is designed for the
good of the whole, not a majority," asserted Ezekiel Chambers, an Eastern Shore Democrat who backed secession in 1861. "Government is a
system of restraints, not indulgences." In response, Baltimore's all-
Democratic delegation to the convention tried to convince plantation-
district legislators that slavery, the minority interest alluded to in most
Southern critiques of majority rule, would be secure under a system
that decreased their power. Baltimoreans led the convention in pledg-
ing to maintain all laws that defended slavery, in declaring that slaveholders had been ill served by the compromise of 1850, and in banning
slavery's future abolition. Urban representatives supported fiscally conservative plans to pay the public debt and restrict internal improvements. They defeated nativist proposals to limit immigrant voting, regulate alcohol, and promote Protestant values in education. Convention
Democrats pleased downstate Whigs, who supported slavery and opposed public works, but they alienated urban Democrats concerned
about morals and economic development.[25]

The Democrats' stronger ties to rural conservatives helped make
them the new majority party in Maryland. Between 1847 and 1851,
Democrats broke the Whig hold on state offices. The Whig failure in
the 1852 presidential election accelerated the party's decline. Winfield
Scott, the national Whig nominee, disavowed Fillmore and the compromise and thereby forced Southerners either to reject him or to defend his lukewarm support of the Fugitive Slave Law. Whigs, who were
formerly recognized as slavery's champions, lost their immunity to hy-
perbolic Democratic charges that they were abolitionist fellow travelers, and Whig leaders who gave priority to Southern rights moved
closer to the Democrats.

In 1853, Henry May, a Baltimore lawyer who fought against emancipation during the Civil War, quit the Whigs to run for congress as a
Democrat. Reverdy Johnson, another party switcher, argued before the
Supreme Court in 1857 against Dred Scott's freedom. In 1855, Thomas
Bowie, a diehard Whig congressman from southwest Maryland, ran a
proslavery campaign against an opponent who defined himself as a
"Union Whig." In 1854, bipartisan support from southern Maryland
legislators enabled Senator Pearce to win reelection. That year, Pearce
and Pratt sided with Democrat Stephen Douglas in favor of the Kansas-

Nebraska Act, and in 1856 they endorsed James Buchanan and voted as Democrats. In 1859, Pearce presided over the slaveholder convention that advanced C. W. Jacobs's proposal to banish or reenslave free blacks.[26]

Slavery also contributed to the Whig collapse in New Orleans, but as in Baltimore questions of culture and political corruption intertwined with sectionalism. In New Orleans, Whigs fit support for slavery's extension into a critique of immigration and Democratic malfeasance. They claimed that Democrats harvested fraudulent ballots from nonnaturalized immigrants who lacked enthusiasm for slavery and who would soon have numbers sufficient to overwhelm their cynical masters in the Democratic Party. In 1852, an Independent ticket dominated by reform-minded Whigs won the elections for a new citywide government that had replaced the old division of the city into separate municipalities according to residential concentrations of Anglo-Americans, Creoles, and recent immigrants.[27]

Louisiana's constitutional reform came on the heels of the spring municipal election. As in Maryland, the party that pushed reform, in this case the Whigs, exacerbated its internal divisions. Whig businessmen coupled calls for popular control with demands for business loans and liberalized bank laws. One such urban Whig said that "the Constitution . . . has fettered the enterprise and industry of the people . . . [and made] one man in any other parish of the state . . . politically equal to two men in New Orleans." In the new 1852 constitution, reformers won on business development, but they did not expand urban political power. The apportionment of legislative seats by total population, including nonvoting African Americans, benefited slave-rich parishes and hurt New Orleans, which possessed one-third of Louisiana's eligible voters. Backlash over the constitution coincided with Scott's disastrous presidential campaign. Some rural Whigs switched to the Democratic Party. In New Orleans, Democrats castigated Whigs for bargaining away poor-white representation in state government and used the issue to sweep the fall elections for state and federal offices.[28]

Missouri Whigs fared better in 1852 because the rupture between friends and foes of Thomas Hart Benton limited the ability of Democrats to profit from Scott's debacle. Nevertheless, Missouri Whigs suffered from state and municipal divisions like those afflicting them in Maryland and Louisiana. Democrats won most Missouri federal races in 1852 and returned Benton to Washington as a St. Louis congressman. Whigs survived by exploiting Democratic divisions and stepping up criticism of immigrants. Edward Bates, a St. Louis Whig leader, warned that "under [Democrats'] corrupt, ruinous system, the United States may find themselves, in another generation, outvoted by the heathens whom they have conquered or bought." Mayor Luther Kennett charged his foes with supporting "Abolitionism, Free-Soilism, Socialism, Red Republicanism, Communism, and all the isms combined." Kennett won reelection in a violent contest marked by a battle between his supporters and Germans who backed a pro-Benton nominee.[29]

Whig nativism and their national leaders' equivocation on slavery cost them St. Louis's large immigrant vote. Foreign-born supporters of slavery turned to the Democrats. John Hogan, an Irish Protestant who ran for mayor in 1855, had been, according to his daughter, "a very active and prominent Whig . . . but after the death of President Taylor, in 1850, the questions of slavery and 'states rights' became the leading issue and . . . my father, as a citizen of Missouri, a slave state, himself a slave-owner, was naturally carried into the Democratic Party." On the other hand, immigrants opposed to slavery had the option of bypassing Whig nativists and voting for Benton's free-soil Democrats.[30]

In all three major Southern cities, the decline of Whig power at the state and federal level took away patronage resources that had been vital to holding followers to the party standard. Aware of this problem, a Missouri Whig told a St. Louis leader that "ours is a routed party. . . . Senatorships, Speakerships, Bank Directors, Public Printers, all gone."[31] Partisan convergence on economic issues created another problem for urban Whigs. Prosperity invalidated Whig predictions that Polk's free trade tariff would close factories. In Maryland, Pearce opposed a river and harbor bill, and Whigs backed the new constitution's limits on internal improvements. Both actions violated traditional Whig support for state aid to the economy. In 1853, Louisiana Democrats stole some of this ground from Whigs by approving new bank charters and railroad loans.[32] Between the end of the Mexican War and the presidential campaign of 1852, Southern Whigs had lost the issues and electoral base that for two decades had made them competitive.

Democrats made gains across the South as Whig voters looked for a more reliable defender of slavery, but in the cities labor issues and the same antipartisan mood that vexed the Whigs would hurt them. Conflicts inside of Baltimore's Democratic Party illustrate this process. In 1851, in response to an independent Union Party ticket, Democrats nominated men without government or party experience to one-half of Baltimore's ten seats in the state lower house. The slate triumphed in a low-turnout election, and in 1852 Democrats bragged that their mayoral nominee, John Smith Hollins, "had not been known as an active politician by either party."[33] Giving power to reformers addressed popular criticism of insider control, but it introduced issues that exacerbated Democrats' internal divisions. This dilemma manifested itself when a Baltimore educator, Martin J. Kerney, a Catholic who was elected as one of the party's new faces in 1851, sponsored bills to fund Roman Catholic schools publicly and establish a ten-hour workday.

Kerney's bills typified republicanism's egalitarian reform strain in that they enlisted the state in behalf of constituents with limited access to the social goods of education and a good job. Kerney traced his beliefs to "the old Jacksonian doctrine . . . equality of political privileges— no distinctions between the man of wealth and the humblest individual who earns his bread by the sweat of his brow. . . . No man to be known by his country or his religion."[34] This rhetoric could not sustain party unity at the level of specific policy because Protestants opposed funding parochial schools and rural slaveholders stymied legislation for urban wage earners. Kerney's bills sharpened sectarian and class tensions in his party, and this in turn cast doubt on Democrats' ability to campaign effectively on Kerney's brand of egalitarian reform.

Kerney's school bill won the support of Baltimore's burgeoning Catholic immigrant vote. However, Democratic Party leaders who feared provoking the city's Protestant majority joined thousands of nativist petitioners in protest of "the plan"—one that, a Baptist editor said, "is beyond all doubt of Jesuit origin." Realizing that his bill had no hope, Kerney tabled it. A milder version submitted in 1853 also failed. Baltimore's political demography, specifically its native-born electoral majority, hurt parochial school funding. Officials governing cities with immigrant voting majorities, like New York, enacted measures to support Catholic schools with public funds.[35]

Opposition within the Democratic Party, this time from rural legislators, also defeated the ten-hour bill. In 1853, a year after slaveholders in the state senate killed the original proposal, Baltimore delegates exempted free blacks from the bill's jurisdiction to allay planter suspicions of government interference with their workforce. Nevertheless, the urban-rural divide held and the measure failed, as did a final attempt at passage in 1854. The conflict over shorter hours touched on the growing influence in the Democratic Party of proslavery Whig converts. In 1853, Davis crowed that "our Locofoco friends have been . . . carving each other to pieces . . . in the selection of their candidates." He traced the struggle to "old line" Democrats unwilling "to fight and starve" while Whig "renegades" won nominations and to animosity between Democratic "secession and abolition wings."[36] Davis exaggerated in saying that the Democratic Party in a Southern state had an "abolition wing," but he did identify nonslaveholders' frustration with planter sensitivity to anything that hinted of a threat to slavery. Rather than express itself as a criticism of slavery or planters, Democrats voiced this dissatisfaction in complaints about the general unresponsiveness of party leaders. In this way, party corruption became a catchall issue that brought together Whig and Democratic dissenters.

Events in 1853 gave Baltimore's insurgent politicians an opportunity to break the Democratic hold on city politics by exploiting the class and cultural divisions exposed in Kerney's proposals. The spring's two-month ironworker strike stimulated labor organizing and emboldened wage earners to criticize inattentive party leaders. The strike coincided with a temperance campaign that emphasized themes of Protestant moral reform popular among native-born workers. The independent campaign of 1853 found a way to connect general suspicion of political parties to the specific concerns of skilled labor and native-born Protestants.

The Baltimore ironworkers' strike, a sign of growing friction between skilled labor and employers that coincided with strikes across urban America, drove workers from the Democratic Party while making the Democrats more attractive to Whiggish businessmen. Although Democrats on the city council had urged the B&O to raise wages for its machinists, a strike leader complained that "in political times we were styled the 'bone and sinew of the country,' but when these exciting seasons passed away, the mechanic and laborer only existed as 'hewers of wood and drawers of water.'" After the strike, a General Mechanics Union formed to "resist the encroachment of capital and the injustice of employers." It nominated strike leader John Michael Clarke as an independent candidate for sheriff. Although Democratic leaders succeeded in killing Clarke's candidacy, organized labor remained active during the fall's election season. At least three trades were on strike, factory hands lobbied for the ten-hour day, and the short-lived General Mechanics Union reconvened under a new name. Three leaders of the iron strike later ran for office as independents or Know-Nothings, whereas employers who resisted the strike shunned the American Party, and three of them, two of whom were former Whigs, became prominent Democrats.[37]

Strike leaders who later joined the nativist American Party likely noticed that Democratic leaders Mayor Hollins and Governor Lowe refused to address the strikers but appeared at a March meeting of the Irish Benevolent Society. Nativist agitation on political questions like the Kerney school bill coincided with ethnic rivalry between iron workers that encouraged native whites to define themselves in opposition to both employers and immigrants. American-born whites comprised two-thirds of city iron workers. Germans made up the largest immigrant contingent. Early rallies included speeches in German, and politicians praised German-born strikers. In return, Germans joined the turnout, and the German Mechanics Association donated money. However, strikers acted through separate ethnic trade associations, and nativists alleged that German workers had gone back without a raise.[38]

Anti-Catholic sentiment peeked out from the edges of the strike. After the strike, Clarke addressed carpenters in a Protestant church, an inhospitable venue for Catholic workers. An early February rally against the arrest of Protestant missionaries in Italy attacked "the intolerance of the Roman Catholic States." Although its organizers had no affiliation with the iron strike, the rally drew headlines in the *Clipper*, the newspaper most sympathetic to the ironworkers. The *Clipper's* editors, William Tuttle and Edward Bull, had a long record of supporting labor and nativism. They belonged to the typographical union and had been active in the 1830s Workingmen's movement. In 1845 their paper endorsed the anti-immigrant American Republican Party, and Bull was a friend of an outspoken Baptist minister. In 1853, *Clipper* editorials attacked immigrant job competition and linked the persecution of Italian Protestants to the Kerney school bill.[39]

Along with stoking xenophobia, the strike reinforced enthusiasm that some native-born workers felt for evangelical reform. Strikers acted through the Order of United American Mechanics (OUAM), which made evangelical Protestant values and native-born identity the basis for solidarity and whose founders had been active in Philadelphia's 1844 nativist riots and the American Republican campaign in that city. The OUAM discouraged drinking and Sabbath breaking, rejected foreign-born applicants, shunned ties with immigrant voluntary societies, and urged members to buy only from American-born mechanics. This brand of artisan moral reform was familiar to Baltimore workers active in temperance societies like the Washingtonians, popular in the early 1840s, and their successor, the Sons of Temperance. These reformers encouraged drinkers to master their will and reassert control of their households. Such solutions appealed to craft workers steeped in artisan-republican traditions that considered economic insecurity and moral corruption as constant threats to independence. The *Clipper* and the OUAM offered nativism as an ideological bridge between American-born workers and Protestant moral reformers.[40]

Those affinities helped moral reformers stage an independent challenge to the Democrats in the fall elections. At the October municipal contest, a mix of Whig and independent candidates cut the Democratic city council majority from eight representatives to two. A month later, a new Maine Law ticket, a name evoking Maine's 1851 alcohol ban, won Baltimore's races for the lower house and the sheriff's office. The temperance slate included five Democrats and five Whigs, but only Democrats fielded candidates against what they called "disorganizers." Independent victories in Baltimore coincided with a Whig resurgence elsewhere that gave Maine Law delegates the balance of power in the lower house and secured a Whig majority in the state senate. Democrats took consolation from winning Baltimore's congressional seats and the governorship.[41]

The November election presaged the new configuration of voters and issues that Know-Nothings solidified after 1854. Patterns of party support in Baltimore had been remarkably consistent prior to 1853. From 1828 through 1852, excepting the aberrant 1850 mayoral contest, there was little variation in the percentage of votes that Democrats received in each of the city's twenty wards. In the 1830s and 1840s, occupation correlated strongly with the Democratic vote—working-class wards backed Democrats and white-collar ones opted for Whigs—while place of birth was a less powerful predictor of partisanship. In 1853, the ward-by-ward percentage of Democratic votes deviated dramatically from the earlier pattern, signaling a citywide realignment of Democratic Party support. In that election, workers fell away from the Democrats and ethnicity came to the fore as an indentity that divided voters. Most damaging to Democrats was their loss of support among American-born craftsmen, the largest ethnic/occupational block in the electorate.[42]

This shift in the electorate reflected a new partisan debate on nativism and protection for skilled labor that Know-Nothings would sharpen in the coming years. The new issues manifested themselves in the Third District election for the U.S. House, where Democrat Joshua Vansant narrowly defeated independent William P. Preston. Both candidates supported the iron strike, so there was some irony in the fact that, while Preston, a lawyer, advocated labor's cause, Vansant, a former hatter associated with artisan politics, accused him of being a "trades union" candidate who would harm business interests. Vansant shunned a factory operatives' ten-hour convention that greeted Preston with "rapturous applause." The Democrat endorsed a new German Citizens Convention that Preston "utterly opposed" because immigrants' "native nationality [should] merge in the land of their adoption." In this vein, the United Sons of America, an American Party (and Know-Nothing) forerunner, endorsed independent candidates and warned that "foreigners will render our elections a curse instead of a blessing."[43]

The new statewide arrangement of Democratic Party power was also at issue. In 1853, city Democrats reinforced their ties to downstate slaveholders by leading the state assembly's lobbying effort to have Pennsylvania strictly enforce the Fugitive Slave Law. In return, Eastern Shore slaveholders assisted local campaigns, including Vansant's. Like other states, Maryland parties introduced nominating conventions late in the Jacksonian era. This new method of party discipline provoked cries of corruption when a losing candidate believed that the outcome had been prearranged. Preston, a career Democrat, ran as an independent to protest Vansant's victory in the party convention and what Preston believed was a state general assembly gerrymander of the district in Vansant's favor. Owen Bouldin, another candidate denied a Democratic nomination, ran as an independent and boasted that he "has not the advantage of being recommended by a 'Convention of Politicians.'"[44]

Preston's campaign typified the efforts of urban reformers to plug the social changes of the 1850s into complaints about political corruption. For example, in 1853 New Orleanian Charles E. A. Gayarre, a former Democratic U.S. senator, bolted his party to protest the convention nomination of William Dunbar, an ally of Gayarre's rival John Slidell. A supporter told Gayarre, "I can see no difference in principle between the French giving their liberties to the keeping of Louis Napoleon and the Americans to the self constituted conventions of a few house politicians." Dunbar won, but Gayarre and his followers cried foul and charged Democrats with recording four thousand illegal votes from nonnaturalized immigrants.[45]

Although reformers claimed to represent political outsiders, Baltimore's independent candidates of 1853 had either led the old parties or resembled the politicians who did. Maine Law sheriff Samuel Hindes was a prosperous hatter and a relative of two Whig activists. Although three-fourths of officeholders in temperance organizations had no connection with party bureaucracies, they fielded independent tickets in 1845 and 1850 and consistently endorsed candidates who supported alcohol-control laws. The leaders of temperance societies owned seventeen times more wealth than the average Baltimorean.[46] Temperance was a comparatively mild reform that wealthy social leaders hoped poorer men and women would adopt rather than a grassroots movement for radical change. Its organizational pattern of elite control with greater class diversity in the membership characterized most voluntary associations and political parties. The 1853 campaign foreshadowed the problem that veteran officeholders in the American Party would have in advocating reform while continuing to support aspects of the old political order, not the least of which was their own access to power.[47]

As in 1850, when Jerome won Baltimore's mayoralty by adding to his Whig base the votes of native-born Democratic workers seeking a protest vehicle, the 1853 elections represented a protest by the electorate's Democratic majority against party leaders, rather than a triumph for temperance as a single issue. Temperance advocates had earlier run for office, but they did so in elections where the major parties had not been beset by internal divisions, and they had failed miserably. In 1853, temperance candidates appealed to affluent Whigs better than a straight-out labor ticket, yet, unlike self-identified Whigs, a vote for them expressed labor activists' opposition to major parties. While the correlation between occupation and voting changed in 1853, white-collar wards still opposed Democrats, and Maine Law candidates received nearly the same proportion of votes from businessmen and professionals as they did from native-born mechanics. Democratic victories in races uncontested by Maine Law candidates suggest that Democratic voters remained loyal to their party in those elections, but otherwise opted for Maine Law candidates, some of whom were nominal Democrats. The reform victory in the 1853 legislative contests showed that partisanship was fraying, but Whig and Democratic victories elsewhere on the ballot left the major parties with considerable power.

As they had with Martin Kerney, veteran politicians held an advantage over outsiders lacking an organized constituency or an institutional party. Once in office, Maine Law delegates accommodated Whigs, who had tacitly endorsed them in the city and who, outside of Baltimore, reaped the benefits of anti-Democratic sentiment. Even with Whig support, the lower house's bill to outlaw liquor met with enough public criticism to allow the Maryland senate to reject it. Meanwhile, Whigs used Maine Law legislators to reelect James Pearce to the U.S. Senate. A Whig legislator explained to Pearce that "the Temperance faction you know control the House when all are present, but the Whigs of that representation are a majority and pledged to you in the end." Maine Law delegates needed a stronger organization and a broader appeal to swing voters, and Whig and Democratic leaders frustrated with internal factionalism needed the voters attracted to reform activists if they were to build a new party.[48]

The American Party, the result of that effort, enjoyed a meteoric rise. In 1854, Maryland's American Party, which had been organized as a secret society the preceding year, won victories in two western towns and then captured Baltimore's mayoralty and a majority on the city council.[49] Democrats battled back in 1855, but thereafter Know-Nothings swept city races for state and federal offices and dominated municipal government until 1860. Know-Nothings controlled the Maryland state assembly from 1856 to 1859 and the governorship from 1857 to 1861.

Know-Nothings succeeded in building the durable coalition that temperance reformers and other independents had not created. They did so by finding ways to bring diverse constituencies together under a few common themes and by attracting skilled veterans of the old parties, especially former Whigs, to lead their organization. On the campaign trail, American Party candidates found ways to use nativism, their signature issue, to address groups of voters whose interests sometimes clashed. By adapting hostility to foreigners to the republican-plot formula that power-seeking conspiracies threatened liberty, Know-Nothings articulated a republican nativism that gave coherence to their stands on culture, work, government reform, and slavery.

Perhaps the Know-Nothings' most prominent use of nativism was their portrayal of Roman Catholic immigrants as the foot soldiers of a papal plot to take over the United States and subvert the republic, a point made in the national party's pledge "to resist the insidious policy of the Church of Rome, and all other foreign influence against our republican institutions." The 1854 American tour of papal legate Gaetano Bedini, who had come to coordinate governance of new Catholic parishes, gave nativists a convenient symbol of Vatican power. Following Protestants in St. Louis and other cities, Baltimore protesters fired shots at Bedini and burned him in effigy, and local Know-Nothings called him "one of the most monstrous instruments of Papal vengeance" who "butchers Protestantism with one hand and Republicanism with the other." The *Clipper* applied the same ideas to the defeated Kerney school bill. "Roman Catholics," the editors argued, planned to "destroy the public schools, and thus have the children of the poorer classes of society either entirely uneducated, or educated only under the direction of Catholic priests." Another American Party editor compared Democrats to the ancient Gauls who invited Romans to help them fight local enemies and then lost their nation to the Romans. According to the logic of this metaphor, "the people of Ireland and Germany have been called in to suppress the will of the children of the soil." The conspiracy theory linked nativism to fears of political corruption. In this way, Know-Nothings offered to voters who were stimulated by antiparty rhetoric reasons to connect their fears for political virtue to the alarm that many Americans felt over the massive increase in immigration during the late 1840s and early 1850s.[50]

The nativist conspiracy theory also helped Know-Nothings court Whigs, a party that had criticized immigration more often than did Democrats. Appealing to Whigs, the *Clipper* asserted that Democrats elevated immigrants above natives for partisan gain. "An American citizen is proscribed because he happens to have belonged to the old Whig Party . . . yet an Irishman or a German or any other foreigner can come among us, remain a short time, announce himself a DIMEKRAT and he is worthy of holding office."[51]

Whig-to-American converts across the South shared the Baltimore argument. Kenneth Rayner, a former Whig and North Carolina's leading Know-Nothing, called Roman Catholicism un-American and anti-republican, and he excoriated corruption among Democrats who "can be bought, not only for the price of a negro, but for a pistareen." John Macpherson Berrien, a onetime Whig U.S. senator who chaired Georgia's American Party convention in 1855, came to the party to combat political "Romanists" and to "stand firm, battling for the rights of our country" against "little pettyfogging demagogues." When Whigs talked about power conspiring against liberty, they emphasized demagogic manipulation of unenlightened voters that they first attributed to Andrew Jackson. They could easily accept the argument that power-seeking Democrats tricked ignorant foreigners out of their votes.[52]

In the South, urban and rural Know-Nothings shared nativism, but it was only in the cities that party leaders used the plasticity of nativism to bring American-born workers into a coalition with Whigs from the social elite. In Baltimore, labor activism continued past 1853. In 1854 and 1855, quarry diggers, B&O workers, and craft apprentices staged separate turnouts to protest longer hours and low pay. Know-Nothing officeholders supported the railroad strike, and at the limestone quarries strikers assaulted foreign-born replacements.[53] Campaigning for Congress in 1855, Henry Winter Davis traveled to Washington, D.C., to address "700 or 800 Baltimore workmen" there on temporary jobs. In another campaign venue, he said that foreigners "were now swarming in such numbers over the land as to have not only become a dangerous element in politics, but a serious competitive power against our mechanics." Nativism spoke to rivalries in trades invaded by immigrants and to the way that social change had taxed skilled labor's resources. A party editorial told workers that "you are laboring daily to support more than two hundred and fifty thousand foreign criminals, vagrants, and paupers, now confined in the various prisons, penitentiaries, alms-houses and hospitals of the United States." In this nativist analysis of skilled labor's problems, immigrants represented an agent of destructive capitalist competition.[54]

In addition to rhetorical appeals, Baltimore's American Party administration won over wage-earning voters by creating jobs in public works. The city council allocated $35,000 "to give employment to the mechanics and laborers now out of work." Know-Nothings increased water spending from $78,920 in 1855 to $704,094 in 1860 and brought fresh water to an additional twelve thousand homes, most of them in newer working-class neighborhoods. In step with professionalization in other cities, Samuel Hinks, a Quaker flour merchant who won the mayoralty in 1854, raised the number of police officers to 350 and increased their pay above the standard manual wage. Davis promised new federal projects and attacked incumbent Democrat Henry May for voting against the spending of $120,000 in improvements to Baltimore's harbor. In sops to their nativist base, the city council restricted hiring by city agencies (e.g., police and construction crews) to the American-born and funded only those militia units that had a native-born membership of at least two-thirds. An early estimate of Hinks's patronage policy predicted that "mechanics and the poorer classes of good habits will reap a large share of his rewards."[55]

Labor had less influence in the initial Know-Nothing campaigns in New Orleans. In 1854, the American Party won a majority on the board of alderman by campaigning as reformers who would erase Democratic budget deficits, stop immigrant vote fraud, and police morals by licensing liquor sales. Under Mayor Charles Waterman, a Whig hardware merchant from New York, Know-Nothings balanced the budget, even as they increased municipal funding of railroads. Although unable to enact a voter registration law, Know-Nothings won control of district courts that administered naturalization oaths. The absence of a politicized strike akin to that of Baltimore's iron industry and the identification of Louisiana's Whig businessmen with political reform made labor issues less salient in the mid-1850s New Orleans elections.[56]

St. Louis Know-Nothings had less success than their counterparts in Baltimore and New Orleans. American Party failure in St. Louis highlights the unique political demography of the other cities where Know-Nothings flourished. In 1854, Luther Kennett, Whig mayor since 1850, joined the American Party and upset Benton in a race for the congressional district that encompassed the city. In 1855, a Know-Nothing won the mayoral election. That victory provoked counterorganizing by the city's large immigrant voting population. In 1860, foreign-born residents comprised 60 percent of St. Louis's population, compared with 25 percent of Baltimore's and 38 percent of New Orleans's. The presence of so many recent German arrivals, many of whom were freesoilers, enabled self-styled "emancipation Democrats" to capture city government in 1856 and to reorganize as Republicans later in the decade. In a city with an immigrant majority, the American Party attempt to build a majority around nativism was doomed from the outset. St. Louis's status as the Southern city with the most enfranchised wage earners and most immigrants allowed Republicans to bear the standard of urban protest that the American Party represented in Baltimore and New Orleans.[57]

In Baltimore, immigrants were numerous enough to produce an American-born backlash, but not so omnipresent as to outvote a determined nativist majority. However, not all American-born whites bought into Know-Nothing rhetoric. In Baltimore, nativism spurred partisan competition, rather than starting a one-sided onslaught against immigrants because it engendered enough voter opposition to encourage Democrats to challenge it. In the three elections held in Baltimore in 1854 and 1855, thirteen of twenty wards switched back and forth between parties. Average turnout, another sign of heightened competitiveness in those three elections, rose 30 percent above the years 1850–53 and far outstripped population growth. This was a remarkable increase for contests below the level of president or governor.[58]

With the hard core of Kerney's Protestant foes having defected to the Know-Nothings, Baltimore Democrats counterattacked nativists on antiparty, civil-libertarian grounds. That position attracted immigrants, and it appealed to the broader public's suspicion of partisan manipulation. Arguments that connected civil liberties to political reform motivated Whigs who disowned national chauvinism—like the Irish Protestants in the party who led local immigrant-aid societies. In 1854, Richard T. Merrick, a former Baltimore Whig, told his colleagues that they "owe an obligation to the institutions of the country before which all animosities must cease. . . . Its high privileges could not be more endangered . . . than in the rule of men united by religious fanaticism, and combined for the purpose of proscribing and disfranchising a large portion of the American people for the crime of following in religious matters, the dictates of conscience." Merrick's criticism fit into Southern antiparty fears of Know-Nothing secrecy that, to them, smacked of corruption and, according to a North Carolina Whig, was "dangerous to liberty."[59]

Baltimore Democrats made city spending another marker of party division by attacking the assumption that government owed labor special favors and by arguing that public works raised taxes and corrupted government. In 1855, the *Republican,* a Democratic Party organ edited by 1830s laborite Beale H. Richardson, complained that "common laborers refuse to work for one dollar and a half a day, and mechanics refuse to continue working for two and a half per day! And these are the parties who join in the clamor for corporation help." Richardson warned that "the credit of the city itself may be seriously effected, or the rate of taxation be rendered so onerous as to drive capital from us." As did lower-South fire-eaters, Richardson compared his enemies to the demagogic excesses of the French Revolution: "Louis Napoleon, to gain over the masses to his ambitious designs against the Republic of France, would take this course and order work to be found for the sans Culottes of Paris." Twenty years earlier, Richardson led artisans in refusing to pay an indemnity to the Bank of Maryland's directors, but in the mid-1850s he, like labor's other former Democratic friends, criticized workers who wanted the state to redress class inequities. In the process of party realignment, Democrats sounded more like conservative Whigs worried about labor demagogues than champions of the common man.[60]

While the parties differed over immigration and the rights of labor, each presented itself as slavery's best defender and demonized its rival as an enemy of Southern interests. Baltimore Democrats, who in their rapprochement with downstate planters had baited Whigs as abolitionists, accused Know-Nothings of being antislavery accomplices. Their allegations ranged from the plausible yet false assertion that Know-Nothings wanted to ban slavery in Kansas to the outlandish claim that they enrolled African Americans in secret lodges and encouraged slave revolts. Democrats also tied their abolitionist smear against the Know-Nothings to fears of majority rule and mistrust of extreme partisanship that ran through Southern politics. "Let Southern men remember," said one Baltimore editor, "that should this new order become triumphant in the Southern states, it is bound by its oath of membership to be governed by the will of the majority; and that majority has shown itself deadly hostile to them." In the American Party's early days, members of its secret lodges pledged to vote only for others enrolled in the Know-Nothing order. Although the party abandoned secrecy and other aspects of fraternalism soon after it gained the national stage, Southern Democrats argued that the grouping's tradition of party discipline was especially dangerous to the South because slave-state Know-Nothings would be bound to the free-soilers who dominated several American Party state organizations in the North.[61]

Similar to the way that Know-Nothings used nonpartisan reform themes to unite different voting blocks in the city, urban Democrats' antiparty counterattack against Know-Nothings created common ground for an alliance between themselves and Democrats in the rural South. Criticisms of party discipline as practiced by Know-Nothings resonated with the ethics of honor that were a touchstone of Southern politics. Honor, an ethical tradition dating to the ancient world, regulated relationships between free citizens. Honor addressed the tension between equality and hierarchy that was endemic to America's market culture but that had special meaning in the South because of slavery's influence on perceptions of status. Men of wealth, rank, and talent dominated Southern society, yet racial mores, which encouraged white unity in defense of slavery, treated all white men as free and equal to each other. Honor's emphasis on integrity and independence mattered most when Southern white men confronted questions about their freedom and equality. As society's governors, free men needed to trust each other to behave responsibly. They saw integrity, or consistent adherence to shared ethical standards, as essential to creating mutual trust. The rebellion of a servant, financial reversal, or a simple confrontation from a rival could compromise a white man's claim to equality. To defend that claim, a man of honor needed an independent character, an instinct for courageous self-assertion. An honorable man was neither a liar nor a servile puppy of another's will, and voters who prized honor in their political leaders could easily accept the criticism that party loyalty sacrificed integrity and independence for the sake of partisan victory.[62]

Drawing on these values, Southern nationalists turned the urban critique of Know-Nothings as a conventional political party into a more fundamental indictment of them as an anti-Southern party. Southern nationalists argued that national political parties, as opposed to purely Southern ones, supported Northern domination in federal politics and negated a public official's claim to moral leadership by requiring him to compromise his principles in order to serve his party. In 1855, a friend told William Porcher Miles to run for mayor of Charleston, South Carolina, on a ticket calling itself Southern Rights, because Miles's "independent and resolute character" was needed to combat Know-Nothings who "are shrewd and selfish men who don't care a damn about their principles . . . now or never can you indicate your manhood." Even those secessionists who remained loyal Democrats, like Virginia's John C. Rutherfoord, expressed "skepticism towards democracy" and worried that Know-Nothing party discipline and oath taking undermined the manly independence required of politicians in a slave society.[63]

By equating resistance to federal and party power with honor-based gender identities, Southern nationalists forced Know-Nothings to explain how a voter could support their political stands and still be true to himself as a man. Democracy's temptations to deceive also troubled Southerners. Know-Nothings made an issue of Democratic manipulation of immigrant votes, and in return Southern Democrats claimed that because Know-Nothing secret oaths bound them to Northern free-soilers, American candidates necessarily lied about their devotion to slaveholders' rights.

Southern Know-Nothings running in plantation districts or seeking statewide office combated these charges by adopting a posture of republican sincerity and disavowing conventional partisan methods. Under personal attack by Democrats in Tennessee's 1855 governor's race, Meredith P. Gentry, the American nominee, refused to reciprocate. "I know . . . what rules of honorable conduct among gentlemen require," Gentry explained. "I cannot degrade my manhood, even if my competitor does do so, no, not even to secure my election." North Carolina's Kenneth Rayner would not actively campaign for an American Party nomination because he believed that "this struggling and scrambling for office and promotion was one of the very great evils it was the object of our organization to remedy." In Mississippi, "American Party spokesmen employed antipartyism even more pointedly than their predecessors" and "expressed grateful relief" when national leaders permitted state organizations to abandon secrecy. In 1855, Virginia's Know-Nothing candidates for statewide offices eschewed speaking on the stump despite an unprecedented Democratic canvas that one derided as "campaign demagogy." Honor and republicanism put Southern Know-Nothings in a double-bind by proscribing partisanship in a political system that lent itself to collective organization.[64]

Attacks on political corruption dominated Know-Nothing rhetoric throughout the slave states, but the honor-based ethics that discredited partisan behavior in rural areas and statewide campaigns had less influence in big cities. Consequently, Know-Nothings in the urban South took a more nuanced approach to traditional party politics. Metropolitan politicians relied on Jacksonian party practices to reach non-slaveowning wage earners, and they could not renounce conventional electioneering tactics even if Southerners associated them with lying and manipulation. Instead, urban Know-Nothings presented themselves as enlightened partisans, or statesmen possessed of strong morals and exceptional cleverness who could use questionable methods for honorable purposes.

This concept of enlightened partisanship found expression in a work of fiction written by New Orleans Charles Gayarre in 1854 as he pondered switching from Democrat to Know-Nothing. Gayarre's *A School for Politics* explores how a statesman could achieve the public good through corrupt means. The novel can be read as a blanket condemnation of political hypocrisy. Ambition drives most characters to indulge vices like lying, bribery, and mobbing that they professed to abhor, and the hero, John Washington Randolph, pretends to "care not for politics; I will not meddle with the dirty trash," yet he deceives friend and foe alike to become governor. However, Gayarre makes Randolph, a planter who bears the names of two republican icons, a true hero rather than just one more wire-pulling villain. Randolph proves himself a good leader who engineers the happiness of others, including that of his enemies. Speaking through Randolph, Gayarre says, "Let men lay their snares. . . . I will profit by their weakness—their lies—their vices—their treachery—but I will keep free from contamination. I will not corrupt anyone—but I will use the corrupt for noble and patriotic purposes."[65] Politicians were not confidence men, but many of them thought that artificiality and insincerity had to be employed to gloss over divisions between constituents that, if fully expressed, would prevent collective action. For leaders like Gayarre, republican intolerance of hypocrisy in elected officials had to be tempered with an awareness that public masking of inner feeling was not only unavoidable but also beneficial.[66]

Although they differed in their attitudes toward partisanship, urban Know-Nothings followed their rural colleagues in vigorously advocating for slaveholders' interests in order to rebut Southern Democratic charges that they were slavery's enemies. The American Party joined its defense of slavery to a defense of the Union from attacks by sectional extremists. In Baltimore, Know-Nothings described themselves as "warm friends and advocates of the Union against the fire-eaters and free soilers." According to a local American editor, "the issue involved [in the Kansas-Nebraska Act of 1854] is union or disunion—the Constitution as it is, with its provisions for the protection of slave property, or its utter destruction." Similarly, Maryland's Anthony Kennedy, an American Party U.S. senator and John Pendleton Kennedy's brother, supported the Lecompton Constitution that permitted slavery in Kansas because he thought it would preserve the Union. Many of Baltimore's American Party officers owned slaves or grew up in families that did, and they either vocally supported the institution or took Henry Winter Davis's advice that "the way to settle the slavery question is to be silent on it."[67]

New Orleans Know-Nothings made similar arguments, emphasizing the manipulation of abolition-inclined foreigners by the Democratic Party and voting for slavery-extension measures. They had good reason to do so. Theodore Hunt, the only Know-Nothing congressman from Louisiana to oppose the Kansas-Nebraska Act, lost reelection in 1856.[68]

In Missouri, the American Party stood for slavery and preservation of the Union. As one party follower put it, "If the American Party succeeds, the Union is safe and our domestic institutions will remain untouched, but if it fails, the horrors of intestine war, and all the appalling consequences of disunion must ensue." Whigs and Know-Nothings cooperated with anti-Benton Democrats, and Luther Kennett won the 1854 St. Louis congressional election by railing against immigrants and attacking Benton for opposing popular sovereignty in Kansas.[69]

That slave-state Know-Nothings could advocate a proslavery Unionism seems unremarkable; prior to 1860, most Southern politicians did so. More intriguing is their twin conspiracy theory in which the Vatican colluded with abolitionists to topple republican freedom. Anna Ella Carroll, a member of a prominent Maryland political family and confidant of Millard Fillmore, called attention to a provision of the Kansas-Nebraska Act that allowed nonnaturalized residents to vote. "The bogs,

alms-houses or prisons of Europe," she claimed, "can make their tenants, in six months, voters at the American ballot-box, in many of the
Western States and Territories." Baltimore's Davis worried that "foreigners owing allegiance to European Sovereigns now have a final voice
in deciding . . . the question of freedom or slavery in its fundamental
law." In 1855, Davis said that "generally foreigners were Free-Soilers or
Abolitionists—deeply prejudiced against Southern institutions." A Baltimore Know-Nothing editor called New York Republican William H.
Seward "this conspirator against the Union" and argued that "by means
of foreign Catholic votes . . . he hopes to effect the abolition of slavery
and the destruction of the Union." According to this logic, leading New
York free-soilers "encourage immigration to this country on the very
ground that foreign labor is to compete with slave labor, and eventually
drive it out of the market." Baltimore Know-Nothings argued that abolitionists and Catholics used immigrants as pawns to undermine the liberty and living standards of slave owners and white workers alike.[70]

This linkage of nativist and proslavery arguments offers a counter-
point to scholarship showing that northern Know-Nothings switched to
the Republican Party after 1856 because, among other reasons, their
papal-plot ideas merged with the Republican claim that a Slave Power,
as Republicans called the slaveholder influence in government, con-
spired against liberty.[71] In the North, the absence of slaveholders and a
strong proslavery vote made the Slave Power conspiracy less controversial than in Baltimore, where its advocates faced intense opposition.
Building a majority in Louisiana, Maryland, and Missouri required
support from slaveholding counties outside the city. Along with pressure from other districts to support slavery, the South's urban voters remained committed to the proslavery consensus of the old parties. If, for
example, Baltimore Know-Nothings had tried to connect nativist and
free-soil arguments (and little evidence suggests they wanted to), they
might have been driven underground by mob violence, as was the city's
feeble branch of the Republican Party.[72] Only in St. Louis, where nativism proved unworkable, could Republicans win, and when they did
the city became an outcast in state politics. In slave-state cities, Know-
Nothings rallied their varied supporters around the common theme of
immigrant subversion, and, in regard to slavery, they reversed the
northern fusion of nativist and slave-power ideas by syncopating attacks on immigrants with the proslavery drumbeat against abolitionism.

The Know-Nothing-versus-Democrat battles of 1854 and 1855 continued the Jacksonian-era South's politics of slavery. The institution re-

ceived bipartisan support, but each side tried to cast the other as in-sufficiently proslavery.[73] Similarly, Know-Nothings and Democrats fit nativism into the conventions of republicanism; each claimed to defend the public good from power-seeking conspirators in the rival party. This style of debate echoed the Jacksonian era in that parties differentiated themselves to voters while still agreeing on popular issues like support-ing slavery, republican government, and commercial expansion. Points of agreement helped reconcile partisans to a temporary loss of power after electoral defeat and had been one of the ways that Jacksonian par-ties had contained democracy within orderly boundaries.

The politics of slavery reinforced another practice that Know-Nothings inherited from the Jacksonian era—the exclusion of poor men and political newcomers from positions of power. As it did in so many aspects of Southern life, slavery led Baltimore's political nativists down a more conservative, order-reinforcing path than the road trav-eled by those Northern Know-Nothings who eventually became free-soil Republicans. Southern Know-Nothings' commitment to upholding the status quo on slavery went along with their defense of established institutions as such. To the extent that support for slavery reinforced mistrust of groups that called for social and political change, the poli-tics of slavery weakened American Party leaders' attachment to the grassroots constituencies of workers and evangelicals whose support they needed.

Therefore, in addition to ideological continuity, Know-Nothings carried forward earlier patterns of party leadership by restricting ma-jor offices to veterans of the old parties who also belonged to wealthy families. A close look at who actually held office under the American Party illustrates this point. Two-thirds of Baltimore Know-Nothings oc-cupying major offices—in the state-party bureaucracy, holding city-wide elected office, or in state and national government—had held posts in the old parties, especially with the Whigs, a pattern typical of the American Party's urban experience. Although Know-Nothings had more fresh faces in lower-party echelons, men with political careers predating the American Party's emergence served in most of the new party's major offices and half of its minor, ward-level, offices.

Merchant and professional domination of party bureaucracies, a pat-tern of the Jacksonian era, increased under competition between Know-Nothings and Democrats. Between 1854 and 1860, three-fourths of the minor offices in both parties went to nonmanual workers. High-status professionals, half of them lawyers, held four-fifths of the major offices.

In contrast, skilled workers occupied a mere 9 percent of the top posts. The 1860 property means of $59,900 for major officeholders and $27,937 for minor ones dwarfed those of $3,000 for eligible voters and $899 for adult whites. Baltimore Know-Nothings, like the Whigs before them and the Democrats they competed against, assigned their offices to men from the social elite who were used to exercising political power. These trends angered outsiders, who complained that a "circle of court flatterers" and "regular bum suckers" controlled nominations.[74] This pattern characterized city politics across America. In St. Louis and New Orleans, former Whigs ran the American Party, and their wealth and occupations resembled those of leaders of the old parties. In some northern states, Know-Nothings ran inexperienced candidates for office, but in the urban South the old Whig elite led the new party.[75]

By drawing on familiar models to construct their bureaucracy, Baltimore Know-Nothings opened themselves to charges of hypocritically selling old wine in a new, reform, bottle. And, despite Know-Nothing protests to the contrary, it was true that veteran officeholders struggled to keep power in their own hands even as they mobilized new constituencies with a call to reform conventional politics. The complex relationship between American Party leaders and evangelical Protestants, one of the social groups that generally backed Know-Nothings, illustrates this contradiction in the American Party and shows what party leaders gained and lost by refusing to make their organization into a grassroots social movement.

Understanding the relationship of evangelicals to the Know-Nothings is a complicated task because, despite distrust between politicians and clergy, religion influenced party politics in several ways. Party leaders joined churches out of a sincere faith commitment, Christian themes colored political debate, and voters' faith often correlated with party preference.[76] The distinction to keep in mind is that in the urban South, the leaders of parties, the institutional bases for political mobilization, refused to merge their organizations with churches, the institutions of religious subcultures. Clergy reciprocated by shielding their congregations from the parties because they regarded politics as a corrupt distraction from spirituality. Voters who took religious criticism of party politics seriously mistrusted Know-Nothings, notwithstanding their endorsement of church-supported moral reforms. For their part, American Party leaders believed that enlightened statesmen should guide the people, and they refused to give power to constituencies led by men inexperienced in politics and government.

Protestant ambivalence toward the Baltimore American Party manifested itself in the small percentage of church members who were party activists and the even partisan split among those who were. Congregation membership lists from 1850s Baltimore showed that only 29 of 386 Methodists and 22 of more than 400 Presbyterians had experience in parties or government, and active Democrats matched the number of Know-Nothings and former Whigs.[77] Church membership reflected a special dedication to a congregation, just as involvement in party governance demonstrated a commitment to politics that went beyond the act of voting. Had Protestant denominations been the driving force of Know-Nothingism, more church members would have taken up the party's labors and fewer Democratic activists would have belonged to congregations aligned with their rivals.

Politicians exercised disproportionate influence in congregational governance, but that involvement signified general civic leadership, rather than a fusion of faith and party. One-fourth of the Methodists' sixty congregational officers were party activists, and Presbyterian bureaucracies included twice as many politicians as did the general membership. Similarly, Baltimoreans with party experience occupied one-third to one-half of the offices in private charities, fraternal societies, volunteer fire companies, and corporate boards. To avoid antagonizing partisans on either side, churches and other voluntary societies divided offices evenly between the parties.[78] Politicians kept their names before the public by leading a variety of economic and civic organizations, and, in assessing their enthusiasm for nativism, we should consider the Protestant faith of Know-Nothing officeholders in relation to other aspects of their identity as well-educated, well-traveled, public figures.

While critical of the antirepublican implications of Roman Catholic immigration, Baltimore's American Party leaders had cosmopolitan backgrounds that tempered sectarian prejudice. Thomas Swann, the Know-Nothing mayor from 1856 to 1860 and a benefactor of Irish charities, believed that "Rome in its present condition is far from inspiring to us," yet he thought that Catholic France's absolutist monarchy had "implant[ed] in the bosom of the poorest citizen the seeds of contentment and happiness." Brantz Mayer, a Know-Nothing publicist, said that in Rome "it appeared as if all the ordinary impulses of society were disregarded . . . and the whole people had devoted themselves to Religion" but he also wrote that "there is a peculiar and charming power in the Catholic religion . . . it is a democratic as well as dramatic religion." A devout Episcopalian, Henry Winter Davis disliked the antihierarchical emotionalism of evangelicals, and he called Bishop Henry Johns "a low church loco foco" who acted "little better than Methodists" because he preached at interdenominational services. In an 1854 tour of Europe, Davis condemned the Austrian monarchy for suppressing Hungarian nationalism, but in Germany he admired Roman Catholic churches and convents, and in Paris he felt "as much at home here as if I had lived here half a life." He claimed that Know-Nothings distinguished "between proscribing people for holding religious dogmas and preventing people from doing mischief by invoking sectarian interests to bear on political affairs." The experienced politicians who led the American Party lacked the nativist fervency of some rank-and-file supporters.[79]

This ambivalence informed the lukewarm support Know-Nothing legislators gave the convent-reform campaign of Presbyterian minister Andrew B. Cross. Cross, who had railed against Catholic convents since the 1830s, argued that in nunneries "the soul of the individual is under the guidance, and the body under the control of men, who have gloried in tyranny, reveled in licentiousness, while they have boasted of extra holiness." In 1856 and 1858, Maryland's House of Delegates, where Know-Nothings held a five-to-two majority, rejected petitions gathered by Cross for a law "for the protection of young women in the convents of the State." A select committee of two Democrats and three Know-Nothings, two of them from Baltimore, concluded that Cross's accusations lacked proof, and if "the charge be true . . . the laws of the land . . . furnish an effectual and complete remedy." In fact, the Know-Nothing state legislature, usually with the Baltimore delegation's assent, rejected many nativist moral reforms, including longer naturalization requirements, prohibitions on alcohol, and stronger Sabbath statutes. Cross also stood out for his involvement in African-American charities, and although Cross downplayed racial equality in his political work, his radical brand of reform likely tripped alarms about "ultraism" in the minds of politicians.[80]

Moreover, Know-Nothing legislators had little fear of electoral defeat from radical anti-Catholics like Cross, who was exceptional as a cleric who wanted to engage the parties. Some of Baltimore's Protestant clergy, like Episcopal Bishop William R. Whittingham and Unitarian minister George Burnap, decried political agitation against Catholics. While many other Protestant clerics disapproved of Roman Catholicism, they also disdained involvement in party politics. For example, John Williams, a Baltimore Baptist minister, attended a Catholic mass long enough "to be disgusted," yet he wrote that "I have always felt it was the duty of a Pastor to 'give himself wholly to the work of the ministry.'"[81]

The distance between party leaders and Protestant radicals was even more acute in New Orleans, where Know-Nothings campaigned for Catholic votes. Creoles, descendants of Louisiana's French and Spanish colonists, saw themselves as the state's true natives and were skeptical of Catholic clerical authority. Some agreed with Know-Nothing claims that recent European arrivals undermined economic opportunity, threatened slavery, and blindly followed Vatican dictates. Louisiana Know-Nothings nominated Catholics for high office, including governor, and in 1855 they sent Charles Gayarre, a New Orleans Catholic, to represent them at the national American Party convention. When the convention ejected Gayarre on religious grounds, the Louisiana delegation walked out. New Orleans had Protestant bigots who during Know-Nothing rule wrecked the presses of a Catholic newspaper, but it also had Protestant clergy who spoke for toleration. Unitarian minister Theodore Clapp believed that that "church despotism belongs to things forever gone by," and he urged compassion for the Irish, who existed "in the extremist need and destitution, should we not open our arms to receive them with a cordial welcome?" Although their presence angered American Party members in other states and in heavily Protestant parishes of northern Louisiana, Know-Nothing politicians in Creole-rich New Orleans and south Louisiana distinguished the practice of the Roman Catholic faith from "Jesuitism," or Vatican influence in politics.[82] In the big cities, emphasizing political corruption over Protestant sectarianism addressed popular criticism of party politics and made Know-Nothings less offensive to the influential minority of urban Catholic Whigs. The South's most zealous anti-Catholic Know-Nothings tended to live in rural areas, where sectarianism met little resistance from an established Catholic presence.[83]

Not only were urban Know-Nothing politicians ambivalent about Protestant radicals, but a religiously informed view of politics could just as easily convince Protestants to vote against Know-Nothing corruption as it could persuade them to support the party on nativist grounds. Henry Slicer, Baltimore's leading Methodist minister, was "an unchangeable Democrat," a friend of national party figures like James Buchanan, and chaplain to the U.S. Senate in the 1830s and 1850s. Slicer worked for moral reforms that the American Party also advocated (such as temperance and Sabbath observance), but he opposed using the pulpit for partisan ends and he said that Know-Nothings "had dragged the city down to the lowest point of degradation" for abusing immigrants and gambling via public lotteries.[84] Clergymen participated in reform activities that politicians also supported, but they rarely endorsed a particular candidate: to have done so would have infected congregations with the worldly distraction of party politics.

The distance between American Party leaders and the subculture of Protestant evangelicals illustrates the dilemma facing reform-minded politicians in Southern cities. Men from the metropolitan social and political elite who joined the Know-Nothings struggled to balance their suspicion of partisanship with an appreciation of its practical utility. Loyalty to party had brought together diverse coalitions in state and national politics to enact legislation that cities needed, such as internal improvements, that might not otherwise have passed. Nevertheless, urban politicians feared that, when taken to extremes, party loyalty could be manipulated by demagogues to harm the public good.

Like other well-off Southerners, urban politicians worried less about elite control of government than about a party system that required them to play to the masses in ways that reduced them from honorable statesmen to lowly spoilsmen. Gayarre switched from the Democrats to the Know-Nothings because he believed that the lure of office had disgraced the old parties. Whigs and Democrats, Gayarre argued, had an "august mission . . . to become the teachers and apostles of the people in enlightening their intellect and purifying their morals, whilst serving and securing at the same time their material interests. . . . Gradually corrupted by ambition and the pride of power, the apostles became the pimps of the populace, and by losing their primitive character, lost their own esteem and that of the world."[85] Along with pimping, decay as an attribute of the old parties factored into Know-Nothing's self-image as unsullied by past ethical lapses. "Of this great breaking up in parties— which I have long looked for and heartily rejoiced in," said Henry Winter Davis, "I am for no old fogey measures." He expected Know-Nothings to "attain power with a degree of moral force that will enable them to illustrate the nature of republican government."[86] In the early years of American Party success in the urban South, Know-Nothings were led by political insiders like Gayarre and Davis who sought to purify party politics of what they considered to be its general corruption. Doing so did not entail an end to traditional practices so much as it required an extra effort by Know-Nothing leaders to use the potentially corrupt means of party politics for virtuous republican ends.

In 1855, the urban South's veteran politicians could congratulate themselves for having rescued their profession from the threat of insurgency manifested in 1853. In 1854, Whigs departed the scene and a new party stepped in with an issue, nativism, that reinvigorated voter interest. Equally noteworthy, party leaders staged this revival without dismantling the established rules of political competition. The American Party drew its leaders from an elite experienced in governing the city who hoped that the new party would relieve fears that party politics was inherently corrupt. In the short run, nativism and the Know-Nothings remedied an ailing system of party competition.

However, this rescue of Jacksonian political norms showed many signs that it would not last. In Baltimore, riots, an occasional byproduct of antebellum politics, broke out at the 1854 and 1855 elections and shook confidence that vote totals expressed the people's will. The prominence in American Party mobs of gangs associated with crime and taverns alarmed evangelicals. A Baltimore Methodist editor who otherwise backed the Know-Nothings "demand[ed] that some measures be taken to nip in the bud this spirit of rowdyism," but he believed that "the muddy stream of party politics is, in this country, too generally suffered to taint the pure fountain of justice." Know-Nothing coercion undermined the party's reform credentials.[87]

Class conflict internal to the American Party was another source of instability. Already restive with the Democrats in 1853, a majority of Baltimore's native-born skilled workers voted Know-Nothing thereafter. In 1855, Know-Nothings reminded them that several Democratic candidates had wanted to arrest the 1853 iron strikers for breaking conspiracy laws. "Remember Mechanics this fact!" read one editorial, "That those who now solicit your votes, three years ago were anxious to incarcerate you in prisons, for asking for an increase of your wages." In an exception to the rule of candidates being wealthy, Baltimore Know-Nothings nominated for the House of Delegates an iron-strike leader, Jehu B. Askew, a former Democrat who symbolized labor's abandonment of their old party. Speaking in Askew's behalf, J. Morrison Harris asked an audience, "Why will you . . . place lawyers on your tickets? No lawyer can serve you better and secure your success more triumphantly than such men from the working people." Harris was an attorney, a veteran Whig activist, and a candidate for Congress, and his question could easily have been turned against the Know-Nothings. Events in 1856 and after proved that working-class Know-Nothings would not indefinitely ratify a system of political competition that required their involvement but denied them power.[88]

Four

Southern Free-Labor Politics
Workers and the Urban Opposition,
1856–1859

The new party organizations created in 1854 and 1855 had a short life span in the rural South. In the lower South, Democrats exercised unquestioned dominance and grew more intransigent in their defense of slavery. Party competition persisted in the upper and border South, but in 1857 foes of the Democrats reorganized, either as Whigs or as a generic "Opposition," and abandoned nativism and the Know-Nothings.[1]

The three largest Southern cities diverged from this pattern. Not only did the party labels and issues that drove the mid-1850s insurgency against the Democrats persist, but, as a result of the new power that workingmen exercised in the opposition parties, party conflict intensified so as to upset the orderly routines of voting and legislating. Working-class political activism polarized the parties along lines of class and ethnicity and entangled city government in social struggles that had heretofore been kept out of formal politics. The party realignment that began in the early 1850s as an attempt to salvage the best features of Jacksonian-era partisanship had, by the end of the decade, turned into a partisan war that critics viewed as a distillation of party politics' worst features. Attacks on party politics had class overtones because they also entailed criticism of the new political actors—the workers who, disregarding respectable political norms, had helped the urban opposition to breast the South's rising Democratic tide.

Urban workers in the late-antebellum South experimented with a brand of labor politics associated for two decades with New York, America's largest city. By 1830, New York's population approached two hundred thousand. That surge in population enabled the new, impersonal wage-labor system to push aside the older model of urban paternalism. Simultaneous with the rise of Whig-versus-Democratic Party competition, New Yorkers from laboring backgrounds stopped deferring to politicians from the social elite and took control of neighborhood-level party bureaucracies.[2] Although occurring later in big Southern cities, this type of politics arrived there as economic and demographic growth weakened patron-client relationships in work and ward politics.

Across the country, a combination of factors stimulated workers' interest in party politics in the late 1850s. Cities in the North and West experienced the same growth in their working-class electorates as had the cities of the South. The urban recession that started in 1854 and worsened with the panic of 1857 sapped resources from nonpartisan labor-reform organizations that had flourished early in the decade. Pushed by hard times and emboldened by new clout at the polls, workers sought redress from better-funded political parties. Characterized by ethnic conflict between workers as well as struggles against employers, labor's political militancy in the largest cities of the slave states was mild compared with that in the North, yet it was radical by the standards of smaller Southern cities.

The most populous Northern cities had a large percentage of voters at the bottom of the social order who could on occasion push working-class candidates and issues into the realm of electoral politics. Class-based collective action was strongest in smaller industrial Northern cities, like Lynn, Massachusetts, where a single industry and minimal cultural differences enhanced labor solidarity.[3] In comparison, wage earners in the South's smaller cities had weaker trade unions and less electoral power. Charleston, Mobile, Richmond, and Savannah had fewer workers in their general populations, and a greater share of those who earned wages consisted of nonvoting recent immigrants and African Americans. In these cities, nativism played better to wealthy Whig moral reformers. Conversely, nativism strengthened Democratic support among the sizable proportion of immigrants in small Southern city workforces.[4]

To explore the distinctiveness of the largest Southern cities, as in other chapters primary attention is here paid to Baltimore. Industrial Baltimore is at center stage because it provided the optimal demographic and political conditions for Know-Nothings to thrive as the party of workingmen. On the one hand, the nativist class argument that foreign competition took jobs away from locals had a ring of truth because immigrants were in fact replacing white Americans as the wage workforce's majority. On the other hand, native white mechanics had the electoral power to use government to combat ills they associated with immigration and employer exploitation. Immigrant numerical strength took longer to show itself in politics than in the workplace because of the minimum five-year lag between a foreign man's arrival and his attainment of voting rights. In 1850, native-born workers accounted for 47 percent of Baltimore's eligible voters, and foreign-born manual workers made up 17 percent. Ten years later, those figures had changed to 40 percent and 29 percent, respectively. A coalition of immigrant wage earners and wealthy natives could outvote American-born workers, but the latter group remained the city's principal voting block.

The power of native-born workingmen to swing elections manifested itself in citywide voting patterns. The demise of the Democrats, who began losing elections in 1853, and the rise of the American Party, who won consistently between 1854 and 1859, coincided with a switch in the pattern of support given to Democrats by American-born workers, who went from preferring Democratic candidates prior to 1853 to strongly opposing them thereafter.[5]

The same demographics characterized New Orleans, another city where Know-Nothings thrived. In its population of working-age white men, New Orleans possessed more foreigners than natives, but franchise rules related to residency and citizenship disqualified most immigrants and left natives in the majority at the polls. By contrast, in St. Louis, where Republicans replaced Know-Nothings in 1856, immigrants outnumbered natives by three-to-two, and they were even more numerous among white adults.[6] Despite these variations, workers in all cities had a common demand that municipal government provide more public jobs and discontinue its belligerence toward workers engaged in strikes and other on-the-job struggles. Patronage and favorable treatment in workplace conflict constituted the tangible rewards for labor's involvement in Southern big-city politics.

That city officials fulfilled these demands greatly disturbed conservative businessmen and rural onlookers, who were accustomed to economy in government finance and who expected police to quell strikes. Alarmed by such actions, some critics of the urban opposition claimed that municipal government had been given over entirely to disorderly workers. They exaggerated. For the most part, veteran politicians from elite social backgrounds ran the American and Republican Party administrations of the South's big cities. In exchange for actions on their issues, workers upheld the stands of their party leaders on other questions, like sectionalism and government aid to business development. Workers wielded more power in late-1850s city politics, but men from other social classes continued to hold the top offices in party and government.

Although they never seized full control, wage-earning partisans nonetheless created a crisis for city politics by destabilizing the coalition of social groups that had traditionally been represented in municipal government. Inside of the administrations of the urban South's opposition parties, conflicts over who should wield power brought veteran officeholders and working-class newcomers into conflict, as did their disagreement over the direction that reform should take. Where politicians from the business elite saw danger in unchecked mob rule, workingmen perceived businessmen's lock on political power as a greater evil.

The mobilization of workingmen by opposition parties in Baltimore, New Orleans, and St. Louis also caused problems beyond the city limits. Even though urban politicians defended slavery, their working-class supporters appeared to threaten the South's balance of power because they opposed the proslavery Democratic Party and its rural, slaveholding constituency. Only in St. Louis did municipal leaders ally with free-soil Republicans. Baltimore advocates for white labor narrowly sidestepped free-soilism, and New Orleans Know-Nothings tried to outdo Democrats in advocating Southern rights. That these metropolitan regimes were independent of the planters who dominated state legislatures and state-party bureaucracies alarmed rural Southerners more than did the specific positions city workers took on the sectional crisis.

Opponents of big-city Know-Nothings and Republicans had cultural reasons to rally behind the Democrats that went beyond the practical problem that autonomous urban administrations posed for Southern unity. Although, to Southern city workers, promoting their cultural style mattered less than did winning jobs and having police protection, they nonetheless brought to elections and government a repertoire of working-class behaviors that violated the norms of middle-class respectability and turned conventions of Southern honor against planters and their allies in the urban elite. Where Know-Nothing politicians from white-collar backgrounds had carefully sought to distinguish partisan politics from conduct unbecoming to Southern culture, politicized street gangs recklessly disregarded the ethics of honor in the name of advancing their partisan interests. Having found that party politics could alleviate some problems associated with the economic and social consequences of urban growth, Southern city workers held tightly to partisan attachments and invested the battle against the Democrats with what contemporaries called the "violent spirit of party."[7] Observers outside the gangs understood violent partisanship as the antithesis of good government and a moral public order.

The unraveling of municipal Whig and Democratic competition had originated in a crisis over slavery in national politics, and in the late

1850s the battle over sectional issues in the federal government continued to influence city politics. Baltimore's experience illustrates this process. In 1855, the pledge of the national American Party convention not to interfere with slavery in federal territory angered free-soil delegates. Later that year, American Party congressmen split along sectional lines over the choice for Speaker of the House of Representatives, and Know-Nothings lost Virginia's gubernatorial election. In Maryland, Democrats retained control of the governor's office, and in 1855 they recaptured a majority on the Baltimore City Council. Baltimore Know-Nothings narrowly won the state and federal elections, but sectionalism thwarted their bid for national power.

In February 1856, the American Party's national convention abandoned secrecy, permitted Roman Catholic participation, and called for the "maintenance and enforcement of all laws," a reference to controversial measures like the Fugitive Slave Law and the Kansas-Nebraska Act. Northern free-soil delegates left the convention in protest of the latter measure. For Baltimore's John Pendleton Kennedy, the departure of "Northern ultras" meant that "things now move on harmoniously," but events in the spring of 1856 eroded centrism's appeal. The caning of Massachusetts senator Charles Sumner by a proslavery congressman and sectional violence in Kansas (popularly referred to as Bleeding Kansas) made Know-Nothings' nativism and sectional neutrality seem irrelevant to Northerners alarmed at slaveholder aggression. Disaffected Northern Know-Nothings turned to the Republican Party and its critique of the Slave Power. Conversely, Southern members of the American Party fearful of threats to slavery disliked the equivocal sectional stand taken by Know-Nothing presidential nominee Millard Fillmore, the favorite of Kennedy and Southern moderates.[8]

These national conflicts shaped the party battle in Baltimore. Politicians in both parties wove together the issues of sectionalism, violence, and class struggle in a debate over who would best preserve order. The caning of Sumner and Bleeding Kansas introduced political violence into the national debate over slavery. The same concern found expression in city politics, where each party added charges that the opposition promoted lawlessness to claims that their rival threatened the Union and slavery.

In 1856, Baltimore Democrats continued to associate local Know-Nothings with free-soilers in the Northern branch of the party. Democrat Beale H. Richardson's *Republican* asserted that slavery "is a great blessing," and said that "almost every man elected by the self-styled

American Party, throughout the North and West, are Abolitionists in principle and practice."[9] Yet Baltimore Democrats had to qualify the Southern-rights refrain in order to allay city dwellers' fears that disunion would harm commercial interests and bring political chaos. Similar to their opponents, urban Democrats argued that defending established institutions, especially the Union and the Constitution, defended slavery. Demanding respect for the law as a proslavery measure addressed the concerns of their local coalition of businessmen and immigrants without challenging the larger Southern Democratic stand in the sectional conflict.

By implying that little distinguished Know-Nothings from Republicans and then characterizing Republicans as foes of the Union, Baltimore Democrats could support slaveholders' interests without embracing secession. Democratic rallies featured a United States flag with a sash proclaiming "The Union Forever!" and party editors argued that "Black Republicanism alone stands up as an enemy of peace and the Union." In 1856, Henry Winter Davis, an American Party congressman, refused to support a South Carolina Democrat for Speaker of the U.S. House. In response, the *Sun,* a self-proclaimed nonpartisan newspaper that nonetheless favored Democrats, stated that "Baltimore must make her election for the South or against her—[and] must not hope to do as her representative did, give a side blow, more injurious to the South, more insidious, than a direct Black Republican one."[10]

Events in Baltimore in tandem with ones beyond its boundaries fed the attack on Know-Nothings as lawless majoritarians. In August 1856, Americans on the city council proposed dividing the larger western wards and consolidating central wards with smaller populations. Democrats opposed increasing the representation of west Baltimore, which by 1856 was solidly Know-Nothing. Equating the ward issue with abolitionism, the *Baltimore Republican* claimed that "none but a Know-Nothing or an Abolition higher law man could for a moment tolerate such an opinion. . . . [Know-Nothings] belong to that higher law party which is ready to trample upon the laws of the country and the eternal principles of justice whenever they may stand in the way of their partisan movements." Redistricting failed, but the controversy introduced a debate over law and order that displayed a willingness by both sides to rewrite basic rules of governance for partisan advantage. These issues and tactics remained part of city politics for the rest of the decade.[11]

The Democrats' law-and-order theme encompassed the defense of immigrant civil liberties from Know-Nothing attacks. It also addressed business disapproval of the labor militancy that had stimulated the 1853 independent victories, and Democrats, some of whom had treated the 1853 iron strike as an illegal conspiracy, continued to describe strikes as threats to civic order. Early in 1855, a work stoppage by employees of the Baltimore and Ohio Railroad (B&O) won support from Know-Nothing city councilmen but drew criticism from Democrats, who claimed that "those who do not choose to work, have a perfect right to play if they like it better—but they have no right to interfere in any manner to prevent others from working."[12] Just as Know-Nothings had done with nativism, Democrats used law-and-order as an ideological least common denominator that united their stands on sectionalism, democratization, and class.

In 1856, Know-Nothings continued to talk about the dangers of immigration and the need for government reform, but they gave more attention to rebutting the charge of lawlessness. They also looked for ways to strengthen their local voting base in light of the diminishing chances for their party's national success. In regard to sectionalism and democratization, Americans called Democrats "disunionists" and criticized their opposition to redistricting the wards as a violation of the principle that "under our Republican form of government majorities are to rule."[13]

That appeal meshed with the Know-Nothings' growing popularity among wage earners. They reasserted arguments that foreign competition threatened the independence of American workers; directed patronage and public works to the native born; and nominated workers for a few high offices. In January 1856, Know-Nothings won a special election in the traditionally Democratic Fifteenth Ward that straddled the industrial west side and the shipyards south of the Basin, thus achieving a tie on the First Branch (the legislative branch) of the city council. The Democrats ran George P. Kane, an Irish Protestant businessman and renegade Whig. Immigrants supported him, as did Kane's fellow businessmen, but he fell flat with American-born manual workers, and they made up a majority of the ward's eligible voters. These workers preferred the Know-Nothing candidate, Joseph Simms, a stove manufacturer who, although no worker, shared ethnicity with American mechanics and knew them in his capacity as an industrial employer. Kane's claim that gangs of "Know-Nothing bullies" intimidated Democratic voters marked a pattern of anti-Know-Nothing fraud accusations that linked illegality with the party's working-class supporters.[14]

In the fall 1856 elections, Know-Nothing leaders, most of them Whig businessmen, promised workers prosperity and protection from anti-labor Democrats. The former argument spoke to the nonpartisan economic concerns of all city dwellers; the latter issue emphasized divisions based on class and party that intensified the hard feelings manifested in the January special election. Know-Nothings nominated for mayor Thomas Swann, a former Whig and the recently retired president of the B&O. Swann campaigned on his record as a skilled executive who had completed the B&O's link to the Ohio River and who would "give prosperity to all commercial, industrial and mechanical pursuits." Jehu B. Askew, leader of the iron strike and a Know-Nothing state legislator, reminded voters that in 1853 Swann's opponent, Robert Clinton Wright, another railroad executive, had opposed raising iron workers' pay, while Swann's B&O quickly reconciled with its employees. Although Swann had privately opposed the wage hike, Askew called him the "mechanic's friend."[15]

Because the B&O had borrowed millions from the city under Swann, Democrats called him a spendthrift "stock jobber" who would bankrupt government. They defended Wright as "the people's candidate and the people's man," but Democrats also promoted his appeal to businessmen. The *Sun* hoped that Wright's "brethren of the mercantile community with whom he has been so long, so intimately, and so pleasantly associated, will it is to be trusted take sure steps to manifest their regard." The new, close identification of Democrats with employers undercut their overtures to workingmen, while the claims of both parties that their opponents schemed against the republic encouraged partisans to take the law into their own hands.[16] Swann won the election with 13,887 votes to Wright's 12,339. Violence, discussed below, broke out at several polling places.

The intensification of party conflict in 1856 touched on two interrelated problems: how far should majority rule go, and what role should propertyless men have in politics? Both parties worried about the majoritarian excesses of poorer voters, but where Southern Democrats saw the demon of abolition, Know-Nothings identified corrupt demagogues who manipulated foreigners and fear-mongered on slavery. Democratization, a background issue in the Jacksonian debates over banking, slavery, and moral reform, moved to center stage in mid-1850s cities as a result of violence associated with the Know-Nothings. Urban election riots by mobs of wage earners threatened civic order, and in the ensuing public alarm conservatives were able to marshal opposition to workers' political involvement.

One reason that violence accompanied elections involving the Know-Nothings was the party's success in attracting to the polls citizens who heretofore had been nonvoters. The new voters, unfamiliar with the routines of elections, were more receptive to American Party claims that Democrats stole elections with unqualified immigrant votes. Nationwide, the conviction that Democratic officials connived with immigrants to cheat their way into office spurred the initial bursts of Know-Nothing violence in 1854 and 1855. In Memphis, the Know-Nothing mayor called out the militia in anticipation of an invasion by Irish rioters from St. Louis. Rumors of German tampering with ballot boxes prompted an election riot in Cincinnati and in Louisville sparked the Bloody Monday riots that resulted in twenty-two deaths. Prior to the election in Louisville, an editor warned "foreigners [to] keep their elbows to themselves today. Americans are you ready? . . . [L]et heaven have mercy on the foe." Days before Mobile's 1855 elections, nativists coupled speeches against immigrant vote fraud with raids on Irish neighborhoods. In San Francisco, a self-styled Vigilance Committee that included many former Know-Nothings killed five men suspected of corrupting elections.[17]

As elsewhere, Know-Nothing election riots in the three largest Southern cities began as efforts to stop immigrant vote fraud. In St. Louis, violence, which had already occurred at the 1852 mayoral election, broke out again at the 1854 congressional elections. Before the vote, Know-Nothings published the names of two thousand allegedly unqualified voters and urged supporters to defend the "purity of the ballot box." On election day, nativist mobs attacked a fire company in a heavily Irish ward, destroyed the presses of a free-soil German newspaper, and fought with the police, many of whom were Irish-Americans. It took three days to quell violence that an observer attributed to the "strong feeling around the importance of the election."[18]

In New Orleans, foes of the Democrats remembered the "Plaquemines Frauds" of 1844 in which John Slidell, a leading Democrat and U.S. senator, carried two boatloads of immigrants to a nearby country parish and had them vote several times at polls situated along the route. The charge reemerged in 1853 when Democrats garnered the highest municipal total in memory despite an epidemic of yellow fever that sent thousands out of the city. In 1854, the newly formed American Party vowed to stop Democratic chicanery that had been highlighted in investigations of immigrant Democrats who could neither read nor name the candidates for whom they voted. At the March municipal elections, two policemen died in a riot that began when Know-Nothings accused Democrats of repeat voting. Before the fall elections for state offices, Know-Nothing editors told supporters that "they must be fully prepared to baffle all attempts at fraud, and destroy the machinations of evil-minded and designing party leaders." Tensions at those elections produced a broad-ranging, week-long riot. Nativists concentrated their fury against the Irish, enthusiastic Democrats who, as in St. Louis, dominated the police force. "The Native Americans are turned out strong against the Irish," an American Party merchant wrote. "There will be a lot of blood spilt before the Irish find out which stall they belong in." [19]

The same concerns about immigrant vote fraud infused Know-Nothing rhetoric prior to the 1855 election riots in Baltimore. Local American Party publicist Anna Ella Carroll argued that the Vatican plotted to destroy "religious liberty and political equality . . . by the open assault of foreigners, particularly at the ballot-box." Know-Nothings believed that Democrats had won the October 1855 city council races by using "money and lies" and by naturalizing immigrant voters at the last minute. [20]

In the month between municipal and federal elections, Baltimore Know-Nothings took an aggressive stand against Democratic fraud. In October, the Rip Raps, a street gang affiliated with the American Party, clashed with a Democratic gang. Later that month, Know-Nothings got the better of a gun battle that disrupted a city council special election. A friendly editor said of this riot that "[Democrats] cannot march through the streets, VILLIFY and KNOCK DOWN whom they please, without being whipped; or at least being driven off with bruised heads." American Party enthusiasts came to the November contest for state and federal offices convinced that laws had failed and that only a show of force could secure an honest election. [21]

As a congressional candidate, Henry Winter Davis claimed massive Democratic fraud in November 1855. "[President Franklin Pierce's] cabinet sent at least from 40 to $50,000 into my district. The Catholics poured out money like water. Every man who could be bribed was bribed. The Irish were armed to the teeth. Voters were moved by the hundred from [the neighboring] district to mine." Expecting foul play, the American Party prepared for war. On election day, John Pendleton Kennedy reported to his diary, "Great determination on the part of the Americans to resist all bullying. The whole town is armed I may say." Davis wrote that "[t]here were thousands of men armed to the teeth that day in Balto; and it was a sheer question of nerve and wit and not of legal votes who would carry the day. If we had broken down at any point we were gone. . . . It was the battle of the American Soldiers." A conviction that their foes disregarded republican fairness legitimated the election violence that occurred in almost every city in which Know-Nothings campaigned.[22]

Know-Nothing riots enabled Democrats to justify their own excesses as justifiable responses to their rivals' lawlessness. In the 1856 campaign, Baltimore Democrats promised to "do all things essential to recover our city from the reign of plunder, rowdyism, and rioting, and murder." Democrats referred to their leading rowdies as "highly respectable" and victims of "unquestionable animosity existing on the part of the K.N. police." They also condoned assaults on Know-Nothings. Commenting on an attack on the offices of the *Clipper* by William "Country" Thompson, a Democratic gang leader, the *Republican* joked, "We do trust he will no longer annoy the amiable folks of the Clipper—their nerves are weak and cannot stand it—something dangerous may be the result." Like their foes, Democrats imbued the 1856 elections with monumental significance. "You are in the midst of a great battle," one editor wrote, "a battle . . . for principle and freedom itself."[23] Baltimore's climactic 1856 election riots occurred in this context of heated rhetoric and prior violence.

Baltimore's mayoral balloting on October 8, which Know-Nothings won handily, produced a higher level of violence—there were seven deaths—than at any city election in memory. The worst fighting occurred in west central Baltimore, where the Rip Raps laid siege to the engine house of the New Market Fire Company, the city's most prominent Democratic gang, which had a long history of election rioting.[24]

After the October riots, Democrats said that "a crisis has arrived" and asked Mayor Samuel Hinks to station militia at the upcoming state and federal elections. Claiming municipal authority to be adequate, Hinks refused. The *Clipper* assured readers that under the Know-Nothings "licentiousness and rowdyism will be controlled."[25]

Despite this promise, the November 6, 1856, elections produced even more bloodshed than those of October, and the character of rioting on that day showed that it had become systematic and citywide in scope. Thirty armed men followed by boys dragging cannons marched from the predominantly Democratic Eighth Ward to the polls of the neighboring Sixth Ward. A Know-Nothing "concourse of equally as wild and infuriated men and youths, armed with muskets and pistols" confronted the Democrats, and a battle raged until nightfall. Simultaneously, Know-Nothings seized the polls in the eastern Second Ward. When Democrats tried to force their way to the voting window, Americans called on reinforcements from the Fourth Ward, and another running gun battle developed. In the west central Twelfth Ward, rioters shot a Democratic candidate for magistrate, and his son. Violence also interrupted voting in the five west-side wards. Ten people died in the riots, and as many as 250 suffered injuries. Between October and November, the American Party raised its majority by 10 percent, or more than five thousand votes. Without his landslide in the city, Fillmore would have lost Maryland, the only state carried by Know-Nothings in the presidential contest. The pattern of violence at multiple sites characterized elections for the next three years.[26]

The November 1856 election riots solidified Know-Nothing majorities in several ways. The terror of that campaign convinced many Democrats to refrain from voting until their safety could be guaranteed. The riots also injured Democratic political gangs. On November 6, Know-Nothings again attacked the New Market Fire Company headquarters, and this time destroyed it. After 1856, Know-Nothing rowdies raided Democratic meeting halls during campaign season. Police facilitated such conquests by arresting Democratic gang leaders and confiscating arms from their followers and from immigrant militia companies, whose funds Hinks had cut off in 1855.[27]

In 1856, New Orleans Know-Nothings also stepped up electoral coercion. In the June contests for city offices, Democrat Thomas Wharton recorded "[s]cenes of outrage and bloodshed at the polls. Naturalized citizens were the objects of enmity and very often not permitted to vote at all." Armed partisans controlled three polling places, police refused to make arrests, and rioters killed two Italians immigrants. At the November presidential balloting, which Fillmore won in the city, Wharton noted "much intimidation" and "many outrages committed." Rowdies beat two Democratic judges, one of whom was the brother of Democratic chieftan John Slidell.[28]

In both cities the turn to coercion by Know-Nothings enabled the local administration to hang onto power amid the national party's collapse. The American Party governed New Orleans until 1862. In Maryland, Know-Nothings controlled Baltimore until 1860, commanded majorities in the legislature from 1855 to 1859, and elected Thomas Hicks governor for the 1858–61 term. In Maryland's party realignment, Democrats made gains in slaveholding counties and lost ground in the farms of the north and west and in towns. In 1859, most rural counties with slaves supported Democrats; western Maryland split its votes; and Baltimore remained in American Party hands. Without their lopsided big-city majority, Maryland Know-Nothings would have faded like their counterparts in most other states.[29]

A close look at the mechanics of election rioting illustrates how the repeated use of this tactic implicated party officials in coercive practices that went beyond legal boundaries and that deepened partisan animosities. To influence ballot totals, election rioting required cooperation between party officials and loosely affiliated gang members, and that cooperation increased the importance to parties of the working-class partisans in the gangs. The foothold in party politics that election rioting gave to the gangs presented problems to party leaders seeking to maintain respectability. In the case of the Know-Nothings, it alienated voters who supported party policy but could not stomach being associated with the gangs.

Partisans needed overwhelming force to overcome the safeguards for fair elections that subjected voters to maximum public scrutiny. Prior to 1860, Baltimore's mayor and city council designated one polling place for each ward. Polling booths were either makeshift shacks, or, if indoors, a room with a "window" through which voters passed their ballots. Parties printed easily identifiable, foot-long ballots, or "tickets," which prominently displayed the party logo and candidate slate. Maryland law designated judges of election, who had the power to make arrests, as the guardians of the polls. Clerks assisted judges by recording voter names and ballot totals. Each party could post a challenger outside the booth to inspect a voter's qualifications. Police officers and crowds of interested onlookers stood nearby. The most effective way to breach these barriers was to drive rival voters from the polls and stuff the ballot box with bogus tickets.[30]

Contemporary claims about election rioting should be regarded with caution because partisan motivation encouraged each side to exaggerate the other's misdeeds while denying their own. However, the available evidence indicates that American Party officials assisted electoral coercion.[31] Systematic coercion could not have succeeded without the permission of the police, and Baltimore police did their part to promote Know-Nothing success. Police facilitated election violence by either joining the mob or standing idle while roughs attacked Democrats. In 1857, a Baltimore police officer led a mob that seized control of the Sixth Ward's voting window. A witness to the 1859 elections testified that "the police appeared to head the rowdies openly." More often, police did nothing to stop violence against rival voters. For example, at the 1857 elections a gang member on the police force permitted assaults on immigrants on the grounds that "if they would come there to be beaten, he could not help it."[32]

In trying to assess the malicious intent of election rioters, we are returned to the partisan debate of contemporaries: a Democrat's gang villain was a Know-Nothing's heroic guardian against vote fraud. While the evidence cannot answer to their virtue, it does show that men schooled in urban violence found new roles to play in party politics as a result of election rioting. Know-Nothing officials promoted police intervention in elections by appointing gang members and poll rioters to the force. A search of municipal employment records for 307 men belonging to pro-Know-Nothing gangs—termed political clubs by supporters—found that 84 of them, or 27 percent, worked as police officers.[33] In 1857, twenty American Party notables, including a Superior Court judge and the state lottery commissioner, recommended that Mayor Swann employ David Huxford as a policeman. They explained that "at the recent Election [of 1856] he received two balls in his right arm while defending the 6th ward polls which will render him unfit to follow his trade for some length of time. The appointment of Mr. Huxford will give general satisfaction to the Members of the American Party." Similarly, Swann hired as a police lieutenant an officer of the Little Fellows gang, whose services to the American Party included, in the words of his supporters, "a wound in his arm secured at the Presidential Election in 1856." In defense of this policy, Swann said that "it is hardly a fair subject of complaint that I have followed what has always been a fixed custom both in the Federal, State and Municipal governments, in making appointments . . . from the dominant party by whom I have been charged with this trust."[34]

As in Baltimore, New Orleans Know-Nothings made control of the police a top priority, and they, too, used force to win elections. Although New Orleans Know-Nothings initially cut the size of the police force, in 1858 Mayor Gerard Stith increased the number of officers above the pre–American Party level of 1855. As in Baltimore, New Orleans Know-Nothings replaced immigrant officers with native-born supporters. At elections, New Orleans police failed to arrest Know-Nothing rowdies and turned a blind eye to violence at the polls. Like Swann, Stith admitted the partisanship of the police. "The force," Stith said, "is mainly constituted of men who are favorable to the principles which are professed by the American Party."[35]

Although Democrats criticized Know-Nothing police hiring, they were no better. Denied access to local patronage, Democrats in port cities lobbied President James Buchanan's administration to hire their rowdies into the federally controlled Customs Service. In 1857, a friend of a New Orleans alderman who had been injured in a recent election riot, told Senator Slidell that the job seeker "was always active, and willing to assume more than his share of 'roughing' incidental to Party struggles." In the late 1850s, at least eleven Democratic gang members and election rioters worked in Baltimore's Customs House. One of them was Patty Naff, the lead brawler of the New Market Fire Company. The Customs Service functioned as a Democratic paramilitary unit in much the same way that Know-Nothings used city police, but in the late 1850s Customs workers could not overawe the more numerous and better-supported policemen.[36]

Other officials besides police abetted electoral coercion. Occasionally, election judges took part in vote fraud in actions that ranged from ignoring poll blocking to actually participating in the riots. Appointed by city government, most judges were partisans of the majority party. Only 19 of 461 Baltimore elections officials serving from 1853 until 1861 worked under both Know-Nothing and Democrat administrations. Although only 35 of these judges were implicated in election fraud, a few corrupt judges could affect the outcome by altering ballot counts in key wards.[37]

For example, J. R. Codet, president of Baltimore's Rough Skins and a Know-Nothing election judge from 1855 to 1859, refused votes from naturalized citizens and cooperated with his gang comrades outside the polling booth. In 1857, municipal authorities situated the Second Ward polls opposite the Rough Skin's headquarters and gave weapons to club members. In 1859, German cooper William Mauer testified that "five or six men came up to me and knocked me down, and then put a ticket in my hand to vote it; I wouldn't; then they drawed my clothes down and pulled me like a dead dog along." The Rough Skins brought Mauer before Codet, who said "never mind [naturalization papers], I want your vote." Know-Nothings opened the office designed to guard against corrupt practices to the most volatile partisans in city politics.[38]

New Orleans Know-Nothings also employed election judges who used violence for partisan ends. One judge boasted that few Democrats voted in his ward. "My speech of the other night had the effect I anticipated. It frightened them out of their wits." C. C. LaCoste, superintendent of elections in the Algiers district of the city, pulled a gun on a

Democrat and encouraged rowdies from a nearby tavern to interfere with the voting. An observer said that "apart from the election days [LaCoste] was an excellent man. On election days he would do anything for his party."[39]

The simple decision of where to locate a polling place could also abet coercion. Know-Nothings situated polling booths near the headquarters of their political clubs and far from the homes of Democrats. Operating on favorable terrain, rioters stationed lookouts a hundred yards or so from the polls to alert partisans near the booth of approaching opposing voters, who for protection often traveled in groups. Thus warned, partisans massed in front of the window and forced voters to push them aside. In New Orleans, messengers on horseback helped coordinate these efforts.[40]

Respectable politicians encouraged these attacks by praising the gangs that carried them out. Most Baltimore Know-Nothing rallies included club contingents, and officeholders like Anthony Kennedy, a U.S. senator, and Congressman Davis attended meetings staged by clubs. Daniel McPhail, Maryland's lottery commissioner, lauded the Tiger club for its actions in the 1856 riots. "Verily was the last election day a day of battle, and the slain of the native born were strewn around the polls as they fell in defense of their birthright against the Foreign party attack."[41]

Baltimore's most notorious American Party call for violence occurred a week before the November 1859 elections. Davis addressed Know-Nothings beneath a banner that depicted a rowdy bashing a Democratic Reformer's head, with the caption, "Reform movement— Reform Man, If you vote, I'll be damned." Blacksmiths operating a forge near the podium produced shoemaker's awls and distributed them to the crowd. Rioters used the awls as election-day weapons. In the intervening week, the Blood Tubs, who earned the nickname from their practice of dunking the heads of opposing voters in vats of animal blood, severely beat Democratic congressional candidate William P. Preston. On election day, clubs and police again suppressed the Democratic vote. That day, the Tigers killed a young Democratic merchant and wounded his brother as these two men tried to distribute opposition ballots in south Baltimore.[42]

Although legal voters freely cast most of the ballots in Baltimore elections, coercion influenced the turnout in key wards and transformed a narrow Know-Nothing majority into a broad one. From 1845 (the beginning of Baltimore's twenty-ward system) to October 1856

(the last election before systematic coercion set in) a small majority of
10 percent or less decided most contests. At the November 1856 federal elections, Know-Nothings won by a 25 percent margin. In the vio-
lence-plagued elections between 1857 and the American Party's defeat
in 1860, Know-Nothings won by landslide margins of 33 percent or
more. Ward-level vote totals also changed. From 1845 to October 1856,
wards returned more victory margins of 10 percent or less than land-
slides of 33 percent or more. From November 1856 to 1860, a majority
of wards turned in landslide majorities, usually for the Know-Nothings,
and closely contested wards almost disappeared. This surge in the margin of victory did not coincide with a higher total turnout. Following
the 1856 riots, Democrats withdrew from the field. Thereafter they
sought to invalidate Baltimore election results via appeals to state and
federal officials. Coercion produced broad Know-Nothing majorities
between 1856 and 1859.[43]

In the rural South, competitive election districts had always been an
exception to the norm of local consensus, but in the cities the parties
contested every ward. Political violence in the late 1850s created landslide ward-level vote tallies, but these should not be taken as indicators
of a new consensus among city voters to support the dominant party. In
Baltimore and New Orleans, Democrats continued to oppose the
American Party, but they could no longer safely register their dissent at
the ballot box. Once they could (i.e., after Know-Nothings lost control
of the police force), ward results returned to the competitive pattern of
earlier years. Furthermore, political violence rarely produced the kind
of party dominance that characterized Know-Nothing rule in Baltimore and New Orleans. Systematic electoral coercion could not succeed in most cities: for that to happen, political and demographic conditions approaching those of Baltimore were required. Across the
country, Know-Nothings wanted to break up ethnic militia units like
the German turnverein that Anna Ella Carroll described as "the priest-
ridden troops of the Holy Alliance," but only in places where the American Party held a decisive legislative majority (e.g., the municipal governments of Baltimore and New Orleans and the state legislature of
Massachusetts) could it disarm its opponents.[44] To function well, antebellum election laws required that each party muster enough partisans
to guard its interests at the polls, preferably without using force. Absent
a credible resort to arms, the redress for coercion lay beyond the
boundaries of local politics; hence, Baltimore Democrats' persistent
calls for state intervention.

Politics in St. Louis, which were no more pacific than in other big cities, showed how a more even balance between the groups capable of using force at elections prevented any party from keeping power through coercion. During the 1854 election riots, German and Irish militia units fought nativist rowdies. St. Louis had more foreign-born residents than natives, and anyone contemplating violence against immigrants knew that they might get more than they gave. Fearful of the large German population, Know-Nothing mobs concentrated on Irish targets, but the Irish used political connections and military organization to discourage would-be rioters. Democrats in state government made sure to fund Irish militia units in St. Louis, and the units reciprocated with loyalty to the Democratic Party. The commander of one such unit told Missouri's Democratic governor that "almost every member of my company voted for your Excellency." Elected mayor in 1855, Know-Nothing Washington King declared police reform "paramount to every other consideration." Like other Know-Nothing mayors, King hired more police, gave preference to party supporters, and used the force in electioneering. But King's police decided not to fight it out with the immigrant militia, who, along with informal paramilitary units, turned back an attack on St. Louis University in 1854 and dissuaded nativists from breaking up the Saint Patrick's Day parade in 1855. Political violence persisted after King lost reelection in 1856, but in St. Louis's three-cornered competition between Know-Nothings, Republicans, and Democrats, no faction had enough power to turn the occasional riot into a tool of party dominance.[45]

In Baltimore, where conditions favored majority coercion, the support of government officials was essential to sustaining violence, but they did not control all aspects of the process. Election rioting was partly a grassroots phenomenon driven by working-class activists who owed their primary allegiance to neighborhood gangs (contemporaries called them clubs), rather than the party bureaucracy.[46] Wage earners used gangs as a conduit to party leaders, and party leaders used gangs as a means for organizing the votes of Baltimore workers. Politicians regarded gangs as both curse and blessing. Gangs belonged to a subculture of taverns and violence that Know-Nothings in other walks of life abhorred, but they lacked the antiparty, class-conscious agenda of trade unions, which provoked even greater worry among white-collar officeholders. For decades, politicians facing close elections had encouraged participation from apathetic groups of voters, even ones that mainstream officials regarded with skepticism. Party outreach to working-class street gangs belonged to this tradition, and, as in the past, such stabs at democratization brought the risk that one's new constituents would push for changes that their sponsors had not anticipated.[47]

Gangs merit special attention because they served as a bridge between workingmen and the parties and because they introduced into city politics a cultural style that clashed with the values of rural Southerners. Like street gangs of today, the gangs that flourished in mid-nineteenth-century cities had homogenous memberships in terms of gender, class, and ethnicity, and most identified with a specific neighborhood. Governance was loose, and levels of individual involvement varied. Violence, too—then as now—characterized gang life;[48] however, the gangs of the past differed in two important respects: adults, most of whom were employed and married, dominated Civil War era gangs, and party politics shaped gang life.

Class status can be difficult to pin down in the fluid economy of nineteenth-century American cities, but occupation and wealth—the measurements of economic rank that are most available to historians—clearly show that gang members belonged to the working class. In 1850s Baltimore, at least a thousand men belonged to more than forty different clubs. Individual gangs usually consisted of between fifty and a hundred members, many of whom had only a fleeting attachment to the organization. Records on 581 Baltimore club members turned up in city directories and the federal census.[49] Most gang members were white, American-born, skilled wage earners in their twenties and early thirties. In terms of occupation, 81 percent of them worked at manual trades, mostly skilled ones, and out of the minority in white-collar occupations, more than one-fourth ran taverns, a job that catered to wage-earning customers. Nearly two-thirds of these men were married; a little more than one-half headed their household; and almost as many dwelled with boarders. Gang members owned an average of $424 in property, in comparison with a mean of nearly $900 for all white Baltimoreans.

Club ties to white industrial workers differentiated them from the total city population. Club members held a greater share of industrial and construction jobs, especially in the metal and building trades, and fewer worked in service, commerce, or transportation. Because they excluded women and blacks and had little appeal for men in well-off families, clubs attracted few workers associated with those groups (e.g., domestic servants, draymen, and merchants). Most foreign-born men who joined clubs picked ones aligned with the Democrats, where they made up one-third of all gang members, and fought nativist gangs aligned with the Know-Nothings. Evidence on the parental nationality of fifty-seven gang members suggests that Democrat gangs had more second-generation immigrants than did American Party clubs, and that both had more children of immigrants than immigrants themselves. Four-fifths of the parents were manual workers. No microcosm of urban society, gangs drew their constituents from the industrial working class.

Gangs participated in what one historian has termed the "traditionalist" subculture of industrial workers. Traditionalists valued their independence as men and economic actors. They fought against the emerging domestic ideals of middle-class culture that sought to tame masculine aggression in public and private settings. Gangs' emergence into politics contained elements of a cultural struggle that pitted traditionalist adherents of a republican "classless masculinity" against a bureaucratized "Christian capitalist order," but the complicated relationship between gangs and political parties cannot by fully comprehended by such a tidy model.[50] Parties were coalitions of social groups, and each constituency had to compromise with the others in order to act collectively. The fact that most officeholders who could help the gangs adhered to standards of middle-class respectability added further incentive for members of working-class gangs to tone down their rowdy behavior when they acted as supporters of their political party. Furthermore, gangs affiliated with the Know-Nothings supported a party committed to reforming public morals in directions that ran counter to the style of the streets, and gang members could not expect to flaunt the values of party leaders and remain in their good graces.

Just as the party elite tried to find ways to balance the Southern gentleman's code of honor with demands for compromise and occasional submission to the will of the masses, club members reined in aggressive behavior associated with tavern brawling traditionalists when they interacted with politicians. In an effort to please party superiors and to advance their own claims to respectability, political clubs turned out for moral reform causes and put on displays of domestic morality. Those reform gestures helped maintain the fragile Know-Nothing coalition, but the otherwise disreputable acts of the gangs alienated genteel professionals. Although gangs did not seek to advance their cultural style through politics, their involvement with the American Party contributed to Democrats' belief that big-city Know-Nothings threatened orderly politics as Southerners understood them.

For those outside of the gangs' cultural world, American Party indulgence of this disreputable type of working-class organization generated different reactions that corresponded to partisan allegiance. For American Party loyalists, gangs were a necessary evil. Without their own cadre of street toughs, Know-Nothings feared that Democrats would retake city government through the even more disreputable tactic of immigrant vote fraud. The lawyers and businessmen at the top of the American Party enlisted the aid of the gangs to stave off the Democrats, but they had no desire to make peers out of the fight-prone tavern keepers who ran the gangs. Just as they did with evangelical moral reformers, American Party leaders tried to reap the benefits of gang activism while keeping these organizations away from the inner sanctuaries of party and government.

Even though Democrats in Southern big cities sponsored their own gangs, they acted as if only Know-Nothings used such groups for aggressive, partisan ends. Urban Democrats highlighted gang violence as a campaign issue because it spoke to their larger attack on American Party lawlessness and because their party allies in the rural South associated negative stereotypes of urban working-class culture with gangs. Planters in the legislatures of Southern states gladly formed tactical alliances with people different from themselves—the Irish of the port cities being a prime example—but they always remained suspicious of the politics in their cities. Rural Southerners and urban businessmen likely to back the Democrats agreed that Know-Nothing gangs threatened cultural values that each group held dear. Gang members tried to appease their party sponsors, but they refused to suppress fully the way of life that made them join gangs in the first place. The alarming aspects of that way of life included brawls at elections and other public venues, sexual license by male members of gangs, and unfeminine self-assertion by their female associates. Neither a respectable family head in the city nor an honorable gentleman in the country liked what he saw when he read about the exploits of big-city street gangs, and each could agree that stopping the party that protected these groups was of vital importance. In short, gangs managed to placate upper-class allies in their own party, but they otherwise offended city dwellers committed to genteel values.

The nuances of this relationship are brought out in the interaction between gangs and government officers. Know-Nothing gangs showed their reluctance to challenge party leaders by adopting a surprisingly deferential attitude toward elected officials. "Dear Sir," wrote a representative of the Jug Breakers, "we beg Leave to ask of you a small favor as one of our Boys was Sent to Jail this morning for throwing Bricks at the 17th Ward Polls yesterday. . . . Do this and you will bestowe a great favor on your Humble Servants." The image of humble servants begging a gentleman's leave is at odds with the actions of their imprisoned colleague. The Rip Raps were equally subservient in asking Senator Anthony Kennedy to cover the cost of a holiday barbecue. "The parties we owe it to are pushing us for it and we are compelled to go out among our friends to raise it," explained the Rip Raps executive committee. "Should you be pleased to give us a Mite toward it it will be kept a secret & greatfully received and properly appreciated by us." The importance of gaining favor with party leaders made club members reluctant to make defiant demands, replete with the curses and rough language of the streets.[51]

Although Know-Nothing gangs ruthlessly abused immigrant voters, they usually cleared the path to the voting window for wealthy and socially prominent men. For example, in 1857, Baltimore Democrat Hugh Auld, a shipbuilder and Frederick Douglass's onetime master, voted without incident. However, when he protested attacks on naturalized citizens a rioter replied, "No Irishman or Dutchman should vote there today." At another election, a merchant claimed, "the poorer class of people, particularly the foreigners, were not allowed to vote." Deference to social rank could overcome ethnic prejudice. In 1859, an Irish Catholic magistrate, Simon Kemp Sr., saw Know-Nothing firemen punch a Democrat after telling him "you shall not vote." Kemp spent the next forty-five minutes asking rowdies for the names of the perpetrators. The firemen left Kemp alone even as they beat other Democrats, and when Kemp wanted to cast his ballot a Know-Nothing said, "Come up squire, *you* can vote." As in Baltimore, New Orleans Know-Nothings vented their fury on immigrant workers rather than rich Democrats. A well-off Democratic observer of the 1855 elections said, "I do not think a Know-Nothing or even witness would have run any risk. This gang seemed desirous to keep laborers away from the polls." In both cities, Know-Nothing mobs left prominent men alone and cleared access to the polls for "old or infirm persons."[52]

Erasmus Levy, president of Baltimore's Regulator club, summed up the gangs' attitude in an election-day encounter with Severn Teackle Wallis, a lawyer and anti-Know-Nothing editorialist. In Wallis's account, Levy said, "he had not done anything; that the boys could have whipped Mr. Brown [a colleague] and myself, if they had pleased but they didn't." Wallis acknowledged that "they had let us vote and they had no objection to gentlemen's voting." According to Levy, "it was only them damned Irish and Dutch they were down on, and by God, they should not vote."[53] Levy voiced the Know-Nothing class-and-ethnic strategy of advancing native white workers by attacking wage earners outside their cultural group. Warring directly against the rich would have challenged men with more resources to fight back, and it would have offended their wealthy sponsors in the American Party.

In their bid to win the favor of their party patrons, clubs performed as if they were ideal types of the nineteenth century's cult of domesticity; that is, gang men were self-controlled, respectable husbands coupled to virtuous, supportive wives. Because Southern nationalist criticism of Know-Nothing manhood focused not only on meek submission to their northern party allies but also on the belligerence of the urban mob, elite officeholders used gang displays of middle-class morality to undercut this impression. At an 1857 ball, wives of men in the Tiger club acted like nurturing partners to their public-spirited husbands. Presenting themselves as supporters of their spouses' patriotism, Sarah Jane Edwards, wife of club president Joseph Edwards Jr., and other partners of the Tigers sewed an American flag for lottery commissioner Daniel McPhail. McPhail thanked the gang in terms familiar to proponents of domesticity. Asserting that "in woman man finds his surest and most steadfast friend," he said that "the American Tiger Club . . . believe themselves to be engaged in that same work of their fathers, and are happy in the reflection that they too can hear the cheering voice and witness the smile of approbation on the face of the mothers and daughters of the present day as a 'lamp to their feet and light to their path.'"[54] Advertised balls where men and women socialized in chaste settings presented club members as protectors of home and family who were committed to middle-class standards of male behavior.

Along with showing respect for the gender conventions of domesticity, Know-Nothing gang members endorsed their party's moral-reform causes. A few—like Emanuel Irons, a brickmaker and city councilman affiliated with the Blood Tubs and the Poor Association— held offices in reform societies, but most limited their moral reform activities to more passive behavior like signing petitions and showing up at party rallies where the issues were discussed. In 1854, the Reubenites paraded with a banner proclaiming "our public schools as they are." In 1857, the Rip Raps joined the funeral procession for the leader of the American Protestant Association. Joseph Edwards Jr. and other Tigers petitioned to build public parks and prevent streetcars from running on Sunday. Four Rough Skins signed a memorial to confine meat sales to public markets in order to prevent "sickness among the community." Hardly the catalysts of Know-Nothing reforms, the clubs nevertheless turned out for these causes when party leaders needed a show of grassroots enthusiasm.[55]

Despite respectable dances and demonstrations for cultural legislation, gang violations of genteel norms belied their commitment to moral reform and exposed the tension between working-class partisans and well-off professional politicians. Away from formal party settings, clubs spent much of their time defying evangelical reformers' cultural values. At the saloons of their leaders or when making the rounds of neighborhood bars, gang members necessarily broke with Know-Nothing temperance advocates, and they frequently committed crimes while intoxicated. The presumption of gang drunkenness was so prevalent that a jury acquitted a Know-Nothing patronage worker for killing a man at a Democratic gang's tavern on the grounds that a severe case of the delirium tremens had rendered the defendant temporarily insane. As a side business, Irons, the officer for poor relief, ran a tavern that the Blood Tubs used as a headquarters. In 1861, a judge fined Irons for violating a Know-Nothing-imposed ban on Sunday liquor sales. Although Joseph Edwards claimed to be a church-going Methodist when on trial for murder, a member of his gang went to jail for disturbing public worship. Another gang officer raided a Methodist Sunday school. Frequent assaults on immigrant congregations persuaded German Lutherans to hold events outside the city and to carry guns. Ministers discountenanced rowdyism and drinking, and it is not surprising that gangs made churches one of several targets of recreational violence.[56]

The display of domestic ideology in club balls contrasted with their members' adulterous affairs and attacks on their wives and lovers. Several examples of domestic violence and criminality illustrate the difference between the social life of gang members and that of the accomplished legislators who ran the parties. George Konig, a Democratic rough, was arrested for spousal violence; and in 1859, a friend hid a woman's corpse on his property.[57] James Manley, a Know-Nothing constable who was reputedly one of "the most desperate characters about the Causeway" (a Fell's Point vice district) and who ran a brothel with his wife, Ann, appeared in court for battering his wife. Police also arrested Ann Manley for beating a prostitute employee while her husband cheered her on.[58] In 1858, Constable William Ford, a relative of men in the Tigers, shot a former police officer who had found Ford with his wife. In 1860, another policeman, Lemuel Gray, tracked his estranged wife to the home of Rip Raps executive officer Thomas Davis, where Gray encountered "Tinker" McIlvain, another Know-Nothing ex-policeman and an affiliate of the Rip Raps and Tigers. McIlvain fled, leaving his lover at Gray's mercy. Gray beat her to death. That same year, Tiger John Segenfoos shot his former lover, prostitute Susan Harris, when she refused to give him money. In these incidents, club members exhibited little concern for standards of conduct more acceptable to the city's upper classes.[59]

For Southerners worried about urbanization, gangs showed how city life undermined gender norms that characterized white society in the countryside. Urban working women who joined in gang brawls defied social expectations of female passivity. In 1857, Sarah Jane Edwards joined the Tigers in a melee against Democratic gangs on Baltimore's Federal Hill. In 1861, Sarah Jackson, described as a "huge woman," helped George Konig steal a hack and go on a driving spree. One wonders what a justice of the peace in a plantation district would have done with the group of people who together tied a white woman to a board and left her exposed overnight in a vacant New Orleans lot. Those involved in the assault were a Hispanic man, a white woman, a free black woman, and two slave women: not only had a white woman committed a violent act, she did so in collusion with a heterogeneous cast of social outsiders.[60]

After the 1856 election riots, a self-described "Lady in the vicinity of the New Market Engine House" praised the firemen's political exploits. Calling herself an "eyewitness of their brave and manly efforts against the combined force of Plug Uglies, Rip Raps, &c.," she distinguished between violence in general and the legitimate violence of partisan gang battles. "Fighting I despise, but when attacked I like to see men defend themselves as you did." Although she presented herself as a virtuous lady seeking the New Market's protection, this woman defended using violence for partisan ends. A historian has pointed out that "to become involved in partisan politics meant that a woman would enter the corrupt and corrupting sphere of men . . . a proper Southern Lady was passive, pious, and home centered." The women who lent their names and sometimes their fists to the partisan cause of the gangs crossed boundaries that limited women's political voice in the rural South.[61]

The wealthy men who chose to stick with the American Party publicly defended their disorderly working-class supporters, but white-collar professionals in the leadership struggled to keep working-class rowdies away from the reins of party power. Although gangs won patronage and office in the American Party ward councils, the most influential posts were beyond their reach. In 1859, the Know-Nothing Superior Council, the top unit of the party's Baltimore bureaucracy, included only six gang workingmen among its more than one hundred members. Business and professional domination of Know-Nothing candidate slates extended down to the level of the city council, which in 1859, after five years of American Party rule, had only six wage-earning manual workers among its twenty-eight Know-Nothing councilmen. Similarly, the leadership posts of the New Orleans American Party remained in elite hands, notwithstanding the victories of a printer and a stevedore for the mayoralty. The highest public office held by a Baltimore club activist was that of acting mayor, and the second most influential gang officeholder was the superintendent of lamps (the acting mayor was the treasurer of the Regulators, William McPhail, a hatmaker who was related to the state lottery commissioner). Most gang members in government worked far below those two exceptions. Of the 36 percent of Know-Nothing gang members identified in demographic records who held a government job, working-class designations fit 89 percent of these jobs, most of which were on the police force.[62]

American Party officials tried to bring gangs under tighter control through the expansion of city services that created more jobs for working-class partisans. Know-Nothing leaders hoped that municipal jobs would shift workers' primary political attachment from the club to the party. Another disciplinary device was a club convention that met in Baltimore from 1857 to 1859. The convention solicited club input in exchange for party loyalty. "The American clubs of the city of Baltimore," the meeting resolved, "know no candidate who is not the regular nominee of an American convention, or American Ward Council."[63]

Worries about club autonomy focused on two aspects of gang life. The most obvious cause for concern was the lawlessness of tavern culture. Less visibly, but still posing a danger to Know-Nothing success, gangs used legal, bureaucratic methods to create a network of political association that bypassed the parties. Although politicians encouraged it, the club convention was one of many signs that Baltimore gangs had an organizational reach that extended beyond their neighborhood and city. In late November 1856, delegates from Cincinnati Know-Nothing clubs came to Baltimore to honor the election-day performance of the gangs. The Shifflers and the Northern Liberties, Philadelphia nativist gangs, visited Baltimore several times in the mid-1850s. They twice participated in election riots, and the Shifflers shielded a fugitive Baltimore gang member from arrest. An 1856 polling place cheer of "Go in Shifflers! Go Fillmore! Go in Rip Raps!" blended regional, national, and local affiliations. In 1857, Baltimore gangs took part in a Washington, D.C., election riot. In 1858, south-side gangs shot off fireworks to celebrate the triumph of New Orleans Know-Nothings in a military confrontation with upper-class reformers. Even the names of gangs like the Calithumpians, Empires, Plug Uglies, and Rip Raps copied those in other cities.[64] Networks of association with nativist gangs across the country helped Baltimore club men when they traveled and increased their awareness of the larger meaning of local issues. At one level, visits from political clubs in other cities resembled the fraternal visits of fire companies. At another, the tribute that Baltimore gangs received from their Cincinnati brethren showed the potential for these autonomous working-class groups to build a translocal network independent of political parties.

The implications of the budding club network were not lost on mainstream politicians. Mayor Swann and John Pendleton Kennedy showed up at the banquet for the Cincinnati visitors and watched as local clubs paraded into the hall to loud approval. The day after the November 1856 election, Kennedy confided to his diary that "the riots yesterday were terrible. We are under the domination of organized bands of ruffians of both parties." One can imagine his discomfort at the banquet. Nevertheless, he and Swann stood up and delivered encomiums to the clubs. Practical politicians recognized the advantages of club support, but they did not view gang members as their peers and they did not want to share power with the Tigers and the Rip Raps. Know-Nothing officeholders balanced their need for club activism against the dangers posed to conventional politics by bringing this type of working-class organization into the halls of power.[65]

Although Swann and other leaders kept an eye on the nonviolent dangers of club autonomy, gangs' everyday lawlessness posed the greater threat to American Party unity. Gang life contradicted the ethical values of genteel society and made well-off Know-Nothings uneasy about associating with a party that winked at immoral conduct. A reporter described Erasmus Levy's tavern as "the resort of characters who will defend themselves, if attacked, to the bitter end; they are such as would attack others without being attacked themselves. . . . Its general reputation is bad." Upper-class city dwellers who supported standards of respectability that Levy's tavern mocked expressed this moral discomfort as a threat to their identity as men. "I was never so un-manned in my life," wrote Baptist minister John Williams in response to a break-in at his home in 1857. "The idea of being surrounded by such miserable beings and not knowing what moment they would assault you made me miserable." Williams sided with the South in the sectional conflict, and like many upper-class Southern nationalists, he loathed the rowdies that flocked to the American Party standard.[66]

The association of Know-Nothings with gangs drove some business-men out of the American Party. Henry Shriver, the son of a small-town manufacturer who began a mercantile career in late-1850s Baltimore, devoted his leisure time to a chess club and dinner parties thrown by business families. Shriver's support for the Know-Nothings evaporated after an omnibus ride with the gangs at the 1858 elections.

> [The bus] had left the starting place about two squares when it was stopped by a crowd of Plugs, Rough Skins, or some other infernal de-nomination. . . . They were all very drunk, and I could not help think-ing that a ride with them was not going to prove very agreeable or very safe. . . . They were continually pulling out their pistols (of which every man had two or three) and examining them by the light and it is astonishing that they did not shoot some of the party accidentally.

Shriver said later that "the informal rascality, which (and it only) makes the American Party triumphant in this city, has considerably shaken my attachment to the cause. I want to be an American, but not a friend of rowdyism." The public displays that gangs made in behalf of domestic values could not overcome the impact of such frightening street encounters on white-collar Know-Nothings.[67]

Yet, as the moral reform gestures of the gangs suggest, men in the gangs did not join the American Party to ridicule middle-class do-good-ers. Economics, not ethics, drew workingmen to the Know-Nothing standard. While no American Party leader delivered a speech about the joy of drinking in neighborhood bars, many of them decried the squeeze on employment and wages that workingmen experienced in the 1850s. A few gang leaders became counterculture celebrities for their political exploits, but action on workplace issues comprised the most significant benefit that workers gained from their involvement with the American Party.

In his 1857 gubernatorial campaign, Thomas Hicks told voters that "[American] mechanics and laboring men had been ostracized. The custom house, the tobacco warehouses were filled with Irishmen which

should be filled with natives of the soil." Replacing foreigners with natives in government employment fulfilled the Know-Nothing promise
to combat immigrant competition. From 1855 to 1860, Know-Nothing
administrators increased municipal spending by 14 percent a year,
twice the rate at which municipal spending grew under mostly Democratic regimes from 1830 to 1850. They added $1.2 million to annual ex-
penditures over the course of five years by raising taxes and borrowing
an unprecedented sum of $5.5 million.[68] By 1860, the city employed
more than one thousand workers in tasks ranging from vaccine physician to street sweeper. Swann's park-building program employed hundreds of laborers at centrally managed sites like Druid Hill Park. The
plan earmarked individual disbursements to ward politicians who oversaw smaller "squares" in their districts. The largest addition to city payrolls occurred when Swann hired almost three hundred new police
officers in 1857. As noted above, clubs members won many of these
jobs, and where possible Know-Nothing officeholders directed patronage to the American-born. Despite their declining share of the general
population during the 1850s, white natives increased their representation in government work from 80 percent to 87 percent because of
Know-Nothing patronage policies.[69]

In addition to creating government jobs, Know-Nothings aided
wage earners by assisting their collective action against employers.
Management relied on police to disperse pickets and protect property,
but Know-Nothing police often turned a blind eye to strike activity and
joined in disturbances on behalf of workingmen. During the Seal Strike
of 1857, B&O conductors and sympathizers in other departments
blockaded tracks west of Baltimore to stop company business. B&O
officials asked the mayor for police to escort trains out of Baltimore.
Swann refused on the grounds that the blockade lay beyond the city
limits and outside of his jurisdiction. The police neutrality enabled
strikers to shut down the B&O for three days. The B&O then went over
Swann's head and enlisted the aid of state government. On May 2, the
Democratic governor, T. Watkins Ligon, warned "all persons . . . to
keep away from the neighborhood of these disturbances" and deployed
state militia on trains outfitted to break the blockade. Fighting between
strikers and the state troops produced one death and many injuries.
Within a week, the state militia had broken the strike.[70]

The Seal Strike drew different reactions from the partisan press.
The *Clipper* concentrated on the injustice of making workers liable for
theft from the cars. "The conductors, very naturally think that if they

are required to give security they should first have an opportunity satisfying themselves that the goods have been entrusted to them as stipulated, and hence refuse to work until an understanding is arrived at." The paper denounced the violence, but tried to pin it on the Calithumpians, a Democratic gang that days before the strike had brawled with the Rip Raps, a club that included B&O workers. Conversely, the *Sun* called strikers "desperate men engaged in this aggravated offense against law and order," who had "advanced to the full development of civil war . . . and attacked the corporate interests of society." From this position, the *Sun* could condone the bayonet charge and rifle volleys carried out by the state militia.[71]

Support for the strike exacerbated antagonism between Swann's administration and the B&O's private investors. B&O managers objected not only to the American Party's behavior in the Seal Strike but also to their opposition to a plan to disburse $3 million in profits as a cash dividend, rather than reinvest it in track and machinery. As a compromise, Swann and the city council offered to issue more stock in exchange for increased payments on the road's municipal debt. Because municipal representation on the B&O board of directors rose by one seat for every twenty-five hundred shares issued, payment in stock had the added benefit of increasing government influence on the executive board. President Chauncey Brooks and his chief adviser, John Work Garrett, both Democrats, opposed this outcome and continued to demand a cash dividend. Partisans from state government and private investors in other cities joined the battle as it dragged out in the courts for the rest of the decade.[72]

The B&O was Baltimore's largest private employer and the city's main hope for commercial growth, and the split between its private investors and interested public officials corresponded to cleavages between business Democrats and Know-Nothing workers. Later in 1857, Garrett, the advocate for private stockholders, won election as B&O president. Garrett's regime, which lasted more than twenty years, eradicated the policies of Swann and like-minded presidents who viewed the B&O as a semipublic corporation with special obligations to government, which had funded it since its inception. Democrats regarded Know-Nothing indifference to labor violence as a threat to property rights, and Garrett's combativeness in the Seal Strike harkened back to the arguments made by the holdout iron makers in 1853. Swann and the American Party enthusiastically supported private enterprise, but they were sensitive to the political consequences of B&O decisions.

Keeping police away from strikers pleased working-class voters in the Know-Nothing stronghold of west Baltimore, while the extra dividend risked the city's multimillion-dollar loans to the B&O and put money into the pockets of Democratic investors that otherwise could have gone to road building that created jobs and supported local industry. The Seal Strike generated tension between businessmen and workers in the American Party, but the extra-dividend fight illustrated why these two groups might want to maintain the uneasy coalition that kept Know-Nothings in power.

In 1858, New Orleans Know-Nothings fought a similar battle to build more railroad track. Democrats in Louisiana's state legislature blocked city government's wish to borrow so as to continue construction on the New Orleans, Jackson and Great Northern Railroad. As in Baltimore, the New Orleans' railroad conflict coordinated the interests of workers eager for jobs with those of Whiggish businessmen seeking trade opportunities.[73]

Municipal assistance to American-born workers also encompassed economic competition with laborers from other cultures. In 1858 and 1859, south Baltimore's Tiger gang exploited their connection to the ruling American Party to carry out a different kind of workplace action, job busting, or the forced removal of rivals from a trade. The Tigers raided shipyards to gain access to jobs in ship caulking, a comparatively high-paying, skilled task that prevented ships from leaking. Prior to the caulker riots, the trade had been almost exclusively an African-American occupation in Baltimore. In addition to showing how white workers used party politics to reorder the workplace, the caulker riots illustrated the emerging free-labor politics of Southern workers that so alarmed slave-state Democrats.

In the spring of 1858, whites in south Baltimore campaigned to take the jobs of black caulkers. Although whites offered to work for fifty cents less per day, which at $1.25 was still a good wage, most employers refused to part with their experienced black workforce. To press their demand, whites led by the Tiger club attacked black caulkers and white shipbuilders. In June and July, the Tigers raided several yards. Two shipbuilders, John S. Brown and William Skinner & Sons, held them off at gunpoint. When police refused their request for assistance, the Skinners were forced to hire twelve white caulkers.[74]

In April 1859, the Tigers caulked the bark *Virginia*. Indicative of their inexperience, two months later the ship began leaking and needed recaulking. This time, the *Virginia's* owners took her to Hugh A.

Cooper, a Fell's Point employer of black caulkers. Wanting Cooper to relinquish the vessel or at least pay them to fix it, the Tigers stormed his dry dock and assaulted any black caulkers that did not flee. Joseph Edwards, the Tigers' president, singled out Cooper for a beating. The Tigers neither took control of the *Virginia* nor got jobs from Cooper, and they made no further attacks on black caulkers. However, because of these riots whites gained access to the caulking trade, particularly in south Baltimore. By 1860, blacks had lost jobs in what was their ninth most common occupation, and on the south side they could work only with the permission of white gang members.

The Tiger club grabbed the biggest share of caulking jobs. Men who belonged to the Tigers, had a relative in the club, or lived with a club member comprised one-third of the white caulkers, and they were almost one-half of the white caulkers living in south-side wards. Like most gangs, the Tigers were comprised of workers who shared ethnic and neighborhood ties. All but four of the fifty-three Tigers for whom occupations could be found practiced manual trades. Fifty of them lived in the two wards that encompassed the south-side waterfront, twenty-one had a relative in the gang, and almost all were born in Maryland to working-class parents. In the depressed economy of the late 1850s, workers likely to join gangs wanted good-paying work of any kind. Job busting was an extreme tactic for gaining entry to a trade. It worked well at Baltimore's economically depressed shipyards, which were concentrated around the harbor and more susceptible to coercive control than trades that dispersed work throughout the city.

Job busting would have failed had municipal government not aided the Tigers. Thirteen Tigers worked for the city, ten as police, and five more had a relative on its payroll. Government support, particularly from gang members on the police force, proved decisive in opening the caulking trade. In several of the attacks, police ignored calls for help and tacitly permitted rioters to control job sites. When arrests were made, club members quickly secured release on bail and enjoyed their liberty with indictments pending almost indefinitely. In the caulker riots, organized workingmen with powerful assistance from municipal government used job busting to gain access to a trade. Had a mob formed on the spot and, opposed by police, tried to reorder hiring at the shipyards, the outcome likely would have been different.

While the panic of 1857 stimulated job competition and assistance from municipal government gave the Tigers the means to carry out their campaign, the politics of white shipyard owners and their connection with skilled African-American workers was an added inducement for the attacks. Owners of slaves and employers of free black labor preferred Democrats to Know-Nothings. Operators of twelve of Baltimore's twenty-six shipyards were either Democratic officials or men who voted for secession. In brickmaking, another source of African-American industrial work, Democratic officials or their relatives ran eleven of twenty-five brickyards, while Know-Nothings operated only three. Although fewer than 1 percent of Baltimore whites owned slaves, slaveholders made up one-fourth of the officers in the City Reform Association, a Democrat-inspired reform movement that toppled the Know-Nothings in 1860.[75]

The shipbuilders who fought on the side of black caulkers—the Skinners, Hugh Cooper, and John S. Brown—were the wealthiest and most stridently partisan Democrats on the waterfront. Their capital reserves enabled them to ride out the panic of 1857 without replacing skilled black caulkers. Moreover, each had been a Democratic officeholder. Skinner had been harbor master. Cooper and Brown had served on the city council, and both lost elections to Know-Nothings. In 1858, Cooper cofounded the Reform Association. Know-Nothings removed Cooper from his municipally appointed seat on the B&O board, and they enforced harbor and wharf taxes on shipbuilders that their Democratic predecessors had let go uncollected.

These shipbuilders also had an interest in slavery. Brown married the daughter of Hugh Auld, a Democratic officeholder related by marriage to Edward Lloyd, an active Democrat and Eastern Shore planter with ties to the politically influential Howard family. Cooper and one of the Skinners were two of the three shipbuilders who owned slaves in 1860. These men, Democratic activists and prosperous employers of free blacks as well as being slave owners, had many reasons to refuse to let a Know-Nothing gang dictate who they hired.

In their attack on free blacks and prominent Democratic shipbuilders, white gangs and the Know-Nothings took aim at the broader patron-client relationship between white employers and free black labor that supported the urban paternalist social order. Shipbuilders maintained an employment agreement with a black caulkers' guild that epitomized the style of patron-client relationships that many employers preferred. Know-Nothing officials undermined the influence of partisan Democratic shipbuilders, and workingmen in the Tigers took jobs from African Americans. Industrial wage earners in gangs had the advantage of police collusion in their campaign against free blacks, whose few friends in the white community were on the outs with city government.

In these ways, the caulker riots showed how workplace and cultural conflicts intersected with party competition in the urban political insurgency. Working-class Know-Nothings removed government support for systems of workplace patronage that political parties had earlier sustained. In reordering the urban workplace, the Tigers demonstrated another facet of opposition politics in the cities. They tied their struggle for advancement to support for white supremacy and slavery. In doing so, the Tigers practiced a uniquely Southern variant of northern workers' free-labor politics.

White supremacist imagery turned up in other aspects of the Know-Nothing struggle. Henry Winter Davis referred to his opponents as "black Democrats," and Know-Nothing election rowdies accused immigrants of failing to vote a "white man's ticket." In 1859, a gang member yelled at a Democrat, "You never voted anything but a black man's ticket anyhow." Rioters in Baltimore and New Orleans sometimes blackened their faces as a means of disguise.[76]

Despite conservative suspicions of their antislavery sentiments, Know-Nothing gangs exhibited little sympathy for slaves or free blacks. In 1860, a ring of Baltimore Know-Nothings that included some Regulators schemed to sell African-American convicts to Deep South slave traders. This was in violation of a statute that, while it enslaved free black criminals, stipulated that they remain in Maryland and serve no more than five years. African Americans were often the victims of gang attacks that were a combination of theft, cruelty, and the activities of young men on a spree. In 1859, Rough Skins aboard a Chesapeake Bay steamer threw free blacks overboard for entering a cabin that the rowdies believed was for whites only.[77]

Compared with the national range of free-labor politics, the behavior of gangs and the American Party situated Baltimore Know-Nothings between two sectional poles. In the North, particularly its western states, both Democrats and Republicans put equality among whites far ahead of interracial humanitarianism, but all Republicans and many Democrats criticized slaveholders and opposed slavery's expansion. Below the Mason-Dixon, Southern nationalists strongly supported slavery. They invoked free-labor egalitarianism to argue that slavery promoted white equality across class lines by exempting poor whites from the lowest forms of manual labor. Southern nativists also thought within this framework of racialized politics. Their belief that greedy bosses and corrupt politicians made tools of white foreigners dovetailed with arguments about slavery that cast blacks as pawns of various plots against the freedom of ordinary white men. By supporting job busting, Baltimore Know-Nothings advanced the principle of white equality by attacking a few employers and a mass of vulnerable black laborers. Neither fire-eaters nor free-soilers, Baltimore's job busters walked a fine line between seeking to reduce slaveholders' power and upholding the racial hierarchy that slavery produced.

Southern workers in other cities manipulated the politics of slavery in ways similar to Baltimore Know-Nothings. Depending on the locality, white Southerners' campaigns against black labor could fit into either opposition to slavery or support for it.

In St. Louis, Republican free-soilers polled well among white workers. Led by Congressman Frank Blair, St. Louis Republicans outdid their colleagues in the free states in claiming to act solely for the benefit of ordinary whites, disavowing interest in elevating the civil status of African Americans. Blair opposed slavery in Kansas out of concern for "a large class of citizens of the southern States—the non-slaveholding people of those States." Reiterating familiar themes of job-competition rhetoric, Blair asserted that "the working men and mechanics of St. Louis have too just a sense of the dignity of their own employments to permit themselves to be degraded by the competition of the negro slaves. A man might as well attempt to educate his negro for the legal profession as to put him at a mechanical trade in competition with the mechanics of my district." Blair's enthusiasm for removing blacks to foreign colonies fit with his constituents' sense that enemies from all sides were overwhelming them.[78]

Other St. Louis Republicans echoed Blair's white-supremacist attack on slavery. In 1857, B. Gratz Brown, Blair's cousin and a state legislator, proposed a gradual end to slavery because he sought to "emancipate the white man from the yoke of competition with the negro." Germans, the St. Louis constituency most opposed to slavery extension, also feared the effects of racial competition. In 1859, a German editor wrote that "it is the Democratic Party that promotes racial amalgamation, while the Republican Party's principles work to restrict slavery and with it racial amalgamation." Noting the prominence of slaveholders, including Blair, in the party, Carl Bernays, a German editor, said that St. Louis Republicans were "those who want the territories given to the free white man and not the slave-baron of the South; but it is not [those who do not own slaves] who are struggling with the slave-owners for the freeing of the slaves." Although they avowed white supremacy, Republicans in St. Louis blasted slaveholders for putting blacks into competition with poor whites.[79]

On the eve of the Civil War, workingmen in the South's smaller cities appealed to white equality to advance their interests, but, unlike St. Louis Republicans, they presented their initiatives as beneficial to slavery. White mechanics in Charleston, South Carolina, argued that banishing free blacks from skilled trades would shore up slavery and promote white unity in the coming war. Richmond cordwainers went on strike against employers who purchased boot pieces from Northern manufacturers for quicker and cheaper local assembly. In an appeal to Southern nationalist sentiment, the cordwainers' president asked, "Is this Southern manufacturing, a Northern leg with a Southern sole?" In North Carolina, urban workingmen allied with the Whig-American opposition petitioned to increase taxes on slaves despite planters' opposition to such legislation. A Raleigh trade federation seeking "justice and equality" of taxation said they did so in the name of white unity. "The antagonism between capital and labor existing elsewhere can never affect the social condition to any extent of an agricultural community like our own; especially when that community has engrafted on it the institution of domestic slavery." Outnumbered as urban workers were in the Carolinas, declarations of sectional loyalty responded to intense pressure from slaveholders. A member of the Raleigh association complained that "the keen scented nostrils of aristocratic patriots smell treason in every movement of our muscles." To allay such fears, the group resolved that should a Republican win the 1860 presidential election, "we will be as willing and as prompt as any to maintain and defend Southern rights, even to spilling of our own blood."[80]

New Orleans, home to thousands of enfranchised workers and the principal city of thoroughly proslavery Louisiana, hosted a more complicated political battle over class and slavery. In 1856 and 1857, local election violence and realignment in state politics made American Party leaders in the city more attentive to working-class voters and more defensive of Southern rights and slavery. In 1856, the Louisiana legislature's Democratic majority evicted three New Orleans Know-Nothing senators who, they claimed, won their seats through fraud. In 1857, state officials considered imposing a property qualification on New Orleans voters. Although that measure failed, the state gave control of election procedures to a superintendent of elections appointed by the governor. Know-Nothings managed to fend off a more drastic version of the law with the help of Pierre Soule's dissident faction within the Louisiana Democratic Party. Soule used New Orleans's beleaguered American Party as a counterweight to the dominant wing of the party headed by his rival John Slidell, the U.S. senator and close friend of President Buchanan.[81] However, Soule was virulently proslavery and anti-Northern, and despite his alliance with Stephen Douglas, of Illinois, he attacked Buchanan and Slidell as foes of the South.

In light of its tenuous alliance with Soule and Louisiana's proslavery stand on sectional issues, the New Orleans American Party stepped up its advocacy of Southern rights. In 1858, local editors endorsed a legislative bill to import "African apprentices," a thinly disguised plan to renew the international slave trade. They excoriated free-soilism in all forms and distanced themselves from the insurgent parties in Baltimore and St. Louis. Instead of reaching out to Republicans or moderate Democrats, Know-Nothings in New Orleans advocated cooperation between nativists and Southern nationalists. "If the South were united upon the anti-foreign policy, enough additional power could be obtained . . . to stop and control the Black Republican agrarians. In no other way can the rapacious march be stayed—in no other way can disunion be avoided."[82]

In 1857, New Orleans Know-Nothings swept the city elections and resorted to coercion in defiance of the new voting law. As they did in smaller Southern cities, business Whigs in the Crescent City, many of whom were foreign-born, Roman Catholic, or both, quit the American Party over sectionalism and nativist violence. Charles Gayarre left over Roman Catholic proscription. In 1856, Judah P. Benjamin, a U.S. senator and Jewish Whig planter who lived in New Orleans, declared himself a Democrat because he believed that "the true parents of the new birth [the American Party] were New England prejudices against slavery and against Catholicism." Christian Roselius, a German lawyer sickened by election violence, led two hundred former Whigs out of the American Party. Benjamin and Roselius disagreed over slavery and secession, yet both agreed that the Know-Nothings threatened civil liberty. In addition to urban defections, the decision of rural Whig planters to align with one or another of the Democratic factions weakened conservative influences on New Orleans Know-Nothings.

Workingmen and their concerns filled the vacuum left by Whig departures. Skilled workingmen staffed the local ward clubs that rallied Know-Nothings to the polls and forwarded nominations for city offices. In 1858, Gerard Stith, a member of the printers' union who had campaigned against immigrant competition in his trade, won the mayoral nomination.[83]

The isolation of the New Orleans regime and the shift of some business Whigs to the Democrats set the stage for a showdown in 1858 between the American Party and the Vigilance Committee, a formally nonpartisan movement devoted to toppling the Know-Nothings. The Vigilantes organized an independent ticket headed by mayoral nominee Pierre G. T. Beauregard, a Democratic planter and army officer who ran the New Orleans Customs House and who was Slidell's brother-in-law.

Know-Nothings called the independent ticket "a hoodwink of the flimsiest sort" that fronted for Slidell Democrats and rich snobs. Referring to reformers' closed-door proceedings, the *Crescent* asserted that "no affair in Downing Street [home of England's prime minister] was ever more genteelly managed, or more exclusive, or more aristocratic." The editors noted that the leaders of the Vigilance Committee "possess great wealth . . . but the possession of great wealth is no consideration in cases like these . . . the American nominees are the equals of their competitors." Know-Nothings also brought race to bear on this argument about white equality. The *Crescent* alleged that Beauregard replaced white workers with slaves in construction of a new customs house. "Negroes are very well in their way, in their proper place and position; but when white men are overslaughed [*sic*] by them by order of a government official . . . it would be well enough for the ostracized classes to remember the fact, and govern themselves accordingly."[84]

As the election approached, the Vigilance Committee armed twelve hundred volunteers and seized government buildings around Jackson Square. The Vigilante's commander was a U.S. Army officer, and his lieutenants had recently returned from William Walker's failed attempt to conquer Nicaragua for slavery, an expedition that Beauregard had contemplated joining. Know-Nothings fought back with their own coercive resources. The board of aldermen impeached Mayor Waterman, who vacillated over the Vigilance Committee's demand that he deputize their troops, and sacked a wavering police chief. Under new leadership, the city police and sixteen hundred volunteers organized by Stith resisted the Vigilantes. Know-Nothings then went on to win a peaceful election. Fearing a backlash, Beauregard's volunteers fled New Orleans. The American Party retained control of the city thereafter.[85]

Despite triumphing over the Vigilance Committee and its well-off supporters, Stith did not attack proslavery interests head on. He doubled city spending above the pared-down level achieved by Waterman, but he kept an eye to efficiency and even-handedness in patronage. Municipal dollars funded more police and projects for new road and levees. The workers who had rallied behind the American Party in 1858 had achieved greater say in city politics without challenging slavery or states' rights.[86]

In New Orleans, Know-Nothings used white supremacy and white equality to rally support against wealthy men in the rival party. Although local Know-Nothings advocated slavery's extension, their charge that rich whites used blacks to undermine the status of poor whites followed the logic of free-soilers like Blair who claimed that white workingmen refused to work alongside slaves. In their struggles for expanded political power, white workingmen across the South invoked racial hierarchy to justify their claims for equality with wealthier whites. However, the cities' divergent responses to the larger politics of their section showed that workers' growing political influence did not uniformly lead them to espouse free-soil views. What looked from a distance to be a home-grown challenge to the South's proslavery consensus appeared on close inspection to be a more flexible and practical political movement. In each city, workingmen focused primarily on their immediate workplace and political struggles and only secondarily on the connection between those conflicts and other levels of American politics.

Baltimore's racist, free-labor politics stood in the middle of this continuum of responses on slavery and Southern rights. Henry Winter Davis was the only Southern congressman besides Blair to vote against a proslavery constitution for Kansas, but unlike Blair, who said he wanted to halt slavery's expansion, Davis welcomed slavery in new territories and declared his vote as a protest of Democratic fraud.[87] Aside from Davis, Maryland's Know-Nothing delegation toed the Southern line on the slavery question, and in Baltimore, advocacy of workers' issues shaded into a defense of slavery, rather than opposition to it.

The mobilization of working-class whites by urban parties produced similar outcomes, although clear opposition to slavery was not one of them. In the 1830s and 1840s, the South's urban workers had operated within a chain of party power (either Whig or Democratic) that allotted control to the business elite in municipal government and gave slaveholding planters the decisive say in state and regional politics. As the power brokers for patronage and for nominations to state and federal government, slaveholders made lieutenants out of urban party leaders. Through this arrangement, planters could dissuade city legislators from enacting populist, egalitarian laws.

In the late 1850s, Know-Nothings in Baltimore and New Orleans and Republicans in St. Louis were urban opposition parties fighting hostile planters in state politics. In Baltimore, American Party politicians supported slavery as a matter of principle: its leaders, after all, had been proslavery men all their lives. However, their ties to proslavery leaders elsewhere in the South were weak. They could therefore allow working-class activists to attack vulnerable black and immigrant laborers and Democratic employers without paying any more serious cost than what had already been exacted in the process of party realignment. No matter what stand urban parties took on the slavery controversy, their status as political holdouts in an increasingly one-party region and social others in a rural world made them doubly threatening. Know-Nothings alarmed not only slaveholders but also urban commercial leaders who enjoyed good relations with country planters and who were habituated to orderly politics.

Some Southern planters had been convinced for more than a decade that secession would best solve the national crisis over slavery. For the most part, men of commerce in Southern cities had steadfastly opposed such a radical measure. By 1859, two political crises that had never been fully separate, the sectional conflict in federal politics and the battle over reform at the municipal level, headed toward convergence. Know-Nothings came to power promising to deliver reform and bolster support for the Union. Urban conservatives initially welcomed the American Party as the answer to a system of party politics that they believed had been disabled by corruption. Four years of election rioting and profligate spending destroyed their confidence that conventional politics, no matter the party, could control the unruly electorates of their cities. The latter phase of the Know-Nothing struggle had made members of the old urban elite receptive to the fire-eaters' case that secession would save republican government from a democracy that had run amok under the rule of party politics.

Five

A Revolution against Party Politics
Reform and Secession
in Baltimore

The fall of 1859 was an exciting and dangerous time in Baltimore politics. On October 16, John Brown raided a federal arsenal on Maryland's border in the hopes of sparking a slave revolution. Panicked Maryland slaveholders responded by asking the state government to reenslave or banish free blacks. The plan won little support, particularly in Baltimore, where free blacks played a vital role as unskilled wage labor, but in the wake of the caulker riots Brown's raid contributed to the urban elite's concerns about the changing racial status quo.

The prospect of an election added to the tension produced by sectional conflict and labor strife. A week before the November 2 elections, the American Party held its infamous rally where Henry Winter Davis spoke beneath a picture of an assault on a supporter of the City Reform Association, an officially nonpartisan group organized by Democrats in 1858 to topple the Know-Nothings. Days later, a rumored attempt on the life of acting mayor William McPhail heightened Know-Nothing determination to stop the Reformers. The Blood Tubs assaulted Democratic congressional candidate William Preston, and the Tigers broke up a south-side Reform rally and threatened to beat those who tried to vote. Referring to Davis's speech, Frederick W. Brune, a second-generation German businessman, said "the outrageous exhibition . . . has . . . disgusted many thinking persons. I hope and pray there will be a bloodless revolution achieved here on Wednesday next." Only a man who took politics very seriously could regard an election for ten state assembly seats and two congressmen as a vehicle for revolution. Equally unfounded was Brune's hope that such a contest would be bloodless.[1]

On the morning of election day, in one of the finest homes in south Baltimore's Fifteenth Ward, George and Adam Barkly Kyle Jr., two aspiring merchants in their late twenties, prepared to head to the polls. They had a lot to carry, and they probably received help from Salley Kelley, the family's slave. Each brother planned to distribute ballots for the City Reform Association. George had given out eighteen pistols to Reform poll watchers, and he and Adam packed guns and knives inside of their long coats.[2] Armed to the teeth and lugging hundreds of ballots, the Kyles knew how dangerous elections had become. They were determined that their party win the day.

The Kyles's family background typified that of Reform Association supporters. Their father, a merchant involved in international trade, joined several Irish Protestant businessmen in immigrating to Baltimore early in the century. Worth $100,000 in 1860, Adam Kyle Sr. was one of south Baltimore's richest men, and like many of his peers he had been a Whig until the party collapsed. In the mid-1850s, Kyle became a Democrat to stop the American Party, which had given him many reasons to worry. Nativism insulted Kyle's heritage; indulgence of gangs upset employment relations for businessmen; and suspicion that local Know-Nothings colluded with Northern Republicans, a charge reinforced by Davis's vote for a Republican Speaker of the House in 1859, alarmed slaveholders like Kyle.[3]

His sons' decision to arm themselves had something to do with the preparations of another voter in the Fifteenth Ward on his way to the polls that morning, Joseph Edwards Jr., the tavern owner and sometime manual laborer who presided over the Tiger club. A neighbor asserted that "every man, woman and even child, who could talk, residing in the fifteenth ward, knows Edwards." His father was a day laborer who by age sixty-four had amassed only $300 in property. The Edwards family, far from living with servants, took in five boarders to supplement their income. Edwards had a shorter walk than that taken by the Kyle brothers because the city council's American Party majority located the polls at his former tavern. It also put the neighboring Seventeenth Ward polling booth a block away. The engine house of the nativist Watchman Fire Company stood nearby. The area, one observer believed, "was generally looked upon as a hard neighborhood."[4]

Around 8:30 that morning, Edwards encountered the Kyles as they approached the polls. Learning that the brothers planned to distribute Reform ballots, Edwards said they would "get plenty of tickets during the day." The Kyles spent a tense two hours at the polls. Outnumbered Reformers suffered insults and occasional rough treatment from the Tigers. At 10:30, Edwards called out, "Snatch the tickets from them sons of bitches," and another man yelled, "Kill the rascals." The mob then surrounded and beat the Kyle brothers. Adam Kyle struggled to his feet, fatally shot a teenage attacker, and ran into the first open door. Ignoring the protests of the family inside, the Tigers broke in and killed Kyle. George, although badly injured, escaped. No arrests were made. The American Party won 75 percent of the citywide vote, and in Ward Fifteen and Ward Seventeen, Reformers garnered only 136 of more than 2,000 ballots cast.[5]

Two days later, leaders of the Reform Association and many of Baltimore's wealthiest businessmen turned out for Adam Kyle's funeral. Their procession, which "number[ed] an unusual quantity of private carriages followed by hundreds of gentlemen arm in arm, four by four," attracted the city's attention. Speakers at the funeral condemned Know-Nothingism and a system of party politics that they believed had sacrificed civic order for partisan victory. "How dreadful that such should be the result of excitement growing out of what some might say good to the government," lamented the wife of a southern Maryland Congressman. "Politics is an evil instead of a blessing, and I should be truly happy to see less interest taken in it." The Reverend John C. Backus praised Kyle as a man "forgetful of personal risk or the demands of business, and impelled by a principle independent of self. . . . He went forth to defend those rights, which in a civil relation were most dear to every citizen, and to rescue the city from the reproach which it bore. . . . He was not a politician, he had not given himself up to the men who aspire to control political parties, but he stood up as all citizens should do to discharge their duties." Backus portrayed Kyle as a martyr to the ideal of the virtuous republican citizen who had an innate dislike for professional politics but was ready to risk all for the public good.[6]

The fight between Kyle, a rich man sympathetic to immigrants and proslavery Democrats, and Edwards, a poor man affiliated with the nativist and strongly Unionist Know-Nothings, illustrated how Jacksonian-era party competition had been transformed. In cities like Baltimore, the parties had talked about class, ethnicity, and sectionalism, but they tried to prevent social divisions related to these and other issues from dividing the voting base. Ideally, politicians could use parties as a filter that distilled the volatility of the electorate into orderly government action. By the late 1850s, social identity and party affiliation had converged, and antiparty rhetoric increased each side's mistrust of the other. Now, party competition intensified, rather than diffused, the class and ethnic hatreds that men like Kyle and Edwards felt for each other. The off-year election of 1859 took on added gravity because it was also a struggle between workers and the wealthy, Unionists and Southern sympathizers, and neither side would rule out extreme measures that might bring victory.

Baltimore's campaign for municipal reform had counterparts in the North and West, where upper-class activists tried to oust prototypes of Gilded Age boss rule. Formulating arguments that would be invoked into the next century, municipal reformers wanted to resolve politicized social conflict by initiating a kind of urban version of the 1810s nonpartisan "era of good feelings" in which the "best element" governed and popular participation and the power of parties were curbed.[7] Slave-state reformers struggled with the same problem of invigorated working-class politics that vexed their counterparts in the North, but their regional location gave them a different set of potential allies. In the South, reformers in the urban elite worked with rural planters in state government, men who saw their region's big-city political machines as a threat to slavery and their power. By 1861, opponents of invigorated municipal government could accept secession as a means of preempting an alliance between the enfranchised urban working class and the Lincoln administration.

The agendas of urban reformers and lower-South planter-politicians differed, but whatever popularity secession had outside the planter class stemmed in large part from the adaptability of its republican themes to local circumstances. Historians have argued that Southern disgust with party politics made secession attractive as a bold measure against government corruption.[8] In the lower South, a region that had done away with party competition by 1860, Democratic leaders united voters in support of Southern nationalism. While they worried more about defending slavery, fire-eaters occasionally cited the combative politics of slave-state cities to argue that the ills of Northern mob rule were infecting the South. Not only would secession protect slavery, Southern nationalists claimed that it would also stop the spread of partisan mob rule.

In the South's big cities, where through the spring of 1861 the Democrats and their opposition continued to compete for power, antipartyism had a different meaning. It made city dwellers unforgiving of their local enemies and convinced many urbanites that the municipal struggle should continue on the elevated plain of a nationwide civil war. Instead of dissolving party differences, treating partisan rivals as foes of republican liberty made party identity and the desire to crush the opposition the springboard for choosing either Union or secession. Bitter municipal conflict not only shaped urbanites' sectional choices, it also induced them to take positions in the vanguard of the war. This partisan past helps explain why the largest cities became bases for mobilizing support for both the Union and secession and why they were the sites of war-related riots in 1861 and 1862. Because of the complexity of secession in the urban South, two chapters are devoted to the topic: in this chapter, Baltimore receives exclusive attention; the rest of the region is treated in full in chapter 6.

Never entirely separate, Baltimore's municipal struggle and the sectional conflict came together over the issue of political violence, which engaged state government in the business of protecting public safety in the city. After Baltimore's bloody election riots of 1856, Democrats demanded a complete overhaul of municipal party politics. They asked Maryland's Democratic governor, T. Watkins Ligon, to deploy state militia at the polls. This request began a drive to circumvent the local Know-Nothing majority by appealing to state government. Ligon gave Baltimore Democrats a precedent in the spring of 1857, when he used state troops to break the Seal Strike on the B&O. Although Ligon planned to use militia at the fall 1857 election, he relented after Mayor Thomas Swann promised to call up extra police and Baltimore militia regiments threatened to disobey Ligon. Swann's accommodation notwithstanding, Know-Nothings refused to be cowed by the threat of force. Davis reported that "we kicked the Governor out, being quite ready to fight." Democrats again claimed that mobs drove their voters from the polls. An infuriated Ligon said that the American Party "is an essential tyranny. It sways a spurious sceptre, over a people despoiled of their rights, and its career must be in profligate antagonism with law, order, and good government."[9]

The conflict between state and local government sharpened in 1858 because of an ambitious Know-Nothing scheme to amend the Maryland constitution. One proposal would have apportioned legislative seats solely on population, and thereby increased Baltimore's share of the House of Delegates to one-third. In the fall 1857 elections, Know-Nothing Thomas Hicks defeated Ligon for the three-year term as governor, and in light of this transfer of power, another proposal tried to reconvert elected judgeships to gubernatorial appointments. Know-Nothings also asked the legislature "to lend its co-operation in abolishing the law which now admits the foreign element to participation in the affairs of your government." In the state legislature, the plan expanded representation for the American Party's urban electoral base at the expense of slaveholding counties, and it removed popular control over some statewide elected offices likely to go to Democrats. At the municipal level, the proposed changes bolstered Know-Nothing dominance by disfranchising naturalized voters.[10]

Constitutional reform alarmed rural proslavery Democrats, who increasingly regarded Baltimore Know-Nothings as threats to slavery and the traditional dominance of rural counties in state government. Democrat Edward Belt, of Upper Marlboro, a small town in Maryland's tobacco country, conjured up the demon of Baltimore's "[municipal] corporation sitting on the throne of power, the emblems of Maryland lying at its feet . . . holding in its right hand the scourge that is all powerful even under existing laws, and just grasping with its left the legislative power itself; so that in the future *its* will may be the Law!" After meeting with Democrats in his birthplace of Frederick, the U.S. Supreme Court chief justice, Roger B. Taney, was "very indignant at the state of things [in Baltimore] . . . and does not seem able to comprehend how it can exist." In a May referendum, Maryland voters rejected the plan despite overwhelming approval in Baltimore. Fear that Know-Nothings would expand their power in Maryland politics helped persuade rural Democrats to support state intervention in municipal affairs.[11]

The alliance between Baltimore conservatives and proslavery Democrats in the countryside encouraged foes of the Know-Nothings to mix allegations of abolitionism into charges that a city government beholden to wage earners had harmed their businesses and encouraged public disorder. That argument bore fruit in the 1859 elections, in which Democrats gained a majority in the General Assembly. Davis believed that "Harper's Ferry was the turning point," because John Brown's Raid increased rural voters' sensitivity to claims that Know-Nothings could not defend slavery.[12]

Badly beaten outside of Baltimore, Know-Nothings had not been entirely eradicated beyond the city limits. In the House of Delegates, twenty of twenty-nine Know-Nothings represented non-Baltimore districts; Americans held ten of the twenty-two senate seats; and an American, aided by a three-to-one landslide in Baltimore, was elected comptroller. Nevertheless, Democrats had the majority, and some rural Know-Nothings disliked their Baltimore brethren, particularly Henry Winter Davis.[13]

Democrats' heightened concern for Southern interests reached into seemingly nonsectional municipal affairs. For example, they blocked Mayor Swann's plan for a commuter railway by claiming that it would empower abolitionists, labor radicals, and corrupt politicos—sometimes one and the same entity for Democrats. A group led by a Know-Nothing state legislator won the city contract to build the railway, beating out Chauncey Brooks, former B&O president and a staunch Democrat. It then sold its interest to a Philadelphia consortium headed by Republican Jonathan Brock, who offered bribes and subcontracts to firms run by American Party city councilmen. Brock also had ties to Simon Cameron, a Pennsylvania Republican U.S. senator who, according to a contractor, had made "some reference to the possession of a road that had considerable patronage, and might be useful for political purposes." As a symbol of Northern capital and Republicans, Brock stimulated cooperation between proslavery voters and Baltimore businessmen competing with New York and Philadelphia. One anti-Brock meeting resolved that "we are in this, as in every other public matter especially jealous of our rights as southerners, when they are invaded by sinister and dishonorable means by northern men, who are more than suspected of hostility towards our institutions."[14]

Labor militancy also worried Brock's foes. In March 1859, the Tigers and other Know-Nothing clubs raided an anti-Brock rally, and in June two hundred workers demonstrated against the low wages paid for jobs in track construction. As they had in earlier labor disputes, Know-Nothing police refused requests to disperse the pickets, forcing the builders to forfeit their contract to a company willing to raise pay. Workers celebrated with a banner that read "Victory Gained." Critics protested that "those who had charge of [the railway's] management subjected it in a great measure to the influence of men notorious as the most lawless in this community."[15] In the winter of 1859–60, Brock's opponents petitioned the legislature and filed an injunction challenging the city's authority to charter a railroad. The General Assembly debate sparked a knife fight on the rotunda of the state house. Democrats, now in the majority, suspended Brock's charter.[16] Although Brock eventually completed the railway, in the spring of 1860 Reformers had convinced the state to strike back at their municipal enemies by associating a prosaic public works project with sectionalism, class, and political corruption.

Reformers understood police tolerance of the railway picketers as a symptom of city government's support for labor activism. Although well-off businessmen held most major offices under the Know-Nothings, American Party indulgence of workers made the Reform Association attractive to the wealthy. Merchants and professionals comprised roughly four-fifths of the officeholders in the City Reform Association. Concern for public morals, once a Know-Nothing issue, went along with class-based preferences for the Reform movement. Democrats predominated, but 48 of 208 Reform Association officers had been Whigs or Americans, and one-third held a post in a moral-reform organization or church bureaucracy. George P. Kane, one such Whig convert, told a Democratic senator that "the good gentlemen of the late Whig Party have redeemed the slate . . . [while] your rank and file upon whom you have so much relied are now the bravest soldiers of the K N clubs." Although supportive of the Know-Nothings, the editors of the *Baltimore American* advised them that "[w]e want men in the City Council chambers who have some personal interest in the prosperity of the city, and the less they know of party tactics the more acceptable they will be." The national failure of political nativism, the panic of 1857, and the crisis over slavery's expansion pushed Know-Nothings to highlight class and sectionalism over religion and culture, and that change in policy drove some upper-class moral reformers out of the party.[17]

After the 1859 elections, the Reform Association asked the General Assembly's new Democratic majority to clean up what one delegate called a "God-forsaken and God-accursed city." Reformers successfully lobbied for passage of the Baltimore Bills, laws that gave the state control over the city's police, militia volunteers, and juries, and reduced crowds at polling places by subdividing each ward into four election precincts. Citing fraud and intimidation at Baltimore's polls, the legislature unseated the city's representatives. It also dismissed a criminal court judge, Henry Stump, who habitually acquitted Know-Nothing defendants. Finally, should local officials fail to keep the peace, the state militia was given unambiguous authority to suppress civil disorder.[18]

Reformers presented these measures as cures for labor violence and economic depression. "As long as lawlessness was supreme here," asserted Frank Key Howard's *Daily Exchange*, "it was idle to hope for better times, for neither capital nor enterprise can develop themselves unless protection is assured them." Rural Democrats tacked on their own concerns about urban free-soilers by amending the police bill to bar "Black Republicans" from the force. That stipulation and the straight partisan vote on the Baltimore Bills showed how the class and corruption issues of urban Reformers had become alloyed to the party and sectional concerns of rural legislators.[19]

While police reformers everywhere in the 1850s agreed on the need for uniforms, arms, and salaried officers, advocates of these changes in cities acting out the drama of machine politics found that partisanship also entered the debate. The Baltimore Reformers' scheme of transferring police administration to a state-appointed agency imitated plans tried out first in New York and then in other cities, often ones where a party powerful at the municipal level fought against a rival dominant in state government. Despite claims to nonpartisanship, this brand of reform usually resulted in a simple shift in patronage hiring to the majority party in the state capital, not an elimination of party-inspired appointments.[20]

For the City Reform Association, passing the Baltimore Bills required their support for the Democratic Party and its pro-Southern stand on sectional issues. The Democratic legislature staffed the police department's new governing board with men sympathetic to their views on slavery and the Know-Nothings. The board chairman, Charles Howard, a speaker at Kyle's funeral and an 1859 Reform candidate, belonged to a leading Democratic family and had close ties to proslavery politicians through his presidency of the Maryland Colonization Society; John W. Davis had been a Democratic state legislator and customs appointee; William Gatchell, a slaveholder, ran a business with a co-owner of the *Exchange,* the Reform organ edited by Charles Howard's son; flour merchant Charles Hinks, brother of a former Know-Nothing mayor now in the Reform Association, had called for better enforcement of the Fugitive Slave Law; Police Marshal George P. Kane owned slaves and offered to resign after Lincoln's election.[21] Invested with power in February, the new board purged the force of Know-Nothings: only four of fifty-nine officers identified in correspondence were Swann holdovers. It then arrested violent gang members. Among the notable cases, in August 1860 Joseph Edwards and other Tigers went on trial for the murder of Adam Kyle. "What a great change since November last," remarked Frederick Brune in the fall of 1860. "The rowdies are nowhere, except in jail."[22]

To counteract accusations of abolitionism, the Know-Nothing city council asked slave-state governments to fund a Baltimore "steam service between the Southern States and Europe" to compete with New York's trans-Atlantic lines. The South's Democratic legislatures rejected the request because they considered Baltimore's American Party an unreliable defender of Southern interests. North Carolina's governor, John Ellis, a secessionist, agreed that "an independent Southern trade with Europe is certainly much to be desired," but he refused to endorse the plan because "a representative of the City of Baltimore aided in placing at the head of one branch of our government a member of the Abolition party—a party whose aim is the overthrow of Southern independence and the destruction of Southern property"—a reference to Davis's vote for a Republican Speaker of the House.[23]

Supported by regional leaders, state government, and local police and courts, Baltimore Reformers approached the fall 1860 city elections with optimism. Reformers campaigned as the advocates of honest, nonpartisan government against the forces of violence and corruption. The backdrop of Know-Nothing outrages and claims that "the blood of the Kyles cries from the ground" framed this appeal. Reformers pledged "the retrenchment of expenditures to the lowest point" and vowed to "zealously cooperate with, and cordially aid, the Police Board . . . in its efforts to preserve and conserve the peace of the city, and redeem it from the disgrace of past lawlessness." Hitting their broadest theme, Reform editors stated that "while, therefore, we earnestly desire to see the present administration of the city wholly gotten rid of . . . that desire is altogether secondary to the paramount anxiety which we feel for the suppression of partisan municipal government altogether." The 1860 Reformers echoed the antipartisan ideals that contributed to the realignment of the Jacksonian parties, but instead of seeking to reconcile party differences, as earlier nonpartisans had done, the City Reform Association argued that Baltimore would be "redeemed" only by eradicating all traces of the American Party.[24]

Like most of his Reform colleagues, George William Brown, the movement's mayoral nominee and a former Whig, was a seasoned politician, but he nevertheless presented himself as an antiparty administrator who reluctantly came forward to serve the public good. Prophesying victory, Brown gloated that "the politicians are not as well satisfied as the people." However, instead of purifying government with new men, veteran Whigs and Democrats reinstated in office their old leaders and drove out Know-Nothings who had disrupted established government routines and agitated divisive social questions.[25]

Know-Nothings fought these charges by hurling antiparty rhetoric back at the Reformers. Baltimore Know-Nothings derided the Vigilance Committee, which tried to oust the New Orleans American Party regime as a crass ploy designed to put government into "the arms of the old Democratic wire workers." Daniel H. McPhail, Maryland's lottery commissioner and a gang favorite, warned that "already have desperate politicians . . . begun to talk of a Vigilance committee in the 'Monumental city.'" Criticizing the use of state militia in municipal elections,

Governor Hicks said "the reverence for law and order, and for the as-certained popular will . . . seems to be in danger of utter extinguish-ment by that violent spirit of party, which can invoke such means to overawe the free right of suffrage, and which may finally attempt to se-cure to itself the possession or continuance of power at the expense of civil war." Know-Nothings had their own antiparty tradition, and the use of this rhetoric by both sides deepened their mutual dislike.[26]

This mean-spirited competition could disrupt the cross-party friend-ships that politicians usually enjoyed. Away from the campaign trail, Henry Winter Davis had helped opposition leaders with personal busi-ness that came before Congress. Such deals were often arranged at the Friday Club, a lawyers' discussion group that included leading Demo-crats and Reformers like Brown. In late 1859, the club expelled Davis for his role in election violence. Days before the 1860 presidential elec-tion, Brown and his brother-in-law, Frederick Brune, encountered Davis on the streets. "Though we determined to speak to him and looked at him to do so," Brune wrote, "he sternly looked ahead—and wouldn't give us a chance." Davis dismissed the Friday Club as a haven for "Brecks" (i.e., supporters of Southern Rights presidential candidate John C. Breckinridge). Later, Davis warned President Lincoln that Bal-timore's Reformers "were generally disunionists." Baltimoreans con-fronted the secession crisis after having fought an intensely partisan local battle that disrupted normal political practice and fused those grudges onto the national divisions emanating out of the sectional conflict.[27]

In 1860 the Baltimore Bills and the enthusiasm of Democrats for a coercion-free election proved too much for the Know-Nothings. In a day of peaceful balloting, Brown triumphed by nearly two votes to one over American Samuel Hindes, one of the nonpartisan candidates to upset Democrats in 1853. Brown's overwhelming majority in 1860—he won every ward—included votes from Know-Nothings, one of whom admitted that the party had been defeated "by our own votes." Brown did particularly well in the wealthiest wards, receiving the fewest votes in ones with concentrations of native-born workers, a further indication that businessmen had abandoned the Americans.[28]

Brown's nonpartisan argument won over many Know-Nothings, but partisanship had not evaporated. Less than a month later, Baltimoreans split their presidential ballots between Breckinridge, who won a 49 per-cent plurality, and Constitutional Unionist John C. Bell, who finished second, with 42 percent. Voting corresponded to the Know-Nothing-era pattern. Breckinridge won in areas of traditional Democratic strength; Bell carried American wards, including those of wealthy Know-Nothings who had supported Brown. Bell won working-class west Baltimore and three of the five wards with high concentrations of white-collar workers. The association of Know-Nothings with Unionism made Brown, a pro-Bell Reformer, "dislike the company in which it places me" and helped persuade his Democratic supporters to back Breckinridge. Breckinridge lost the support of Brown voters outside of the old Jacksonian Democratic base.[29]

Despite the Reformers' hope for the suppression of partisan municipal government, conflict based on party identity shaped the presidential election. Pro-Breckinridge Reformers argued that their revolution against the disruptive politics of the late 1850s could be secured only when Know-Nothings lost the chance to regain power via federal intervention. The *Exchange* tried to fuse local and sectional arguments by telling readers that "the Bell and Everett party is . . . the discarded and defeated Know-Nothing faction," and the "plainest duty of the people of Maryland" was to "defend the principles for which the South now contends."[30]

The successive shocks to public opinion leveled by a presidential election, secession, an economic panic, the outbreak of war, and a major riot accelerated the process through which Baltimoreans turned their inclinations on Union and secession into firmly held convictions. However, despite shifts in momentum that short-term events gave to each side, the Civil War came to Baltimore primarily as an extension of the earlier fight over its insurgent American Party regime. From November to April, outright secession and unconditional Unionism had few Baltimore advocates. Enfranchised city dwellers supported stricter enforcement of the Fugitive Slave Law and the Crittenden Compromise—a plan to eliminate federal involvement in the slavery controversy—and they listened with interest to John Pendleton Kennedy's proposal for a border-state confederacy that would eventually force all parties back into the Union. Firm Unionists pledged that, should such schemes fail, "we will and do adhere to the union of the States and the constitution with all the tenacity of affection that we may command so long as it may be possible to dispense justice to every section under them."[31]

That position differed from the view of men who put a priority on slavery and states' rights and who wanted Governor Hicks to let the General Assembly debate disunion or at least pledge Maryland's opposition to coercion of the seceding states. A January meeting expressed this cautious commitment to the South by resolving that in the event of an impasse, they would "cast our lot with Virginia and the other slave-holding states of this confederacy." Within an overall consensus that valued peace and preservation of the Union with slavery, political participants divided between firm Unionism, on the one hand, and sympathy with the South and a conditional Unionism, on the other. Probably the most accurate contemporary assessment of the city's view on secession came from businessman Henry Lowe. "There is a strong Union feeling here, but no dispensation to aid the government against the South."[32]

The durability of 1850s party allegiances demonstrated in November also characterized support for the winter's public meetings held by Unionists and Southern sympathizers. A majority of rally officers had been active in party politics. Among the Unionists, Know-Nothings and Whigs predominated, but enough Democrats joined them to lend credence to a federal sympathizer's January boast that "the Union meeting here was a crusher, composed as it was of all parties." Their opposition drew more exclusively on Democrats. Of the ninety-three officers of Southern Rights meetings, more than half were Democrats and only six had been Whigs or Americans.[33]

The survival of 1850s partisan identities contributed to the failure of Republicans to win over Baltimore Unionists. In 1856, mobs broke up Republican rallies, and John C. Fremont, their presidential nominee, received less than 1 percent of Baltimore's vote. Baltimore's Republican leaders—a Quaker, a New Englander, and a German communist—lacked political experience or mainstream credentials, unlike prominent St. Louis Republicans Frank Blair, a former Democrat, and Edward Bates, a former Whig, who had held office under the old parties. In 1860, violence still threatened Republican Party meetings in Baltimore, and Lincoln finished last in the city with one-tenth as many votes as Bell. Know-Nothings refused to abandon their standard for the Republicans.[34]

During that campaign, Americans promoted Bell over Lincoln, routinely derided Republicans as "nigger-worshippers," and mobbed a meeting of the state Republican committee. A local Republican reported to a national leader that "our enemies are growing bolder in their interpretations of us, and they do not spare the rod when they get a chance to put it on thick. The Bell men are really worse upon us than the Democratic wings." In June, only 12 out of 160 members in the Baltimore Republican Association had been Know-Nothings. Most ex-Americans had the notation "11th hour man," or late arrival, next to their name. William Schley, one of these latecomers, assured American Governor Hicks that he supported slavery. If the Republican Party "interfere . . . with the domestic institutions in all of the States, or in any State, I would in a second separate myself from it." In April 1861, Hicks admitted to Lincoln that "I had done all properly in my power to prevent your election." Democrats erred when they cast doubt on Know-Nothings support for slavery. When given the chance to back Lincoln, Baltimore's American Party refused.[35]

After Lincoln's victory, Know-Nothings, who still represented Baltimore in federal offices despite their municipal defeat, adopted the "Union party" label, but continued to denounce abolition. In December 1860, John Pendleton Kennedy blamed secession on an irresponsible "parade of idle and mischievous debate" over sectional issues, not a substantive difference over slavery, which he said was "a clear gain to the savage it has civilized." His brother Anthony walked a similar line, asking the U.S. Senate in January 1861, "[I]s there no real cause for alarm in the Southern States . . . when Mr. Seward declares boldly that the election of Lincoln is the downfall of slavery?" Congressman James Morrison Harris proposed a compromise that would have had Southern legislatures repeal secession ordinances in exchange for a constitutional amendment prohibiting federal interference with slavery in the territories. Although they were Unionists, Baltimore Know-Nothings continued to adamantly defend slavery.[36]

Henry Winter Davis was the most likely convert from American to Republican, but even he tried to keep the parties separate and thereby avoid the proslavery backlash that fusion would bring. Unlike other Baltimore Know-Nothings, Davis advocated an end to slavery's expansion. Lincoln even offered him the vice presidential nomination, but Davis declined because Lincoln refused to abandon the Republican Party. "You know the power of names enough," Davis told his brother, "to know that till [Lincoln's] presidency is developed and our people begin to feel confidence in him personally it will be impossible to carry the state for him under the name Republican." After November, Davis pressed Lincoln to downplay free-soilism. Arguing that the ratio of Republicans to Know-Nothings in Maryland was "as 2,000 is to 40,000," Davis believed that his party brethren "can be won to support your administration if you will allow them to see in it something besides the representatives of a northern antislavery policy."[37]

While American Party leaders saw themselves as responsible Unionists opposed to Republican "mad men," the small contingent of Baltimore Lincoln voters deeply resented Know-Nothing tactics. A Republican lawyer complained that "Davis is cowering from the reproach of
Republicanism but planning to derive the highest honors from its success." To distance themselves from charges of colluding with free-soilers, Know-Nothings joined in the attack on the Republicans, but in so
doing they contributed to the proslavery mood that inhibited support
for unconditional Unionism during the secession winter of 1860–61.[38]

Whereas Know-Nothings worried about national politics and allegations that they coddled abolitionists, Brown's Reform administration
saw danger in a local challenge from disgruntled workers that could
bring civil war to the city because of strong associations of past labor
conflicts with party identities that had now become sectionalized. The
Brown administration succeeded in cleansing city government of Know-
Nothing partisans and dismantling Swann's patronage machine. Brown
followed through on his campaign promise to sack municipal employees "concerned in the many outrages that have been perpetrated on the
citizens of Baltimore for the last five or six years."[39] To rein in spending
on public works, Reformers eliminated or consolidated several departments, blocked construction of the city passenger railroad, cut money
to deepen the harbor, and forced private subscribers to fund the purchase of Druid Hill Park. In their short reign, Reformers slowed the
growth rate of municipal borrowing by one-fourth and nearly halved
the floating debt used to pay off existing claims.[40]

Spending cuts pleased businessmen unhappy about debt's impact
on commerce and taxes, but such parsimony angered working-class voters, who had welcomed Know-Nothing public works relief in past re-
cessions and who had lost jobs during the secession-related economic
slowdown. Both rich and poor worried about the troubled economy. As
early as November 1860, a merchant noted "an utter want of confidence"
among his colleagues. Two banks failed, port arrivals and rail traffic declined, canneries and foundries reported layoffs, and a builder claimed,
"There is much less doing at this moment than ever before in my
knowledge." In the first half of March 1861, more than five thousand
people sought aid from the Poor Association, more than in the entire
month a year earlier, and according to one estimate fifteen thousand laborers were out of work. The crisis continued into late April, at which
time a city dweller said that "all kinds of business that I know anything
about is prostrate. I really do not know where very many get bread."[41]

Calls for relief mounted in the spring of 1861. One group asked for jobs in public works on the grounds that "a large number of Mechanics and laboring men have been thrown out of employment and . . . many are suffering for the necessaries of life." East-side "citizens and tax payers" urged the city council to build roads to ease the burden on private charities. "Many there are in our midst that are entirely destitute of food to support their needful wants, although the more fortunate have given liberally yet it does not appear reasonably that this class can give that relief that would be desirable." Petitioned steadily since February, on March 27 the council appropriated $20,000 for park building.[42]

Negotiations for public works touched on old wounds related to the labor activism of the 1850s. On April 5, a new association of the unemployed led by Thomas Saville, a former Know-Nothing policeman and future Union volunteer, proposed a march with banners reading "Work or Bread!" Saville claimed that "the merchants and bosses desired to crush the poor working man." Arguing that the relief daily wage of 75 cents could not support families, he warned that "it is necessary that something should be done in relieving the necessities of the unemployed, otherwise, as necessity knows no law, and self-preservation is the first law of nature, they will be forced to seek for sustenance for themselves and families in any manner that presents itself." Although some Democratic leaders had endorsed the earlier relief campaign, only one of the April 5 rally officers had been a politician, while eight were veterans of the Know-Nothing police, of gangs, or of both.[43]

Reformers viewed this and other labor unrest as a question of law and order. The city council refused to consider the April petition, and the *Exchange* declared that "when the threat is openly made, that if [the city council] do not give bread . . . bread will be taken by force in spite of them, they will owe it to themselves and the people they represent, to make the most determined stand, at the threshold, against any and every such inadmissible and criminal resolution." The next week, Reformers applied this doctrine to a strike at the iron foundry of Adam Denmead, a Whig and early Know-Nothing who, in 1859, had quit the party to run for state office as a Reformer. When some employees turned out to protest wage cuts, a judge issued arrest warrants for strike leaders, one of whom went to jail for conspiracy.[44]

Remarkably, both sides in the debate over public works backed away from a showdown. Saville's group softened its rhetoric. On April 10, they told the council that they were "grateful to your honorable body for the appropriation of $20,000 you have already made, and feel assured that it is only necessary to make known to your honorable body the sufferings now in our midst to procure your sympathy and aid." Accepting this overture, the city spent an additional $22,918 to dredge the harbor and Jones Falls. Despite their cost-cutting rhetoric, Reformers created more than one thousand relief jobs in hopes of avoiding a confrontation with labor that in combination with national events threatened their destruction.[45]

The compromise over public works prevented a recurrence of strike-related violence that had broken out in 1853 and 1857, but because of the Reform administration's otherwise hostile treatment of Know-Nothing partisans and their policies, this olive branch failed to establish bipartisan support for city government. Instead of getting rid of partisanship in city politics, Reformers had simply gained the upper hand over their rivals, who continued to look to their own leaders for direction on local and national issues. An absence of community consensus predisposed Baltimoreans to fall out with each other as the Civil War approached.

Having set aside political violence in the fall of 1860, Baltimoreans turned to it again as the secession crisis intensified. The first major public disorder related to sectionalism occurred on February 23. Between ten thousand and fifteen thousand people who had gathered for Abraham Lincoln's arrival on his way to his inauguration demonstrated in anger upon discovering that he had passed through secretly the evening before. By April, each morning brought hundreds to the newspaper offices to read the latest headlines posted on bulletin boards. Unionists congregated at the *Baltimore American*'s posting sometimes scrapped with Southern sympathizers at the nearby *Sun* building.[46]

The firing on Fort Sumter on April 12 and Lincoln's call three days later for seventy-five thousand volunteers to defend federal property in the seceding states threw gasoline on these smoldering sectional feelings. "Never before," a reporter observed, "have the citizens . . . been laboring under such a perfect *furore* of excitement." On April 13, Unionists led by the Minute Men militia, formerly a pro-Bell political club, attacked a North Carolina man wearing a secession cockade. Shortly thereafter, the Minute Men and local German turnverein militia left to defend Washington, D.C. On April 15, two thousand Unionists and Southern sympathizers clashed in downtown Baltimore. Smaller battles broke out at flag raisings and rallies. Striving to preserve order, Kane's police closely watched Know-Nothing gangs. They arrested Erasmus Levy and two other Regulators—both of whom later served in the Union army—for disrupting a public rally. As Northern troops began arriving in Baltimore en route to Washington, hostile crowds were menacing, but let them pass without bloodshed. On April 18, after learning that Virginia had moved toward secession, Southern sympathizers vowed to "repel, if need be, any invader who may come to establish a military despotism over us."[47]

The explosion occurred on April 19. That morning, a train carrying seventeen hundred Union volunteers from Massachusetts and Pennsylvania arrived at President Street Station, terminus of the Philadelphia, Wilmington, & Baltimore Railroad. President Station was located just east of the Basin, and more than a mile from Camden Station to the Basin's southwest, starting point for Washington-bound trains. To get there, the troops, like all other travelers, had to cross city streets. For four hours, a crowd of thousands jeered, set up barricades, and physically assaulted Massachusetts soldiers struggling to make their way along Pratt Street toward the southbound train. Friends of the Union battled on the side of the troops. Some fighting occurred away from the rail stations. Southern sympathizers destroyed the presses of the German-language antislavery newspapers. On the south side's Federal Hill, between one hundred and five hundred industrial workers, including some former Tigers, routed a smaller party trying to fire a salute to the Confederacy. The political elite also fell out. At City Hall, Judge Benjamin C. Presstman threatened to cut off the nose and ears of Judge Hugh Lennox Bond, a Unionist. The violence ended when the Sixth Massachusetts Regiment departed for Washington, and the hapless Pennsylvania volunteers either fled on foot or returned north on the train that brought them. Thirteen soldiers and twelve civilians died in the riot, and scores more were injured.[48]

In the three-week period of "armed neutrality" that followed, Southern-sympathizing Reformers pushed Baltimore toward secession. City government garrisoned itself against federal attack. Police and militia burned the northbound railroad bridges, cut the telegraph to Washington, removed navigational buoys from the harbor, and patrolled the outskirts of the city, paying special attention to Union encampments at Cockeysville and Fort McHenry. Brown embargoed commerce and asked local financiers for $500,000. Bowing to intense pressure, Hicks convened the legislature. On April 24, Baltimore elected an uncontested slate of self-proclaimed Southern and States' Rights candidates to replace the ousted Know-Nothing delegation.

Municipal officials quickly enrolled approximately fifteen thousand men into militia units to defend Baltimore from invasion. The volunteers included adventure seekers from the countryside, government workers, and Democratic rowdies. Militiamen raided armories and gun shops. Brown, while denying the riot's secessionist impulse, admitted that militia volunteers "hoped for war," and many later joined the Confederate armed forces. Governor Hicks had enough doubts about the militia's loyalty to confiscate their weapons in late May.[49] With help from Kane and Brown, militia commander Isaac Trimble, later a Confederate general, paid Virginia's military for munitions. Since March, the Confederate government had been recruiting troops in Baltimore, and after the riot, Jefferson Davis sent a representative to the Maryland legislature to promise $2 million in aid should they secede. North and South Carolina also sent arms, and Virginia troops at Harper's Ferry debated marching to Baltimore.[50]

The weekend after the riot, mobs raided the armory of the German Turner militia and stoned the home of a Lincoln customs appointee. Prominent Unionists like Henry Winter Davis and abolitionist rabbi David Einhorn fled north, while city police and militia arrested and disarmed those who stayed behind. When Henry Hoffman, Lincoln's choice to head the Baltimore customs house, tried to enter the city on April 22, train passengers cried that a "Black Republican traitor . . . was aboard & ought at once be taken from the cars." Hoffman reached Baltimore, but after witnessing "the excited state of feeling" he returned to his native Cumberland. Brown ordered national flags lowered to discourage attacks on Unionist homes. Although they would later deny it, Lincoln believed that the post-riot actions of Brown and other city officials demonstrated their "unmistakable complicity with those in armed rebellion against the Government of the United States."[51]

Shouting "Keep back, men, or I shoot," Police Marshal George P. Kane enabled the Massachusetts volunteers to escape by placing himself and fifty officers between them and the mob. Police wanted to avoid the consequences attending federal casualties, and the mob cooperated because it considered the police to be allies in their larger cause. However, police efforts to avoid bloodshed should not be taken as support for the Union. Kane later served as a Confederate colonel. During the riot, he walked with a man bearing a South Carolina flag that had been paraded in front of the Massachusetts troops. Kane also telegraphed Frederick secessionist Bradley T. Johnston to "send expresses over the mountains and valleys of Maryland for the riflemen to come without delay. Fresh hordes will be down on us tomorrow. We will fight them and whip them or die."[52]

Police quickly released the few rioters they chose to apprehend. One officer told rioters he would make no arrests and urged them to loot arms stored at City Hall. Another claimed that policemen disliked a colleague "as he was a Union man." The police board also funded weapons for Southern-sympathizing militia. A militia volunteer recalled that after the riot, city government directed his unit to "assist the police to scatter the body of armed men who called themselves 'Union' men. . . . Word was passed around among the men to give them no quarter if we got a chance to attack them."[53]

Like the Reform police, state troops that defended the city in late April had earlier fought Know-Nothings and workers. In 1857, the First Light Division had put down the B&O strike and stood ready to guard Baltimore polls. After John Brown's raid, it patrolled the vicinity of Harpers Ferry. Their chief, George H. Steuart, a slaveholder who later commanded the Confederacy's Maryland Line, believed the secessionist fable that black votes in the free states had given Lincoln the presidency. He protested as "a violation of my rights . . . the deliberate and intentional extension of the elective franchise to a single negro." Like other urban secessionists, militia volunteers blended local partisan grudges with racial and proslavery arguments publicized farther south.[54]

Appointed by Democratic presidents prior to 1861, Southern sympathizers in the customs service acted as street-level enforcers of the ideological fusion of sectionalism and party identity. At least eleven customs employees rioted on April 19. They showed off captured Massachusetts rifles and proclaimed "this will tell the time of day." John Thompson Mason, the collector of the port, used his office as the headquarters for Southern Rights organizing, joined the April riot, and later took a commission in the Confederate navy. In early May, thirty-seven customs officials followed Mason's earlier decision to resign in protest of Lincoln's policies.[55]

During the height of Know-Nothing election violence, Democrats used the U.S. Customs House as a paramilitary base, a function similar to the one taverns served for nativist gangs. John Lutz and Samuel McElwee, customs workers involved in the attack on Union troops, had brawled for Democrats at the Eighth Ward polls. Customs officials sometimes provided bail money for Democratic gang members arrested by Know-Nothing police. Augustus Pennington, a Fifteenth Ward Reform candidate in 1859, had been threatened on election eve and was attending to the wounded George Kyle the next day when friends urged him to find cover. "I proceeded down to the United States Customs House," Pennington said, "which I considered the only safe place in the city except the eighth ward." What organization the April 1861 riot had came from armed customs workers like Lutz, captain of the customs police, who was observed "leading a crowd and saying he knew where to get guns."[56]

Lincoln's victory ended Democratic control of the customs house and closed off an important counterweight to Know-Nothing municipal power. Early in 1861, a Democratic patronage official lamented that "it is all a scramble now for the spoils, and the American Party are making desperate efforts to get control of the Balto Post Office and Custom House." Customs officials had close ties to Democratic merchants trading on the seas, and in 1861 these groups stood together in defiance of the new Republican federal administration that threatened the commerce of the slave states and the political fortunes of Democrats.[57]

The April 19 rioters and the supporters of armed neutrality are prime subjects for analyzing the constituency of secession in slave-state cities like Baltimore. Social data exist for 159 men identified as either attacking the troops or demonstrating for the South.[58] Most important in this group were "gentlemen of property and standing" involved in water-born commerce and the Democratic Party. A smaller number of immigrant workers joined them. These groups forged a patron-client alliance resembling that of black caulkers and white shipbuilders or New York City's draft-resisting Irish dockers and Democratic merchants trading with the South.[59] This Southern-sympathizing minority traced its lineage back to the six-year struggle against the Know-Nothings.

Although many local businessmen opposed secession, the most common occupations for rioters were merchant, clerk, or other commercial pursuit. More than one-half of the identifiable rioters practiced nonmanual trades; more than one-half were employed in commerce or transportation; and fewer than one-eighth worked in industry. The mob averaged $9,879 in real and personal property listed in the federal census. There were more rioters worth upwards of $1,000 than there were ones with no property at all—this in a city where the median holding was zero. As one trader wrote, "the merchants and all the best citizens (not the rowdies) armed themselves to prevent more troops from passing through the city."[60]

The majority of the rioters (68 percent) hailed from Maryland or one of the other slave states; one-fourth came from a foreign country, and very few had Northern roots. Irish workers sympathized with the South to a greater degree than Germans, the other significant non-Anglo immigrant bloc. The Irish made up the largest group of foreigners rioting on April 19, Irish surnames stand out in the 24 April poll book of Southern Rights and States' Rights voters, and a smaller share of Maryland's Irish fought for the Union than did Germans. Nine of the seventeen Irish rioters identified in census records practiced unskilled and semiskilled trades, and they were all but two of the rioters holding such occupations for whom nativity could be determined. The Gamecocks, a predominantly Irish gang, composed a song to commemorate the April 19 actions of "gallant" John Quinn, a customs house boatman and storied Democratic rioter.[61]

In addition to Irish laborers, other subsets of the working class took part in the riot. George Konig, the secession flag bearer, was a second-generation German tavern keeper and Democratic brawler. Corsican barber Cypriano Ferrandini allegedly plotted Lincoln's assassination in February, and he helped threaten Judge Bond during the riot. Reminiscent of the cooperation between black caulkers and white shipbuilders, African-American sailors helped merchants construct barricades on Pratt Street and cheered Jefferson Davis. These rioters represented the various elements of low-skilled minority labor that nativist gangs had targeted in election riots and hate strikes during the 1850s.[62]

The demographic backgrounds of the rioters resembled those of the 9,578 men who voted on 24 April. Voters could either stay home, as thousands of Unionists did, or cast a ballot for the uncontested Southern and States' Rights ticket. Wealthy Maryland natives and poor immigrants comprised the bulk of the voters, while the middle class of skilled artisans shunned the polls. Voters held a median of $500 in property, and their per capita wealth was ten times the median for white Baltimoreans as a whole. Two-fifths worked in commerce, an economic field that employed only one-eighth of all city workers. Skilled artisans were underrepresented, given their share of the general population and electorate, whereas unskilled and semiskilled workers, who normally cast ballots at half the rate of their eligibility, voted in proportion to their share of the electorate. The Irish, 8 percent of Baltimore whites, made up 14 percent of the voters, and Germans turned out at a rate just ahead of their 17 percent share of the white population. Three-fourths of voters holding low-skilled jobs were born abroad, half of them in Ireland. Conversely, American natives, two-thirds of them Marylanders, made up 91 percent of the Southern Rights voters who practiced high-status, white-collar professions. Combining occupation and nativity, wealthy Maryland-born merchants were the most numerous, followed by penniless Irish laborers. Immigrant unskilled workers had innumerable informal contacts with Baltimore-bred merchants and clerks, who hired them on a need basis to move their commodities from wharf to market to rail depot. Their common battle against the Know-Nothings reinforced that bond, and their alliance continued to hold in the crisis atmosphere that followed the riot.[63]

In line with the dynamics of municipal reform, on April 24 propertyless immigrants voted for wealthy Democratic leaders, rather than their fellow workers. Reform publicist and attorney Severn Teackle Wallis led the Southern Rights delegation. Other candidates included John C. Brune, Frederick's brother, who was president of the Poor Association and the board of trade; T. Parkin Scott, a Roman Catholic attorney critical of nativism; and iron maker Ross Winans, whose opposition to strikes in 1853 and 1857 led him to the Reform cause. Winans's outspoken secessionism—he produced Confederate arms and, on April 18, urged resistance to federal troops—made him the first Baltimorean arrested for treason against the federal government. The non-elected leadership "was composed chiefly of old democrats," according to an insider, and included Adam Kyle Sr., who wanted to run to avenge "the assassination of his gallant son, by the roughs at the polls."[64]

The same upper-class and partisan Democratic cast characterized the "law and order" militia companies that Southern sympathizers, aided by $70,000 in state funding, had organized in the wake of John Brown's raid. The Maryland Guard, cofounded by George Kyle, was the most important of these units. One volunteer stated that on April 19 "we were on the side of the mob and we were sorely exercised in our mind as to how far our duty required us to go in the matter." Afterwards, the unit helped police burn the railroad bridges and arrest and disarm Unionists. Unlike working-class gangs and fire companies, young Democrats from merchant families predominated in the militia units. Clerks, merchants, and customs officials made up 69 percent of the Maryland Guard's 303 members. Confirming a federal officer's October assertion that "the Maryland Guard is in Virginia fighting for secession," 49 out of the 111 Guardsmen sampled, including Kyle, fought for the Confederacy, a rate five times higher than that for white men statewide. Maryland guardsmen belonged to prominent families like the Gilmors and the Howards, and they helped channel the energy of Reformers in the mercantile elite into the campaign against federal coercion.[65]

"Should this continue," wrote a Baltimore clerk a week after Lincoln's election, "I think all the merchants have to go overboard which are heavy engaged with the Southern States." The majority of businessmen, including representatives of large firms like Alexander Brown & Sons and eventually John W. Garrett at the B&O, backed the Union. They did so largely because of their extensive trade with the free states. Businessmen active in the secession movement, by contrast, tended to trade with the South and stood to gain by curtailing their dependence on Northern creditors. In the 1850s, they had expanded markets in the South and in Latin America, with some successes in dry goods, textiles, and fertilizers. Rioters involved in these efforts could rationalize the economics of secession, especially when business interests dovetailed with family and politics. After the riot, Samuel Wethered, a textile maker with Southern investments, urged his brother-in-law Daniel Barringer, a leading North Carolina politician, to send "arms and men" to stop the approaching "hordes from the North."[66]

For some businessmen, loyalty to Democrats and slaveholders inclined them toward secession in spite of their economic interests. Democratic shipbuilder John S. Brown, a veteran foe of Know-Nothing gangs and a relative of Eastern Shore slaveholders, backed secession, and his son joined the Confederate army. This decision hurt Brown financially. According to an acquaintance, he lost a federal patronage post "due to sympathy for the Southern cause," and closed his shipyard "in which he could not have remained much longer due to his Confederate sympathies."[67] Visiting Baltimore just before the riot, English reporter William Howard Russell believed that "the whole feeling of the landed and respectable classes is with the South." He attributed their motives to cultural sensibilities instead of financial concerns. "The dislike to the Federal Government at Washington is largely spiced with personal ridicule and contempt of Mr. Lincoln. Your Marylander is very tenacious about being a gentleman and what he does not consider gentlemanly is simply unfit for anything."[68] Rather than a simple question of profit, association with slaveholders farther South and involvement with local Southern-sympathizing Democrats persuaded some rich Baltimoreans to adopt the sectional views of their preferred civic leaders.

Immigrant supporters of secession exposed other facets of its flexible appeal. Some were wealthy merchants like the Brunes, the Kyles, and Robert W. Davis, an Irishman shot by Massachusetts troops. The Friedenwalds, a family of German-Jewish dry goods merchants who traded extensively in the upper South, advanced familiar ideas about abolitionist fanaticism and financial ruin, but they also connected states' rights arguments to German liberal fears of government tyranny. After Lincoln's election, Moses Friedenwald wrote that "if there is yet a bosom in the Old World wherein there is a spark for the freedom of man let it be smothered. Man must be oppressed, the Iron heel of tyranny must be felt, self government, I say, is a failure." A year later, Jonas Friedenwald, then a captain in a Virginia regiment, said that Union victory would "palsy the fervent emigrant from attempting to embark to a land of dissension, the asylum of the oppressed of all nations will be a land without law and Liberty." All sides claimed to defend freedom, but for immigrants involved in Southern commerce and suspicious of Know-Nothing Unionists, the Confederacy looked like the better defender of economic opportunity and civil liberty.[69]

As the demographic data show, upper-class leaders of the secession movement had some success in attracting immigrant workers near the bottom of the economy. Catholic owners of slaves in southern Maryland, Catholic politicians T. Parkin Scott and Roger B. Taney, and the Roman Catholic Church newspaper, the *Catholic Mirror,* lobbied the South's cause with Baltimore's Irish. Secessionist editor Thomas Hall, one of Robert W. Davis's pallbearers, played on the cultural insecurity produced during the Know-Nothing era. He ridiculed "the idea of Irishmen coming on here to fight the battles of a party that a very few years ago deprived them of the right to carry arms belonging to the state in Massachusetts, while the negro enjoyed the privilege of forming military companies—thus making the negro not equal but superior to the adopted citizen!" Long the targets of nativist politicians, some Irish workers allied with these wealthy Southern sympathizers, rather than cast their lot with former enemies who now dominated the Union movement.[70]

Secession's wealthy leaders drew workers to them via patron-client relationships that Democrats had earlier used to win loyalty from wage-earning blacks and immigrants persecuted by the American Party. Unlike New York's Civil War draft protesters, Baltimore's anti-Union rioters left African Americans alone. Some black sailors joined the April riot, and on April 22 approximately 350 free blacks "offered their services" to the Reform administration for local defense. Although Reform police monitored free black assemblies, a conference of the African Methodist Episcopal Church in late April offered a "vote of thanks" to city officials for their protection.[71]

Addressing the unemployed, Hall promised that "there will be work enough for all, to the remotest generation, in supplying the demands of Southern Commerce." A Reform public-works recipient claimed that on April 20 a factory owner asked "if I was out of work. [He] asked me to join the Southern Army." On the Monday following the riot, the city council appropriated an additional $3,000 for jobs in public works. A machinist who made Confederate arms explained that "he was a Union man, but had to work for a living." Notwithstanding the April strike at his ironworks, the employees of Reformer Adam Denmead, who built weapons for the militia, were among the few industrial workers to demonstrate for secession. Cypriano Ferrandini cut the hair of the mercantile elite at Barnum's Hotel, a rallying point for the April riot, and he used those connections to finance a militia unit that he commanded during the 1857 B&O strike and that Ross Winans funded in 1861. On April 22, a friend urged Mayor Brown to buy arms, expel federal troops from Maryland, and fund soup kitchens like one started by Winans's son Thomas and the widow of secessionist merchant George S. Brown. "It is important not only in view of the calls of humanity," read the advice, "but for other reasons which your known intelligence must perceive." By linking Southern rights to unemployment relief, the writer reminded Brown of the local and national dimensions of the crisis. He urged that patron-client relationships be used to broaden secession's urban appeal beyond a clique of merchants and lawyers.[72]

While slavery and states' rights mattered to Baltimore secessionists, the movement's coherence and its intensity derived from the association that Southern sympathizers—most of whom were Democrats and/or Reformers—made between Unionists and Know-Nothing rowdies. A secessionist paper called the federal sympathizers who rioted on April 19 "ex-members of Mayor Swann's police and Joe Edwards's crew of Tigers Eubolts &c.!" A merchant agreed that "all the disorder we have now is from the old clubs of 'Tigers, Roughs, and Plugs,' who are to a man 'Black Republicans,' and the only ones that we have in Baltimore." A militia volunteer claimed that city Unionists "were the same lot of Roughs whose killing of Adam Kyle was the reason for the formation of the Maryland Guard." McHenry Howard, Charles Howard's son, linked the battle against gangs to the defense of Southern rights.

"The outbreak of April 19th was not a return of mob law as Northern papers say. The roughs are Unionists. It resulted from the irrepressible indignation of the people at seeing armed men pass over our soil to subjugate our brethren of the South." The "roughs" had connections to the American Party of the 1850s, just as Howard, a Maryland guardsman and future Confederate officer, did to the Democrats.[73]

Although these justifications of the riot referred to local politics, their theme of responsible citizens standing up for their civil rights against street toughs and federal soldiers adopted the same imagery that secessionists in the lower South used in their appeal to the border states. In December 1860, Jabez L. M. Curry, an Alabama congressman representing the Confederate government, pitched secession to Governor Hicks as a defense of slaveholders' rights in the face of fanaticism and majoritarian tyranny. "I am firmly of the opinion that Maryland will not long hesitate to make common cause with her sister States which have resolutely and wisely determined not to submit to Abolition domination." Curry warned that "[w]hen Mr. Lincoln is inaugurated, it will not be simply a change of administration . . . but a reversal of the former practice and policy of the Government so thorough as to amount to a revolution. . . . The States whose property is thus condemned, are reduced to inferiority and inequality."[74]

Five months later, on May 2, 1861, Beale H. Richardson's *Republican* made the case for secession by associating the cause with Southern honor's emphasis on manly independence and equality. "There can be but two parties now in the state of Maryland—the friends of freedom and state's [sic] rights and the craven vassals of submission." Richardson described "this latter class" as those "who, for the paltry consideration of a temporary pecuniary gain, are willing to sacrifice the honor, the glory, and the interests of the state." Baltimore secessionists shared Curry's concerns about domination by a revolutionary majority, but they said less about defending slavery and instead emphasized their visceral partisan dislike for their local enemies, who many conflated with the Republican regime in Washington. Richardson made the connection clear. "Know-Nothing leaders and their ruffian bullies . . . have been taken up and are now the special pets of Lincoln and his administration." Equating submission to local foes with submission to national ones, Richardson vowed that "Baltimore will not be humiliated under Know-Nothing ruffianism again, under any name or flag which they choose to assume."

In the early 1850s, Baltimore's leading Democrats had moved closer to rural planters in their party. This alliance transformed local party allegiance so as to drive Democrats from power in 1854, even as it bound them more firmly to the sectional concerns of rural Marylanders. When, in 1860, Democrats regained control of city government under the guise of the Reform Association, they owed a great deal to their planter allies in the state legislature who had taken control of the police force and who worried about the city's loyalty to slavery and Southern rights. By late April 1861, circumstances had given Southern sympathizers in the Reform administration the momentum needed to stage the riot and the armed-neutrality standoff. Their brief ascendancy represented the maturation of a decade-long process of party competition that began with a crisis over sectional issues and, after attaching party loyalties to class and cultural divisions in urban society, returned in 1861 to those same concerns.

By the same token, the federal occupation of Baltimore gave leaders of the defunct American Party an opportunity to recapture office, but to do so they would have to reconcile themselves to the sectional policies of their Republican benefactors. Despite the outpouring of Southern sympathy on April 19, within days of the riot a few Unionists demonstrated in public. By early May, Unionists had regrouped to agitate for an end to the embargo and the dispersal of the pro-Southern militia. Meanwhile, federal troops occupied Annapolis and secured the rail connections around Baltimore. On May 13, General Benjamin Butler peacefully entered the city. Within a week, federal commanders had established military control that would last until war's end.[75]

Federal control of Maryland gave Baltimore Unionists less to fear from the abolitionist smear and more to gain by demonstrating their loyalty to Lincoln. Consequently, they moved closer to national Republican policy and made more strident attacks on Southern sympathizers. The day after Butler's arrival, an east-side rally called the April rioters "domestic traitors" and pledged its support for the Union military. Kennedy continued to attack antislavery agitation, stating that "we deplore the unfortunate ascendancy of the Republican Party," but he also predicted that "Maryland . . . must soon become a Free State." Although Henry Winter Davis was locked in a patronage fight with Montgomery Blair, Lincoln's postmaster general and Frank Blair's brother, he campaigned for reelection on an unconditional Union platform.[76]

The overwhelming prominence of sectionalism as a political issue in 1861 helped bring about the Know-Nothing rapprochement with Germans, a common theme of Unionist strategy in the urban South and the free states. During the congressional campaign, Davis addressed a meeting of German Unionists alongside Leopold Blumberg, a militia officer and merchant who began recruiting for the Union military after rioters looted his store. Liberal German immigrants had been among the few early supporters of the Republicans; the percentage of Germans serving in Maryland Union regiments (11 percent) nearly doubled their representation in the state's population (6 percent); and Germans made up a sizeable part of Baltimore's Union vote. Former Know-Nothings dropped their virulent nativism when they realized that German ballots would be essential for wartime political survival.[77]

As witnessed by the joint appearance of Davis and Blumberg, Unionism pushed the concerns of American-born workers and Protestant evangelicals into the background and thereby drew a broader coalition of supporters to the American Party in its new Union guise. American Party Unionists won over some former foes in the business community, most notably Garrett and the B&O. Industrialists and their creditors tended to back the Union. Manufacturers did more business with the North, had no use for slave labor, and resented rural opposition to state support for industry. Displaying the American Party version of the patron-client ties that had allied black caulkers and Irish laborers with secessionist merchants, on January 9, 1861, three thousand workingmen rallied for the Union at a meeting headed by industrial employers.[78]

Although Union and secession drew different types of businessmen to their standards, there were enough Southern sympathizing industrialists like Winans and slave-owning ironmaker Peter Mowell, on the one hand, and Unionist immigrant merchants like Blumberg and dry goods importer Charles Lenz, on the other, to blur a strict correspondence between allegiance and economic field. The most ardent advocates of either cause had formerly been active in party politics. Businessmen with little partisan history, for example Unionist banker Johns Hopkins, disengaged from party politics after 1861, while those who had been American Party officeholders, like Archibald Stirling, a banker who led the way in drafting Maryland's antislavery constitution in 1864, remained politically active after the initial crisis passed. That predisposition to rush headlong into political conflict separated these sectional activists from the mass of businessmen, who, like the major commercial associations, remained noncommittal during the secession crisis.[79] Muting one's partisanship made practical business sense in a city of the border South. A friend of iron makers Hayward, Bartlett, &

Company explained that "during the war, the firm, like most of Baltimore's business houses, evidently followed Br'er Fox's example and 'lay'd low,' for it was no time for any concern doing business in both the North and the South to seek publicity for fear of a partisan label."[80]

Because of Germans and some employers who had voted for Reformers in 1860, the Union cause in Baltimore drew on a broader base of support than had the late-1850s American Party. Nevertheless, former Know-Nothings constituted the militant vanguard of Baltimore Unionism. American-born workers and their street gangs, the core partisans of Know-Nothingism, were Unionism's paramilitary counterpart to Southern-sympathizing police and militia. On April 28, 1861, the Blood Tubs ignored police threats and circled the harbor in a schooner festooned with U.S. flags.[81] Two days before Butler's troops entered Baltimore, men in the Tigers enrolled in the second company of Union volunteers organized in Maryland. Later in May, the Black Snakes, a gang supportive of Henry Winter Davis, attacked friends of John Pendleton Kennedy, Davis's conservative rival for the Union Party congressional nomination. In June, James Manley, a Know-Nothing rowdy who fled to Philadelphia after attacking a policeman at the 1860 elections, returned to Baltimore in a Pennsylvania regiment and called for the hanging of George P. Kane. At a fall Democratic campaign rally, Rip Raps Gregory Barrett Jr., who later served as a Union army officer, and John Horner, described as "formerly a Swann policeman, and sometime inmate of the penitentiary, now an employee in the Custom House," sparked a melee by rushing the stage and giving "three cheers for the star spangled banner." In December, Davis said that his most loyal support came from Baltimore's "great mechanical class."[82]

When the war began, 48 percent of American Party gang members took up arms for the Union.[83] That level of service (more than double the 23 percent rate for fighting-age Maryland white men) was at par or above the average for all loyal states. By contrast, their rivals in Democratic gangs joined the federal military at the lower statewide rate and were more likely to don a Confederate uniform. Almost two-thirds of Know-Nothing gang members volunteered in 1861 and 1862, prior to effective federal conscription, which created more incentives to volunteer. The high rate of gang volunteers early in the war indicated gang members' commitment to the Union cause.[84]

The elements of a Republican electoral majority were in place by the summer of 1861, but unconditional Unionism, even with support for slavery, had yet to gain majority status with voters. In special elections for the U.S. House of Representatives on June 13, Henry May, a Democrat who proclaimed himself an "Independent Unionist," defeated Henry Winter Davis in the Fourth Congressional District. Unionists won an equivocal victory in the Third District. Know-Nothing Congressman J. Morrison Harris declined the Union nomination because he rejected "the idea of subjugating and holding the Seceded States by force." His replacement, Cornelius L. L. Leary, won, but he endorsed "Southern rights" and opposed the Republican Party's 1860 platform. Together, the Democratic candidates, neither of whom endorsed secession, garnered 54 percent of 25,284 ballots cast in Baltimore. The June elections showed that no sea change had occurred on slavery and that party divisions remained vital.[85]

In a matter of weeks, however, federal military intervention altered the balance of party power. Even before the riot of April 19, Republicans looked at Baltimore as a threat to military security and Maryland's loyalty. New York editor Horace Greeley contributed to this view by stating that Baltimore's "government was in the hands of the Breckinridge Democracy, who had seized it with the cry of reform; and the leaders of the Democracy were deep in the counsels of treason."[86]

As federal occupiers saw it, aside from helping the Sixth Massachusetts Regiment escape the mob, the Reform police had acted in league with the Confederacy. Howard and Kane refused to cooperate with searches for hidden arms. In late May, the police board investigated officers who testified against it to a grand jury. The board also fired eight men who refused to take down a U.S. flag. Individual officers continued to speak out for secession and got into scrapes with Unionists. Convinced that the Reform police "stealthily wait to combine their means and forces with those in rebellion," Middle Department commander Nathaniel P. Banks on June 27 arrested Kane and replaced him with a provost marshal responsible to the army. The subsequent discovery of arms caches in City Hall and other locations furthered federal suspicions of a police plot against the government. In August, John A. Dix, Bank's replacement, wrote that "we have no doubt the old city Police are busy stirring up disaffection. I shall arrest any one of them who is so engaged if I can obtain the proof." Other conspiracies allegedly included the militia volunteers and "men of rank Secession proclivities who have heretofore stood high in the estimation of our citizens." Rumored plots along with the threat of Confederate invasion, which appeared more likely after the federal defeat at Bull Run on July 11, motivated Unionists and federal authorities to apply a hard hand to Southern sympathizers.[87]

Lincoln's commitment to purging secessionists from Baltimore city government manifested itself in the imprisonment of Mayor Brown, the police board members and other municipal officials, and Baltimore's Southern Rights and States' Rights legislators later in the summer. Other indications that municipal government had someone looking over its shoulder included the stationing of federal troops at strategic points throughout the city and a ban on the display of Confederate symbols. In June, a young secessionist who had not left for Virginia wrote, "Tis by George an awful sight to see so many men with muskets, marching down to kill a fellow's best friends." By August small acts like cheering for Jefferson Davis could lead to arrest. In mid-September, Dix stopped publication of two pro-Southern newspapers and arrested their editors. That month, the state's attorney redressed the Reformers' lax prosecution of the April rioters by bringing several suspects to trial. By the time of the October city council election, the police had been reorganized, suppression of secessionists had increased, and local Unionists routinely denounced political opponents as traitors. Days before the vote, the *Baltimore American* asserted that "the union party in the state should omit nothing which can insure the utter demolition of the treacherous organization opposed to them."[88]

Federal intervention in local politics and the increasing association of Democrats with secession helped Know-Nothings consolidate their power in the Union party. Unionists nominated thirteen former Know-Nothings and no former Democrats to run for twenty First Branch (the legislative branch) city council seats. Pro-Union Democrats lost out to former Americans in ward-level nominating conventions, and those chosen by independent ward meetings refused to run. The unopposed Union slate won, but it polled only twenty more votes than the Southern and States' Rights ticket of April 24. These elections did not measure enthusiasm for the candidates' sectional stand so much as they showed that participation dropped off in contests with a preordained outcome.[89]

The final blow to Democratic power occurred at the November state elections. Democrats, this time called National Democrats, nominated for governor Benjamin Chew Howard, a member of a prominent political family, several of whom were either in federal prisons or Confederate units on election day. Although absent from most Maryland voting districts, Banks stationed federal troops at Baltimore's polls to "protect Union voters and to see that no disunionists are allowed to intimidate them, or to interfere with their rights." Election judges disqualified votes from suspected rebels, and federal police arrested 164 people, including some Democratic candidates, for acts of resistance to the government. Democrats cast their ballots freely, but the presence of soldiers dampened turnout (the 21,529 ballots represented the lowest total for a gubernatorial election since 1850) by convincing some Southern sympathizers to stay home. These tactics, along with Howard's association with secession and a poor campaign, contributed to the decisive triumph of Augustus W. Bradford, the Union nominee. In Baltimore, Bradford won 78 percent of the vote, and Union nominees swept the city's other races.[90]

As would occur throughout the South, the strongest proponents of disunion were the most likely to flee in advance of Union troops. Their departure meant that a large chunk of voters abstained from wartime elections. As early as April 28, 1861, Southern sympathizer Edward Spencer claimed that "5000 of the best citizens of Baltimore" had gone South to fight for secession. Modern estimates of Baltimore's Confederate volunteers run from four thousand to seven thousand, confirming Spencer's guess. Out-migration and loyalty oaths that disfranchised Confederates shrank by approximately one-third the base of Democratic voters pursued by its heirs, the Southern Rights and Conservative Union parties. Furthermore, the taint of disloyalty that hung over the Reform administration convinced some Democrats to drop the party.[91]

In the fall of 1860, both of Baltimore's major parties had defended the Union and slavery and had been competitive at the polls. In the course of one year, sectionalism had become so intertwined with party affiliation that former Know-Nothings dominated the city's Union municipal administration, and their old Democratic foes struggled to stay out of federal prison. In the midst of war, former Know-Nothings succeeded in convincing their voters and their federal allies to treat Democrats as the enemy.

The core group that moved from Reform to Breckinridge to decrying federal coercion and ultimately to secession failed miserably in bringing the rest of the city along to their final destination. Furthermore, while they had success against the Know-Nothings before April 1861, their revolution against political parties did not work out exactly as planned. Unlike the lower South's revival of one-party, or "no party," government in the late 1850s, big cities like Baltimore had socially diverse electorates that had been polarized in local struggles and could not be easily unified, especially by leaders strongly identified with recent conflicts. If the elimination of party competition made the lower South look northward for the ever-present threat to republican liberty, then antiparty rhetoric in cities like Baltimore encouraged a search for local as well as external agents of tyranny.[92] Instead of resolving local partisan differences, secession raised the stakes in an already bitter struggle.

Six

Redefining Southernness
Secession and the Civil War in Slave State Cities

The twin stories of secession and reform in Baltimore resembled events in the South's two other major cities, St. Louis and New Orleans. A comparison with these and smaller Southern cities highlights unique features of Baltimore's history and shows how party competition in the largest urban centers brought them into the Civil War on terms different than those experienced in most other slave-state communities. In the big three cities, the local contest between Democrats and an insurgent opposition party became enmeshed in state politics and the question of Union or secession. When the politics of the cities collided with the politics of the sections, municipal class and ethnic struggles became part of the battle that outsiders waged to bring the cities around to their side.

Having a municipal administration that was independent of the state legislature's Democratic majority did not automatically make a Southern city Unionist: Know-Nothings governed New Orleans, but secessionists won a majority there in a January 1861 special election. Rather than foster a uniform climate of opinion on sectional issues, the battle over opposition party politics created deep partisan divisions that attached themselves to urbanites' differing views on secession. Although Baltimoreans and their counterparts in St. Louis and New Orleans had plenty of reasons to avoid the perils of civil war, their recent political past predisposed them to apply the combative spirit of local politics to the divisive questions that tore apart the nation.

In smaller Southern cities, which also experienced conflict between Unionists and secessionists, party competition had vanished from their politics by the spring of 1861. Without a tradition of partisan mobilization, a smaller city's minority on the sectional question—Unionists in much of the South, but secessionists near the border—lacked the means to sustain an effective challenge to the consensus viewpoint reached by the local political elite. By 1861, partisanship had come into disrepute in Southern political culture. As did other Southerners, big-

city politicians disparaged partisan excess, but unlike government officials in places like Richmond and Savannah, they continued to struggle
with real party competition and its potential to spark collective violence.

The survival of politically driven antagonisms in the big cities fostered a unique brand of wartime social conflict not shared by the rest
of the South. Political partisanship not only made big cities organizing
ground for both Unionists and Confederates, it also set comparatively
rational and orderly boundaries for the internecine conflict that characterized the Civil War in some Southern subregions.

On the one hand, the introduction of divisive social conflicts over
class and ethnicity into party competition in the 1850s had made politics
more volatile and violent. On the other hand, the decade's new voters
had learned to act on local grudges through bureaucratic institutions —
parties before 1861 and armies thereafter. These institutions provided
a structure that contained social conflict even if it did not immediately
end it. In contrast, the split over Union and secession in the most divided
regions of the wartime South, the highland counties of Appalachia and
the Ozarks, descended into disorganized feuding that was difficult to resolve after the larger war ended. Unlike the big cities, wartime grudges
between individuals in the Southern Mountains persisted long past
1865 in the form of bloody ambushes on country roads and dynastic
quarrels between extended families. Guerilla war in the high country
made its mark on society and culture, rather than on politics. In large
cities, battles on the streets had intersected with battles on the campaign
trail before Fort Sumter, and the Civil War reinforced that identification
of political partisanship with deeply felt social antagonisms.

In the 1850s, Baltimore, New Orleans, and St. Louis diverged from
the political culture of their region. By the decade's end, Southern nationalists seeking to create an independent government for what they
argued was already an independent society began reading these pockets of political heterodoxy out of the list of Southern places. Already
under suspicion as un-Southern before 1861, the biggest cities of the
slave states entered the Civil War on their own unique terms and
drifted further from the regional norm as the war progressed.

Postwar Southerners looked back on their history from the perspective of a region characterized by military defeat, economic ruin, a
racial caste system, and one-party politics. In escaping the worst fighting of the war and in their diverse economies and populations, the
largest cities broke with these post–Civil War definitions of Southern-
ness. Yet the same held for Memphis and the New South's Birmingham,

and although they had been in the vortex of wartime conflict, life in postwar Richmond and Atlanta bore little resemblance to the experience of farmers in the Mississippi Delta or the Georgia Piedmont. Atlanta, Birmingham, Memphis, and Richmond remained part of the South because Southern identity was not exclusively rural. If the Civil War ended a tradition of combative party politics across the slave states, then the survival of that tradition in the largest Southern cities may be the most important marker that differentiated them from the section that surrounded them. Secession was a political act, and politics above all else explain how a city of regional anomalies like Baltimore fits into the history of the nineteenth-century South.

As in so much of its antebellum history, Baltimore's battle over municipal reform resembled but did not replicate events in other large Southern cities. Central to the political dramas playing out in Baltimore, St. Louis, and New Orleans was the survival of an opposition party in the face of a strong Democratic majority in the rest of the state and region. However, geography and demography led each municipal regime to approach party and sectional allegiance differently in 1860 and 1861. In comparison with the South as a whole, the onset of civil war in St. Louis and New Orleans shows how the dynamics of Southern urban growth shaped a common early wartime experience for the biggest cities. Yet when compared with each other, the history of the secession crisis in the slave states' two other major metropolitan centers puts into relief Baltimore's middle-of-the-road stand on Union and secession.

In St. Louis, ethnicity, sectionalism, and the panic of 1857 redrew the lines of party affiliation. In 1856, self-styled Emancipation Democrats, opponents of slavery's expansion, won the major city offices and sent Frank Blair, whom the Republican Party also endorsed, to Congress. That election ended Know-Nothing rule in St. Louis, but it did not bring unquestioned free-soil dominance. In 1858, Blair lost his seat to a proslavery National Democrat, Richard Barrett. A Know-Nothing candidate siphoned anti-Democratic votes away from Blair, and mobbing by what a Blair supporter called "a ring of Irish bullies" aided Barrett. In that year's state senate contests, Democrats defeated B. Gratz Brown, who had recently advocated gradual emancipation.[1]

When St. Louis free-soilers regained office in 1859 and 1860, they did so with a new label, Republican, and an altered coalition of supporters, Germans and antislavery former Know-Nothings. In their early 1850s break from the Democratic Party, free-soilers had done better among lifelong Democrats, and because free-soilers also opposed nativism they won votes from all immigrant groups, including the Irish. The decline of the Know-Nothings ended the temporary alliance of German and Irish behind the followers of Thomas Hart Benton. The Know-Nothing common enemy had disappeared, and immigrants more concerned with the civil rights of the foreign-born than with stopping slavery's expansion resented free-soil leaders, like Blair and Edward Bates, a former Whig, who had flirted with nativism.[2]

The 1858 elections showed free-soilers that German votes would be central to their future in St. Louis. The presence of a Know-Nothing negated any support Blair might have won from foes of immigration (he garnered only 10 percent of the non-German vote), yet Blair still managed to finish fewer than five hundred ballots behind Barrett. Thereafter, Republicans stepped up their appeals to Germans, and Blair recruited a cadre of armed German "Wide Awakes" to counteract Democratic gangs.[3]

Meanwhile, proslavery Democrats won back the support of the city's Irish. Friends of the South distinguished between the "black Dutch," allied with Blair, and the Irish, who had a stronger bond to the Democratic Party. As in Baltimore, St. Louis's Irish Catholic minority sought federal patronage from the Buchanan administration as a reward for voting Democratic. In one such request, J. V. Huntington, a local Roman Catholic journalist, asked a prominent Missouri Democrat "whether the party in the State, owes us anything, either for local support, or for our support of the cause of the South generally?"[4]

Along with such material incentives, ethnic conflict with Germans pushed the St. Louis Irish toward the Democrats. In St. Louis, German Protestants and free-thinkers accused the "miracle-working" Roman Catholic Church of delivering fraudulent votes for the Democrats. Native-born Republicans exacerbated the split by showing more animosity toward the Irish than the Germans. In a diary entry, a young, U.S.-born merchant loyal to the Republicans praised both a German celebration of Schiller's birthday ("Schiller's Hundredth birthday. May his name long live with the many works he left behind") and reported with satisfaction that fire companies had allowed buildings in the "*Star of Erin*" neighborhood to burn "to the ground, and everybody seemed to be very happy on the '*Strength*' of it."[5]

The boldness of Blair's Wide Awakes produced a reaction by the city's Irish militia, the Montgomery Guards and the Washington Guards. They decided to cooperate with the Minute Men, who, unlike the Baltimore group, were a Southern-sympathizing militia unit. In 1860, Irish units joined an expedition to drive free-soil Jayhawker paramilitaries from western Missouri. Rising bitterness between Irish and German militiamen peaked during the Camp Jackson riot in May 1861, when six Irish Catholics died at the hands of German Union volunteers.[6]

The economics of urban growth also affected partisanship. In general, business leaders were conservative, hoping first and foremost for peace. That outlook resonated with St. Louis's status as a border city that traded with both sections and that hoped to expand trade via federally supported rail connections to the west. Among political partisans, businessmen who in 1850 had been Whigs opposed to Benton's hard money policies joined the Republican coalition after Benton retired and former Whigs like Bates gained prominence in the party. Republican businessmen tended to concentrate on manufacturing and railroading, industries that drove the city's late-antebellum growth. For example, Oliver and Chauncey Filley, Republican mayors during the late 1850s and the war, belonged to a family of Connecticut stove makers that moved to St. Louis in the 1830s. By the end of the decade, Blair and the Republicans had won over St. Louis entrepreneurs opposed to the proslavery and antiurban sentiments of Democrats in state government.

As in Baltimore, Democrats drew support from a different segment of the business community—families who either traded with the South or were involved in older enterprises like the fur trade and real estate. Hard times associated with the panic of 1857 and the proslavery image that had been earned for Missouri by Democrats' intervention in Kansas reversed the Jacksonian-era influx of New England businessmen. Smaller merchant houses that traded with the lower Mississippi and Ohio River systems took the places vacated by northeasterners, and they adopted the proslavery allegiance of the city's old-money Creole families—like the Bertholds, who turned their estate into the headquarters of the Minute Men militia. As in Baltimore, St. Louis secessionists came from the upper classes, but they recruited allies among working-class Irish immigrants. For example, the Minute Men drew their leaders and most soldiers from mercantile families, but they also admitted some Irish dock workers.[7]

In St. Louis, party affiliation, which by 1860 also indicated sectional allegiance, corresponded fairly neatly to place of birth. Republicans drew their strength from free-state natives and immigrants from continental Europe, whereas Democrats counted on the Irish and settlers from the South. The early arrival of Republicans in St. Louis helped to clarify lines of ethnic allegiance on sectional issues that the lasting presence of nativist Know-Nothings had muddied in Baltimore and New Orleans.

The alliance between German liberals and native-born Unionists helped to make the opposition party leaders in St. Louis outspoken critics of slavery in ways that politicians in Baltimore and New Orleans avoided. Exchanges of partisan vitriol were both cause and effect of the Republican inability to attract rural allies. Echoing the charges of corruption and abolitionism that Maryland Democrats hurled at Baltimore Know-Nothings, Missouri's Democratic governor, Claiborne Fox Jackson, called his foes "Black Republican[s] of the blackest hue." St. Louis German radicals reciprocated by calling Southern nationalists "burned-out and demoralized mongerers of human flesh." This mutual hatred gave Missouri Republicans little hope for a victory beyond the confines of St. Louis. In 1860, Abraham Lincoln won a plurality in St. Louis, marking his only significant showing in a slave state, yet he and the Republican gubernatorial nominee garnered few votes elsewhere in Missouri. A German editor stated that "St. Louis has the character of a free state, a virtual enclave in this region of slavery. This circumstance places it in political isolation . . . and cripples its influence."[8]

In 1860, Baltimore Know-Nothings remained a viable party in state politics (they had recently elected a governor from the slaveholding Eastern Shore), and they sidestepped criticism of slavery or praise of Republicans in order to attract sectional moderates. In each big city, the opposition party won votes by standing against the planter-dominated Democratic Party that controlled the state legislature. However, only St. Louis Republicans included criticism of slavery in their attack on rural domination. In the convention balloting, moderate Unionists captured 80 percent of the votes and captured almost all of the seats. Although four St. Louis Republicans won election to the convention, the majority of city dwellers occupied a middle ground that supported the Union as long as Lincoln defended slavery and avoided coercing states that had already seceded. Aware of this sentiment prior to the presidential election, Republican Thomas Gantt believed that "[d]isunion has no friend here . . . but those who are most anxiously looking to what the fools of the South may do are to be counted by the thousands."[9]

The polarization of city and countryside set the stage for a clash between Union and secession forces in St. Louis in May 1861 that was analogous to Baltimore's April riot. Despite endorsing Union Democrat Stephen Douglas for president, after Lincoln's victory Governor Jackson and the legislature's Democratic majority called an election for a convention to reconsider Missouri's relationship to Washington. In the run up to the February 18 election, the state legislature tried to undermine Republican influence in St. Louis. In January, Lieutenant Governor Thomas Caute Reynolds traveled to the city to drum up support for the Minute Men, and various state officials made heavy-handed inquiries about the weapons stored at the federal arsenal in St. Louis. The Republican city administration responded by organizing a Committee of Safety on January 11 to counteract secessionist threats. By the middle of February, federal troops at the arsenal had been reinforced and had acquired an energetic junior officer in Captain Nathaniel Lyon, an antislavery veteran of the Kansas troubles. The Minute Men, now incorporated into the state militia, drilled at the Berthold Mansion, preparing for an opportunity and an order to seize the 60,000 muskets and 90,000 pounds of gunpowder under federal guard.[10]

The February convention initially met in Jefferson City, but lack of accommodations and what Unionists perceived as local hostility persuaded delegates to reconvene in St. Louis a week later. On March 9, the convention voted in favor of remaining in the Union, and it defeated a secessionist resolution by a majority of almost three to one.[11] Although disheartened by the convention vote, Missouri secessionists continued to press their cause. Sensing rural animosity, Richard Johnson, a St. Louis Republican, wrote that "Union men were elected from here for the Convention, but this represents a very small portion of the State and if they thought they could injure St. Louis by seceding they would do it for spite." In March, the state legislature transferred control of city police from municipal government to a board of commissioners appointed by Governor Jackson, a move similar to that enacted by Maryland Democrats the year before. Jackson staffed the board with Democratic stalwarts. One of them, Basil Duke, the commander of the Minute Men, said that "the Police Bill was in reality a war measure, designed to enable our people to control St. Louis. . . . I knew the meaning of the measure . . . and tried to carry it into action." Anti-Republican forces scored another victory on April 1, when Daniel G. Taylor, a Democrat aligned with Governor Jackson and the Creole fur traders, defeated unconditional Unionist John How. Emboldened by police reform and the city election, secessionists used the crisis that followed Fort Sumter to attempt to take full control of the city.[12]

Governor Jackson refused Lincoln's call for volunteers and activated the state militia. He deployed a force of seven hundred at Camp Jackson, a newly christened bivouac near the St. Louis federal arsenal. Awakened to the danger of losing the arsenal, Lincoln allowed Blair and Lyon to arm local Home Guard volunteers. Simultaneous with the armed-neutrality standoff in Baltimore, in late April and early May federal and secession forces prepared for a showdown in St. Louis. Confederates smuggled cannon to their St. Louis supporters, while Lyon and Blair trained their volunteers and added recruits until they outnumbered the force at Camp Jackson by ten to one. On May 10, Lyon moved on the state militia and won their surrender without a battle. Federal soldiers, most of them St. Louis Germans, confronted an angry crowd while escorting their prisoners to jail. Exchanges of insults and rocks escalated to shooting. At the end of the violence, twenty-eight civilians, two federal soldiers, and three secessionist militiamen had been killed. Two more days of sporadic rioting followed.[13]

Camp Jackson brought the Civil War to Missouri. After the riot, Governor Jackson put state government on a war footing against the Union, and over the course of the summer armies marched across Missouri to decide its fate. In St. Louis, Lyon's seizure of Camp Jackson quelled the rising tide of Southern sympathy and put the city firmly under Union control. In April, Democrats had been using the authority of the new police board, the Democratic mayor, and state militia to promote the Confederacy and intimidate Unionists. After May 10, Unionists turned the tables. U.S. marshals seized Confederate arms cached around the city, including a supply at police headquarters. St. Louis's Southern sympathizers continued to criticize Union policy publicly until August 14, when John C. Fremont, the new commander of federal forces in Missouri, declared martial law in the city, suppressed antiadministration newspapers, and reorganized the police. Lincoln removed Fremont shortly thereafter, but Fremont's actions along with the organizing efforts of Blair and B. Gratz Brown had given unconditional Unionists control of St. Louis politics months before their takeover in Baltimore.[14]

Sectional polarization in St. Louis emerged out of the party struggle of the 1850s. The city's unconditional Unionists were Republicans, and local Republicans organized the Home Guard and the Committee of Safety. While not every St. Louis Democrat became a secessionist, the leading Confederates of the city shared that partisan background.

Thomas Caute Reynolds, titular Confederate governor of Missouri and an ardent prewar Democrat, practiced law in St. Louis during the 1850s with help from Basil Duke, commander of the Minute Men and a Confederate general. Another St. Louis attorney, Thomas Lowndes Snead, edited a pro-Breckinridge newspaper and advised Sterling Price, prewar Democratic governor and head of Missouri's Confederate forces. Daniel M. Frost, another Confederate general from St. Louis, supported the anti-Benton Democrats before the war and, in 1860, he ran for a state senate seat. Although St. Louis produced many more commanders and foot soldiers for the U.S. Army, this roll call of its Confederate leaders testifies to the commitment and partisan past of the city's Southern sympathizing minority.[15]

As in Baltimore, state militia units from St. Louis served as a conduit for prewar Democrats seeking to transform themselves into Confederates. In July 1860, Frost led militiamen in asking the city to cover the costs of a recent encampment. Mayor Filley refused because camp organizers used the event to promote the Democratic Party. Angry at Filley's rebuke, an artillery officer, who in civilian life was an active Democrat and philanthropist, prophesied the role that he and his fellow volunteers would play the next year. "If this Union by political maneuvers is to be destroyed, I shall be on the Southern division. . . . I am not to be bullied out of St. Louis; it is my home and my country. I have given to the city and the State a college and museum not worth less in value than two hundred thousand dollars. . . . I shall stay in . . . St. Louis unless driven out; but it will be when every dwelling is wrapped in flames and the streets running with blood." Having considered themselves a bulwark against Republican rule before 1861, St. Louis's Democratic militiamen were well prepared to take on the Confederacy's struggle.[16]

St. Louis Republicans felt the same antipathy toward their former Democratic Party enemies now arrayed under the Confederate flag. After the riot, Sarah Hill, the wife of a Republican businessman and Union officer, observed that "the disruption and separation permeated all classes and a feeling of suspicion and uncertainty hung heavy as a pall." Another federal sympathizer boasted that "we are determined to make the rebel ears tingle before we are through with them." Galusha Anderson, an antislavery Baptist minister, summed up the impact of Camp Jackson: "The suddenness of this outburst of patriotism for a time threw those who had been struggling in doubt and gloom to prevent the secession of Missouri into a delirium of joy." Anderson nevertheless acknowledged that "secessionism in St. Louis was neither dead nor hopeless."[17]

The location of Baltimore and St. Louis near slavery's border gave their anti-Democratic politicians more latitude to dissent from Southern nationalism than was afforded to Know-Nothings in New Orleans, the principle city of the Gulf Coast. The political economy of the lower South made support for slavery an article of faith for any candidate seeking office, even in New Orleans. Louisiana had many more slaves, slaveholders, and nonslaveholding whites who earned a living from slave-related businesses than did Missouri. New Orleans also possessed a smaller proportion of the groups most likely to oppose slavery—free-state migrants and Germans. Germans comprised only 11 percent of the Crescent City's population, compared with 31 percent in St. Louis, and New Orleans had few of the liberal refugees who settled further north. A New Orleans editor asserted that "an overwhelming majority of Germans in this city and state are true to the section of their adoption and detest the infernal doctrine of the Arch Abolitionists as strongly as we do." With few exceptions, New Orleans's Roman Catholic clergy, the spiritual guides for most immigrants, supported slavery and states' rights.[18]

Of the three largest cities in the South, New Orleans had the highest ratio of black to white, with slaves outnumbering free blacks. The African-American presence in the city and the surrounding countryside made all the proslavery arguments—the threat of slave revolts, racial amalgamation, white benefits from slave ownership, and the dangers of social equality—appear more real to New Orleans voters. Where St. Louis showed the potential for urban opposition politics to bring Republicans into the slave states, New Orleans demonstrated that hostility toward the planter-dominated Democratic Party could mobilize voters without stirring the masses to support the Union and emancipation.

Like their counterparts in late-antebellum Baltimore and St. Louis, New Orleans Democrats sought to topple their local foes via an appeal to rural party allies in control of state government. Those requests set in motion the 1857 election reforms and the 1858 confrontation between the New Orleans Vigilance Committee and the Know-Nothings. During that crisis, Louisiana Democrats expressed fears about their largest city similar to those voiced by Belt and Taney in Maryland. Governor Robert C. Wickliffe, a lawyer and planter from east Louisiana's

Florida parishes, accused New Orleans's government of showing "disregard for the law and its ministers, and a contempt for the rights of the persons and property of large classes of our fellow-citizens." At the height of the June 1858 impasse, followers of the Vigilance Committee listened to a minister compare New Orleans with "the then prosperous condition of Jerusalem and her then approaching doom—and showing the terror that should fill every Christian bosom when he sees a large city around him full of wickedness." An editor friendly to Senator John Slidell, leader of the state's Democratic Party, called New Orleans "this political Sodom." In Louisiana, as in Maryland and Missouri, urban reformers gathered rural support by linking their criticisms of city politics to proslavery antiurban arguments that equated abolitionism with a general disregard for law and traditional morality that country folk had long associated with cities.[19]

In Baltimore, Know-Nothings countered this attack by vilifying Democrats and trying to keep alive the few party outposts in the Maryland countryside. Although they later became isolated within Missouri politics, St. Louis Republicans started their fight against rural domination as a Democratic Party splinter movement led by Senator Thomas Hart Benton, an affiliation that won them country allies who either revered Benton or, more rarely, opposed slavery's expansion. During the mid-1850s, New Orleans Know-Nothings pursued the Baltimore strategy of seeking aid from party leaders in other parishes, but after 1857 the Louisiana American Party had been vanquished outside of New Orleans. At that point, Crescent City Know-Nothings turned to dissidents inside the Democratic Party to counter the alliance between city reformers and the majority faction of Democrats who were led by Senator Slidell. The character of Democratic infighting shaped the choices that New Orleans Know-Nothings made in the secession crisis.

In Louisiana, competing factions of slavery expansionists vied for control of the Democratic Party. The dominant group, led by Slidell, strongly supported the Buchanan administration and its efforts to open Kansas to slavery. Pierre Soule headed Slidell's challengers. Soule backed Stephen Douglas in national politics and favored proslavery filibustering in the Caribbean and Latin America as an alternative to the Kansas deadlock. That policy accommodated Douglas's views and maintained Soule's standing as a slavery expansionist. Soule, a Creole, drew some support from immigrants who opposed the American Party but disliked the Anglo-American cotton planters allied to Slidell.

Louisiana lacked a renegade Democrat comparable to Benton, an influential officeholder who gave the free-soil argument legitimacy. As the lead dissident in the Missouri Democratic Party, Benton paved the way for his city supporters to agitate against slavery's spread. By contrast, New Orleanians looking for an ally to fight Slidell heard from Soule that the Democrats had done too little to help slavery expand. The politics of slavery left New Orleans Know-Nothings little room for maneuver on the sectional issues. They staved off defeat in 1857 and 1858 by combining their control of political violence inside the city with aid from Soule's Southern nationalists in the state legislature. The showdown with Pierre G. T. Beauregard's Independent Reform ticket in 1858 brought about a kind of ceasefire between city and state government. Slidell Democrats remained suspicious of New Orleans, but they had few cards to play after the 1857 voting law failed to quell rioting and the American Party overawed the Vigilance Committee. Instead of going it alone like the St. Louis Republicans, New Orleans Know-Nothings combined a tough stand against their city foes with outreach to disgruntled Democrats.

In 1859, that alliance grew stronger when Soule's "New Line" Democrats held rallies in concert with Americans, and both sides agreed to support candidates opposed to Slidell's "Old Line" nominees. Soule welcomed Know-Nothings who were "willing to stand by our side, and combat with us, in the cause of popular rights and popular independence." Besides working with Soule, New Orleans Know-Nothings had other proslavery credentials. The *Crescent*, their most pro-Southern newspaper, hoped that "a dissolution of the present Union would make New Orleans, in five years, what New York is now." City delegates in the state legislature proposed a tax on Northern traders who were "in any way subserving solely Northern interests by underselling Southern merchants." Mayor Gerard Stith, a typesetter, and his successor John T. Monroe, a stevedore, practiced manual trades but were associated with Southern proslavery policies. Both took measures to curtail black liberty in the city, like requiring white supervision of black religious services, and both were native Virginians. Plenty of Unionists supported the New Orleans Know-Nothings, but the city party had enough Southern nationalists to reconcile Democratic fire-eaters to municipal independence.[20]

New Orleans Know-Nothings complemented their search for allies in the state capital by accommodating some former foes within the city. In 1859, Democrats again tried to oust the Americans via an Independent Citizens ticket, and they again failed in an election clouded by the murder of an Irish supporter of the Independent Citizens. By then, American Party overtures to Germans and the alliance with Soule had made inroads on the foreign-born vote, notwithstanding the enduring enmity of the Irish. In 1860, Monroe won the Creole-rich Second District, and Christian Roselius, a German lawyer and prominent anti-nativist, endorsed Constitutional Unionist John C. Bell, the Know-Nothing choice for president.[21]

Know-Nothings also healed some wounds with reform businessmen. A month after the 1858 showdown with the Vigilance Committee, the Know-Nothing board of aldermen appointed two of Beauregard's assistants to the school board. In 1860, Thomas K. Wharton, one of these appointees, described the American municipal ticket as "a very good showing of honest and capable men." Mayor Stith enhanced the economy by providing much-needed improvements to streets, water, and schools. Sectional accommodation, broad-based local support for the American Party, and fear of Know-Nothing violence convinced influential Democrats to refrain from another intervention in city politics.[22]

In 1860 and 1861, proslavery Democrats challenged the opposition parties in all three cities, and only in New Orleans did the opposition hold uninterrupted control of city government. Crescent City Know-Nothings fought off the Democrats by neutralizing Southern reform arguments that an independent regime supported by white labor's votes threatened slavery. However, accommodation to the Southern nationalist tide in state politics brought other problems for an urban opposition that still counted preservation of the Union among its core principles. In the 1860 presidential campaign, Slidell Democrats pursued a rule-or-ruin strategy for their party's nomination that alarmed New Orleans Unionists but nonetheless required them to demonstrate their Southern loyalty. At Louisiana Democrats' March 1860 convention, Slidell's followers endorsed him for president and resolved "[t]hat in case of the election of a President on the avowed principles of the Black Republican Party . . . Louisiana should meet in council with her sister slave-holding states, to consult as to measures for future protection." At the next month's national party convention in Charleston, Slidell worked with other Southerners to stop the nomination of Stephen Douglas, whose opposition to the Lecompton Constitution had cost him proslavery support. Deadlocked, the convention disbanded without a nominee. In June, after a second effort to reach consensus had failed, Southern Democrats nominated Vice President John C. Breckinridge on a separate ticket. During the fall campaign, Slidell

Democrats stumped for Breckinridge and interpreted his candidacy in secessionist terms. In addition to bringing Alabama fire-eater William Lowndes Yancey to speak in New Orleans, Slidell told voters that "unless some great, and, to me, unexpected revolution shall take place in the sentiment of the people of the free States, we cannot with safety and honor continue the connection much longer."[23]

Tennessean John Bell, who promised to maintain the Union and Constitution as they were, offered New Orleans Know-Nothings a proslavery, pro-Union choice to combat the sectional extremism of Slidell Democrats. The inaugural Bell meeting in New Orleans resolved that "[t]here is value in the federal Constitution and the Union which warrants an honest effort to maintain it 'at any price.'" However, the need to deflect Breckinridge criticisms that they were abolitionist fellow travelers led Constitutional Unionists to identify themselves as "patriots of Louisiana! Patriots of the South!" The Breckinridge campaign posed a conflict for those who simultaneously identified with the South and the nation, and it led New Orleans Bell supporters to qualify their "at any price" commitment to the federal government. Exemplifying this attitude, Roselius told a crowd, "Our rights in the Union, if we can, out of the Union if we must."[24]

Bell's campaign succeeded in New Orleans, where he garnered 48 percent of the vote. Of the three largest slave-state cities, all known for their moderate Unionism, only New Orleans gave Bell a plurality. Despite finishing third in New Orleans, Breckinridge took enough rural parishes to narrowly defeat Bell statewide by 2,477 ballots. Caught between Breckinridge's victory in Louisiana and Lincoln's triumph overall, New Orleans's Bell voters quickly had their conditional Unionism put to the test.[25] Led by Democrats in high offices, Louisiana secessionists used the month after the presidential election to alter political conditions in their favor. Thomas O. Moore, the new Democratic governor, called a special session of the state legislature for December 10 to address the "extraordinary occasion" of "the election of Abraham Lincoln . . . by a sectional and aggressive antislavery party." The Democratic U.S. senators Slidell and Judah P. Benjamin demanded Louisiana's "speedy separation." Benjamin said "no prospect remains of our being permitted to live in peace and security within the Union." At their December meeting, the legislature called for an election of a secession convention and appropriated $500,000 for a military board appointed by Governor Moore "for protection of the state from domestic or foreign violence." By these actions, secessionist Democrats promoted disunion as an inevitability for Louisiana.[26]

Several obstacles hampered New Orleans Know-Nothing efforts to stop secession. Unlike the issues at stake in their earlier struggles against the Democrats, New Orleans Know-Nothings did not agree on secession. Secessionist Know-Nothings included the party's one-time Catholic supporter Charles Gayarre and the new mayor, John T. Monroe. Other well-placed Know-Nothings, like Congressman Randall Hunt, led the Union campaign. Nor did American Party power in New Orleans help Unionists in an election that would be decided by statewide results.

Candidates for the January 7, convention election divided into two camps. One was united behind the policy of immediate secession; the other, labeled Cooperationists, opposed independent state secession but disagreed on related issues. Some Cooperationists, like Pierre Soule, supported secession but wanted Louisiana to act in concert with other slave states and thereby achieve a more orderly break from the Union. Others, like Roselius and Thomas Durant, a Douglas Democrat who broke with Soule over disunion, wanted Southerners in Congress to secure slaveholders' rights and thereby preserve the Union. If rebuffed, they vowed to secede. Unconditional Unionists opposed to secession regardless of Lincoln's actions made up the smallest Cooperationist contingent. They occasionally heard fiery Union rhetoric from other Cooperationists, but otherwise lacked their support. The *Picayune,* a New Orleans Cooperationist journal, asserted, "There is no voice in the state for quiet yielding to the North. There is no desire to stay in the Union without the settlement, and the settlement now, of the slavery question." Unlike the case for the Union made by St. Louis Republicans and Baltimore Know-Nothings, New Orleans Cooperationists conceded the point that Louisiana must, if pushed too far, secede in order to defy Northern aggression.[27]

Along with secessionist activism, the absence of a strong unconditional Unionist voice helps explain what one historian has called "the paradox" of Louisiana's secession, a surprise given the Unionism of New Orleanians and tariff-dependent sugar planters.[28] However, the wave of secessionist enthusiasm that swept much of the rural South failed to wipe out support for the Union in New Orleans. In the January convention election, secession candidates won a majority of the New Orleans races, but the total city vote split almost down the middle, secessionists eking out a one-hundred-vote (2 percent) majority. Despite a close 4 percent margin for secession statewide, in most country parishes one side or the other polled a lopsided majority. Out of the state's forty-nine parishes, thirty-one provided victory margins of two-thirds or more for either secession or cooperation, and eleven of the remaining parishes had victory margins above 10 percent. Cooperationists won ten of the twenty-five seats contested in New Orleans and its environs, making the city one of only eleven parishes to split its delegation. If the election is viewed as a measure of sectional opinion in New Orleans prior to war, it showed strong support for both viewpoints. As the *Bee* put it, "Public sentiment in N.O. is nearly equally divided with a slight preponderance in favor for secession."[29]

Although secession triumphed in New Orleans in 1861, the city's experience with the politics of disunion better resembled that of Baltimore and St. Louis than that of smaller Southern cities. New Orleans stood apart from other lower-South cities with Unionist minorities because its federal sympathizers continued to act on behalf of their cause after secession had been officially declared. The antisecession minority in New Orleans acted like the anti-Union minority in Baltimore and St. Louis. Outnumbered and outgunned, they refused to give up on their beliefs in the name of community consensus.

After losing the January elections, New Orleans Unionists resisted secessionist pressure to abandon their dissent. By the time the convention delegates arrived in Baton Rouge, the state capital had turned into the parade ground of disunion. Immediately after the election, thousands of young men signed up for service in military units sponsored by and loyal to state government. On January 10, Governor Moore seized federal arsenals and forts within Louisiana. Ignoring the closeness of the election and a 20 percent drop in turnout between November and January, Moore claimed that "the vote of the people has since confirmed . . . that the undivided sentiment of the State is for immediate secession." The next day, two hundred fully equipped New Orleans volunteers arrived in Baton Rouge to help capture the local federal arsenal. When the handful of U.S. soldiers stationed in Louisiana decided not to challenge the property seizures, secessionists celebrated what they hoped would be one of many bloodless triumphs. In Missouri, prosecession demonstrations in the state capital persuaded the Unionist majority to relocate the convention to St. Louis. In Louisiana, the delegates remained in Baton Rouge until secession had been enacted. Outnumbered by disunionist delegates inside the convention hall by

106 to 66, outside the hall Cooperationists confronted a near fait accompli for secession manifested by the legislature's steps toward independence and the soldiers and civilians who encouraged them.[30]

In this anti-Union environment, it took nerve to oppose the secession ordinance. Most of those who did so came from New Orleans. Convention delegate Charles Bienvenu introduced a resolution to have the January vote totals published, an act that would undermine secessionist claims of a mandate. Once secession passed the convention, Bienvenu tried to kill the measure by putting it to a vote of the people. Another New Orleans delegate, Joseph A. Rozier, introduced the Cooperationist plan for submitting Southern terms to the North in hopes of averting secession. Roselius protested a resolution stating that the convention "unqualifiedly approved" of confiscating federal property. Moore's supporters attacked Roselius with "harsh language" and easily passed their motion. On January 26, the convention voted 116 to 17 in favor of immediate secession. Most Cooperationists either abstained or switched sides. Six of the seventeen who voted against disunion had been elected in New Orleans. To put this in perspective, only one-fifth of the Cooperationist delegates elected outside of New Orleans voted no, whereas three-fifths of those from the city did so. Except for a defiant speech by James G. Taliaferro of Catahoula Parish and an East Felicianan's call for united Southern secession, all major floor actions against disunion were initiated by New Orleans delegates.[31]

No immediate harm came to these Cooperationist diehards, but on the streets of New Orleans outspoken Unionists faced intimidation and arrest. At a Unionist rally after the capture of Fort Sumter, counter-demonstrators jeered and paraded with an effigy of the principal speaker, a federal judge. Police arrested a Michigan-born federal sympathizer for boasting that "Lincoln would shell Charleston and cut the levees of New Orleans." Pinched for supplies by the federal blockade and Confederate military demands, city officials confiscated Unionist property and searched homes for firearms. In the spring of 1862, Confederate commanders ordered all citizens to profess their loyalty to Richmond under penalty of arrest or expulsion. With the power of the police and government on their side, secessionists took the same kind of coercive action against their local pro-Union foes as Unionists took against secessionists in Baltimore and St. Louis.[32]

As in other big cities, New Orleans secessionists, some of them American Party nativists, viewed some immigrants with suspicion. Police helped Confederate authorities coerce immigrants, including foreign nationals, into the army. Confederates also censored the press. An antislavery German claimed that "possession" of a New York newspaper "would have been deemed sufficient reason for hanging any man." Less than two months after Sumter, British journalist William Howard Russell reported daily arrests of abolitionists in New Orleans, and he claimed that "persons found guilty not of expressing their opinions against slavery, but of stating their belief that the Northerners will be successful, are sent to prison for six months. The accused are generally foreigners, or belong to the lower orders, who have got no interest in the support of slavery." Although hundreds of foreign-born New Orleanians volunteered for regular Confederate units, secessionists doubted the loyalty of nonslaveholders unacquainted with Southern culture.[33]

Coupled with coercion, secession's leaders searched for ideological arguments that would win over the diverse, nonslaveholding population of New Orleans. In the election campaigns of 1860 and 1861, several secessionist rationales—white supremacy, sectional loyalty, and the promise of a better economy under the Confederacy—appealed to wage-earning voters. Their misgivings about foreigners notwithstanding, Slidell Democrats reminded immigrants that Bell was the choice of the American Party, who "accepted . . . all the proscriptive principles of Know-Nothingism." After Lincoln's election, Mayor Monroe gave his full assistance to secession, and some of the native-born workers in the American Party went with him. Anthony P. Dostie, a Northern-born professional and one of the city's most vocal unconditional Unionists, attributed Confederate domination to Monroe and his loyal following of 1850s gang leaders, citing as an example Lucien Adams, "chief of the Thugs of New Orleans."[34]

To insure the Know-Nothing regime's loyalty, state officials strengthened their authority in city government. New patronage appointments went to Slidell-ites. Army officers handled defense-related aspects of municipal administration. Beauregard held one of the top commands in the Confederate military, and his protégé Thomas Wharton took charge of public works, the main patronage vehicle for working-class partisans. In 1861, Wharton noted that "political times have drawn out *the fighting instincts* of the South." His move from an embattled foe of city government to one of its insiders showed how secession had enabled Democratic Reformers to gain influence in city government that Know-Nothings had earlier denied them.[35]

Although a few Unionists, like Dostie, left the South rather than submit to Confederate rule, most New Orleanians, including the working-class constituents of the American Party, accepted the new government as the least-troublesome way to continue their prewar routines. However, they demonstrated little enthusiasm for the economic sacrifice and actual fighting required to maintain their new sovereign's independence. The economic panic induced by secession prompted Hugh Kennedy, editor of the pro-Douglas *True Delta* and a self-styled labor spokesman, to spell out a condition of working-class Confederate loyalty. "Gov. Moore . . . is a cotton planter of large means and grand possessions, and within the range of his personal associations, privation of any kind may be an unknown visitor . . . therefore it is that we would counsel him to give some heed to what is daily occurring in this, the principal city of the state . . . where thousands are unsure that bread to eat can be obtained for their honest and willing labor from week to week." City workers' support for secession would fade, the paper implied, if the Confederate cause looked like a "rich man's war and a poor man's fight."[36]

Some white workingmen devoted themselves to the Confederacy; others battled against it. But the largest number exercised the same kind of conditional commitment to their new nation that working-class Bell and Douglas supporters had given the Union a year earlier. The experience of two workers' voluntary associations illustrates the complexity of Confederate loyalty for New Orleans free labor. Gerard Stith, the former president of the Typographical Union and former mayor, served on the board of aldermen in Monroe's Confederate municipal administration, and other typesetters volunteered for the army. However, an equal number went to the free states, and those still at work admitted new members from New York. The printers' union rejected a resolution calling on members to swear allegiance to the Confederacy. It also formed a home-defense unit that exempted its members from serving in the national army. One printer recalled that "the 'Home Guard' seemed more suited to the arts of peace than those of war." When Union forces captured New Orleans in April 1862, the printers, "like all others, quickly discarded their military uniforms and clothed themselves in the garb of peace-loving citizens."[37]

The American Hook and Ladder Company, a volunteer fire unit composed of wealthy professionals as well as craftsmen, upheld the Confederate cause with greater unanimity than the printers. They often declared their commitment to "our Country, struggling as it is for liberty and a national existence," and a large proportion of their members volunteered for Confederate service beyond the city limits. Those

that stayed behind sent supplies and money to their departed colleagues. However, war and its economic consequences hampered their
ability to support Southern independence. Army enlistment and
scaled-back contributions from businesses and city government de-
pleted the company treasury and diminished its effectiveness in fighting fires. By the spring of 1862, indebtedness forced the firemen to sell
their horses and equipment. Although they pledged funds for Monroe's
poor-relief efforts, in March the firemen stated that "the financial condition of this company will not permit it to render any pecuniary assistance." By September 1862, federal authorities had paroled all members of the American Hook and Ladder Company, and the organization
returned to fighting fires. Only three members resigned rather than
serve as an auxiliary of a Unionist city administration. The printers and
firemen showed how ideological qualms and a concern for home and
family that overrode political principle undermined labor's commitment to the Confederacy.[38]

As these examples suggest, the war intensified material strains on
secessionist loyalty. In May 1861, U.S Admiral David Farragut took
control of one of the passes at the mouth of the Mississippi, and by the
next year his blockade had effectively shut the port down. Closed commerce drove up prices, eliminated thousands of jobs on the levee, and
created food shortages that stirred resentment against Monroe's government. In June, Russell reported that "the municipal authorities, for
want of funds, threaten to close the city schools and disband the police;
at the same time employers refuse to pay their workmen on the ground
of inability." In August 1861, Monroe began distributing free food to
the poor. By October, he had fixed the price of bread. The buildup of
federal forces downstream so pressed city government that in February 1862 Monroe replaced civilian government with the Committee of
Public Safety, staffed by prominent citizens to coordinate military defense and civilian administration.[39]

Confronted with the ideological pressure of Confederate coercion
and the material pressure of the bad economy, many New Orleans
Unionists acquiesced to Confederate rule. Some, like Michael Hahn, a
German attorney and free-soiler who refused to swear loyalty to Richmond but served as a notary public, made minor compromises that tacitly acknowledged Confederate authority. Others enlisted in the Confederate military, often under threat of arrest or as a remedy for
unemployment, but they tried to enroll in units assigned to defend the
city and thereby avoid distant service in Tennessee and Virginia. These

quasi volunteers included prominent Union leaders like Roselius and Durant, as well as ethnic and occupational groups that secessionists viewed with suspicion. Free people of color formed the famous Louisiana Native Guards, which initially offered its services to the Confederacy. Confederate commanders distrusted using these guards for active military duty and withheld weapons and supplies. State government also denied military supplies to some immigrant regiments whose effectiveness and loyalty were in doubt (one Irish unit chose to arm itself with pikes rather than rifles). New Orleanians who enrolled in home-defense units simultaneously escaped the stigma of Unionism and ducked the request for new recruits from Confederate commanders enduring heavy casualties in far-off theaters.[40]

However, by January 1862 General Mansfield Lovell, commander of Confederate defenses in lower Louisiana but whose best troops had been sent to commands in other states, welcomed anyone who would serve locally. When volunteers ran out, Lovell forced unemployed workers, often Northerners and immigrants, into hastily organized garrison regiments. The quasi volunteers' low morale contributed to the federal capture of New Orleans in April. Some conscripts mutinied when ordered to serve outside the city; and those stationed at Fort Jackson, a river redoubt key to Lovell's strategy, mutinied after coming under Union fire. Lovell, showing his low regard for home-defense volunteers and conscripted workers, left all such conscripts behind when he evacuated New Orleans on April 25. In their failed effort to hold New Orleans, Confederates had to combat the apathy of the people they defended in addition to fighting Farragut's fleet.[41]

On May 1, 1862, after five days of negotiations with a defiant but defeated Monroe administration, General Benjamin Butler disembarked his soldiers from Farragut's ships and established effective federal control over New Orleans. Led by Monroe and Soule, the city's Confederate majority vehemently protested occupation and provoked a harsh reaction that earned Butler the nickname "Beast." Conversely, the Unionist minority welcomed Farragut and Butler as liberators and joined with them in establishing a new Union government for Louisiana. The proportion of bedrock Unionists among white New Orleanians approximated the share of Confederate sympathizers in the populations of Baltimore and St. Louis. Roughly 6,400 white New Orleanians volunteered for federal military service and 14,500 swore loyalty oaths prior to the threat of property confiscation should one refuse.[42] This sizeable demonstration of Union loyalty set New Orleans apart from other lower-South cities struggling with federal occupation. Around 24,000 New Orleanians, its slaves and free blacks, had fewer hesitations about supporting the Union and its implicit promise of emancipation and civil rights. Nevertheless, the city's white Confederates outnumbered the combined strength of all Unionists.

Louisiana moved faster toward Reconstruction than west Tennessee or coastal South Carolina, other areas that federal troops captured early in the war, because New Orleans, the center of federal control, had a politicized Unionist community that drew on the city's recent political past to rebuild a loyal government. Before the end of May 1862, Unionists rallied in public and, on June 4, created the Union League of New Orleans, the nucleus of the new civilian government. In response to threats from Confederate sympathizers, the Union League adopted the Know-Nothing tactics of secrecy and paramilitary violence. After Butler arrested Monroe and his cronies in mid-May, the army quickly restored civilian control over most aspects of public administration apart from police. Unionists experienced in 1850s city government, including notable figures in Reconstruction like Hahn, Rozier, and Roselius, staffed the new municipal regime. Among the most influential was Benjamin Flanders, appointed a commissioner of public works, in place of Wharton, in August. Flanders had been a late-antebellum school commissioner, but he had left New Orleans in 1861 under a Confederate ban.[43]

Butler cultivated the city's white wage-earners with a public-works program that he paid for by taxing Confederate bondholders. Playing to the class resentment alluded to by the *True Delta* newspaper in 1861, Butler told unemployed workers that "this hunger does not pinch the wealthy and influential, the leaders of the rebellion." He asked, "How long will you suffer yourselves to be made the serfs of these leaders?" Less exalted Union soldiers held similar views of workers' political role. Nathan W. Daniels, a white commander of a black Union regiment, wrote that "when this cursed system of slavery shall have been eradicated, when just labor shall have been established and the colored man given all his rights, . . . then will New Orleans . . . rival New York and become the great metropolis of the south—but it must undergo first a severe discipline—the rich must become poor and old classes change their character." At an 1863 celebration by a local chapter of the Workingmen's National Union League, New Orleans workers shouted, "That's True!" in response to Judge Josiah Fisk's statement that "among the large slave holders, a poor white man, no matter what may be his moral or intellectual worth, is not looked upon with as much respect as a slave belonging to a rich nabob." Fisk went on to exhort "the workingmen of this city . . . to form a government which will afford protection to the poor as well as the rich—a government giving freedom to all." Native and foreign-born whites mingled in the league's audience, one of many signs that prewar ethnic tension had eased, while the antagonism between rich and poor had intensified.[44]

Although they supported emancipation, New Orleans white workers had not abandoned their prewar racism. As Baltimore's job busters had done before the war, whites in wartime New Orleans attacked slaveholders but upheld the racial hierarchy that slavery produced. When they drafted a new antislavery constitution in 1864, New Orleans delegates tried to prevent black suffrage, and they opposed public education for former slaves. Confederate retreat from cities like New Orleans allowed the South's Unionist white workers to renew their challenge to the standing relationship between rich and poor of their own race, and as a result of wartime politics they made emancipation, but not racial equality, part of that fight. It fell to African Americans to stretch the boundaries of that struggle so as to challenge the South's status quo on race.[45]

The congressional elections held on December 3, 1862, capped the quick political revival of New Orleans Unionists. Operating with federal protection, candidates competed for each of the two seats representing the city. Flanders won 90 percent of the vote in his election, while Michael Hahn, who, like all Unionists, endorsed emancipation but opposed African-American civil and political rights, defeated a more radical candidate favored by the army. The total vote of 7,760 fell 41 percent below the turnout for the same seats in 1859, but compared with the 1861 secession election the ballot total had dropped only 11 percent, lending credence to claims that in 1861 Unionists in districts running two types of secessionists had stayed home. The diversity of Unionist positions expressed in the campaign and in Hahn's victory over the choice of Union commanders showed that competitive politics had returned to the city within nine months of the Confederates' departure.[46]

Union military control and an antislavery civilian government in New Orleans opposed to a proslavery, Confederate administration in most other parishes pushed the traditional opposition between city and country in Louisiana politics to its logical extreme. Crescent City Unionists had little in common with rural Confederates. Although they often disagreed with each other, naturalized immigrants and Northern-born whites dominated the Union government. Seeking civil rights and an end to slavery, free people of color, including the Louisiana Native Guards, supported Butler, and escaped slaves flooded the city in search of freedom. Behind Confederate lines, Southern planters kept power, and African Americans remained in slavery.

All of this helps to make clearer how Southern urban politics had become entangled in sectional issues. There was nothing peculiar to Maryland, the Mid-Atlantic, or the sectional border that inclined Baltimoreans to oppose the Democratic Party. Across the South the party in control of the state legislature represented the interests of farmers and rural voters, and while it also courted urban votes, the dominant party sided with the country when its claims countered those of the city. Opposition parties had won majorities in the largest urban centers by paying attention to local concerns like immigration and by standing up to rural domination in state government. By 1860, sectionalism outshone all other issues for Southern state governments. Consequently, urban Democrats seeking aid against the municipal opposition phrased their requests in terms that fulfilled the sectional imperatives of rural Southerners.

Baltimore Know-Nothings stood in the middle of a spectrum of big-city responses to Democratic domination and secession. When Democrats recaptured Maryland state government in 1859, they suppressed the coercive power of police and gangs and engineered the fall of the Baltimore American Party. The nature of the Reform victory allowed for a broader debate over Baltimore's stand on disunion than had the outcomes of opposition politics in St. Louis and New Orleans. St. Louis elected Republicans at all levels of government in 1859 and 1860. These votes committed city government, but not all city residents, to unconditional Unionism. New Orleans Know-Nothings pursued a coalition with Soule's dissident faction of the Democratic Party that, because of its states' rights views, covered their Southern nationalist flank. That alliance also encouraged Know-Nothings to join Louisiana Democrats in perceiving Lincoln's election as a provocation to the South. For all of their sectional rhetoric, Baltimore's Democratic Reformers and their Know-Nothing foes had not taken such clear stands on Union or secession. Up close, events in Baltimore appeared to have reached the level of the Civil War before 1860, but when compared with the two cities most like it in the South, its partisans of either side had more room to maneuver on sectional issues.

Along with highlighting Baltimore's distinctiveness, this overview of the secession crisis in the big slave-state cities illustrates what they shared. Baltimore, St. Louis, and New Orleans were neither bastions of the Union nor strongholds of secession. Instead, they served as organizing bases for both camps, with outcomes varying according to state and local balances of power and the presence of federal troops. Smaller Southern cities followed a different pattern. After an initial contest between Union and secession, their political leaders closed ranks around the majority sentiment and prevented the kind of political turmoil that visited their larger cousins. In the largest Southern cities, party hatreds nurtured during the 1850s, and larger, less-tractable electorates prevented political leaders from achieving such a consensus. Unlike Baltimore's secession rioters or New Orleans's Unionist diehards, politicians in the South's smaller cities valued community consensus over a go-for-broke attachment to faction. In Southern cities ranked four through ten in size of population, people argued over the fate of the Union prior to Fort Sumter, but their failure to sustain effective political opposition to the reigning party prevented sectional minorities from holding out after government leaders had united on their choice.

In the lower South, Know-Nothings briefly ruled the midsized cities, but the Democratic attack on the American Party as a threat to Southern unity succeeded in driving them from power by the late 1850s. Unlike the vocal Unionist minority in the New Orleans American Party, politicians in smaller lower-South ports who opposed secession had no base of voters or friends in city office to back them, and Unionist protest was feeble after a Republican won the presidency.

In 1855, Know-Nothings won control of municipal government in Savannah, Georgia, but their defeat in the elections of 1856 and 1857 eliminated "effective opposition" to the Democracy. Democrats campaigned on the sectional implications of a Know-Nothing victory, which, they argued, would aid the Republicans and harm the South. Although poorer voters, like Savannah's Irish workers, voted Democratic, the party's municipal leaders were almost exclusively merchants, planters, and professionals. After the end of party competition in 1857, business leaders united behind the Democrats. This unity did not entail commitment to the states' rights doctrine of Georgia's leading Democrats. In 1859, People's Democratic candidates defeated Savannah's "regular" party nominees by arguing that their opponents' sectionalism and "cliqueism" had distracted attention from municipal issues like education and street repair. Known in 1860 as "the Citizens

Ticket," these Democrats quietly endorsed Bell against Breckinridge, the mainstream party nominee, but this was muted Unionism. The Citizens nominated a Breckinridge supporter for mayor, and their sole demonstration for Bell consisted of displaying his name on their newspaper masthead without editorial comment. Breckinridge carried Savannah's presidential vote, and, after Lincoln's national victory, few spoke out against secession. Even immigrant wage-earners, whites with the least material interest in slavery, demonstrated for the Confederacy. According to one historian, "the militant Unionism that frustrated immediate secessionists did not exist as a political force in Georgia in late 1860 and early 1861."[47]

Unlike the conditional secessionism of New Orleans, Savannah's support for the Confederacy withstood the strain of war. After capturing the Sea Islands that skirted Georgia's coast in November 1861, federal troops were within easy reach of the city. Preferring to defend more strategic positions inland, Confederate commanders provided minimal aid to Savannah. Although the situation afforded opportunity for local Unionists to assist in a federal takeover, Savannahans put up a united defense that convinced Union troops to refrain from attacking until 1864.[48]

In Mobile, Alabama, the Democratic Party, as in Savannah, drove Know-Nothings out of office by exploiting sectionalism. In 1856, Jones M. Withers, the Know-Nothing mayor, switched parties because he believed the Americans had betrayed the South's interests. After 1857, planters who had earlier backed the Whigs persuaded Alabama's anti-Democrats to outflank the dominant party by claiming it did too little, rather than too much, to protect slavery and the South. The Southern nationalism of Know-Nothing planters left Mobile's pro-Union businessmen further isolated in state politics. Enough Mobile Democrats advocated moderation in the 1860 presidential contest to enable Stephen Douglas to win a municipal plurality. Nevertheless, again as in Savannah, cautious Unionism quickly yielded to secessionism after Lincoln's victory. The day after the election, a pro-Douglas editor published a call for a secession convention over the objections of Douglas, who was in Mobile at the time. In the coming months, Northern-born businessmen sympathetic to the Union avoided public rallies and kept their opinions to themselves out of fear for their safety.[49]

City dwellers in the upper South were more forthright in their defense of the Union, but although they sustained opposition to the Democratic Party past the presidential elections, by April 1861 they, too, had succumbed to secession fever. Richmond, Virginia, illustrates this pattern. In the early 1850s, Whig businessmen who eschewed partisanship in local elections governed Richmond. After the national Whig Party died, its Richmond followers adopted the Know-Nothing label. As it did in many Southern places, the arrival of Know-Nothings increased the partisanship of local elections because the new party discountenanced split tickets and, in reaction, Democrats encouraged supporters to vote against Americans at all levels of government. Democrats unseated the Know-Nothings in 1857, but unlike Savannah and Mobile the opposition battled back in 1859 to recapture local and state offices. In 1860, Bell won the presidential vote of Richmond and of Virginia. Some white workers, a group aligned with the Democrats, broke with their pro-Breckinridge leaders to support Douglas.[50]

In the secession winter of 1860–61, Unionists and secessionists demonstrated for their causes. On February 4, 1861, Richmonders elected two conditional Unionists and one secessionist to a convention called to consider severing relations with Washington. Richmond's ratio of conditional Unionists to secessionists mirrored the statewide outcome, a result that gave moderates hope that disunion could be averted. All of this changed on April 12, the day of Fort Sumter. A recent study of the city argues that Lincoln's call to suppress the rebellion "transformed [Richmond] from an American city to a Southern place practically overnight." Secessionist mobs now held sway in city streets. Many European immigrants and Northerners fled. Immediate secessionists won only 45 percent of the February convention vote, but in a May referendum secession passed unanimously with just sixty-three fewer ballots than the combined vote total of the earlier, closely contested, election.[51]

Compared with the cities of the lower South, where friends of the Union went underground in November 1860, Richmond looked like a hotbed of militant Unionism. Yet, when set alongside Baltimore and its sister big cities, Richmond Unionists lose their radical edge. Despite voting and demonstrating for the Union, Richmond did not have a core of Union paramilitaries who fought secessionists on city streets in April and May, as they did in Baltimore and St. Louis. Although Unionism had strong rural support and, prior to Sumter, could be advocated without fear of attack in Richmond, the city failed to elect an outspoken Unionist to its convention to match the New Orleanians who defied secessionists in a much more hostile political climate. After secession, Richmond became the Confederate capital and, despite acts of dissent like foot dragging by immigrant soldiers and the famous bread riot of 1863, served the cause of Southern independence. By contrast, each of the big cities contributed thousands of volunteers to federal regiments, a much more significant measure of Union strength than the kinds of covert actions taken in Richmond and other cities behind Confederate lines.

The failure of Richmond's Whig-American opposition to win enfranchised workers away from what a historian terms Virginia's "very prosouthern Democratic Party" helps explain this relatively weak Unionism. States' rights supporters in the local American Party favored an attack on foreign antislavery "radicalism," rather than making a nativist appeal to American-born white workingmen. This strategy reflected the poor prospects for creating a version of Baltimore's class-and-ethnic majority in Richmond. Disenfranchised African Americans made up roughly one-half of all wage-earners, and immigrants, often nonvoters because of naturalization delays, comprised a majority of working-class whites.[52] Unlike the big cities that had experienced party competition in municipal races for more than a generation, Richmonders had a short, five-year, history of partisan local elections, and poor white voters had exercised the franchise only for ten years. Late-antebellum Richmond averaged 3,700 ballots per election. The all-time high, in 1860, was 4,281. By contrast, more than 25,000 Baltimoreans regularly went to the polls, more than 30,000 did so in 1860, and Baltimore had a larger share of wage-earners in its electorate. In the Virginia capital, politicized wage-earners were few in number, they disagreed on secession (workers made up almost one-half of the signatories of one Breckinridge memorial), and the Unionists among them lacked advocates in government office.[53]

A final comparison point for the cities of the South during the secession crisis is the South's most pro-Union city, Louisville, Kentucky, situated across the Ohio River from a free state. In 1860, whites made up 90 percent of Louisville's population of 68,000, and a majority of them were native-born. In the 1850s, the city elected Whigs, then Americans, and finally Constitutional Unionists. Although early in the decade middle-class newcomers had broken the political control exercised by an established elite, local offices remained in the hands of wealthy businessmen and professionals. Wage-earners had little say in government. In a rare occasion when a self-described "workingmen's advocate" openly criticized the political power of businessmen, he lost his newspaper column. One historian asserts that "organized labor in

Louisville prior to the Civil War . . . was not a major influence in the economic or political affairs of the city."[54]

City government favored economic development projects, most notably the Louisville and Nashville Railroad. These measures sometimes clashed with the fiscal conservatism of the Kentucky legislature, which by the late 1850s had fallen into line behind the Democratic Party. Yet despite hostility toward proslavery Democrats in state government, no major Louisville politician supported the Republicans or free-soil. In 1860, the city and state voted for Bell.[55]

During the secession crisis, Kentucky maintained its neutrality longer than any other state. Benefiting from a resilient prewar party organization that grew out of the Know-Nothings and their Louisville base, Unionists finally prevailed in an election for a special convention held on August 5. They garnered a majority of seats statewide and swept the elections in Louisville. During the Civil War, Jefferson County, Louisville's home, produced the most federal volunteers of any Kentucky county (6,578). Although many secessionists lived in Louisville, the city had no major public disorder associated with disunion, unlike Baltimore and St. Louis, where the secessionist minority tried to take power by force of arms. Even when the Confederate army approached the city in the summer of 1862, Louisville Southern sympathizers failed to challenge Unionists openly.[56]

Louisville's quiet Unionism stands in contrast to the hotly contested battles over sectional allegiance in larger Southern cities near the border. While the people of Louisville favored the Union and Richmonders ultimately opted for secession, the comparative unity of the political leadership in both communities prevented the kind of bitter disruptions experienced in the big cities. After the Bloody Monday riots of 1855, Louisville civic leaders clamped down on public disorder and reduced partisan conflict in local elections. Know-Nothings remained in office until 1859. Their firm control of city politics, albeit without violence, meant that antislavery Germans lacked a viable free-soil party, as they had in St. Louis.[57] Unity among wealthy civic leaders combined with the absence of an institutional vehicle for secession to challenge this consensus made Louisville's entry into the Civil War a much more peaceful exercise than that experienced in other border cities.

Situating Baltimore in this continuum of responses to the sectional crisis clarifies some aspects of its Civil War history and of the South's secession. The big cities kept alive the prewar partisan divisions that had either disappeared before 1860 in much of the South or evaporated after war broke out in the spring of 1861. Divisions over Union and secession existed throughout the South in 1861, but once war came, communities closed ranks around the majority choice. As in Louisville, in areas where Unionism had widespread support, like northwestern Virginia, opposition to secession cut across the lines of class and ethnicity. Similarly, rich and poor whites joined hands in places that gave secession hearty majorities. Although supporters of the minority viewpoint tried to undermine the majority in the strongholds of Union and secession, peace reigned behind the battle lines.[58] The big cities were not the only Southern places to experience internecine conflict over sectionalism, but their partisans stood apart from the rest of the region because they applied to the war the allegiances and organizing strategies that had been learned in the process of party competition.

To illustrate the uniquely political character of the Civil War in the big cities, a final point of comparison is in order. Outside of the cities, residents of the Appalachian and Ozark mountain ranges, places with large majorities of white nonslaveholders, were the Southerners who divided most evenly over secession or Union. In much of America, support for secession and Union transcended class and ethnic background, but historians of the Civil War in the Southern Mountains have found a correlation between sectional allegiance and social identity. Secession was caught up in an ongoing struggle that pitted modernizers involved in far-flung commercial markets against rural traditionalists isolated from those markets and their culture. By contrast, in the big cities, sectional allegiance attached itself to more a complicated mix of social markers, and each side used party identity to bridge social divisions within their coalitions.

The guerilla war in the mountain South reversed the larger social struggle of the divided nation. Except for western Virginia, where economic ties to the free states inclined business leaders to back the Union, Confederates in the backcountry tended to be younger, urban, and more involved in trade with the lowland markets of the South than were the mountain counties' staunch Unionists. The orientation of ambitious mountain townsfolk toward planters and cotton factors made them sympathetic to secessionist arguments. By contrast, mountaineers loyal to the federal government had less money and lived away from the railroad heads and river towns that served as the gateways between their homeland and the rest of the South. As an extension of conflicts attending social changes in the Mountain South, the Civil War in Appalachia and the Ozarks more often pitted neighborhood against neighborhood, rather than neighbor against neighbor.[59]

A comparison of sectional allegiance in western North Carolina, where most highlanders backed the Confederacy, and neighboring East Tennessee, which produced twenty-seven thousand Union soldiers, illustrates how integration into the larger Southern economy affected support for secession. In western North Carolina, Unionists and secessionists campaigned for their respective causes up until Fort Sumter, at which point conditional Unionists abandoned Lincoln to rally around the Confederate cause. Western North Carolina's community leaders suffered less wartime infighting than their neighbors in Tennessee because Carolina highland counties lacked the divisions in economic and social orientation that characterized their neighbors to the west. From the settlement of western North Carolina by Europeans in the 1700s, North Carolinians there generated wealth by trading with Georgia and South Carolina. Furthermore, they enjoyed family and political partnerships with the eastern sections of their own state. Some diehard unconditional Unionists went underground or braved the hostility of secessionist mobs, but in the first year of war, dissent was as scarce in North Carolina's mountains as it was in the state's low country. Anti-Confederate activity increased as battlefield reverses, conscription, and federal military incursions created motives and opportunities for mountain Unionists to emerge from the shadows; nonetheless, North Carolina's piece of Appalachia "never became the Unionist stronghold that existed across the state line." Ties of kin and commerce convinced mountaineers to fight alongside their fellow North Carolinians, rather than against them.[60]

East Tennessee had a stormier relationship with its low country. Settled before the rich farmlands to the west, the political and economic influence of the east declined steadily during the nineteenth century—a process symbolized by the permanent transfer of the state capital from Knoxville to Nashville in 1834. Differential economic development fed eastern animosity toward the west. East Tennesseans had always produced crops for cash and used the surplus to build railroads, towns, and industry, but commerce had an uneven impact on the highlands. The broad valley of East Tennessee bisected the Unaka (Smoky) Mountains on its eastern side and the Cumberland Plateau on its western side. Serviced by the East Tennessee and Virginia Railroad, in 1860 the economy of the valley fostered the same kinds of cultural and economic bonds with the cotton plantations and market towns of the lower South that the Buncombe Turnpike created in western North Carolina. However, the commercial network of the Tennessee Valley failed to extend far up the slopes of the surrounding high country. In the late 1850s, commerce in the valley was often conducted by young men or newcomers to the region who had no status or influence in the community networks of mountain hollows and isolated plateaus that were uninvolved in their economy.

East Tennessee's federal sympathizers defended their cause after Fort Sumter. In June 1861, twenty-five of the thirty-one counties in the region voted against separation from the Union. Local secessionist leaders tended to be the young townsmen of the valley. Unionists also had some wealthy leaders, but their rank and file came from poorer settlements at a remove from lowland commerce. The greater isolation of some East Tennessee mountaineers from the economy and community of the plantation South accounted for the higher level of Union activism in that region after the fall of Fort Sumter.[61]

Politics set the mountains apart from the big cities. The market's arrival in Appalachia did not divide voters into a party of self-sufficient yeomen against one representing merchants, planters, and townsfolk. Instead, the role of the market in mountain politics was to increase party competition in those places it penetrated. In market towns and county seats, cultural diversity and rivalries over trade promoted competition in a variety of public arenas, including elections and government. An absence of party competition characterized homogenous, self-sufficient mountain hollows, where either Whigs or Democrats dominated.

Party affiliation proved a less-reliable predictor of Union or Confederate loyalty than did factors related to cultural background or economic status. After Lincoln's election, voting on secession conventions in the mountains of Tennessee and North Carolina followed social, rather than party, distinctions, with slaveholding comprising the single-strongest predictor of support for secession. Once war began, political notables put aside party animosities for new, wartime allegiances. Andrew Johnson, East Tennessee's premier Democrat, cooperated in support of the Union with his prewar Whig nemesis, William G. Brownlow. On the Confederate side, General Felix Zollicoffer, a prewar Whig senator, worked with the Democratic governor, Isham G. Harris, to subdue homegrown Unionists. Two scholars of western North Carolina conclude that federal loyalism in wartime "differed from the Unionism of the antebellum or secession period in that it was not as politicized."[62]

Guerilla fighting in the mountain South stood out for its desperate violence. Neither Confederate nor Union regulars could establish firm control over East Tennessee or southwestern Missouri. As civil order broke down, it fell to groups identified by kin and neighborhood friendship to provide what law there was, and by the war's end many guerilla fighters had shed broader allegiances to sections in favor of feuds over family and personal honor that persisted beyond 1865.[63]

In the cities, politics played a greater role in shaping Civil War allegiance than did the competing visions of the economic future that operated in the backcountry. Cities lacked the juxtaposition of self-reliant small producer and market-oriented entrepreneur that characterized much of the countryside. Because they lived at the center of the market revolution and its modernizing social changes, few big-city residents understood their stand on the war as a choice between republican simplicity or worldly sophistication, self-sufficiency or economic interdependence.

Baltimoreans carried their existing party loyalties into the secession crisis, and for many city dwellers those allegiances prepared them to take up arms for the Confederacy or the Union. In the cities, party identity and the experience of party combat conditioned sectional choices in ways not shared by most rural Southerners, but it would be an exaggeration to say that the constituencies backing the Democrats and Know-Nothings in the 1850s remained locked in place thereafter. The social factors that corresponded to partisanship—income, class, occupation, religion, and family networks—had been reshuffled in the 1850s and would continue to change during the war. For example, in all three big cities discussed in this book, the Union movement brought German immigrants into a coalition with some of their old Know-Nothing foes. In fact, it was the malleability of party politics that made the bitter divide over sectionalism in the big cities so unique. Rather than reflect a division in urban society that attached itself to war, urban partisan conflict reflected a culture of political behavior that pertained to cities, but was unfamiliar to most Southerners. Whereas, the sectional crisis marked the beginning of Democratic domination in most of the South, in the cities it intensified party conflict and entrenched, rather than eradicated, political partisanship as a principal of urban civic life.

For the South's free laborers, the difference between rural quiescence and urban partisanship profoundly shaped their involvement in the Civil War. In the antebellum countryside, even the boldest wage-earning roughs either ignored elections and government or took their political cues from well-off landowners. Following Fort Sumter, Unionists among the rural South's propertyless whites had no organizations, leaders, or friendly editors to rally around. They expressed their dissent by refusing to participate in the elections for secession conventions, an act of defiance that rejected rather than engaged formal politics. When war broke out, the rural South's landless Unionists again made their greatest impact through inaction. They refused to volunteer for the army, dodged the draft in 1862, and deserted their units upon the first opportunity. Only after 1862, when wartime hardships hit home and Confederate provost marshals confiscated supplies and hauled off draft-age men, did poor white Unionists organize guerilla resistance.[64]

In contrast, workingmen in Southern big cities had long experience in politics, and their ready assumption of the duties and opportunities of war reinforced their involvement in government and civic life. The career of James Caulk, a Baltimore boilermaker and a member of the Tiger gang, illustrates how prewar political engagement led urban workingmen to immerse themselves in the Civil War and its politics. In 1857, Caulk, having been recently wounded in an election campaign riot, won a job on the Know-Nothing police force. Just before the 1860 presidential election, Caulk joined the Republican Party and was later rewarded by the Lincoln administration with a job in the customs service. In September 1861, he enlisted in a federal artillery unit. Caulk saw combat in Virginia and rose to the rank of sergeant before being posted to Baltimore in 1864. Upon his return to the Seventeenth Ward, Caulk became active in the Unconditional Union party, and, in 1865, he was elected to the first of two terms on the city council. In the cities, workers had their own political clubs and had friends among influential legislators like Baltimore's Henry Winter Davis. They formed the vanguard of Southern federal units and returned from war ready to take on leadership roles in local politics.[65]

In antebellum America, people living in the slave states' largest cities, places that today seem "un-Southern" or atypical of the region, saw themselves as Southerners, as did other residents of their section. Baltimore, New Orleans, and St. Louis lost that designation by taking a different road to the Civil War than the one traveled by most Southerners. At the time that most slave-state voters gave up on a system of party competition that clashed with ideas about honor, manly conduct, and communal harmony, city dwellers pushed the Jacksonian model of competitive party politics in the opposite direction. They made party identity a surrogate for social conflicts that had theretofore been latent in most electoral struggles, and they attached a vital significance to party victory that made violence the norm rather than the exception to the routines of government.

As a primary expression of public culture, big-city politics grew increasingly dissimilar from the politics of the South. After the Fifteenth Amendment, municipal party leaders forged coalitions that included not only white foreigners but African Americans. As a result, city politics remained open to a wider array of viewpoints than became permissible in the Solid South of the late 1800s. The pluralism, cacophony, and disorder of urban life had always provoked reactions from country folk, but because the voters of Atlanta, Birmingham, and other New South cities ruled by the Democratic Party ratified the new political orthodoxy, few sought to write them out of their region's history. It is worth considering that when those inherently urban phenomena worked their way into the fabric of political life as opposed to the tapestry of the streets, Southerners began to wonder if a particular city was truly their own.

Appendix
Baltimore's Economy and Politics

Table 1. Employment of Baltimore adults by economic sector, 1850–1860

Economic sector and sector subcategory	1850 (%)	1860 (%)	Change, 1850–1860 (%)
Primary (farming/extractive)	1	0.4	−45
Secondary sector subfields			
Manufacturing subfields			
Textile & leather	1	1	−30
Apparel	9	13	33
Wood	8	6	−18
Metal	8	7	−13
Food	4	4	−1
Luxury	1	1	81
Other	2	4	82
All manufacturing	33	36	10
Construction	10	7	−28
Common labor	10	12	18
All secondary fields	53	55	4
Tertiary sector subfields			
Commerce	16	16	2
Transportation	12	9	−30
Service	9	13	48
Professional	3	2	−22
Education	0.5	1	35
Government	1	1	39
All tertiary fields	41	42	2
No occupation	6	3	−46

Sources: 1850 U.S. Census, Baltimore City, Pop., NAMS M-432, rolls 281–87; 1860 U.S. Census, Baltimore City, Pop., NAMS M-653, rolls 458–66.
Notes: Percentages sum to within 1 percent of 100 in each column.

    To come as close as possible to giving a random sampling of each group, 4,000 names were selected from the city's 20 wards. The number of names selected per ward was weighted according to each ward's share of the total city population. For example, in 1860, 10 percent of all Baltimore workers lived in Ward 18. Therefore,

400 names were sampled from its census schedule. Smaller wards had smaller samples taken to reflect their proportional share of city workers.

Individuals were selected by dividing the number of pages in a given ward's manuscript census schedule and selecting one person from each consecutive page as determined by the dividend. On each page, names were taken from the same line, or from the first relevant case in descending order from that line. For example, to find 200 working-age individuals in a ward consisting of 400 manuscript pages, a name is selected on the tenth line of every second page. For this method see Stanley Nadel, *Little Germany: Ethnicity, Religion, and Class in New York City, 1845–80* (Urbana, 1990), 10.

The sample represents 4 percent of the 1850 and 3 percent of the 1860 working population. Only one individual was recorded for each household. Assuming five residents per household, approximately 12 percent of 1850 households and 8 percent of 1860 households are included in this table.

Economic sectors and skill categories are based on definitions in Theodore Hershberg, Michael Katz, Stuart Blumin, Laurence Glasco, and Clyde Griffin, "Occupation and Ethnicity in Five Nineteenth-Century Cities: A Collaborative Inquiry," *History Methods Newsletter* 7 (19/4): 174–216, 187–89.

Table 2. Ethnicity and employment of Baltimore adults by economic sector, 1850–1860

Economic sector and sector subcategory	1850			1860		
	Native white (%)	Foreign white (%)	African American (%)	Native white (%)	Foreign white (%)	African American (%)
Primary (farming/extractive)	68	6	26	53	18	29
Secondary sector subfields						
Manufacturing subfields						
Textile & leather	63	37	0	53	37	11
Apparel	48	49	3	43	55	2
Wood	63	28	8	60	37	3
Metal	64	32	3	57	41	2
Food	46	48	7	44	53	3
Luxury	38	62	0	38	62	0
Other	70	29	1	50	48	2
All manufacturing	57	38	4	50	48	2
Construction	63	16	21	65	20	14
Common labor	19	53	28	15	66	19
All secondary fields	51	37	12	45	48	8

Tertiary sector subfields

Commerce	67	31	2	66	33	1
Transportation	50	21	29	39	33	28
Service	22	29	49	18	35	48
Professional	82	17	1	75	21	4
Education	30	60	10	48	52	0
Government	79	18	3	87	11	2
All tertiary fields	53	27	20	47	32	21
No occupation	55	24	22	62	31	8
All city workers	52	32	16	46	41	13

Note: Percentages sum to within 1 percent of 100 by row and year.

Table 3. Social status and political involvement in Baltimore, 1840–1860

Level of political involvement	Ten-year resident (%)	High-white-collar job (%)	Per-capita wealth in 1850	Native-born white (%)
Working-age, 1850	51	5	$243	52
Continuous resident, 1850–60		8	$927	58
Eligible voters, 1850		9	$947	76
1840 voters	65	15	$854[a]	83
Minor politicians	72	36	$3,836	96
Major politicians	89	80	$7,468	97

Sources: "List of the Voters in Baltimore, at the Election held on October 7, 1840," (n.p., n.d.), at the MdHS Library. The only extant voter lists for Civil War–era Baltimore either are incomplete or record votes at the April 24, 1861, election, which because it had only a single ticket did not reflect the full range of Baltimore voters. 1850 U.S. Census, Baltimore City, Pop., NAMS M-432, rolls 281–87. Records yielded data on 836 activists in the Democratic and American Parties, 1854–1855. Of 54 Know-Nothings holding major offices, 27 were Whigs and 8, Democrats. Eighty percent of 46 Democratic major officeholders were active Democrats before 1854.

Prior party affiliation database exceeds 1,500. *Sources: American Democrat, Baltimore American, Clipper, Republican, Exchange, Patriot,* and *Sun.* At the BCA, *Officers of the Corporation,* 1840–1866, mayor's papers, city council papers, RG 16, ser. 1, 1847–61. At the MdHSSC, see papers of the Howard family, William P. Preston, Thomas Swann, James A. Pearce, J. Morrison Harris, Henry W. Davis, Mayer family, Glenn family, and Brune-Randall Collection. Ridgway, *Community Leadership in Maryland,* esp. 87–88, 98, 102–3, 153–54; W. Wayne Smith, "Jacksonian Democracy on the Chesapeake: Class, Kinship and Politics," *MdHM* 63, no. 1 (1968): 60–62. To get a comparable estimate of wealth, data from the 1850 census are used. The discrepancy between the 1850 and 1860 census figures makes the numbers questionable in comparisons across the decade. Sample numbers are as follows: working-age and eligible voters = 4,000; persisters, 1850–1860 = 399; persisting 1840 voters = 203; minor politicians = 220; major politicians = 80. Persistence rates for eligible voters were not tracked.

The lower-wealth data for the 1840 voters are offset by the high average wealth of persisting voters from the Eleventh Ward's 1858 voter list. They had a mean reported wealth of $4,704. Their numbers have not been used because the wealthy were overrepresented in that ward.

[a]Refers only to those 1840 voters who appeared in the 1850 census.

Table 4. Occupations in Baltimore and the 1850 electorate

Occupational category	Working-age population (%)	Eligible voters (%)	Change, population to electorate (%)
High-status white-collar	5	9	74
Low-status white-collar	14	19	29
Skilled manual	44	48	11
Semiskilled manual	20	14	−30
Unskilled	11	7	−41
No job listed	6	3	−40
Total	100	100	

Source: 1850 U.S. Census, Baltimore City, Pop., NAMS M-432, rolls 281–87. Eligible voters are defined as white males aged twenty-one and older, either born in the United States or having a blood relative born in the United States before 1846 and therefore presumably qualified to meet the five-year residency requirement for naturalization. The use of such a positive identification for a foreign-born man's eligibility undercounts the number of foreign-born voters, but to accept every foreign-born man over twenty-one as an eligible voter—the only alternative to the blood-kin test—would dramatically overrepresent immigrants in the electorate. Since the heaviest wave of immigration to antebellum Baltimore occurred in the decade 1845–54, it is plausible that in 1850 a higher proportion of adult immigrants were nonnaturalized, and therefore disfranchised, than would have been the case at other times.

Table 5. Linear regression coefficients showing the relation of demographic characteristics of wards and Baltimore's Democratic vote, 1850–1860

Year	Native B (R^2)	Native skilled	German	Irish	High-white-collar
1850	−0.54(0.19)*	0.37(0.15)*	0.68(0.24)**	0.58(0.04)	−0.72(0.49)***
1851	−0.71(0.19)*	0.29(0.04)	1.01(0.30)**	0.07(0.00)	−1.04(0.39)**
1852	−0.49(0.16)*	0.48(0.25)**	0.66(0.24)**	0.17(0.00)	−0.87(0.64)***
1853	−0.83(0.67)***	−0.23(0.08)	0.72(0.42)**	0.73(0.12)	−0.28(0.09)
1854	−1.04(0.80)***	−0.53(0.31)**	0.84(0.45)***	0.93(0.15)*	−0.11(0.01)
1855	−0.74(0.46)***	−0.39(0.17)*	0.59(0.25)**	0.75(0.11)	−0.08(0.01)
1856	−0.97(0.40)**	−0.51(0.14)	0.59(0.13)	1.41(0.20)**	−0.15(0.01)
1857	−0.03(0.00)	−0.33(0.04)	−0.64(0.10)	2.19(0.32)**	0.44(0.05)
1858	−0.09(0.00)	0.21(0.01)	−0.30(0.02)	1.37(0.10)	−0.21(0.01)
1859	0.38(0.03)	−0.23(0.01)	−0.70(0.11)	1.13(0.08)	0.85(0.13)
1860	−0.49(0.44)***	−0.33(0.21)**	0.28(0.13)	0.68(0.21)**	−0.08(0.01)

* $p \leq 0.10$ ** $p \leq 0.05$ *** $p \leq 0.01$

Notes: Numbers in parentheses are R^2. $N = 20$ wards for all years.

Each column of the table represents the results of a bivariate linear regression analysis using the percentage of Democratic vote for each year as the dependent variable and each of the demographic variables as an independent variable. The Democratic ward percentage is used for all, rather than the percentages for all parties in all contests, in order to give readers a consistent variable measurement over time and to make a concise table. In years with more than one election, the contest for federal or statewide office was chosen to measure the Democratic vote, with two exceptions, 1856 and 1860, where the mayoral results were selected rather than the presidential results. In 1856 the October mayoral contest had less violence and fraud than the November federal election, and in 1860 the four-way November presidential race makes for a more complex and less relevant measure of local party strength than do the results from the October mayoral election where Democrats/

City Reformers ran against Know-Nothings. Sources for elections are *Baltimore American*, Oct. 3, 1850; Oct. 9, 1851; Nov. 3, 1852; Nov. 8, 1853; Oct. 12, 1854; Nov. 5, 1856; Oct. 14, 1858; Nov. 4, 1859; *American Democrat*, Nov. 9, 1855; *Clipper*, May 28, 1858; *Daily Exchange*, Oct. 11, 1860.

The demographic categories draw on information gathered in the federal manuscript censuses of 1850 and 1860. Native skilled indicates the percentage of American-born eligible voters who practiced skilled jobs as defined in Hershberg et al., "Occupation and Ethnicity in Five Nineteenth-Century Cities." The same source defines high-status white-collar jobs. Germans and Irish indicate percentage of eligible voters per ward born in those countries.

Census data for demographic characteristics are available for only 1850 and 1860. A constant rate of change between decades was assumed to determine figures for the intervening years. For example, the 1853 native percentage was imputed as the 1850 value plus 0.3 times the total difference between 1850 and 1860.

Several questions might be raised about the appropriateness of the method of analysis. For example, it would be possible to do an analysis with all the years lumped together, using interaction terms of the form, e.g., native x year to detect changes in the effects of native, native skilled, etc., over the 1850–60 period. However, as is well known, such an analysis would ignore the time-series aspects of this data, with potential for serious biases in the R^2 estimate (Charles W. Ostrom Jr., *Time Series Analysis: Regression Techniques*, Sage University Paper Series on Quantitative Applications in the Social Sciences, 07-001 [Beverly Hills, Calif., 1998]).

While it is possible to adjust for such issues, using, e.g., a panel-corrected time-series analysis to account for the repeated measurement of wards over time, such as that implemented in Stata's *xtpcse* procedure (StatCorp, *Stata Statistical Software: Release 7.0* [College Station, Tex., 2001]), such complexity seemed excessive for the simple point under consideration here. With these considerations in mind, and the goal of presenting an analysis relatively comprehensible to the reader, it was decided instead to run a simple regression analysis for each independent variable on each year of the data. While the sample size for each year is only 20, note that there is no need or attempt to infer beyond the current data, which should lessen concerns about the modest sample size.

With the preceding caveats in mind, consider the actual meaning of the table. For each demographic variable, the B (slope) coefficient from the regression analysis indicates the predicted effect of a one-unit change in this variable on the percentage Democratic vote. For example, the slope of -0.54 for native percentage in 1850 indicates that a ward that was 1 percent higher in native population had, on average, a 0.54 percent lower Democratic vote. The R^2 values here can be used as a relative indication of the reliability or dependability of this predicted average. So, while the slope for Irish percentage in the 1859 election shows what appears to be a relative large average effect, 1.1, note that the relative small R^2 of 0.08 suggests this is a relative weak and undependable relationship, which leads us to discount the importance of the apparently large slope.

In brief, these data reaffirm other evidence showing that U.S.-born workingmen were core constituents of the Know-Nothings. The slope for the native-born workers factor, which had heretofore indicated support for the Democratic Party, between 1854 and 1856 becomes negative and therefore shows opposition.

Table 6. Nativity and economic sector employment for the Baltimore electorate, 1850 and 1860

	Industry (%)	Construction & labor (%)	Commerce (%)	Transport & service (%)	Professions, government, & no occup. (%)	All eligible voters (%)
1850 electorate						
Native whites	28	12	17	13	7	77
Foreign whites	9	5	5	3	1	23
All eligible voters	37	17	22	16	8	100
1860 electorate						
Native whites	22	11	16	7	6	62
Foreign whites	16	10	7	4	1	38
All eligible voters	38	21	23	11	7	100

Notes

Abbreviations

Baltimore newspapers are cited as *American Democrat, Baltimore American, Clipper, Exchange, Patriot, Republican, The South,* and *Sun.*

BCA	Baltimore City Archives, Baltimore, Maryland
LC	Manuscripts Division, Library of Congress, Washington
LHQ	*Louisiana Historical Quarterly*
LSU	Louisiana and Lower Mississippi Valley Collections, Special Collections, Hill Memorial Library, Louisiana State University, Baton Rouge
MdHM	*Maryland Historical Magazine*
MdHSL	Library of Maryland History, Maryland Historical Society, Baltimore
MdHSSC	Special Collections, Maryland Historical Society, Baltimore
MoHR	*Missouri Historical Review*
MoHS	Missouri Historical Society, St. Louis
MSA	Maryland State Archives, Annapolis, Maryland
NAMS	National Archives Microfilm Series
NARA	National Archives and Records Administration, Washington, D.C.
NOPL	New Orleans Public Library
TUL	Special Collections, Howard-Tilton Library, Tulane University, New Orleans
UNCSC	Southern Historical Collection, Wilson Library, University of North Carolina, Chapel Hill
WHMC	Western Historical Manuscripts Collection, University of Missouri, Columbia

Introduction

1. Eric Foner, "Free Labor and Nineteenth-Century Political Ideology," in *The Market Revolution in America: Social, Political, and Religious Expressions,* ed. Melvyn Stokes and Stephen Conway (Charlottesville, Va., 1996), 111.

2. Ibid., 117.

3. Paul Boyer and Stephen Nissbenbaum, *Salem Possessed: The Social Origins of Witchcraft* (Cambridge, Eng., 1974), 166, 172; Gary B. Nash, *The Urban Crucible: The Northern Seaports and the Origins of the American Revolution* (1979; rpt., Cambridge, Mass., 1986), 1.

4. Thomas Jefferson, *Notes on the State of Virginia* (1785; rpt., New York, 1964), 157–58; Thomas P. Slaughter, *The Whiskey Rebellion: Frontier Epilogue to the American Revolution* (New York, 1986), 70, 187 (quotation); Reginald Horsman, *The New Republic: The United States of America, 1789–1815* (Harlow, Eng., 2000), 12.

5. Howard P. Chudacoff and Judith E. Smith, *The Evolution of American Urban Society*, 4th ed. (Englewood Cliffs, N.J., 1994), 69–70. Unless otherwise noted, population data are in J. D. B. DeBow, *The Seventh Census of the United States: 1850* (Washington, D.C., 1853) and Joseph C. G. Kennedy, *Population of the United States in 1860* (1864; rpt., New York, 1990).

6. Tyler Anbinder, *Five Points* (New York, 2001), 145; Paul Gilje, *The Road to Mobocracy: Popular Disorder in New York City, 1763–1834* (Chapel Hill, N.C., 1987), 140–41; Sean Wilentz, *Chants Democratic: New York City and the Rise of the American Working Class* (New York, 1984), 107 (quotation), 175, 382–83; Mary P. Ryan, *Civic Wars: Democracy and Public Life in the American City during the Nineteenth Century* (Berkeley, Calif. 1997), 34; David M. Henkin, *City Reading: Written Words and Public Space in Antebellum New York* (New York, 1998), 12.

7. Morton and Lucia White, *The Intellectual versus the City: From Jefferson to Frank Lloyd Wright* (Cambridge, Mass., 1962) 23–24.

8. Mark Voss-Hubbard, *Beyond Party: Cultures of Antipartisanship in Northern Politics before the Civil War* (Baltimore, 2002), 42, 211.

9. William W. Freehling, *The South vs. the South: How Anti-Confederate Southerners Shaped the Course of the Civil War* (New York, 2001).

10. Leonidas W. Spratt, *The Philosophy of Secession: A Southern View* (Charleston, S.C., 1861), 8.

One. The Specter of Mob Rule

1. James Henry Hammond, "Speech on the Admission of Kansas . . . in the Senate of the United States Mar. 4, 1858," in *Selections from the Letters and Speeches of James Henry Hammond, of South Carolina* (1866; rpt., Spartanburg, S.C., 1978), 319.

2. Stephanie McCurry, *Masters of Small Worlds: Yeomen Households, Gender Relations, and the Political Culture of the Antebellum South Carolina Low Country* (New York, 1995), 226.

3. Edmund Ruffin, *African Colonization Unveiled* (Washington, D.C., 1859), 2; Edmund Ruffin, *The Political Economy of Slavery* (Washington, D.C., 1857), 29.

4. "A Citizen of Virginia," *The Union, Past and Future; How It Works and How to Save It* (Washington, D.C., 1850), 26–27.

5. Charles Davis to William P. Miles, Dec. 8, 1859, William Porcher Miles Papers, UNCSC.

6. Alexander Stephens, "The Cornerstone Speech," Mar. 21, 1861, in *Defending Slavery: Proslavery Thought in the Old South,* ed. Paul Finkelman (Boston, 2003), 89–95, 92. Clement Eaton, *The Growth of Southern Civilization, 1790–1860* (New York, 1961), 247; Lyle W. Dorsett and Arthur H. Shaffer, "Was the Antebellum South Antiurban? A Suggestion," *Journal of Southern History* 38, no. 1 (1972): 93–100; James M. McPherson, *Ordeal by Fire: The Civil War and Reconstruction,* vol. 1, 3rd ed. (Boston, 2001), 35.

7. Carter Vaughn Findley, "An Ottoman Occidentalist in Europe: Ahmed Midhat Meets Madame Gulnar, 1889," *American Historical Review* 103 (Feb. 1998): 18.

8. John Coles Rutherfoord, *Speech of John C. Rutherford of Goochland County, in the House of Delegates of Virginia, 21 Feb. 1860 in Favor of the Proposed Confederation of Southern States* (Richmond, Va., 1860), 18.

9. J. D. B. DeBow, *The Interest in Slavery of the Southern Nonslaveholder* (Charleston, S.C., 1860), 4–5. Eugene D. Genovese, *The World the Slaveholders Made: Two Essays in Interpretation* (New York, 1969), 203; Raimondo Luraghi, *The Rise and Fall of the Plantation South* (New York, 1978), 68–69.

10. David R. Goldfield, *Urban Growth in the Age of Sectionalism: Virginia, 1847–1861* (Baton Rouge, La., 1977), xxviii, 265–69; David R. Goldfield, "The Urban South: A Regional Framework," *American Historical Review* 86, no. 5 (1981): 1011, 1014, 1034; David R. Goldfield, *Cotton Fields and Skyscrapers: Southern City and Region* (1982; rpt., Baltimore, 1989), 29, 32; Blaine A. Brownell, "Urbanization in the Old South: A Unique Experience?" *Mississippi Quarterly* 26 (Spring, 1973): 105–19; McPherson, *Ordeal by Fire,* 27–35; Claudia Dale Goldin, *Urban Slavery in the American South, 1820–1860: A Quantitative History* (Chicago, 1976). Daniel W. Crofts, "Late Antebellum Virginia Reconsidered," *Virginia Magazine of History and Biography* 107, no. 3 (1999): 253–86; Daniel W. Crofts, *Reluctant Confederates: Upper South Unionists in the Secession Crisis* (Chapel Hill, N.C., 1989), 132, 315; William G. Shade, *Democratizing the Old Dominion: Virginia and the Second Party System, 1824–1861* (Charlottesville, Va., 1996), 286; Midori Takagi, *"Rearing Wolves to Our Own Destruction": Slavery in Richmond, 1782–1865* (Charlottesville, Va., 1999), 75–79; Gregg David Kimball, "Place and Perception: Richmond in Late Antebellum America" (Ph.D. diss., University of Virginia, 1997), 98, 110; Michael D. Naragon, "Ballots, Bullets, and Blood: The Political Transformation of Richmond, 1850–1879" (Ph.D. diss., University of Pittsburgh, 1996), 258; William A. Link, "The Jordan Hatcher Case: Politics and a Spirit of Insubordination in Antebellum Virginia," *Journal of Southern History* 64, no. 4 (1998): 632; Steven E. Tripp, *Yankee Town, Southern City: Race and Class Relations in Civil War Lynchburg* (New York, 1997), 87, 89.

11. Wilmington, Delaware, also fits this definition, but it had only four slaves, was closely tied to Philadelphia, and its politics diverged from the rest of the South.

12. A. A. Echols to [Massachusetts] Governor E. Washburn, Nov. 10, 1860, Thomas Butler King Papers, UNCSC; Harriet E. Amos, *Cotton City: Urban Development in Antebellum Mobile* (Tuscaloosa, Ala., 1985), 237; Kathleen C. Berkeley, *"Like a Plague of Locusts": From an Antebellum Town to a New South City, Memphis, Tennessee, 1850–1880* (New York, 1991), 66; Gerald M. Capers,

The Biography of a River Town: Memphis: Its Heroic Age (New Orleans, 1966), 112–18; Anthony Gene Carey, *Parties, Slavery, and the Union in Antebellum Georgia* (Athens, Ga., 1997), 247; Brian E. Crowson, "Southern Port City Politics and the Know-Nothing Party in the 1850s" (Ph.D. diss., Knoxville, University of Tennessee, 1994), 259–63; Eric H. Walter, *The Fire-eaters* (Baton Rouge, La., 1992), 278; Frederic Cople Jaher, *The Urban Establishment: Upper Strata in Boston, New York, Charleston, Chicago, and Los Angeles* (Urbana, Ill., 1982), 362–69; Walter J. Fraser Jr., *Charleston! Charleston!: The History of a Southern City* (Columbia, S.C., 1989), 241–43.

13. DeBow, *The Interest in Slavery of the Southern Nonslaveholder,* 8.

14. Henry Chase and C. H. Sanborn, *The North and South: Being a Statistical Overview of the Free and Slave States* (1857; rpt., Boston, 1972), 15–16; Bureau of the Census, ed., *The United States on the Eve of the Civil War* (Washington, D.C., 1963), 61–62; William J. Cooper and Thomas E. Terrill, *The American South: A History* (New York, 1991), 206. Unless otherwise noted, population data are in DeBow, *The Seventh Census . . . 1850,* and Kennedy, *Population of the United States in 1860.*

15. University of Virginia Geospatial and Statistical Data Center, *United States Historical Census Data Browser,* online, 1998, University of Virginia; available at http://fisher.lib.virginia.edu/census/ (May 6, 2003).

16. Nash, *The Urban Crucible,* 2–4; Jon C. Teaford, *The Municipal Revolution in America: Origins of Modern Urban Government, 1650–1825* (Chicago, 1975), 68, 73–74; Charles G. Steffen, *The Mechanics of Baltimore: Workers and Politics in the Age of Revolution, 1763–1812* (Urbana, Ill., 1984), xiii; Billy G. Smith, *The "Lower Sort": Philadelphia's Laboring People, 1750–1800* (Ithaca, N.Y., 1990), 147; Richard Ostreicher, "The Counted and the Uncounted: The Occupational Structure of Early American Cities," *Journal of Social History* 28, no. 2 (1994): 351–61.

17. Joseph H. Ingraham quoted in *My Native Land: Life in America, 1790–1870,* ed., Warren S. Tryon (1952; rpt., Chicago, 1962), 162–63.

18. Spratt, *The Philosophy of Secession,* 2.

19. William H. Trescott to William P. Miles, Feb. 1860, Miles Papers, UNCSC.

20. Thomas J. Pressly, *Americans Interpret Their Civil War* (1952; rpt., New York, 1964), 94 (quotation). Historians have paid great attention to the causes of the Civil War and Southern secession. For this study, it is important to note that scholars disagree over the degree of Southern white unity behind secession. For examples of arguments for the importance of internal as well as external divisions in late-antebellum Southern politics, see William A. Link, *Roots of Secession: Slavery and Politics in Antebellum Virginia* (Chapel Hill, N.C., 2003); Freehling, *The South vs. the South;* Michael P. Johnson, *Toward a Patriarchal Republic: The Secession of Georgia* (Baton Rouge, La., 1977); William L. Barney, *The Secessionist Impulse: Alabama and Mississippi in 1860* (Princeton, N.J., 1974). For historians who contend that unity outweighed internal divisions, see Gary W. Gallagher, *The Confederate War* (Cambridge, Mass., 1997); George C. Rable, *The Confederate Republic: A Revolution against Politics* (Chapel Hill, N.C., 1994); William E. Cooper, *The South and the Politics of Slavery, 1828–1856* (Ba-

ton Rouge, La., 1978); Steven A. Channing, *Crisis of Fear: Secession in South Carolina* (New York, 1970).

21. This view of secession informs most scholarly work on the topic and has been incorporated into four premier survey texts of the period. McPherson, *Ordeal by Fire,* 37 (1st quotation), 144 (2nd quotation); David Herbert Donald, Jean Harvey Baker, Michael F. Holt, *The Civil War and Reconstruction* (New York, 2001), 131; William L. Barney, *Battleground for the Union: The Era of the Civil War and Reconstruction, 1848–1877* (Englewood Cliffs, N.J., 1990), 125; Richard H. Sewell, *A House Divided: Sectionalism and Civil War, 1848–1865* (Baltimore, 1988), 78.

22. Philip J. Ethington, *The Public City: The Political Construction of Urban Life in San Francisco, 1850–1900* (Cambridge, Eng., 1994), 15.

23. Chapter 6 explores in detail the secession crisis in Louisville and other cities.

24. Allan Pred, *Urban Growth and City Systems in the United States, 1840–1860* (Cambridge, Mass., 1980), 62–65. E. J. Hobsbawm, *The Age of Capital, 1848–1875* (New York, 1975), 229 (1st quotation); Barbara Burlison Mooney, "Racial Boundaries in a Frontier Town: St. Louis on the Eve of the American Civil War," in Simon Gunn and Robert J. Morris, eds., *Identities in Space: Contested Terrain in the Western City since 1850* (Alderhsot, Eng., 2001), 83 (2nd quotation). For claims that Baltimore, St. Louis, and New Orleans were not truly Southern, see Peter Kolchin, *American Slavery, 1619–1877* (New York, 1993), 177; Elizabeth Fox-Genovese, *Within the Plantation Household: Black and White Women of the Old South* (Chapel Hill, N.C., 1988), 77–78.

25. Harry Jansen, *The Construction of an Urban Past: Narrative and System in Urban History* (Oxford, 2001), 37–39.

26. *Debow's Review* 21, no. 5 (1856): 548; Edward W. Belt, *The Reform Conspiracy* (Baltimore, 1858), 35, 39, 40.

27. Joseph H. Lamotte to Ellen LaMotte, Sept. 16, 1854, Lamotte correspondence, MoHS; William B. Napton diaries, Aug. 25, 1856, p. 183, MoHS; William K. Scarborough, ed., *The Diary of Edmund Ruffin,* 2 vols. (Baton Rouge, La., 1972–76), 1:294, 2:108, 455.

28. J. B. Cotton, *Report of the Superintendent of Elections, to the Legislature of the State of Louisiana* (New Orleans, 1858), 6; L. A. Quitman to Rice C. Ballard, Nov. 14, 1856, Rice C. Ballard Papers, UNCSC; William Howard Russell, *My Diary North and South,* ed. Eugene D. Berwanger (1988; rpt., Baton Rouge, La., 2001), 168.

29. *Official Journal of the House of Representatives of the State of Louisiana, Session of 1859* (Baton Rouge, La., 1859), 6.

30. Laurence Keitt to William P. Miles, Oct. 3, 1860, Miles Papers.

31. Louis T. Wigfall, *Speech of the Honorable Louis T. Wigfall of Texas on the Relations of States* (Washington, D.C., 1860), 29.

32. Benjamin F. Evans to William P. Miles, May 20, 1861, Miles Papers.

33. Voss-Hubbard, *Beyond Party,* 14; Michael F. Holt, *The Rise and Fall of the American Whig Party: Jacksonian Politics and the Onset of the Civil War* (New York, 1999), 957.

34. Anson F. Ashley to his father, Apr. 11, 1855, St. Louis History Collection, MoHS.

35. Spratt, *The Philosophy of Secession*, 4.

Two. From Urban Paternalism to Free Labor

1. For this system, see Carole Shammas, *A History of Household Government in America* (Charlottesville, Va., 2002), esp. 53–82.

2. Richard B. Stott, "Artisans and Capitalist Development," in *Wages of Independence: Capitalism in the Early American Republic*, ed. Paul A. Gilje (Madison, Wis., 1997): 101–16; Seth E. Rockman, "Working for Wages in Early Republic Baltimore: Unskilled Labor and the Blurring of Slavery and Freedom" (Ph.D. diss., University of California, Davis, 1999), 15–18; Christopher L. Tomlins, *Law, Labor, and Ideology in the Early American Republic* (Cambridge, Eng., 1993), 218, 278–79, 283; David Montgomery, *Citizen Worker: The Experience of Workers in the United States with Democracy and the Free Market during the Nineteenth Century* (Cambridge, Eng., 1993), 50; Richard Ostreicher, "The Counted and the Uncounted: The Occupational Structure of Early American Cities," *Journal of Social History* 28, no. 2 (1994): 357.

3. Gary L. Browne, *Baltimore in the Nation, 1789–1861* (Chapel Hill, N.C., 1980), 9–11, 24, 55–57; Charles G. Steffen, *From Gentlemen to Townsmen: The Gentry of Baltimore County, Maryland 1660–1776* (Lexington, Ky., 1993), 139, 141, 146, 148, 158, 163; James Weston Livingood, *The Philadelphia-Baltimore Trade Rivalry* (Harrisburg, Pa., 1947), 13, 15, 21; G. Terry Sharrer, "Flour Milling in the Growth of Baltimore, 1750–1830," *MdHM* 71, no. 3 (1976): 322–33.

4. Tench Coxe, *A Statement of the Arts and Manufactures of the United States of America, for the Year 1810* (Philadelphia, 1814), 79–87; United States, Secretary of State, *Digest of the Accounts of Manufacturing Establishments in the United States, and of Their Manufactures* (Washington, D.C., 1823).

5. D. Randall Bierne, "Hampden-Woodberry: The Mill Village in an Urban Setting," *MdHM* 77, no. 1 (1977): 8; Bill Harvey, *The People Is Grass: A History of Hampden-Woodberry, 1802–1945* (Baltimore, 1988), 9–10; John W. McGrain, *From Pig Iron to Cotton Duck: A History of Manufacturing Villages in Baltimore County* (Towson, Md., 1985), 335; Lynda Fuller Clendenning, "The Early Textile Industry in Maryland, 1800–1845," *MdHM* 87, no. 3 (1992): 262–63; Bayly Ellen Marks, "Clifton Factory, 1810–1860: An Experiment in Rural Industrialization," *MdHM* 80, no. 1 (1988): 54–55.

6. William George Hawkins, *Life of John H. W. Hawkins* (Boston, 1863), 5, 19.

7. Richard M. Bernard, "A Portrait of Baltimore in 1800: Economic and Occupational Patterns in an Early American City," *MdHM* 69, no. 4 (1974): 354; T. Stephen Whitman, *The Price of Freedom: Slavery and Manumission in Baltimore and Early National Maryland* (Lexington, Ky., 1997), 18–21, 168–69.

8. Whitman H. Ridgway, *Community Leadership in Maryland, 1790–1840: A Comparative Analysis of Power in Society* (Chapel Hill, N.C., 1979), 71–87; Thaddeus P. Thomas, *The City Government of Baltimore* (Baltimore, 1896), 18; Steffen, *The Mechanics of Baltimore*, 13, 44, 75–81, 97, 143, 166, 171–75, 189; Mary Jane Dowd, "The State in the Maryland Economy, 1776–1807," *MdHM* 57,

nos. 2–3 (1962): 90–132, 93, 102; Tina H. Sheller, "Artisans, Manufacturing, and the Rise of a Manufacturing Interest in Baltimore Town," *MdHM* 83, no. 1 (1988): 3–17, 6–9, 10–11.

9. William Bruce Catton, "The Baltimore Business Community and the Secession Crisis, 1860–61" (master's thesis, University of Maryland, 1952), 3–6; Browne, *Baltimore in the Nation*, 25–28, 168–69, 171; Frank R. Rutter, *South American Trade of Baltimore* (Baltimore, 1897), 16–49.

10. James D. Dilts, *The Great Road: The Building of the Baltimore and Ohio, the Nation's First Railroad, 1828–1853* (Stanford, Calif., 1993), 28, 36–38, 42–44, 49–50, 143. Sherry H. Olson, *Baltimore: The Building of an American City* (Baltimore, 1980), 77, 79; Norman G. Rukert, *Historic Canton* (Baltimore, 1978), 19–20; Edward K. Muller and Paul A. Groves, "The Emergence of Industrial Districts in Mid-Nineteenth Century Baltimore," *Geographical Review* 69 (1979): 165.

11. U.S. Secretary of State, *Statistics of the United States of America* (Washington, D.C., 1841), 216; Joseph C. G. Kennedy, *History and Statistics of the State of Maryland* (Washington, D.C., 1852), 53; U.S. Secretary of the Interior, *Manufactures of the United States in 1860: Compiled from the Original Returns of the Eighth Census* (Washington, D.C., 1865), 220–23.

12. See tables 1 and 2 in the appendix.

13. Glen E. Holt, "The Shaping of St. Louis, 1763–1860" (Ph.D. diss., University of Chicago, 1975), 280, 366; Glen E. Holt, "St. Louis' Transition Decade, 1819–1830," *MoHR* 76, no. 4 (1982): 367; Richard C. Wade, *The Urban Frontier: Pioneer Life in Early Pittsburgh, Cincinnati, Lexington, Louisville, and St. Louis* (1959; rpt., Chicago, 1967), 201–02; James Neal Primm, *Lion of the Valley: St. Louis, Missouri, 1764–1980*, 3rd ed. (Columbia, Mo., 1998), 193–97; James Neal Primm, "Yankee Merchants in a Border City: A Look at St. Louis Businessmen in the 1850s," *MoHR* 78, no. 4 (1984): 379; Jeffrey S. Adler, *Yankee Merchants and the Making of the Urban West: The Rise and Fall of Antebellum St. Louis* (Cambridge, Eng., 1991), 113; Russell M. Nolen, "The Labor Movement in St. Louis Prior to the Civil War," *MoHR* 34 (Oct. 1939–July 1940): 23, 31.

14. Louise E. Newman, "Commercial Life in New Orleans on the Eve of the War for Southern Independence" (master's thesis, Louisiana State University, 1942), 39–40; Ruby Nell Gordy, "The Irish in New Orleans, 1845–1855" (master's thesis, Louisiana State University, 1960), 15; Roger W. Shugg, *Origins of Class Struggle in Louisiana* (Baton Rouge, La., 1939), 113, 318; Robert C. Reinders, *The End of an Era: New Orleans, 1850–1850* (New Orleans, 1964), 20; Joseph G. Tregle Jr., *Louisiana in the Age of Jackson: A Clash of Cultures and Personalities* (Baton Rouge, La., 1999), 17. Jonathan W. Nader vs. William C. Quirk, Dec. 19, 1855, First District Court papers, NOPL (quotation).

15. Shammas, *A History of Household Government*, 108, 124.

16. Barbara Jeanne Fields, *Slavery and Freedom on the Middle Ground: Maryland during the Nineteenth Century* (New Haven, Conn., 1985), 4–5, 62; Christopher Phillips, *Freedom's Port: The African-American Community of Baltimore, 1790–1860* (Urbana, Ill., 1997), 38–45; Joseph Garonzik, "Urbanization and the Black Population of Baltimore, 1850–1870" (Ph.D. diss., State University of New York at Stony Brook, 1974), 142–44; Stephanie Cole, "Servants and

Slaves: Domestic Service in the Border Cities, 1800–1850" (Ph.D. diss., University of Florida, 1994), 64–65.

17. Serena Johnson Papers, MdHSSC.

18. 1850 U.S. Census, Baltimore City, Pop., NAMS M432, rolls 281–87.

19. William W. Brown, *The Narrative of William Wells Brown: A Fugitive Slave* (1848; rpt., Reading, Mass., 1969), 8; List of Free Negroes, n.d. [1841–1859], Dexter Tiffany Collection, box 63, folder 6, MoHS; Ira Berlin, *Slaves without Masters: The Free Negro in the Antebellum South* (New York, 1974), 276–77; Leonard P. Curry, *The Free Black in Urban America, 1800–1850: The Shadow of a Dream* (Chicago, 1981), 22–26, 29, 39–44.

20. Thomas N. Ingersoll, *Mammon and Manon in Early New Orleans: The First Slave Society in the Deep South, 1718–1819* (Knoxville, Tenn., 1999), 332; John W. Blassingame, *Black New Orleans, 1860–1880* (Chicago, 1973), 10; Gwendolyn Midlo Hall, "The Formation of Afro-Creole Culture," in *Creole New Orleans: Race and Americanization,* ed. Arnold R. Hirsch and Joseph Logsdon (Baton Rouge, La., 1992), 58–87; Herman C. Woessner III, "New Orleans, 1840–1860: A Study in Urban Slavery" (master's thesis, Louisiana State University, 1967), 21–23, 27–28.

21. Fields, *Slavery and Freedom,* 4–5, 33, 37, 62; Phillips, *Freedom's Port,* 155, 199; Patricia C. Click, *The Spirit of the Times: Amusements in Nineteenth-Century Baltimore, Norfolk, and Richmond* (Charlottesville, Va., 1989), 38; Jeffrey R. Brackett, *The Negro in Maryland: A Study of the Institution of Slavery* (1889; rpt., Freeport, N.Y., 1969), 210; James M. Wright, *The Free Negro in Maryland, 1634–1860* (1921; rpt., New York, 1971), 95–98, 101, 113–19, 133, 185; Bettye Gardner, "Free Blacks in Baltimore, 1800–1860" (Ph.D. diss., George Washington University, 1974), 130–31, 136, 156, 161, 179–80, 210; Baltimore City Criminal Court docket, Oct. 1853, Oct. 1857, MSA; "An Act Relating to Paupers, Beggars, Vagrants, Vagabonds and Disorderly Persons in the City of Baltimore," *The Laws of Maryland,* chapter 116, Mar. 10, 1854; Baltimore City register of wills, indentures, 1851 and 1857, MSA; Berlin, *Slaves without Masters,* 316–27; Ira Berlin and Herbert G. Gutman, "Natives and Immigrants, Free Men and Slaves: Urban Workingmen in the Antebellum American South," *American Historical Review* 88, no. 5 (1983): 1198.

22. Judy Day and M. James Kedro, "Free Blacks in St. Louis: Antebellum Conditions, Emancipation, and the Postwar Era," *Bulletin of the Missouri Historical Society* 30, no. 2 (1974): 118–19; Free Negro Bonds, 1846–61, Tiffany Collection, ser. 14, A, box 62, MoHS.

23. Frank Towers, "Job Busting at Baltimore Shipyards: Racial Violence in the Civil War-Era South," *Journal of Southern History* 66, no. 2 (2000): 221–56; *Baltimore American,* July 8, 1858 (quotation).

24. Towers, "Job Busting at Baltimore Shipyards"; D. Randall Bierne, "The Impact of Black Labor on European Immigration into Baltimore's Oldtown, 1790–1910," *MdHM* 83, no. 4 (1988): 337; Dilts, *The Great Road,* 138–39; Frederick Douglass, *Narrative of the Life of Frederick Douglass* (1845; rpt., New York, 1968), 101–2. Richard C. Wade, *Slavery in the Cities: The South, 1820–1860* (New York, 1964), 325–27.

25. *Exchange,* Mar. 7, 1860 (quotation). Phillips, *Freedom's Port,* 231–34. Cf. Berlin, *Slaves without Masters,* 375.

26. James Thomas, *From Tennessee Slave to St. Louis Entrepreneur: The Autobiography of James Thomas,* ed. Loren Schweninger (Columbia, Mo., 1984), 90.

27. Shammas, *A History of Household Government,* 116.

28. "An Act Relating to Paupers, Beggars, Vagrants . . . in the City of Baltimore"; records of the Baltimore Alms House, 1852, BCA; "An Act in Aid of the Benevolent Objects of the Corporation of the City of Baltimore," *The Laws of Maryland* chapter 429, Mar. 9, 1858; Katherine A. Harvey, "Practicing Medicine at the Baltimore Almshouse, 1828–1850," *MdHM* 71, no. 3 (1979): 223, 234.

29. Poor-relief petitions to the St. Louis County Court, 1841–1859, Tiffany Collection, folder 1, boxes 36-37; James B. Clemens to his father, Jan. 30, 1854, Mary C. Clemens Papers, Special Collections, St. Louis University; "Report of the Inspector of the Workhouse," *The Revised Ordnances of the City of St. Louis, 1853* (St. Louis, 1853); Earl F. Niehaus, *The Irish in New Orleans, 1800–1860* (Baton Rouge, La., 1965), 35, 117; Reinders, *End of an Era,* 19, 90. Joshua Civin, "Jacob Cohen and Jewish Black Encounters," paper presented at the Society for Historians of the Early American Republic, Baltimore, July 20, 2001.

30. Harold P. Williams, *History of the Hibernian Society of Baltimore* (Baltimore, 1957), 9–10; financial records, box 4, and minute books, Apr. 4, 1859, Hibernian Society of Baltimore Papers, MdHSSC; Association for the Relief of the Poor, minute book, 1849–1850, MdHSSC; H. Brockenau to William W. Glenn, Sept. 20, 1853, Glenn Family Papers, box 1, MdHSSC (quotation). Frederick M. Spletstoser, "Back Door to the Land of Plenty: New Orleans as an Immigrant Port, 1820–1860" (Ph.D. diss., Louisiana Sate University, 1979), 316–17, 351–58; Niehaus, *The Irish in New Orleans,* 13.

31. Moses Merryman account book, MdHSSC.

32. Port warden's reports, 1853–58, monthly reports, RG 39, BCA.

33. Port warden's reports, Mar. 1858-Sept. 1860. Costigan, a Democratic holdover, ignored Know-Nothing preference for white natives.

34. Joshua Vansant, "The Autobiography of Joshua Vansant," n.d., manuscript, BCA; U.S. 1850 U.S. Census, Baltimore City, Pop., Eleventh Ward and Fifth Ward, NAMS roll 432-T283, p. 111.

35. Recollections of George A. Frederick, vertical file, MdHSSC; William Otter, *History of My Own Times: Or the Life and Adventures of William Otter, Sen.,* ed. Richard B. Stott (Ithaca, N.Y., 1995); Dilts, *The Great Road,* 143, 361; Ridgway, *Community Leadership in Maryland,* 109, 268; James H. Logan Papers, MdHSSC.

36. Ridgway, *Community Leadership in Maryland,* 97; Mark H. Haller, "The Rise of the Jackson Party in Maryland, 1820–1829," *Journal of Southern History* 28, no. 3 (1962): 320–23; W. Wayne Smith, "The Whig Party in Maryland, 1826–1856" (Ph.D. diss., University of Maryland, College Park, 1967), 59–99.

37. Browne, *Baltimore in the Nation,* 152; Anita Rosalyn Gorochow, "Baltimore Labor in the Age of Jackson" (master's thesis, Columbia University, 1949), 15.

38. John P. Kennedy, "Address to the Whigs of Baltimore," n.d. [1844], in Kennedy, *Miscellanies, Political and Literary,* vol. 2, n.p., n.d., Peabody Library,

Baltimore; Smith, "Whig Party in Maryland," 77, 200. R. D. Millholland, Matthew Kelley, et al., *Address to the Voters of the 5th Congressional District of Maryland, Residing within the First Five Wards of the City of Baltimore* (Baltimore, 1834); R. J. Matchett, *Matchett's Baltimore Director . . . for 1837–8* (Baltimore, 1837); 510 out of 1,190 cases were unidentifiable; cf. Amy Bridges, *A City in the Republic: Antebellum New York and the Origins of Machine Politics* (1984; rpt., Ithaca, N.Y., 1987), 67–68; Thomas B. Alexander, et al., "The Basis of Alabama's Two-Party System," *Alabama Review* 19, no. 4 (1966): 249, 252.

39. Perry H. Howard, *Political Tendencies in Louisiana* (rev. ed., Baton Rouge, La., 1971), 51, 63–64; Shugg, *Origins of the Class Struggle in Louisiana*, 146, 148; Tregle, *Louisiana in the Age of Jackson*, 282–94. Maximillian Reichard, "Urban Politics in Jacksonian St. Louis: Traditional Values in Change and Conflict," *MoHR* 60, no. 3 (1976): 260, 269; Primm, *Lion of the Valley*, 170–72; John Vollmer Mering, *The Whig Party in Missouri* (Columbia, Mo., 1967), 71–85.

40. See tables 3 and 4 in the appendix; *Exchange*, Oct. 13, 1860.

41. DeBow, *The Seventh Census . . . 1850;* Dennis C. Rousey, "Aliens in the WASP Nest: Ethnocultural Diversity in the Urban South," *Journal of American History* 79, no. 1 (1992): 155–56.

42. Berlin and Gutman, "Natives and Immigrants, Free Men and Slaves," 1182–83, 1195; Randall M. Miller, "The Enemy Within: Some Effects of Foreign Immigration on Antebellum Southern Cities," *Southern Studies* 24, no. 1 (1983): 50–51; Fred Siegel, "Artisans and Immigrants in the Politics of Late Antebellum Georgia," *Civil War History* 27, no. 3 (1981): 225; Christopher Silver, "A New Look at Old South Urbanization: The Irish Worker in Charleston, South Carolina, 1840–1860," *South Atlantic Urban Studies* 3 (1979): 154, 160.

43. Shugg, *Origins of the Class Struggle*, 146, 148; Merlin Elaine Owen, "The Presidential Elections of 1852, 1856 and 1860 in New Orleans" (master's thesis, Tulane University, 1957), 43.

44. List of voters, 1837; Registration Books, 1838; "List of the Voters in Baltimore, at the Election held on 7th Oct., 1840" (n.p., n.d.); list of voters, Eleventh Ward, 1858–1859, all at the MdHSL. Demographic sources include 1850 U.S. Census, Baltimore City, pop; 1860 U.S. Census, Baltimore City, Pop., NAMS roll M-653, T-463; city directories for the late 1830s and the 1850s. Eleventh Ward sample numbers: Working-age, 507; eligible voters, 477; voters, 1,197. The total 1860 ward population was 10,571. Voters found in demographic sources comprised 82 percent of the list of 1,425 names. Many nontraceable names were duplicates. Although a wealthier Baltimore ward, the Eleventh housed factories, quarries, and high numbers of semiskilled servants. Eleventh Ward adults had zero median property holding; the electorate's was $1,650; for voters it was $3,000. John B. Jentz, "The Antislavery Constituency in Jacksonian New York City," *Civil War History* 27, no. 2 (1981): 111–14. In *Journal of Interdisciplinary History* 16, no. 4 (1986), see Gerald Ginsberg, "Computing Antebellum Turnout: Methods and Models," 579–611, and Walter Dean Burnham, "Those High Nineteenth-Century American Voting Turnouts: Fact or Fiction?" 613–44. Inter-University Consortium for Political and Social Research, *Study 00003: Historical Demographic, Economic, and Social Data: U.S., 1790–1970* (Anne Arbor, 1999). Turnout sources: Gorochow, "Baltimore Labor," ix–xii, 21; Kennedy, *History and*

Statistics of Maryland, 23; Kennedy, *Population of the United States in 1860,* 210–15; *Baltimore American,* Oct. 20, 1840, Oct. 10, 1850; *Sun,* Nov. 17, 1860. An adjustment for a 10 percent census undercount has been made. See above, and in *Social Science History* 15, no. 4 (1991), see Peter K. Knights, "Potholes in the Road of Improvement? Estimating Census Underenumeration by Longitudinal Tracing: U.S. Censuses, 1850–1880," 517–26, and Kenneth Winkle, "The U.S. Census as a Source in Political History," 565–77.

45. W. Wayne Smith, "Jacksonian Democracy on the Chesapeake: Class, Kinship, and Politics," *MdHM* 63, no. 1 (1968): 60; Ridgway, *Community Leadership in Maryland,* 87–88, 98, 102–03, 153–54.

46. Robert W. Fogel, *Without Consent or Contract: The Rise and Fall of American Slavery* (New York, 1989), 359.

47. *American Democrat,* Sept. 27, 1855. 1850 U.S. Census, Baltimore City, Pop., Wards 1–4, 9, 15–17; 1860 U.S. Census, Baltimore City, Pop., Wards 1–4, 9, 15–17.

48. *Baltimore American,* Feb. 23, 1857; Philip Scranton, *Proprietary Capitalism: The Textile Manufacture at Philadelphia, 1800–1885* (Cambridge, Eng., 1983), 83.

49. Philip Kahn Jr., *The Four Seasons of Baltimore's Needle Trades* (Baltimore, 1989), 4; Paul A. Muller and Edward K. Groves, "The Changing Location of the Clothing Industry: A Link to the Social Geography of Baltimore in the Nineteenth Century," *MdHM,* 71, no. 3 (1976): 404–10.

50. Etan Diamond, "Kerry Patch: Irish Immigrant Life in St. Louis," *Gateway Heritage* 10, no. 2 (1989): 27; Bruce Levine, *The Spirit of 1848: German Immigrants, Labor Conflict, and the Coming of the Civil War* (Urbana, Ill., 1992), 297.

51. Reinders, *End of an Era,* 18; Robert T. Clark Jr., "The New Orleans German Colony in the Civil War," *LHQ* 20 (Oct. 1937): 993.

52. David R. Goldfield, "Pursuing the American Dream: Cities in the Old South," in *The City in Southern History: The Growth of Urban Civilization in the Old South,* ed. Blaine A. Brownell and David R. Goldfield (Port Washington, N.Y., 1977), 56; Rousey, "Aliens in the WASP Nest," 156; Berlin and Gutman, "Natives and Immigrants, Free Men and Slaves," 1182–83; Miller, "The Enemy Within," 34.

53. Alexander I. Burckin, "The Formation and Growth of an Urban Middle Class: Power and Conflict in Louisville, Kentucky, 1828–1861" (Ph.D. diss., University of California, Irvine, 1993), 119–22, 132, 186, 240, 249, 251, 260–61.

54. Kimball, "Place and Perception," 51, 61–62; Naragon, "Ballots, Bullets, and Blood," 186–89.

55. Berkeley, *"Like a Plague of Locusts,"* 16,21, 32; Capers, *Biography of a River Town,* 77, 99–100; Joe Brady, "The Irish Community in Antebellum Memphis," *The Western Tennessee Historical Society Papers* 40 (Dec. 1986): 29.

56. Ernest M. Lander Jr., "Charleston: Manufacturing Center of the Old South," *Journal of Southern History* 23, no. 3 (1960): 331, 334, 337, 349–50; Silver, "A New Look at Old South Urbanization," 147–48; Frederic Cople Jaher, "Antebellum Charleston: Anatomy of an Economic Failure," in *Conflict, Class and Consensus: Antebellum Southern Community Studies,* ed. Orville V. Burton and Robert C. McMath Jr. (Westport, Conn., 1982), 219.

57. Whittington B. Johnson, *Black Savannah, 1788–1864* (Fayetteville, Ark., 1996), 56–57; F. N. Boney, "The Emerging Empire State, 1820–1861," *A History of Georgia* (Athens, Ga., 1977), ed., Kenneth Coleman, 152–73, 172; Richard H. Haunton, "Savannah in the 1850s" (Ph.D. diss., Emory University, 1968), 56–57; Edward M. Shoemaker, "Strangers and Citizens: The Irish Immigrant Community in Savannah, 1837–1861" (Ph.D. diss., Emory University, 1990), 316, 318–19; Dennis C. Rousey, "From Whence They Came to Savannah: The Origins of an Urban Population in the Old South," *Georgia Historical Quarterly* 79, no. 2 (1995): 310, 331.

58. Amos, *Cotton City*, 91–92, 212–15.

59. Jane C. Bernstein, "From Anonymity to Unity: The Baltimore Ironworkers Strike of 1853" (master's thesis, University of Maryland, College Park, 1985), 8, 24, 27, 29, 34–44, 58; Ferdinand C. Latrobe, *Ironmen and Their Dogs* (Baltimore, 1941), 9–10, 17, 20.

60. *Sun*, Apr. 12, 1877; *Baltimore Gazette*, Apr. 14, 1877; L. W. Slagle, "Ross Winans," *The Railway and Locomotive Society Bulletin* 70 (1947): 12; Bernstein, "From Anonymity to Unity," 34, 55–59, 64, 73–77. In the Ross Winans Papers, MdHSSC, see payrolls, 1858, box 3, file 63, Ross Winans Day Book, 1860–1867, and agreement between John Marley and Ross Winans, Sept. 9, 1847, box 1; payrolls 1847–51, box 8; payroll book, 1846–51, box 21. McGrain, *From Pig Iron to Cotton Duck*, 245.

61. Slagle, "Ross Winans," 13. In the Winans Papers: payrolls, 1858; indenture contract between Ross Winans and E. Glenn Sept. 18, 1848, and agreement between Winans and George W. T. Cooley, Sept. 30, 1848, box 1, folder 11; Ross Winans to Mr. Runn, Dec. 29, 1853, outgoing correspondence of Ross Winans; John Childe, B&O repair shops, rules for employees, Nov. 15, 1855; also see Denmead & Sons, Mar. 23, 1853, Cortlan & Sons, Feb. 6 and July 14, 1851, register of wills, indentures.

62. Ross Winans, *One Religion: Many Creeds* (Baltimore, 1870), 1, 41–42, 65–66, 95 (2nd quotation), 113 (1st quotation), 133; Ross Winans, *Gleanings from Various Authors*, nos. 1, 3, 5 (Baltimore, 1872), Winans Papers, box 9, v. 13; *Sun*, Apr. 12, 1877; Thomas Winans's soup house account book, June 3, 1861 to May 1862, Winans Papers, box 23, v. 70. Cf. Jonathan A. Glickstein, *Concepts of Free Labor in Antebellum America* (New Haven, Conn., 1991), 25, 30.

63. Winans Papers: memo to mayor and city council of Baltimore from "mechanics and others," n.d. [1858], box 1; Ross Winans, statement on police during the strike, n.d. [1853], box 9, folder 9. Browne, *Baltimore in the Nation*, 184–85; Bernstein, "From Anonymity to Unity," 101 (strikers quoted), 107 (lawyers quoted).

64. Bernstein, "From Anonymity to Unity," 54–55, 86, 88, 105; *Clipper*, Feb. 14, 15, and 23, Mar. 15 and 22, 1853; *Sun*, Oct. 17, 1853.

65. Walter Licht, *Working for the Railroad: The Organization of Work in the Nineteenth Century* (Princeton, N.J., 1983), 13–14, 79–124; Dilts, *The Great Road,* 136, 177–79, 270, 359–60; William B. Catton, "John W. Garrett of the B+O: A Study in Seaport and Railroad Competition, 1820–1874" (Ph.D. diss., Northwestern University, 1959), 142, 145; Childe, rules for employees, 1855.

66. Catton, "John W. Garrett of the B+O," 130, 141, 144–45; in the Baltimore

and Ohio Railroad papers, MdHSSC, see William P. Smith to John W. Garrett, box 92, file 22052; Smith to Henry Tyson, June 27, 1859, and John M. Buck to Garrett, Feb. 9 and 11, 1859, in box 52, file 1573 no. 1. Charles A. Swann to John S. Wilson, Dec. 10, 1860, box 61, file 308 (quotation).

67. Extracts from minutes, board of directors, B&O, Jan. 14, 1857, box 106, and William S. Woodside, "General Order—The Sealing of Loaded House Cars," Apr. 15, 1857, box 107, Robert Garrett Family Papers, LC; *Sun,* May 4, 1857.

68. *Sun,* May 2, 6, and 8 (quotation), 1857; extract from B&O board, May 13, 1857, Garrett Papers; William P. Smith to John W. Garrett, Nov. 11, 1860, box 61, file 3089, B&O papers.

69. For the 1859 reductions, see the B&O papers: "Reductions of Employees 1859 on Western Line," box 92, file 22052; quotations are "Equality and Justice" to John W. Garrett, Aug. 13, 1859; "J.W.H." to Garrett, Apr. 20, 1859.

70. Nolen, "The Labor Movement in St. Louis," 33; Eric Arnesen, *Waterfront Workers of New Orleans: Race, Class, and Politics, 1863–1923* (1991; rpt., Urbana, Ill., 1994), 21; Screwman's Benevolent Association of New Orleans papers, LSU; Richard B. Morris, "Labor Militancy in the Old South," *Labor and Nation* (May-June 1948): 36; Niehaus, *The Irish in New Orleans,* 51, 58.

71. Thomas N. Heald, "History of the New Orleans Typographical Union from May 2, 1852 to Jan. 1, 1901," typescript (n.p., n.d.), 22, 29, 32, and n.p., Aug. 1, 1852 (quotation), in New Orleans Typographical Union no. 17 Collection, Special Collections, Earl K. Long Library, University of New Orleans.

Three. Reform and Slavery

1. *Republican,* Sept. 6, 1855.

2. Joel H. Silbey, *Martin Van Buren and the Emergence of American Popular Politics* (Lanham, Md., 2002), 42, 50.

3. Bruce Levine, *Half Slave and Half Free: The Roots of the Civil War* (New York, 1992), 173–74.

4. Smith, "The Whig Party in Maryland," 222–23; Charles H. Bohner, *John Pendleton Kennedy: Gentleman from Baltimore* (Baltimore, 1961), 171, 176; *Baltimore American,* Oct. 6, 1846, Oct. 7, 1847.

5. McPherson, *Ordeal by Fire,* 65–66.

6. John W. DuBose, *The Life and Times of William Lowndes Yancey* (1892; rpt., New York, 1942), 263; William Lowndes Yancey to Benjamin Cudworth Yancey, Nov. 7, 1851, Benjamin Cudworth Yancey Papers, folder 14, UNCSC.

7. Bernard C. Steiner, *Life of Reverdy Johnson* (Baltimore, 1914), 23–24, 30 (quotation); James Morrison Harris to the Democratic Whig Young Men of . . . Philadelphia, Apr. 4, 1848, James Morrison Harris Papers, box 5, MdHSSC.

8. *Baltimore American,* Nov. 8, 1848. J. Thomas Scharf, *History of Baltimore City and County,* part 1 (1881; rpt., Baltimore, 1971), 123 (quotation).

9. Thelma Jennings, *The Nashville Convention: Southern Movement for National Unity* (Memphis, 1980).

10. John S. Sellman to Philip F. Thomas, Jan. 7, 1850 (quotation), H. C. Scott to Thomas, Jan. 1, 1850, Philip F. Thomas correspondence, MdHSSC; Alan M.

Wilner, *The Maryland Board of Public Works: A History* (Annapolis, Md., 1984), 25 (Thomas quoted); *Baltimore American,* Jan. 18 and 22, 1850; Archibald Hawkins, *The Life of Elijah Stansbury* (Baltimore, 1874), 153, 187.

11. Bohner, *John Pendleton Kennedy,* 201 (Kennedy quoted); Maria Nazarczuk, "Response of Maryland to the Compromise of 1850" (master's thesis, University of Maryland, 1965), 33, 73, 75–83.

12. *Baltimore American,* Sept. 26, 1850.

13. William N. Chambers, *Old Bullion Benton: Senator from the New West* (1956; rpt., New York, 1970), 276; Robert E. Shalhope, "Thomas Hart Benton and Missouri State Politics: A Re-Examination," *Bulletin of the Missouri Historical Society* 25 (Apr. 1969): 179, 188–89.

14. James M. White, deed of sale of slaves to Ferdinand Kenett, Jan. 23, 1860, Rosemonde and Emile F. Kuntz Collection, ser. 3, TUL; Thomas Caute Reynolds to Charles Gayarre, May 3, 1850 (quotation), Charles E. A. Gayarre Collection, box 14, LSU; Mering, *The Whig Party in Missouri,* 78–79; Primm, *Lion of the Valley,* 165; Louis S. Gerteis, *Civil War St. Louis* (Lawrence, Kan., 2001), 41–43, 57–58; Adler, *Yankee Merchants and the Making of the Urban West,* 120.

15. Tregle, *Louisiana in the Age of Jackson,* 240, 261; John M. Sacher, *A Perfect War of Politics: Parties, Politicians, and Democracy in Louisiana, 1824–1861* (Baton Rouge, La., 2003), 81, 307–10.

16. *Proceedings of the Democratic Mass Convention of the State of Louisiana, Held at the City of New Orleans, Jan. 8, 1842* (New Orleans, 1842), 5; Karl J. R. Arndt, "A Bavarian's Journey to New Orleans and Nagadoches in 1853–1854," *LHQ* 23, no. 2 (1940): 494.

17. John Michael Sacher, "The Sudden Collapse of the Louisiana Whig Party," *Journal of Southern History* 65, no. 2 (1999): 222–23; Ryan, *Civic Wars,* 113–14; Louisiana Legislature, *Executive Journal of the Senate, 1852* (n.p., n.d., [Baton Rouge, La., 1852]), 3; Marius M. Carriere Jr., "Joseph M. Walker," in *The Louisiana Governors,* ed. Joseph G. Dawson III (Baton Rouge, La., 1990), 129.

18. Maryland Ten Hour Association, *Address to the Working Men of the State, Sept. 2, 1850* (Ellicotts Mills, Md., 1850), 2–7.

19. Hawkins, *The Life of Elijah Stansbury,* 187.

20. *Sun,* Sept. 30, Oct. 2, 1850; Jacob Frey, *Reminiscences of Baltimore* (Baltimore, 1893), 90. *Baltimore American,* Oct. 3, 4 (Jerome quoted), 7, 10 (2nd quotation), and 11, 1850. For candidates, see *Republican,* Sept. 12, 1855; Ridgway, *Community Leadership in Maryland,* 100, 258; Richard J. Matchett, *Matchett's Baltimore Director for 1851* (Baltimore, 1851); *American Democrat,* Nov. 6, 1855; 1850 U.S. Census, Baltimore City, Pop., NAMS M432, First Ward, roll 281, p. 112, Twelfth Ward, roll 285, p. 248; Wilbur F. Coyle, *The Mayors of Baltimore* (Baltimore, 1919), 81–82.

21. Steiner, *Life of Reverdy Johnson,* 32, 34–35; Henry W. Davis to S. F. DuPont, Nov. 1, 1850, Davis to DuPont, Mar. 13, 1850, Samuel Francis DuPont Papers, Winterthur Manuscripts, Group 9, series B, box 29, Hagley Museum and Library, Wilmington, Delaware. For patronage conflict, see Severn T. Wallis to James A. Pearce, Aug. 10, 1850, and J. J. Crittenden to James A. Pearce, July 22, 1849, James Alfred Pearce Papers, MdHSSC; Smith, "Whig Party in Maryland," 242, 247–52; Birckhead and Peale to William M. Meredith, secretary of the

treasury, Mar. 10, 1849, and Joseph S. Cattreau to Col. George P. Kane, Mar. 16, 1849, applications for customs house officers, Maryland, Civil Reference, Department of the Treasury, RG 59, box 100, NARA; U.S. Secretary of State, *Register of Officers and Agents, Civil, Military, and Naval in the Service of the United States* (Washington, D.C., 1851), 86−89; *Sun,* Apr. 20, 1852.

22. Z. Collins Lee, *The Age of Washington* (Baltimore, 1849), 12; Henry Winter Davis, *Principles and Objects of the American Party* (New York, 1855), 9, 10.

23. Thomas Brown, *Politics and Statesmanship: Essays on the American Whig Party* (New York, 1985), 169; Holt, *The Rise and Fall of the American Whig Party,* 31.

24. James Warner Harry, *The Maryland Constitution of 1851* (Baltimore, 1902), 22, 32; *Sun,* Sept. 30, Oct. 1, 1850; William J. Evitts, *A Matter of Allegiances: Maryland From 1850 to 1861* (Baltimore, 1974), 34−35, 41.

25. Ezekiel F. Chambers, *Speech of Judge Chambers on the Judicial Tenure in the Maryland Convention, April 1851* (Baltimore, 1851); Catton, "The Baltimore Business Community and the Secession Crisis," 74; Harry, *The Maryland Constitution of 1851,* 22−23, 32, 37−40, 43, 46−47, 62−63, 75, 78; Maryland, Constitutional Convention, *Proceedings of the Maryland State Convention to Frame a New Constitution* (Annapolis, Md., 1850), 117; Mary Patrick McConville, *Political Nativism in the State of Maryland, 1830−1860* (Washington, D.C., 1928), 18−19; *Baltimore American,* Sept. 25, 1850; Ralph A. Wooster, *Politicians, Planters, and Plain Folk: Courthouse and Statehouse in the Upper South, 1850−1860* (Knoxville, Tenn., 1975), 24.

26. Evitts, *A Matter of Allegiances,* 51−53; Smith, "Whig Party in Maryland," 265; Holt, *American Whig Party,* 933; *American Democrat,* Sept. 10, 1855; Bernard C. Steiner, "James Alfred Pearce," *MdHM* 17, no. 1 (1922): 37−41; John G. Chapman to James A. Pearce, Jan. 12, 1854, and Henry D. Farnandis to Pearce Feb. 1, 1854, Pearce Papers; *Sun* June 10, 1859.

27. Tregle, *Louisiana in the Age of Jackson,* 308; Chester S. Urban, "New Orleans and the Cuban Question during the Lopez Expeditions of 1849−1851: A Local Study in Manifest Destiny," *LHQ* 22, no. 4 (1939): 1132, 1149; James K. Greer, "Louisiana Politics, 1845−1861," *LHQ* 12, no. 4 (1929): 555−610, 561, 563−64; Sacher, "Collapse of the Louisiana Whig Party," 238.

28. Randell Hunt, *Speech Delivered at the Whig Mass Meeting . . . Oct. 24, 1851* (New Orleans, 1851), 4, 5; Reinders *The End of an Era,* 56; Greer, "Louisiana Politics," 595, 598; Sacher, "Collapse of the Louisiana Whig Party," 245.

29. Mering, *The Whig Party in Missouri,* 186−87, 202 (Kennett quoted); William E. Parrish, *Frank Blair: Lincoln's Conservative* (Columbia, Mo., 1998), 48; Edward Bates, address to Rock Island Convention, Sept. 11, 1852, Edward Bates Papers, WHMC.

30. V. M. Porter, "A History of Battery 'A' of St. Louis: With an Account of the Early Artillery Companies from Which It Is Descended," *Missouri Historical Society Collections* 2, no. 4 (1905): 17; Sophia Hogan Boogher, *Recollections of John Hogan* (St. Louis, 1927), 27; St. Louis, *Anzeiger des Westens,* July 26, 1852.

31. J. S. Rollins to George R. Smith, Jan. 30, 1856, George R. Smith Papers, box 1-2, MoHS.

32. Steiner, "James Alfred Pearce" (1923) 360−61; John M. Sacher, "'A Per-

fect War': Politics and Parties in Louisiana, 1824–1861, vol. II" (Ph.D. diss., Louisiana State University, 1999), 335–36.

33. Enoch L. Lowe to Jervis Spencer, Mar. 4, 1850, vertical file, MdHSSC; *Baltimore American,* Oct. 9, 1851, Jan. 18, 28, 1853; Douglas Bowers, "Ideology and Political Parties in Maryland, 1851–1856," *MdHM* 64, no. 3 (1969): 199–200; *Patriot,* Oct. 9, 1852 (quotation).

34. Martin J. Kerney, *Speech of Mr. Kerney, of Baltimore City, on the Bill Regulating Labor, Delivered in the House of Delegates, April 21, 1852* (Annapolis, Md., 1852); *Sun,* Oct. 11, 1852 (quotation).

35. Petition of the Reverend James Dolan, May 16, 1853, and petition of Miles A. McDonough, May 23, 1853, city council papers, RG 16 ser. 1, BCA; Michael S. Franch, "Congregation and Community in Baltimore, 1840–1860" (Ph.D. diss., University of Maryland, College Park, 1984), 383 (quotation); *Baltimore American,* Apr. 23 and 27–28, May 7 and 9, 1852; Bowers, "Ideology and Political Parties," 203–4; *Sun,* Oct. 11 and 13, 1852; McConville, *Political Nativism,* 23. Bridges, *A City in the Republic,* 101.

36. *Baltimore American,* May 19, 1852; Maryland, House of Delegates, *Journal of the Proceedings of the House of Delegates of the State of Maryland: Jan. Session, 1852* (Annapolis, Md., 1852), 943 and House, *Journal, 1853* (Annapolis, Md., 1853), 23, 44, 61, 64, 86, 111, 123, 157, 175, 178, 282. Maryland, Senate, *Journal of the Proceedings of the Senate of Maryland: Jan. Session, 1852* (Annapolis, Md., 1852), 1117 and Senate, *Journal, 1853* (Annapolis, Md., 1853), 486. George B. DuBois Jr., "The Search for a Better Life: Baltimore's Workers, 1865–1919" (Ph.D. diss., University of Maryland, 1995), 11. H. W. Davis to S. F. Dupont, n. d.[1853], DuPont Papers, box 21.

37. *Clipper,* Feb. 12, 1853 (1st quotation); *Sun,* Oct. 4 and 13–21, 1853; Bernstein, "From Anonymity to Unity," 115 (2nd quotation); Browne, *Baltimore in the Nation,* 288. Levine, *The Spirit of 1848,* 139.

38. Bernstein, "From Anonymity to Unity," 54–55, 86, 88, 105; *Clipper,* Feb. 14, 15, and 23, Mar. 15 and 22, 1853.

39. Franch, "Congregation and Community," 363; *Baltimore American,* Feb. 18, 1853; *Clipper,* Feb. 12, 19–25, 1853; Membership book, 1852–1860, p. 415, Baltimore Typographical Union papers, box 9, Archives and Special Materials, Langsdale Library, University of Baltimore; William R. Sutton, *Journeymen for Jesus: Evangelical Artisans Confront Capitalism in Jacksonian Baltimore* (University Park, Pa., 1998), 248.

40. Bruce Laurie, *Artisans into Workers: Labor in Nineteenth-Century America* (New York, 1989), 93, 98–99; Sutton, *Journeymen for Jesus,* 146, 226–27, 270–72; Jonathan Zimmerman, "Dethroning King Alcohol: The Washingtonians in Baltimore, 1840–1845," *MdHM* 87, no. 4 (1992): 376–78; papers of the Sons of Temperance, Phoenix Division, Branch no. 8, MdHSSC; *Sun,* Oct. 13 and 17, 1853.

41. *Sun,* Oct. 22, Nov. 9 (quotation), 1853; *Baltimore American,* Oct. 13, 1853; Bowers, "Ideology and Political Parties," 208.

42. From 1845 to 1852, the average ward-level standard deviation in Democratic Party support from one election to the next (i.e., the proportional change in party strength) was 8.4 percent. When the 1850 mayoral returns are included,

the standard deviation rose slightly, to 9.5 percent. That level of change produced very small changes in the proportion of votes won by Democrats from election to election. In 1853, the proportion of votes won by Democrats in each ward changed by an average of nine percentage points per ward from the mean level of support that Democrats polled between 1845 and 1852. These changes were most pronounced in the heavily native-born and working-class wards of the west side. In the west Baltimore wards (Wards 17–20) the percentage of votes for Democrats dropped by 17 percent.

43. *Clipper,* Feb. 14, Mar. 18, 1853; William P. Preston, Political scrapbook, pp. 45, 47, 52, William P. Preston Papers, MdHSSC; *Sun,* Oct. 13 (2nd quotation), 20 (1st quotation), Nov. 9, 1853; McConville, *Political Nativism in the State of Maryland,* 29 (3rd quotation); Jean H. Baker, *Ambivalent Americans: The Know-Nothing Party in Maryland* (Baltimore, 1977), 19.

44. *Sun,* Oct. 13 and 18, 1853 (quotation); John Everett et al. to Franklin Pearce, Mar. 20, 1853, vertical file, MdHSSC; Isaac M. Denson to George Gale, George Gale Papers, MdHSSC; Glenn C. Altschuler and Stuart M. Blumin, *Rude Republic: Americans and their Politics in the Nineteenth Century* (Princeton, N.J., 2001), 55.

45. Samuel Hurbanks to Charles Gayarre, Nov. 7, 1853, Gayarre Collection, box 11; Sacher, "'A Perfect War': vol. II," 342–43.

46. For Hindes, see *American,* Oct. 12, 1848, Oct. 2, 1850, Oct. 7, 1851; 1850 U.S. Census, Baltimore City, Pop., NAMS M-432 roll T-483, Fifth Ward. Forty-eight temperance leaders were identified in Baltimore newspapers, 1840–1860; Franch, "Congregation and Community," 367; and Ridgway, *Politics and Community Leadership,* 101. *American,* Oct. 4, 1845, Sept. 10, Nov. 19, 1846; *Sun,* Sept. 30, 1850, Apr. 3, 1852, Oct. 22, 1853.

47. Cf. John W. Quist, *Restless Visionaries: The Social Roots of Antebellum Reform in Alabama and Michigan* (Baton Rouge, La., 1998), 193, 225–27; Stuart M. Blumin, *The Emergence of the Middle Class: Social Experience in the American City, 1760–1900* (Cambridge, Eng., 1989), 196–98.

48. Henry D. Farnandis to James A. Pearce, Jan. 26, 1854, Pearce Papers, box 2; Evitts, *A Matter of Allegiances,* 62; Bowers, "Ideology and Political Parties," 209.

49. Lawrence F. Schmeckebier, *History of the Know-Nothing Party in Maryland* (Baltimore, 1899), 13–19.

50. Schmeckebier, *History of the Know-Nothing Party in Maryland,* 16–17; Franch, "Congregation and Community," 363; *Clipper,* Oct. 2 (quotation), 5, 10–12, and 17, 1854; Anna Ella Carroll Papers, correspondence, microfilm reel 1, Oct. 17, 1854, MdHSL (quotation); *American Democrat,* Sept. 19, 1855 (quotation).

51. *Clipper,* Sept. 26, 1854.

52. Kenneth Rayner, "Speech of Hon. Kenneth Rayner . . . Dec. 8, 1856" (n.p., n.d.), 8, UNCSC; Gregg Cantrell, *Kenneth and John B. Rayner and the Limits of Southern Dissent* (Urbana, Ill., 1993), 83, 87; Royce McCrary, "John Macpherson Berrien and the Know-Nothing Movement in Georgia," *Georgia Historical Quarterly* 61, no. 1 (1977): 37; George Stapleton to James M. Berrien, Nov. 30, 1855, James M. Berrien Papers, UNCSC (quotation); John D. Bladek, "America for Americans: The Southern Know-Nothing Party and the Politics of Nativism, 1854–1856" (Ph.D. diss., University of Washington, 1998), 55–56.

53. *Sun,* June 3, 1854; Evitts, *A Matter of Allegiances,* 70; *Republican,* Jan. 2 and 10, Mar. 21, Apr. 7, 1855.

54. *American Democrat,* Sept. 15, Oct. 10, 1855; Davis to S. F. DuPont, Sept. 22, 1856, DuPont Papers, box 22.

55. *American Democrat,* Oct. 3, 10, and 25, 1855, May 14, 1856; *Republican,* Jan. 16, 18, and 27, Feb. 8, 13, 15 (1st quotation), and 20, Mar. 1, 12, and 24, Apr. 12, Aug. 26 and 30, 1855, Jan. 15, Sept. 1 and 23, 1856; Browne, *Baltimore in the Nation,* 157, 210; Thomas, *The City Government of Baltimore,* 28; New Orleans *Daily Picayune* Oct. 28, 1854 (2nd quotation).

56. Marius M. Carriere Jr., "Anti-Catholicism, Nativism, and Louisiana Politics in the 1850s," *Louisiana History* 35, no. 4 (1994): 461, 464; New Orleans *Daily Picayune* Nov. 9, 1854; Leon Cyprian Soule, *The Know-Nothing Party in New Orleans: A Reappraisal* (Baton Rouge, La., 1961), 62, 78, 83, 88; A Citizen, *What Has the Present Council Done for the City of New Orleans* (New Orleans, n.p., 1856), 7; James K. Greer, "Louisiana Politics, 1845–1861," *LHQ* 13, no. 2 (1930): 284; U.S. Public Works Administration, "Administrations of the Mayors of New Orleans, 1803–1936," unpublished typescript, 1940, p. 100, NOPL.

57. Gerteis, *Civil War St. Louis,* 55, 71; Walter D. Kamphoefner, "St. Louis Germans and the Republican Party, 1848–1860," *Mid-America* 57 (Apr. 1975): 70–71, 73, 88.

58. Gorochow, "Baltimore Labor in the Age of Jackson," xi–xiv; *Baltimore American,* Oct. 4, 1845, Oct. 8, 1846, Oct. 7, 1847, Nov. 8, 1848, Oct. 4, 1849, Oct. 3, 1850, Oct. 9, 1851, Oct. 14, 1852, Nov. 8, 1853, Oct. 12, 1854; *American Democrat,* Nov. 8, 1855; *Sun,* Oct. 2, 1842, Oct. 22, 1844.

59. Richard T. Merrick, *Correspondence to William Meade Addison, Oct. 5, 1854* (n.p., n.d. [1854]), MdHSL; Fayetteville, North Carolina, *Observer,* May 29, 1855.

60. *Republican,* Jan. 19 and 27, Sept. 7, 1855; Sutton, *Journeymen for Jesus,* 232.

61. *Republican,* Mar. 16 (quotation), May 2, 1855.

62. Joanne B. Freeman, *Affairs of Honor: National Politics in the New Republic* (New Haven, Conn., 2001), xv, xx; Kenneth S. Greenberg, *Masters and Statesmen: The Political Culture of American Slavery* (Baltimore, 1985), 20; Bertram Wyatt-Brown, *Southern Honor: Ethics and Behavior in the Old South* (New York, 1982), 35, 45–46, 69; Christopher J. Olsen, *Political Culture and Secession in Mississippi: Masculinity, Honor, and the Antiparty Tradition, 1830– 1860* (New York, 2000), 5, 8.

63. William H. Trescott to William P. Miles, Sept. 6, 1855; box 3, William Porcher Miles Papers, UNCSC; Wallace Hettle, *The Peculiar Democracy: Southern Democrats in Peace and Civil War* (Athens, Ga., 2001), 76 (2nd quotation); Bladek, "America for Americans," 2; Bertram Wyatt-Brown, *The Shaping of Southern Culture: Honor, Grace, and War, 1760s-1880s* (Chapel Hill, N.C., 2001), 199–200.

64. W. Darrell Overdyke, *The Know-Nothing Party in the South* (Baton Rouge, La., 1950), 93 (Virginian quoted), 109 (Gentry quoted); Cantrell, *Kenneth and John B. Rayner,* 92; Olsen, *Political Culture and Secession,* 153–54;

Bladek, "America for Americans," 121–22; Shade, *Democratizing the Old Dominion,* 283–84.

65. Charles E. A. Gayarre, *The School for Politics: A Dramatic Novel* (New York, 1854), 26, 150. For an alternative interpretation, see Sacher, *A Perfect War of Politics,* 238.

66. Altschuler and Blumin, *Rude Republic,* 83–84; Kimberly K. Smith, *The Dominion of Voice: Riot, Reason, and Romance in Antebellum Politics* (Lawrence, Kans., 1999), 60–61.

67. *Patriot,* Sept. 21, 1854 (1st quotation); *American Democrat,* Sept. 12, 1855 (2nd quotation). Anthony Kennedy, *Admission of Kansas: Speech of the Hon. Anthony Kennedy, of Maryland, in the Senate of the United States, March 12, 1858* (Washington, D.C., 1858), 5; Henry W. Davis to S. F. DuPont, Dec. 1857, DuPont Papers, box 24. Robert J. Brugger, *Maryland: A Middle Temperament, 1634–1980* (Baltimore, 1988), 262 (Davis quoted).

68. Sacher, *A Perfect War of Politics,* 247.

69. James Neal Primm, "Missouri, St. Louis, and the Secession Crisis," in Steven Rowan, *Germans for a Free Missouri: Translations from the St. Louis Radical Press, 1857–1862* (Columbia, Mo., 1983), 9; S. H. Woodson to George R. Smith, Feb. 23, 1856, Smith Papers; J. O. Davis to James Rollins, June 13, 1854, James Rollins Papers, WHMC.

70. Anna Ella Carroll, *The Great American Battle: or, the Contest between Christianity and Political Romanism* (New York, 1856), 107; Henry Winter Davis, *The Origin, Principles and Purposes of the American Party* (n.p., 1855), 14; *American Democrat,* Sept. 15, 1855 (Davis 2nd quotation), Oct. 30, 1855 (editors quoted).

71. William E. Gienapp, *The Origins of the Republican Party, 1852–1856* (New York, 1987), 366–67; Michael F. Holt, *The Political Crisis of the 1850s* (New York, 1978) chapter 6. Critics accept the compatibility of the conspiracies. Eric Foner, *Free Soil, Free labor, Free Men: The Ideology of the Republican Party before the Civil War* (New York, 1970), 232; Tyler Anbinder, *Nativism and Slavery: The Northern Know-Nothings and the Politics of the 1850s* (New York, 1992), 45–47, 119–20.

72. *Baltimore American,* Nov. 5, 1856.

73. William J. Cooper Jr., *The South and the Politics of Slavery, 1828–1856* (Baton Rouge, La., 1978).

74. Records yielded data on 836 activists in the Democratic and American parties, 1854–1855. Of 54 Know-Nothings in major offices, 27 were Whigs, 8 Democrats. 80 percent of 46 Democratic major officeholders were active Democrats before 1854. Prior party affiliation database exceeds fifteen hundred. Sources: *American Democrat, Baltimore American, Clipper, Republican, Exchange, Patriot,* and *Sun.* At the Baltimore City Archives, City of Baltimore, *Members of the City Council, Their Clerks, and the Officers of the Corporation* (hereafter cited as *Officers of the Corporation*), 1840–1866, mayor's papers, city council papers, RG 16, ser. 1, 1847–1861. At the MdHSSC, see papers of the Howard family, William P. Preston, Thomas Swann, James A. Pearce, J. Morrison Harris, Henry W. Davis, Mayer family, Glenn family, and Brune-Randall Collection. Ridgway, *Community Leadership in Maryland,* esp. 87–88, 98, 102–03,

153–54; Smith, "Jacksonian Democracy on the Chesapeake," 60–62. Quotations: Andrew J. Bandel to Thomas Swann, Nov. 17, 1857; B. J. Hall to Swann, Mar. 17, 1857, box 29, mayor's papers.

75. Marius M. Carriere Jr., "Political Leadership of the Louisiana Know-Nothing Party," *Louisiana History* 21, no. 2 (1985): 186; Michael F. Holt, *Forging a Majority: The Formation of the Republican Party in Pittsburgh, 1848–1860* (1969; rpt., Pittsburgh, 1990), 154; Bridges, *A City in the Republic,* 96–97; Glenn C. Altschuler and Stuart M. Blumin, "Limits of Political Engagement in Antebellum America: A New Look at the Golden Age of Participatory Democracy," *Journal of American History* 83, no. 4 (1997): 866–67.

76. Daniel Walker Howe, "The Evangelical Movement and Political Culture in the North during the Second Party System," *Journal of American History* 77, no. 4 (1991): 1216–39, 1224; Richard J. Carwardine, *Evangelicals and Politics in Antebellum America* (New Haven, Conn., 1993), xvii, 30–49; James T. Kloppenberg, "The Virtues of Liberalism: Christianity, Republicanism and Ethics in Early American Political Discourse," *Journal of American History* 74, no. 1 (1987): 9–33; Nathan O. Hatch, "The Democratization of Christianity and the Character of American Politics," in *Religion and American Politics: From the Colonial Period to the 1980s,* ed. Mark A. Noll (New York, 1990), 92–120.

77. F. Littig Shaffer, George W. Corner, Rev. Samuel A. Wilson, *History, Official List and Membership of the East Baltimore Station of the East Baltimore Conference of the Methodist Episcopal Church, June 1859* (Baltimore, 1859); *Directory of the First Presbyterian Church* (Baltimore, 1860); Ridgway, *Community Leadership in Maryland,* 78; James E. P. Boulden, *The Presbyterians of Baltimore: Their Churches and Historic Grave-Yards* (Baltimore, 1875), 27, 95, 129; John C. Backus, *Discourse, Containing a Review of the History of the First Presbyterian Church in Baltimore* (Baltimore, 1860), 86. Politicians counted if listed themselves or if a wife, child, or sibling was a member.

78. Association for the Relief of the Poor, minute book, 1849–1850, MdHSSC; *Republican,* Jan. 15, 1855; Baltimore United Fire Company minute books, Jan. 29, 1855, MdHSSC; *Baltimore American,* Feb. 19, 1857; Baltimore Board of Trade, *Ninth Annual Report of the Board of Trade of Baltimore, for 1858* (Baltimore, 1859). Blumin, *Emergence of the Middle Class,* 209.

79. Thomas Swann, "Notes on European Travels," [n.d., 1830s], Thomas Swann Papers, box 3, MdHSSC; Brantz Mayer, "Italy" [n.d.] in Mayer-Roszel Papers, box 3, MdHSSC. H. W. Davis to S. F. DuPont, Nov. 1, 1850, July 9, 1854, Aug. 6, 1854, Aug. 22, 1854, and June 21, 1855, DuPont Papers, box 21; Gerald S. Henig, "A Marylander's Impressions of Europe during the Summer of 1854," *MdHM* 72, no. 2 (1977): 226–37, 231.

80. Boulden, *The Presbyterians of Baltimore,* 79; Andrew B. Cross, *Priests' Prisons for Women* (Baltimore, 1854) 2, 5 (1st quotation); *Republican* Sept. 21, 1855 (2nd quotation); Maryland, General Assembly, House of Delegates, *Report of the Select Committee on Convents and Nunneries* (Annapolis, Md., 1856); Andrew B. Cross, *Memorial of Andrew B. Cross, for the Suppression of Abuses and Protection of Persons Confined in Prisons, Convents and Mad Houses . . .* (Annapolis, Md., 1858); E. J. Hall, *Report of the Majority Committee . . . to the People for their Action a Prohibitory Liquor Law* in Maryland, Senate, *Journal of Pro-*

ceedings of the Senate of Maryland, Jan. Session, 1856 (Annapolis, Md., 1856); Maryland, House of Delegates, *Journal of the Proceedings of the House of Delegates, Jan. Session, 1858* (Annapolis, Md., 1858), 322; Baker, *Ambivalent Americans,* 100–03; Schmeckebier, *History of the Know-Nothing Party in Maryland,* 33–34; Richard R. Duncan, "The Era of the Civil War," *Maryland: A History,* ed. Richard Walsh and William Lloyd Fox (Baltimore, 1983), 316.

81. Baker, *Ambivalent Americans,* 139; Franch, "Congregation and Community," 366–70. J. W. M. Williams, *Reminiscences of a Pastorate of 33 Years in First Baptist Church of Baltimore, Maryland* (Baltimore, n.d. [1854]), 18; diary, vol. 6, July 29, 1856, John W. M. Williams Papers, UNCSC.

82. W. Darrell Overdyke, "History of the American Party in Louisiana: Chapter III," *LHQ* 16, no. 2 (1933): 270; Stephen J. Ochs, *A Black Patriot and a White Priest: Andre Cailloux and Claude Paschal Maistre in Civil War New Orleans* (Baton Rouge, La., 2000), 106; Roger Baudier, *The Catholic Church in Louisiana* (New Orleans, 1939), 381; Theodore Clapp, *Autobiography: Reflections during a Thirty Years Residence in New Orleans* (1857; rpt., New York, 1972), 248, 250; Carriere, "Anti-Catholicism, Nativism, and Louisiana Politics," 463–66; Soule, *Know-Nothing Party in New Orleans,* 66.

83. Primm, *Lion of the Valley,* 168; Cecil S. H. Ross, "Pulpit and Stump: The Clergy and the Know-Nothings in Mississippi," *Journal of Mississippi History* 48, no. 4 (1986): 275–76; Marc W. Kruman, *Parties and Politics in North Carolina, 1836–1865* (Baton Rouge, La., 1983), 166.

84. J. H. Dashiell, *Memoir of Henry Slicer* (Baltimore, 1875); Sutton, *Journeymen for Jesus,* 247. R. McClellan to Henry Slicer, Oct. 18, 1856, Howell Cobb to Henry Slicer, Aug. 14, 1856, Henry Slicer to Isaac Toucey, secretary of the navy, Oct. 17, 1860; Henry Slicer journals, Dec. 7, 1853, Nov. 2, 5 (quotation), 1859, Oct. 30, Nov. 5, 1860, all in Henry Slicer Papers, United Methodist Historical Society, Lovely Lane Museum and Library, Baltimore.

85. Charles E. A. Gayarre, *To the People of Louisiana on the State of the Parties* (n.p., 1855), 6.

86. H. W. Davis to S. F. DuPont, n.d. [Oct. 1854], Mar. 1855, Apr. 1855, DuPont Papers.

87. *Methodist Protestant,* Oct. 25, 1856.

88. For Askew, see Baker, *Ambivalent Americans,* 73; "Testimony . . . on Contested Elections," p. 32, in Maryland, House of Delegates, *Papers in the Contested Election from Baltimore City* (Annapolis, Md., 1860). *American Democrat,* Sept. 23 (2nd quotation), Oct. 10, Nov. 6 (1st quotation), 7, 9, 1855. Scharf, *History of Baltimore City and County,* 193.

Four. Southern Free Labor Politics

1. Crofts, *Reluctant Confederates,* 52; Overdyke, *The Know-Nothing Party in the South,* 262, 267, 271, 274, 285. Americans held a majority in the Kentucky state senate until 1858.

2. Anbinder, *Five Points,* 145; Gilje, *The Road to Mobocracy,* 140–41; Wilentz, *Chants Democratic,* 175, 382–83.

3. Stephen J. Ross, *Workers on the Edge: Work, Leisure, and Politics in In-*

dustrializing Cincinnati, 1788–1890 (New York, 1985), 74, 80; Susan E. Hirsch, *Roots of the American Working Class: The Industrialization of Crafts in Newark, 1800–1860* (Philadelphia, 1978), 126; Alan Dawley, *Class and Community: The Industrial Revolution in Lynn* (Cambridge, Mass., 1977), 103; Montgomery, *Citizen Worker*, 117, 130; Iver Bernstein, *The New York City Draft Riots: Their Significance for American Society and Politics in the Age of the Civil War* (New York, 1990), 94–98.

4. James Marchio, "Nativism in the Old South: Know-Nothingism in Antebellum South Carolina," *The Southern Historian* 8 (1987) 44; Naragon, "Ballots, Bullets, and Blood," 201, 226; Haunton, "Savannah in the 1850s," 200, 209; Alan S. Thompson, "Southern Rights and Nativism as Issues in Mobile Politics, 1850–1861," *Alabama Review* 35 (Apr. 1982): 138; David T. Gleeson, *The Irish in the South, 1815–1877* (Chapel Hill, N.C., 2001), 118.

5. See tables 5 and 6 in the appendix.

6. Dennis C. Rousey, *Policing the Southern City: New Orleans, 1805–1889* (Baton Rouge, La., 1996), 60, 74; Sacher, "'A Perfect War,' vol. II," 298; Walter D. Kamphoefner, *The Westfalians: From Germany to Missouri* (Princeton, N.J., 1987), 148–49.

7. Thomas H. Hicks, *The Inaugural Address of Thomas H. Hicks, Governor of Maryland, Jan. 13, 1858* (Annapolis, Md., 1858), 10–11.

8. John Pendleton Kennedy, journals, Feb. 23, 25, 1856, in John Pendleton Kennedy Papers, microfilm, roll 3, Peabody Library, Baltimore; Baker, *Ambivalent Americans*, 50; Bladek, "America for Americans," 145, 150, 226–28, 239; Anthony Gene Carey, "Too Southern to Be Americans: Proslavery Politics and the Failure of the Know-Nothing Party in Georgia, 1854–1856," *Civil War History* 41, no. 1 (1995): 33; Crowson, "Southern Port City Politics," 154; Anbinder, *Nativism and Slavery*, 207; Cooper, *The South and the Politics of Slavery*, 368–69.

9. *Republican*, May 23, Aug. 16, 1856.

10. Gerald S. Henig, *Henry Winter Davis: Antebellum and Civil War Congressman from Maryland* (New York, 1973), 83; *Sun*, Sept. 25, 1856.

11. *Republican*, Aug., 25, 1856.

12. Ibid., Jan. 2, 1855.

13. Ibid., Aug. 15, 1856.

14. Ibid., Jan. 3, 1856.

15. *Sun*, Sept. 29, 1856; *Republican*, Oct. 6, 1856.

16. *Republican*, Sept. 27, 1856; *Sun*, Sept. 18, 1856, and Nov. 5, 1856.

17. Brady, "The Irish Community in Antebellum Memphis," 43; William A. Baughin, "Bullets and Ballots: The Election Day Riots of 1855," *Historical and Philosophical Society of Ohio* 21, no. 4 (1963): 269; Amos, *Cotton City*, 228; Charles E. Deusner, "The Know-Nothing Riots in Louisville," *Register of the Kentucky Historical Society* 61 (Apr. 1963): 140; Ethington, *The Public City*, 89, 116, 118.

18. John C. Schneider, "Riot and Reaction in St. Louis, 1854–1856," *MoHR* 68, no. 2 (1974): 172; David Grimsted, *American Mobbing, 1828–1861: Toward Civil War* (New York, 1998), 329; St. Louis *Missouri Democrat*, Aug. 7, 8, 10, 1854; Henry Hitchcock to Ellen Hitchcock, Aug. 7–8, 1854, Hitchcock Family Papers, MoHS (quotation).

19. Soule, *The Know-Nothing Party in New Orleans,* 46, 54, 63 (1st quotation); C. E. Taylor to his father, Sept. 11, 1854 (2nd quotation), TUL; Earl F. Neihaus, *The Irish in New Orleans, 1800–1860* (Baton Rouge, La., 1965), 89–90; Rousey, *Policing the Southern City,* 41, 69–70; Placide Canonge vs. William Piles (1855), case 9453, State of Louisiana, Fourth District Court of New Orleans, NOPL. Jonathan W. Nader vs. William C. Quirk, Dec. 19, 1855, First District Court papers, NOPL.

20. Carroll, *The Great American Battle,* 103; Henry Winter Davis to Samuel F. DuPont, Oct. 1855, Samuel F. DuPont Papers, Winterthur Manuscripts Group 9, ser. B, box 22, Hagley Museum and Library Wilmington, Delaware.

21. *American Democrat,* Oct. 6, 19, and 24 (quotation), 1855. Grimsted, *American Mobbing,* 233.

22. Davis to DuPont, Nov. 20, 1855, DuPont Papers, box 22.

23. *Sun,* Sept. 18, 1856; *Republican,* Oct. 8, 1855, Aug. 28, 1856.

24. For a full discussion of these events, see Frank Towers, "Violence as a Tool of Party Dominance: Election Riots and the Baltimore Know-Nothings," *MdHM* 93, no. 1 (1998): 5–38.

25. Democratic city convention, committee minute book—Committee of Law and Order, Oct., 1856, MdHSSC; *Baltimore American,* Nov. 3 and 4, 1856; *Clipper,* Sept. 24, 1856.

26. *Baltimore American,* Nov. 5, 1856.

27. Evitts, *A Matter of Allegiances,* 103; *Republican,* Aug. 12–14, 17–18, 22, 24, and 29, Sept. 7, Oct. 17, 1857; *Baltimore American,* Oct. 8 and 9, 1857; *Clipper,* May 31, 1858.

28. Soule, *Know-Nothing Party in New Orleans,* 73–74, 82; Thomas K. Wharton's private journal, June 3, Nov. 4, 1856, LSU; Rousey, *Policing the Southern City,* 76; A. L. Diket, *Senator John Slidell and the Community He Represented in Washington, 1853–1861* (Washington, D.C., 1982), 460.

29. Jean H. Baker, *The Politics of Continuity: Maryland Political Parties from 1858 to 1870* (Baltimore, 1973), 1–5.

30. Towers, "Violence as a Tool of Party Dominance"; *The Revised Ordinances of the City of St. Louis, 1853* (St. Louis, 1853), 363–65.

31. Democrats provided most testimony on Know-Nothing fraud, and despite American Party cross-examination these sources are open to charges of partisan bias. However, newspapers corroborated court testimony. See the *Republican,* Nov. 5–7, 1857, and *Baltimore American,* Nov. 3–19, 1859.

32. Maryland, House of Delegates, *Baltimore City Contested Election—Papers in the Contested Election from Baltimore City, 1859: Adam Denmead, E. Wyatt Blanchard, Francis B. Loney, et al. vs. Charles L. Kraft, Thomas Booze, Robert L. Seth et al.* Annapolis. Md., 1860 (hereafter cited as *Baltimore Contested Election, 1859*), 52, 88; *Republican,* June 11, 1856; US House of Representatives, 35th Congress, Committee on Elections, *Maryland Contested Election—Third Congressional District: Papers in the Contested Election Case from the Third Congressional District, Maryland—William P. Whyte vs. J. Morrison Harris.* Washington, D.C., 1858 (hereafter cited as *Maryland Contested Election, 1857*), 41.

33. See below for club membership. Police records include *Officers of the Corporation,* 1857, 1860, 1851–1861; police payrolls, 1857 and 1859, in Bills,

Vouchers, Checks, and Payrolls, RG 41, ser. 3, BCA; DeFrancais Folsom, *Our Police* (Baltimore, 1888). Also see John W. Woods, *Woods' Baltimore Directory for 1858–59* (Baltimore, 1859); John W. Woods, *Baltimore City Directory, 1860* (Baltimore, 1860); Richard J. Matchett, *Matchett's Baltimore Directory for 1855–56* (Baltimore, 1856); 1860 U.S. Census, Baltimore City, Pop., NAMS 653 rolls 458–66; 1850 U.S. Census, Baltimore City, Pop., NAMS 432 roll 281–87.

34. Stephen H. Manly, et al. to Mayor Thomas Swann, 1857, and George A. Coleman et al. to Thomas Swann, Feb. 2, 1857, mayor's correspondence, RG 9, ser. 2, BCA. *Baltimore American,* Nov. 6, 1856, 1; *Officers of the Corporation, 1857–58.* Thomas Swann, *Mayor's Message and Annual Reports of the City's Departments to the Mayor and City Council of Baltimore, 1858* (Baltimore, 1858), 16–17.

35. Rousey, *Policing the Southern City,* 66–67, 71–76; Gerard Stith, *Message of Gerard Stith . . . Oct. 12, 1858* (New Orleans, 1858), 12.

36. Soule, *Know-Nothing Party in New Orleans,* 82; Eugene O'Sullivan to John Slidell, Feb. 23, 1857, applications for appointments as customs service officers, 1833–1910, in "Records Relating to Customs Service Appointments, Division of Appointments, General Records of the Department of the Treasury," RG 56, NARA. George T. Mason to Howell Cobb, Feb. 1, 1858, in "Customs House Nominations,—Delaware, Maryland, Georgetown, D.C., Virginia—Mar. 4, 1857 to Mar. 4, 1861," Treasury Department, civil records, NARA. Also see the biannual lists of federal officers for 1855, 1857, and 1859, published in U.S. Secretary of State, *Register of Officers and Agents.*

37. Towers, "Violence as a Tool of Party Dominance," 17.

38. *Officers of the Corporation,* 1857, 13–14; *American Democrat,* Sept. 27, 1855, Nov. 7, 1855; *Baltimore American,* Nov. 4, 1856; *Clipper,* Dec. 11, 1854; U.S. 7th Census, 1850, population schedules for Baltimore City, NAMS 432, roll 284, p. 102; *Baltimore City Directory, 1860,* 79; William P. Whyte, Baltimore Municipal Election testimony, 1857, p. 4, Frederick and William Pinckney Whyte Papers, MdHSSC; *Maryland Contested Election, 1857,* 41–42, 203, 223–24; *Republican,* Nov. 5, 1857. *Baltimore Contested Election, 1859,* 45–46 (Mauer quoted); *Baltimore American,* Nov. 3, 1859.

39. Petition of Henry Peire, Nov. 14, 1855, in Henry L. Peire vs. William A. Nott, First District Court papers; Joseph Brownlee vs. Louis Bertrand, Nov. 12, 1857, Fourth District Court papers, NOPL.

40. Towers, "Violence as a Tool of Party Dominance," 14. Louisiana Senate, *Majority Report and Resolution on the Petition of Henry M. Hyams, Henry St. Paul, and Dr. D. Withers Contesting . . . Their Seats as Senators from the Parish of Orleans* (Baton Rouge, La., 1856), 17; testimony of George Lughenbuhl, Canonge vs. Piles.

41. *American Democrat,* Sept. 17, 1855; *Clipper* Apr. 17 (quotation) and 30, 1857; "Baltimore Pony Gazette," Apr. 27, 1856, Pioneer Hook and Ladder Co. papers.

42. Henig, *Henry Winter Davis,* 116 (quotation); coroner's inquest, n.d. [1859], Health Department records, RG 19 ser. 1, box 26, BCA; *Baltimore American,* Nov. 3–15, 1859; William P. Preston Papers, Historical Manuscripts and Archives Department, McKeldin Library, University of Maryland.

43. Towers, "Violence as a Tool of Party Dominance," 18–22.

44. Carroll, *Great American Battle*, 236; Clark, "The New Orleans German Colony in the Civil War," 997; John R. Mulkern, *The Know-Nothing Party in Massachusetts: The Rise and Fall of a People's Movement* (Boston, 1990), 102.

45. Primm, *Lion of the Valley*, 172–73; G. Engelmann to Soulard, Nov. 11, 1854, Soulard Family Papers, box 2, MoHS; Porter, "A History of Battery 'A' of St. Louis," 17; Washington Guards, minute book, 1853–1855, Feb. 24 (quotation), Aug. 11, 1854, in Missouri Militia Collection, box 1, MoHS; Schneider, "Riot and Reaction in St. Louis," 174, 183–84; Washington King, *Mayor's Message with Accompanying Documents . . . 1855* (St. Louis, 1855); Gerteis, *Civil War St. Louis*, 65, 71, 77; William B. Faherty, *Better the Dream: St. Louis University and Community* (St. Louis, 1968), 103; Michael McInnis, "Know-Nothing Party History," unpublished typescript (n.d.), p. 6, Revolutionary War papers, MoHS.

46. This study categorizes political clubs as organizations that participated in elections and government but that were not direct subsidiaries of the parties.

47. Altschuler and Blumin, *Rude Republic*, 17.

48. Malcolm Klein, *The American Street Gang: Its Nature, Prevalence, and Control* (New York, 1995), 20–21; Martin Sanchez Jankowski, *Islands in the Street: Gangs and American Urban Society* (Berkeley, Calif. 1991), 1–5.

49. City newspapers published in the 1850s include *American Democrat, Baltimore American, Clipper, Exchange, Patriot, Republican,* and *Sun.* At the BCA, see mayor's correspondence, 1853–1861, city council papers, RG 16, ser. 1, 1853–1861, reports and returns, RG 41, ser. 2, 1850–1865; also see *Baltimore Contested Election, 1859; Maryland Contested Election, 1857;* list of officers and members, New Market Fire Co., 1857, Equitable Fire Insurance Co., Baltimore; Pioneer Hook and Ladder Co. papers; Baltimore Republican Association, June 5, 1860, William Gunnison application and papers, applications for appointments as customs service officers, Civil Reference Division, RG 56, no. 247, box 100, NARA; Browne, *Baltimore in the Nation, 1789–1861,* 292; Fields, *Slavery and Freedom on the Middle Ground,* 60. Demographic sources: *Woods' Baltimore Directory for 1858–59; Baltimore City Directory, 1860; Matchett's Baltimore Directory for 1855–56;* 1860 U.S. Census, Baltimore City, Pop., NAMS M653 rolls 458–66; 1850 U.S. Census, Baltimore City, Pop., NAMS M-432, rolls 281–87; *Officers of the Corporation;* U.S. Secretary of State, *Register of the Officers and Agents,* 1852–1862; Treasury Department, customs house nominations—Delaware, Maryland, Georgetown, D.C., Virginia, Mar. 4, 1857–Mar. 4, 1861.

50. For "traditionalists" see Bruce Laurie, *Working People of Philadelphia, 1800–1850* (Philadelphia, 1980). Gail Bederman, *Manliness and Civilization: A Cultural History of Gender and Race in the United States, 1880–1917* (Chicago, 1995), 13; Amy S. Greenberg, *Cause for Alarm: The Volunteer Fire Department in the Nineteenth-century City* (Princeton, N.J., 1998), 164 (quotation); Michael Kaplan, "New York City Tavern Violence and the Creation of a Working-Class Male Identity," *Journal of the Early Republic* 15, no. 4 (1995): 594; Elliott J. Gorn, "'Good-Bye Boys, I Die a True American': Homicide, Nativism, and Working-Class Culture in Antebellum New York City," *Journal of American History* 74, no. 2 (1987): 403.

51. Bresent to Steptoe B. Taylor, Oct. 13, 1859, register's records RG 32, box 36, BCA; Browne, *Baltimore in the Nation*, 292.

52. *Maryland Contested Election, 1857,* 41; *Baltimore Contested Election, 1859,* 54, 62; State of Louisiana, *In the Matter of the Contested Election of L. Burthe, J. J. Michel and G. Burke and also of A. T. C. Morgan* (n.p., 1856), 28, copy at TUL.

53. *Baltimore Contested Election, 1859,* 170 − 71.

54. *Clipper,* Apr. 17, 1857.

55. *Baltimore American,* Oct. 25, 1859; Edward Maddox, et al. to city council of Baltimore, n.d. [Spring 1861], city council papers, box 120; "Remonstrance against Petitioning the Legislature in Favor of Running the City Passenger Railway on Sunday," n.d. [Feb. 1863], city council papers, box 125, WPA no. 125; petition to regulate the sale of meat in public markets, n.d. [1856], city council papers, box 105; *Clipper,* Oct. 10, 1854, Apr. 25, 1857.

56. List of fines and forfeitures, Sept. 1861, reports and returns, box 81; *Baltimore American,* Jan. 27, Feb. 4 and 5, 1857; *Baltimore Contested Election, 1859,* 52; J. Showacre, justice of the peace report, Sixteenth Ward, June 30, 1859, reports and returns, box 79; *Sun,* Jan. 2, 1861. *Exchange,* May 21, 1860; Louis P. Hennighausen, "Reminiscences of the Political Life of the German-Americans in Baltimore during the Years 1850–1860," *Eleventh and Twelfth Annual Report of the Society for the History of Germans in Maryland, 1897–1898* (Baltimore, 1898), 14; Klaus G. Wust, *Zion in Baltimore, 1755–1955: The Bicentennial History of the Earliest German-American Church in Baltimore, Maryland* (Baltimore, 1955), 80.

57. *Baltimore American,* Nov. 7, 1859; *Exchange,* Aug. 27, 1860.

58. *Baltimore American,* May 9, 1851; *Republican,* Nov. 8, 1855; *Sun,* June 16, 1859; *Exchange,* May 18, 1860.

59. For Ford, see *Sun,* Sept. 30, 1858. The Gray murder is in *Exchange,* Aug. 9 and 11, 1860. For McIlvain and Davis, see *American Democrat* Oct. 6 and 8, Nov. 13, 1855; *Republican,* Dec. 19, 1857; Joshua Hynes et al. to Mayor Swann, Feb. 26, 1857, mayor's correspondence; appointments by the mayor, 1859, city council papers. For Segenfoos, see *Exchange,* Sept. 17, 1860; *Baltimore American* Feb. 22, 1861.

60. *Baltimore American,* Sept. 13, 1856; *Exchange,* Apr. 18, 1861; *New Orleans Daily Crescent,* Feb. 17, Mar. 25, 27, and 30, 1858.

61. *Republican,* Oct. 14, 1856; Janet L. Coryell, "Superseding Gender: The Role of the Woman Politico in Antebellum Partisan Politics," in *Women and the Unstable State in Nineteenth-Century America,* ed. Alison M. Parker and Stephanie Cole (College Station, Tex., 2000), 86 − 87.

62. *Clipper,* July 6, 11, 12, 18, and 27, 1859, Sept. 4, Oct. 31, 1860; Baker, *Ambivalent Americans,* 110 − 12; see chapter 4, n. 49. Carriere, "Political Leadership of the Louisiana Know-Nothing Party," 194.

63. *Clipper,* Sept. 8 and 12 (quotations), 1857, July 8, 20, 1859; Baker, *Ambivalent Americans,* 123.

64. *Republican,* Oct. 13 and 14, Nov. 29, 1856; Maryland, House of Delegates, *Testimony Taken before a Committee of the House of Delegates of Maryland on Contested Elections* (Annapolis, Md., 1860), 125; Browne, *Baltimore in*

the Nation, 292; *Baltimore American,* June 2, 1857; *Clipper,* June 10, 1858; Grimsted, *American Mobbing,* 242.

65. *Republican,* Nov. 29, 1856; John Pendleton Kennedy, journal, Nov. 5, 1856.

66. *Exchange,* Feb. 20, 1860; John W. M. Williams, Spring 1857 (quotation), Dec. 1860, diary, vol. 6, Williams Papers.

67. Henry W. Shriver to Frederick A. Shriver, June 7, 1858; n.d. [1858]; Feb. 8, 1859. Andrew Shriver Collection, box 9, Shriver Family Papers, MdHSSC.

68. *Baltimore American,* July 24, 1857 (quotation); returns of the officers of the corporation, in *Ordinances and Resolutions of the Mayor and City Council,* 1852 and 1860, rolls 1227–1228, BCA; J. H. Hollander, *The Financial History of Baltimore* (Baltimore, 1899), 201–2, 223, 380–81; Browne, *Baltimore in the Nation,* 208–13. Because the water department created a one-time jump in spending that was carried out by Whig, Democratic, and American Party administrators, figures for the five-year period 1851–55 do not distinguish parties; see Thomas, *The City Government of Baltimore,* 27.

69. Annual reports omitted precise employment figures. Hundreds of nameless employees on construction projects are not included in the figure citing one thousand employees. *Officers of the Corporation of the City of Baltimore, 1852 and 1861;* Folsom, *Our Police,* 24; Samuel MacCubbin to the mayor, Apr. 23, 1860, city council correspondence, box 11; *Report of the Commissioners of the Public Schools,* in returns of the officers of the corporation, 1852, 159, *Report,* 1860, p. 369, BCA; *Port Warden's Annual Report, Names of Persons Employed, Their Offices, and Salaries in the City Yard,* n.d. [1855], reports and returns, box 71; *Port Warden, Monthly Reports,* 1853–1859, city council papers, monthly reports, RG 39, ser. 3, BCA; Hollander, *Financial History of Baltimore,* 245–47, 305–6.

70. *Sun,* May 2, 4, and 8, 1857; *Republican,* Apr. 27, May 2, 1857.

71. *Clipper,* Apr. 30, May 4 and 5, 1857; *Sun,* May 8, 1857.

72. Catton, "John W. Garrett of the B+O," 166–68.

73. *New Orleans Daily Crescent,* Apr. 14, 1858; Diket, *Senator John Slidell,* 107.

74. For full treatment of this event, see Towers, "Job Busting at Baltimore Shipyards."

75. Three shipbuilders participated in the American Party, although each also had ties to secession and the Democrats.

76. Henry Winter Davis, *Speeches and Addresses Delivered in the Congress of the United States, and on Several Public Occasions,* (New York, 1867), 123; *Baltimore Contested Election, 1859,* 40–41, 43 (quotation); *Maryland Contested Election, 1857,* 37; Soule, *Know-Nothing Party in New Orleans,* 81.

77. *Exchange,* May 19, Aug. 6, Sept. 17 and 20, 1860, Mar. 11, 1861; James Revell to George P. Kane, Apr. 18, 1861, provost marshal, letters received, military records, Middle Department, part 1, box 1, NARA; *Baltimore American,* Oct. 6, 1859.

78. Eugene H. Berwanger, *The Frontier against Slavery: Western Anti-Negro Prejudice and the Slavery Extension Controversy* (Urbana, Ill., 1967), 123; Berlin, *Slaves without Masters,* 370–75; Francis P. Blair Jr., *Speech of the Honorable Francis P. Blair, Jr. of Missouri, on the Kansas Question* (Washington, D.C., 1858), 3, 6.

79. Rowan, *Germans for a Free Missouri,* 76 (3rd quotation), 86 (2nd quotation), 94. Parrish, *Frank Blair,* 67 (1st quotation), 71; Kamphoefner, "St. Louis Germans and the Republican Party," 82; Adler, *Yankee Merchants and the Making of the Urban West,* 148.

80. Michael P. Johnson and James L. Roark, *Black Masters: A Free Family of Color in the Old South* (New York, 1984), 277–79; Naragon, "Ballots, Bullets, and Blood," 291 (cordwainer quoted); Quentin Busbee, et al., *Resolutions and Address of the Wake County Workingmen's Association* (n.p., n.d., [1859]), copy at NCC; Frank I. Wilson, *Address Delivered before the Wake County Workingmen's Association . . . Feb. 6, 1860* (Raleigh, N.C., 1860), 21, copy at NCC; Kruman, *Parties and Politics in North Carolina,* 191.

81. Greer, "Louisiana Politics, 1845–1861," 258–59; Sacher, "'A Perfect War,' vol. II," 383; Soule, *Know-Nothing Party in New Orleans,* 87.

82. Sacher, "'A Perfect War,' vol. II," 369, 385, 391–92, 399; *New Orleans Daily Crescent,* Apr. 24, 28, May 17, 1858.

83. Cotton, *Report of the Superintendent of Elections,* 5; Soule, *Know-Nothing Party in New Orleans,* 89, 91–93; Robert D. Meade, *Judah P. Benjamin: Confederate Statesman* (New York, 1943), 103; Sacher, "'A Perfect War,' vol. II," 396.

84. W. Darrell, Overdyke, "History of the American Party in Louisiana," *LHQ* 16, no. 4 (1933): 614, 618; *New Orleans Daily Crescent,* May 31, June 1, 2, 1858.

85. Rousey, *Policing the Southern City,* 78–79; Wharton's private journal, June 6, 1858; John S. Kendall, "The Municipal Election of 1858," *LHQ* 5 (1922): 364, 366, 370, 373–74; *New Orleans Daily Crescent,* June 2, 1858; T. Harry Williams, *P. G. T. Beauregard: Napoleon in Gray* (Baton Rouge, La., 1955), 42.

86. Reinders, *The End of an Era,* 59–61; Stith, *Message of Gerard Stith, 1858,* 9–10; Charles M. Waterman, *General Message of Charles M. Waterman . . . Oct. 1st, 1857* (New Orleans, 1857), 16; Gerard Stith, *Message of the Mayor, Oct. 11, 1859* (New Orleans, 1859), 2, 16.

87. Davis, *Speeches and Addresses,* 86.

Five. A Revolution against Party Politics

1. Henig, *Henry Winter Davis,* 116; New Orleans *Daily Picayune,* Nov. 6, 1859; Evitts, *A Matter of Allegiances,* 128; *Baltimore American,* Nov. 3–15, 1859; William P. Preston Papers, University of Maryland; Frederick W. Brune to Emily Brune, Oct. 29, 1859, Brune-Randall Family Papers, box 14, MdHSSC.

2. *Sun,* Jan. 31, 1861.

3. 1860 U.S. Census, Baltimore City, Pop., NAMS M653, roll T-464, Fifteenth Ward, p. 511; Boulden, *The Presbyterians of Baltimore,* 79; *Baltimore American,* May 12, 1851; J. Thomas Scharf, *History of Maryland from the Earliest Period to the Present Day,* vol. 3 (1879; rpt., Hatboro, Penn., 1967), 267.

4. *Sun,* Jan. 26, 1861 (quotation); 1860 U.S. Census, Baltimore City, Pop., NAMS M653, roll T-464, Fifteenth Ward; *Baltimore Contested Election, 1859,* 78–79, 277.

5. *Baltimore American,* Nov. 3, 1859 (1st quotation); *Sun,* Jan. 26, 1861 (2nd quotation); *Exchange,* Aug. 31, 1860; coroner's inquest, n.d. [1859] Health De-

partment records, RG 19 ser. 1, box 26, BCA; *Clipper*, Oct. 4, 1860; *Baltimore Contested Election, 1859*, 236–39.

6. Mrs. Benjamin G. Harris diaries, Nov. 4, 1859, MdHSSC; *Baltimore American*, Nov. 5, 1859.

7. Ryan, *Civic Wars*; Ethington, *The Public City*, 129; 150; Jon C. Teaford, *The Unheralded Triumph: City Government in America, 1870–1900* (Baltimore, 1988), 9.

8. Recent statements are in Olsen, *Political Culture and Secession in Mississippi*, 165; Rable, *The Confederate Republic*, 22.

9. *Republican*, Oct. 5, 1857; Evitts, *A Matter of Allegiances*, 116–17; correspondence between T. Watkins Ligon and Thomas Swann, Oct. 28, 1857, and Reverdy Johnson, et al. to Ligon, n.d. [Oct. 1857], Governor's Letterbook, 1854–64, MSA. Schmeckebier, *History of the Know-Nothing Party in Maryland*, 77; Henry Winter Davis to Samuel F. Dupont, Dec. 1857, Samuel F. DuPont Papers, Winterthur Manuscripts, group 9, ser. B, box 24, Hagley Museum and Library Wilmington, Delaware; T. Watkins Ligon, *Message of the Executive of Maryland, to the General Assembly of Maryland* (Annapolis, Md., 1858), 21, 25, 26 (quotation).

10. *Clipper*, May 20, 1858; Duncan, "The Era of the Civil War," 326–27; Swann, *Mayor's Message . . . 1858*, 19, 24–25, 26 (quotation).

11. Belt, *The Reform Conspiracy*, 35, 39, 40; Frederick Brune to Emily Brune, Nov. 8, 1859, Brune-Randall Papers, box 14.

12. Henry Winter Davis to S. F. Dupont, Nov. 11, 1859, DuPont Papers, box 26.

13. Schmeckebier, *History of the Know-Nothing Party*, 102–03; Baker, *The Politics of Continuity*, 33.

14. Maryland, House of Delegates, "Evidence Taken before the Committee on Corporations Relative to the Baltimore City Passenger Railroad," document 2 in Maryland, General Assembly, *Documents, 1859* (Annapolis, Md., 1860), 8, 15 (contractor quoted), 30, 54, 88–91, 107–08, 161; Maryland, House of Delegates, *Majority Report of the Committee on Corporations . . . Relative to the Baltimore City Passenger Railroad* (Annapolis, Md., 1860); John B. Seidenstricker, *Proceedings of a Town Meeting of Citizens of Baltimore Relative to the City Passenger Railway Company* (Annapolis, Md., 1860), 4 (2nd quotation).

15. *Sun*, June 3, 4, 7, and 8 (marchers quoted), 1859; *Clipper*, June 3, 1859; *Exchange*, Feb. 3, 7 (quotation), 10, and 13, 1860.

16. Hollander, *The Financial History of Baltimore*, 278; J. Thomas Scharf, *History of Baltimore City and County from the Earliest Period to the Present Day: Including Biographical Sketches of Their Representative Men* (Philadelphia, 1881), 363–64.

17. Baker, *The Politics of Continuity*, 43; Evitts, *A Matter of Allegiances*, 149. *Baltimore American*, Sept. 25, 1860; George P. Kane to James A. Pearce, Nov. 19, 1859, James Alfred Pearce Papers, MdHSSC. Reformers listed in *Baltimore American*, Nov. 1, 1859. Sources on politicians are in chapter 3, n. 74.

18. *Exchange*, Feb. 2 (quotation), 3, Mar. 1, 1860; Evitts, *A Matter of Allegiances*, 132; Baker, *The Politics of Continuity*, 27, 31; Henig, *Henry Winter Davis*, 138.

19. *Exchange,* Mar. 16, 1860; *The Laws of Maryland,* 1860, chapter 7.

20. Philip J. Ethington, "Vigilantes and the Police: The Creation of a Professional Police Bureaucracy in San Francisco, 1847–1900," *Journal of Social History* 21 (Winter 1987): 201; Roger Lane, *Policing the City: Boston, 1822–1885* (Cambridge, Mass., 1967), 75–77; John C. Schneider, *Detroit and the Problem of Order, 1830–1880: A Geography of Crime, Riot, and Policing* (Lincoln, Neb., 1980), 83–86.

21. John Everett et al. to Franklin Pearce, Mar., 20, 1853, vertical file, MdHSSC; *Baltimore American,* Jan. 9, 1857, Nov. 3 and 4, 1859; William W. Glenn to William H. Gatchell, Aug. 11, 1859, William W. Glenn Papers, MdHSSC; Ralph Clayton, *Black Baltimore, 1820–1870* (Bowie, Md., 1987), 64–65; Clinton McCabe, *History of the Baltimore Police Department, 1774–1907* (Baltimore, 1907), 31; *Republican,* Sept. 25, Nov. 2, Dec. 10, 1857.

22. Letters sent by the Baltimore Board of Police, 1861, military records, Middle Department, RG 393, part 4, NARA. Charles Howard, et al., to Benjamin Herring, n.d. [Feb. 1861], city council papers, RG 16, ser. 1, box 117; *Clipper,* Aug. 31, Oct. 3, 1860; *Exchange,* Feb. 11, Aug. 15 and 17, 1860; R. S. Teal to George P. Kane, Apr. 13, 1861, provost marshal, letters received, military records, Middle Department, part 1, box 1, NARA; Frederick W. Brune to Emily Brune, Oct. 10, 1860, Brune-Randall Papers, box 14.

23. City council, Baltimore, to John W. Ellis, Aug. 2, 1860, and Ellis to city council, Aug. 10, 1860, *The Papers of John W. Ellis,* vol. 2: *1860–1861,* ed. Noble J. Tolbert (Raleigh, N.C., 1964), 447–48, 451.

24. *Exchange,* Sept. 7 (3rd quotation), 25 (2nd quotation), Oct. 6 (1st quotation), 1860.

25. George W. Brown to Frederick W. Brune, Aug. 7, 30, Sept. 6, 1860, Brune-Randall Papers, box 6.

26. *Clipper,* June 5 and 9, 1858; Hicks, *Inaugural Address . . . 1858,* 10–11.

27. Robert T. Merrick to Benjamin C. Howard, Aug. 22, 1856, Howard Family Papers, correspondence of Benjamin C. Howard, box 13, MdHSSC; IIenig, *Henry Winter Davis,* 118–19; Frederick W. Brune to Emily Brune, Oct. 27, 1860, Brune-Randall Papers, box 14; Henry W. Davis to S. F. DuPont, July 1860, DuPont Papers, box 27; Henry Winter Davis to Abraham Lincoln, Feb. 21, 1861, Abraham Lincoln Papers, LC.

28. *Exchange,* Oct. 11, 1860; William Louis Schley to Thomas Hicks, Jan. 16, 1861, Thomas Hicks Papers, MdHSSC.

29. George Brown to Frederick Brune, July 13, 1860, Brune-Randall Papers, box 6. *Exchange,* Oct. 11, 1860; *Sun,* Nov. 7, 1860. A statistical analysis of the ward-by-ward vote for Breckinridge revealed strong affinities between his support and the presence of immigrants. The Breckinridge vote also resembled the 1854–56 pattern of Democratic ward-by-ward support. The Breckinridge ward-by-ward pattern correlated at 0.76 with the presence of foreign-born and at 0.66 with with the earlier pattern of Democratic support. These figures represent the product moment correlation coefficient, a dimensionless index that ranges from −1.0 to 1.0 and reflects the extent of a linear relationship between two data sets. Results close to 1.0 reflect a strong relationship between data sets.

30. *Exchange,* Nov. 6, 1860.

31. *Sun* Jan. 10, 1861 (quotation); William H. Collins, *An Address to the People of Maryland,* 4th ed. (Baltimore, 1861), 7; *Proceedings and Speeches at a Public Meeting of the Friends of the Union in the City of Baltimore . . . Jan. 10, 1861* (Baltimore, 1861), 8; John P. Kennedy, *The Border States: Their Power and Duty in the Present Disordered Condition of the Country* (Baltimore, 1861); Baker, *The Politics of Continuity,* 50–51.

32. *Sun,* Feb. 2, 1861 (quotation). See also Henry May, et al., *"The Federal Union, It Must be Preserved!"* (n.p., n.d. [1860]); Robert McLane, *Speech of the Hon. Robert M. McLane in the State Conference Convention, March 14, 1861* (Baltimore, 1861); *Address and Resolutions Adopted at the Meeting of the Southern Rights Convention of Maryland* (Baltimore, 1861); George L. P. Radcliffe, *Governor Thomas H. Hicks of Maryland and the Civil War* (Baltimore, 1901), 21; Henry Lowe to John Judge, Jan. 12, 1861, John Judge Papers, UNCSC.

33. Schley to Hicks, Jan. 16, 1861; *Sun* Jan. 7, Feb. 1, 1861; Matthew Page Andrews, "History of Baltimore: From 1850 to the Close of the Civil War," *Baltimore: Its History and Its People,* vol. 1, ed. Clayton Coleman Hall (New York, 1912), 166–67; David Perine scrapbook, Perine Family Papers, box 6, MdHSSC.

34. Hennighausen, "Reminiscences of the Political Life of the German-Americans in Baltimore," 57; William Bruns and William Fraley, "'Old Gunny': Abolitionist in a Slave City," *MdHM* 68, no. 4 (1973): 369; *Baltimore American,* Nov. 5, 1856; *Sun,* Nov. 7, 1860.

35. *Exchange,* Oct. 12, 1860; N. H. Pollock to Montgomery Blair, Oct. 13, 1860, correspondence to Montgomery Blair, Blair Family Papers, microfilm reel 28, LC; membership list of the Baltimore Republican Association, June 5, 1860, Gunnison application and papers, applications for appointments as customs service officers, Treasury Department records, Civil Reference Division, RG 56, no. 247, box 100, NARA; William Louis Schley to Thomas H. Hicks, Jan. 16, 1861, and Thomas H. Hicks to Abraham Lincoln, Apr. 26, 1861, Hicks Papers.

36. Kennedy, *Border States,* 37; Anthony Kennedy, *The Position of the Country and the Position of Maryland* (Baltimore, 1861), 6; J. Morrison Harris, Jan. 3, 1861 resolutions, James Morrison Harris Papers, box 3. MdHSSC.

37. Henry W. Davis to Abraham Lincoln, Feb. 1861 (quotation), Henry W. Davis to David Davis, June 28, 1860 (quotation), Davis to Davis, Sept. 1860, Lincoln Papers; Charles Lewis Wagandt, *The Mighty Revolution: Negro Emancipation in Maryland* (Baltimore, 1964), 22.

38. William L. Marshall to Montgomery Blair, May 27, 1860, correspondence to Montgomery Blair, reel 28.

39. *Sun,* Jan. 26, 1861; "Law and Order" to George W. Brown, n.d. [1861] (quotation), William Thompson to Brown, Nov. 12, 1860, Jehu B. Askew to Brown, Nov. 21, 1860, mayor's correspondence, box 30.

40. Resolutions to economize on expenditures, Nov. 22, 1860, city council papers, box 119; Simon J. Martenet to George W. Brown, Feb. 15, 1861, mayor's correspondence, box 30; *Baltimore American,* Feb. 22, 1861; Hollander, *Financial History of Baltimore,* 209, 218, 234–35, 270, 310, 326, 384–85.

41. F. W. Brune to Emily Brune, Nov. 29, 1860, Brune-Randall Papers, box 14; Catton, "The Baltimore Business Community and the Secession Crisis," 53;

Exchange, Mar. 14, 26, and 30, Apr. 1, 1861; Catherine N. Smith to Nelly, May 10, 1861, Civil War file, MdHSSC.

42. Mechanics and workingmen's petition to mayor and city council, Mar. 4, 1861 (1st quotation), mayor's papers, box 30; Peter Mowel et al. to mayor and city council, Mar. 4, 1861 (2nd quotation), report of Joint Standing Committee on Ways and Means, First Branch of city council, Mar. 27, 1861, city council papers, box 119.

43. *Exchange,* Apr. 6 and 9, 1861.

44. Ibid., Apr. 9, 12, 1861.

45. Petition, William L. Garrittee and others, Apr. 10, 1861, city council papers, box 120; *Exchange,* Apr. 11, 1861; Saville refused to endorse the petition. List of employees on Druid Hill Park improvements, Apr. 21–27, 1861, vouchers, 1861, RG 41, ser. 3, box 184, BCA; *Second Annual Report of the Park Commission of the City of Baltimore, 1861* (Baltimore, 1862), published reports, RG 68, ser. 22, BCA.

46. Evitts, *A Matter of Allegiances,* 174; *Baltimore American,* Feb. 25, 1861; Juan Ianni, "The Nineteenth of April, 1861" (seminar paper, Johns Hopkins University, 1975), 12, at MdHSL.

47. Robert W. Schoeberlein, "Baltimore in 1861: A Case Study of Southern Unionism" (master's thesis, University of Maryland, 1994), 35, 39; *Exchange,* Apr. 15 (1st quotation) and 16–19, 1861; Harold R. Manakee, *Maryland in the Civil War* (Baltimore, 1961), 31; *Republican,* Apr. 20, 1861 (2nd quotation).

48. Schoeberlein, "Baltimore in 1861," 50–57; Frank Towers, "'A Vociferous Army of Howling Wolves': Baltimore's Civil War Riot of April 19, 1861," *Maryland Historian* 23, no. 2 (1992): 1–28; Matthew Ellenberger, "Whigs in the Streets? Baltimore Republicanism in the Spring of 1861," *MdHM* 86, no. 1 (1991): 23–38; Charles B. Clark, "Baltimore and the Attack on the Sixth Massachusetts Regiment, April 19, 1861," *MdHM* 56, no. 1 (1961): 39–71; Matthew Page Andrews, "The Passage of the Sixth Massachusetts Regiment through Baltimore, April 19, 1861," *MdHM* 14 (1919): 60–73; Hugh L. Bond's reminiscences of Apr. 19, 1861, Harris Papers, box 5; *Republican,* Apr. 19, 1861; *Clipper,* Apr. 20, 1861.

49. George William Brown, *Baltimore and the Nineteenth of April, 1861* (Baltimore, 1887), 63; Radcliffe, *Governor Thomas H. Hicks,* 97

50. Isaac Trimble to Lt. Col. Morris A. Moore, Apr. 30, 1861, and Frasier I. Thomas to Isaac Trimble, May 5, 1861, Isaac Trimble Papers, MdHSSC; *The South,* Apr. 22, 1861; Linda Laswell Crist and Mary Seaton Dix, eds., *The Papers of Jefferson Davis,* vol. 7: *1861* (Baton Rouge, La., 1992), 52, 149; Charles Howard to General Mason, Apr. 30, 1861, letters sent by Baltimore Board of Police.

51. *The South,* Apr. 23, 1861; *Sun,* Apr. 30, 1861; *Baltimore American,* Apr. 22, 1861; Radcliffe, *Governor Thomas H. Hicks,* 67; Henry W. Hoffman to Samuel P. Chase, Apr. 23, 1861, in John Niven et al., eds., *The Salmon P. Chase Papers,* vol. 3: *Correspondence, 1858–March 1863* (Kent, Oh., 1995), 59; Frank K. Howard to *Maryland Times,* Sept. 22, 1861, Lincoln Papers (Lincoln quoted).

52. Brown, *Baltimore and the Nineteenth of April,* 51 (1st quotation); Andrews, "Passage of the Sixth Massachusetts," 70–71; David Creamer, notes and memorandum, 1861, "in Reference to the Riots in Baltimore &c. before the U.S.

Grand Jury," June term, 1861, LC, copy at MdHSSC, 17, 23; Clark, "Baltimore and the Attack on the Sixth Massachusetts Regiment," 50–51 (Kane's telegram), 65.

53. Washington Hands, Civil War notebook, microfilm copy, MdHSL; *Baltimore American*, Apr. 20, 1861; Creamer, notes and memo, 3–5, 18, 22 (1st quotation), 27, 33–34; Charles Howard to Col. Benjamin F. Huger, May 3, 1861, letters sent by Baltimore Board of Police; William Bowly Wilson's reminiscences of Apr. 19, 1861, Civil War file, MdHSSC (2nd quotation).

54. *Republican*, Oct. 29, 1857; Duncan, "The Era of the Civil War," 322–25; George H. Steuart to *National Intelligencer*, Nov. 19, 1860, James Steuart Papers, box 3, MdHSSC; Daniel D. Hartzler, *Marylanders in the Confederacy* (Silver Spring, Md., 1986), 10.

55. Creamer, notes and memo, 12 (quotation), 17; Hartzler, *Marylanders in the Confederacy*, 220; William W. Glenn, *Between North and South: A Maryland Journalist Views the Civil War*, ed. Bayly Ellen Marks and Mark Norton Schatz (Rutherford, N.J., 1976), 21; *Sun*, May 6, 1861.

56. U.S. Secretary of State, *Register of Officers and Agents . . . 1859*, 64. *Baltimore Contested Election, 1859*, 305 (1st quotation); Creamer, notes and memo, 12 (2nd quotation).

57. Edward Spencer to Braddie Spencer, n.d. [1861] (quotation), in possession of George M. Anderson, S.J., Rockville, Maryland.

58. Creamer, notes and memo; *Sun* Apr. 20, May 6, Sept. 6 and 18, Nov. 7, 1861; *Exchange*, June 27, 1861; *Baltimore American*, Apr. 20, May 10, 1861; *The South*, Apr. 22, May 4, 1861; *Republican*, Apr. 20, 1861; *Clipper*, May 10, 1861; magistrates' reports for quarter ending July 1, 1861, reports and returns, RG 41, ser. 1, boxes 81, 82, BCA; Maryland, House of Delegates, *Evidence of the Contested Election in the Case of Ridgely vs. Grason* (Annapolis, Md., 1865), 24, 39, 44, 76. Demographic sources: 1860 U.S. Census, Baltimore City, Pop.; *Woods' Baltimore Directory for 1858-'59; Woods' Baltimore City Directory . . . 1860;* Baltimore City general property tax records. assessor's tax books, 1856–1861, BCA; Kevin Conley Ruffner, *Maryland's Blue and Gray: A Border State's Union and Confederate Junior Officer Corps* (Baton Rouge, La., 1997).

59. Bernstein, *The New York City Draft Riots*, 117–23.

60. Jabez David Pratt to John C. Pratt, Apr. 27, 1861, Civil War file, MdHSSC. Occupation: N = 118; 14 merchants, 15 clerks; place of birth: N = 80; 18 Ireland, 50 Maryland, 6 North; wealth: N = 82.

61. *Baltimore American*, Nov. 5, 1856; "The Baltimore Boys," Confederate Broadsides Collection, Rare Books and Manuscripts, Reynolds Library, Wake Forest University, Winston-Salem, N.C., online at www.wfu.edu/Library/rarebook/broads.html (Mar. 1, 2003).

62. *Sun*, Sept. 12, 1861; Ferrandini and the Lincoln plot of Feb. 1861, vertical file, Enoch Pratt Free Library, Baltimore; *Exchange*, Apr. 20, 1861; Andrews, "Passage of the Sixth Massachusetts," 67.

63. *Poll Book, 24 April 1861* (Baltimore, n.d. [1861]), at the MdHSL; 1860 U.S. Census, Baltimore City, Pop.; 10 percent of voters in each precinct tracked in the census. The average voter owned $8,109. Place of birth: N = 985; Maryland 52 percent, North 8 percent, South 6 percent, Ireland 14 percent, Germany

18 percent, other foreign 2 percent. Like other voters, most of these were married household heads.

64. Ellenberger, "Whigs in the Streets?" 36; Ross Winans & Co., Day Book, May 4, 1861, Ross Winans Papers, MdHSSC; *The South,* Apr. 25, 1861; *Republican,* Apr. 20, 1861; parole of honor for Ross Winans, May 16, 1861, oaths of allegiance, 1861, 1862–63, military records, Middle Department, box 10; Glenn, *Between North and South,* 31–32 (final quotations).

65. Radcliffe, *Governor Thomas H. Hicks,* 15; Isaac F. Nicholson, "The Maryland Guard Battalion, 1860–61," *MdHM* 6, no. 2 (1911): 117–31. Daniel M. Thomas to "My Dear Sister," Apr. 21, 1861 (quotation), Daniel M. Thomas Papers, MdHSSC; clerk to the general auditor, Oct. 2, 1861 (quotation), "Register of Letters Received and Endorsements Sent," July 1861–June 1862, military records, Middle Department, part 1. Maryland Guard register, adjutant general's papers, MSA; Fifty-third Regiment, Maryland Volunteers, Descriptive Book, MdHSSC.

66. Jonas Friedenwald to Aaron Friedenwald, Nov. 11, 1860, Friedenwald Papers, Jewish Historical Society, Baltimore; Alexander Browns & Sons to Edingburgh, Apr. 18, 1861, letters, 1859–1861, Alexander Brown & Sons papers, LC; Catton, "Baltimore Business Community," 18, 22–23, 29–30, 112; Browne, *Baltimore in the Nation,* 171; Baltimore Board of Trade, minute book, May 3, 12, 1853, Baltimore Board of Trade records, MdHSSC; Samuel Wethered to Daniel M. Barringer, Apr. 19, 1861, Daniel M. Barringer Papers, box 3, UNCSC.

67. "John S. Brown," in William J. Kelly, "Shipbuilding at Federal Hill," unnumbered typescript, MdHSSC.

68. Russell, *My Diary North and South,* 71.

69. Moses Friedenwald to Aaron Friedenwald, Nov. 12, 1860, Jonas Friedenwald to Aaron Friedenwald, Nov. 22, 1861, Friedenwald Papers; Kahn, *The Four Seasons of Baltimore's Needle Trades,* 26–27.

70. Thomas Spalding, *The Premier See: A History of the Archdiocese of Baltimore, 1789–1989* (Baltimore, 1989), 175–76; *The South,* Apr. 30, 1861.

71. Charles Howard to George P. Kane, Mar. 14, 1861, letters sent by Baltimore Board of Police; *Sun,* Apr. 20 and 23, May 8 (quotation), 1861.

72. *The South,* Apr. 23, 1861; Creamer, notes and memo, 1, 21 (workers quoted). For Denmead's employees, see Fifty-third Regiment, Descriptive Book; Maryland Guard register, 1861; Washington Hands, Civil War notebook; *Republican,* Apr. 30, 1861; David Keene to George William Brown, Apr. 22, 1861, Civil War papers, RG 56, ser 1., box 1, BCA; Thomas Winans's soup house account book, Winans Papers.

73. *The South,* Apr. 28, 1861; Jabez Pratt to John Pratt, Apr. 27, 1861; Wilson, reminiscences of 1861; McHenry Howard to Francis G. Wood, May 17, 1861, McHenry Howard Papers, MdHSSC.

74. William R. Smith, *The History and Debates of the Convention of the People of Alabama . . . Jan. 7, 1861* (Montgomery, Ala., 1861), 400, 402 (Curry quoted); Charles B. Dew, *Apostles of Disunion: Southern Secession Commissioners and the Causes of the Civil War* (Charlottesville, Va., 2001), 56–57.

75. *Baltimore American,* Apr. 30, May 2, 6, 8, and 13, 1861; *Sun,* May 3, 1861; Horace Abbott & Sons et al., to mayor and city council, May 4, 1861, city council papers, box 119.

76. *Baltimore American,* May 15, 1861; John P. Kennedy, *The Great Drama: An Appeal to Maryland* (Baltimore, 1861), 14–15; Wagandt, *The Mighty Revolution,* 19. Reinhard H. Luthin, "A Discordant Chapter in Lincoln's Administration: The Davis-Blair Controversy," *MdHM* 39, no. 1 (1944): 25–48.

77. Dieter Cunz, *The Maryland Germans: A History* (Princeton, N.J., 1948), 303, 309.

78. Catton, "Baltimore Business Community," 61–62, 64, 66; *Sun,* Jan. 10, Feb. 2, 1861.

79. Catton, "Baltimore Business Community," 86; *Sun,* Sept. 4, 1861; Maryland State Convention, *The Debates of the Constitutional Convention of the State of Maryland . . . 1864* (Annapolis, Md., 1864), 3.

80. Latrobe, *Iron Men and Their Dogs,* 24.

81. *Republican,* Apr. 29, 1861.

82. Schoeberlein, "Baltimore in 1861," 88, 102; Perine Scrapbook, Sept. 11, 1861; Henry W. Davis to Sophie DuPont, Dec. 18, 1861, DuPont Papers, box 42. L. Allison Wilmer, J. H. Jarrett, and George W. E. Wilmer, *History and Roster of Maryland Volunteers, War of 1861–1865,* 2 vols. (Baltimore, 1898), I:29; *Exchange,* Oct. 12, 1860; *Baltimore American,* June 28, 1861; *Sun* Sept. 20, 1861; Ruffner, *Maryland's Blue and Gray,* 251–52, 355; testimony in examination given by General Dix and Captain Brooks, Mount Clare, May 31, 1862, Baltimore and Ohio Railroad papers, file 562, box 36, MdHSSC.

83. Wilmer, Jarrett, and Wilmer, *History and Roster of Maryland Volunteers;* discharges, 1865, bounty applications, 1862–1865, muster rolls, 1862–65, in Civil War records, RG 56, BCA; petition, "Discharged Soldiers and Sailors of the Volunteer Army and Navy of the U.S.," n.d. [1866], city council papers, box 141; Descriptive Book, drafted men and substitutes, Third District, Maryland, Eighth Subdistrict, Fifteenth Ward, provost marshal, military records, RG 110 no. 3712, NARA; Hartzler, *Marylanders in the Confederacy;* Ruffner, *Maryland's Blue and Gray.* N = 453.

84. Maryland Union participation derived from Brugger, *Maryland,* 286; Kennedy, *Population of the United States in 1860,* 212–13. Estimates of free-state service vary from 37 percent to 50 percent; McPherson, *Ordeal by Fire,* 181; Montgomery, *Citizen Worker,* 94; James W. Geary, *We Need Men: The Union Draft in the Civil War* (DeKalb, Ill., 1991), 78–86.

85. Anonymous letter to J. Morrison Harris, June 4, 1861, Harris Papers, box 6; *Baltimore American,* May 22 (quotation), June 14, 1861.

86. William C. Wright, *The Secession Movement in the Middle Atlantic States* (Rutherford, N.J., 1973), 23.

87. *Baltimore American,* June 28, 1861 (1st quotation); John A. Dix to E. A. Townsend, Aug. 19, 1861, letters sent, vol. 27, Middle Department (2nd quotation); W. R. Mortimer to Thomas Hicks, June 2, 1861 (3rd quotation), anonymous letter to Hicks, May 4, 1861, "Old Guard" to Hicks, June 25, 1861, and S. Guiteau to Hicks, Aug. 16, 1861, Hicks Papers; Schoeberlein, "Baltimore in 1861," 111.

88. Charles C. Shriver to Frederick A. Shriver, June 6, 1861, Shriver Family Papers, MdHSSC (1st quotation); *Baltimore American,* Aug. 9, Oct. 5 (2nd quotation), 1861; *Sun,* Sept. 6, 7, 14, and 20, 1861; John A. Dix to E. A. Townsend, Aug. 12, 1861, letters sent, vol. 27.

89. *Baltimore American,* Oct. 3 and 8–10, 1861; *Sun,* Sept. 11 and 23, 1861.

90. *Sun,* Nov. 7 and 8, 1861; Baker, *The Politics of Continuity,* 69; Bernard C. Steiner, *Citizenship and Suffrage in Maryland* (Baltimore, 1895), 41 (quotation).

91. Anna B. Agle and Sidney H. Wanzer, eds., "My Dearest Braddie: Love and War in Maryland, 1860–1861, Part I," *MdHM* 88 (Spring 1993): 73–88, 83 (quotation). Calculations based on Hartzler, *Marylanders in the Confederacy,* 1; Kennedy, *Population of the United States in 1860,* 210–11. Charles Branch Clark, "Politics in Maryland during the Civil War," *MdHM* 38, no. 3 (1943): 249–50.

92. Holt, *The Political Crisis of the 1850s,* 211, 238, 244; Paul D. Escott, *After Secession: Jefferson Davis and the Failure of Confederate Nationalism* (Baton Rouge, La., 1978), 40; Lacy K. Ford Jr., *The Origins of Southern Radicalism* (New York, 1988), 338–40; Carey, *Parties, Slavery, and the Union in Antebellum Georgia,* 166, 240.

Six. Redefining Southernness

1. Parrish, *Frank Blair,* 66, 73; Gerteis, *Civil War St. Louis,* 66; Samuel Simmons to Montgomery Blair, May 21, 1856, correspondence to Montgomery Blair, Blair Family Papers, reel 20, LC.

2. Parrish, *Frank Blair,* 73; Marvin R. Cain, *Lincoln's Attorney General: Edward Bates of Missouri* (Columbia, Mo., 1965), 82

3. Kamphoefner, "St. Louis Germans and the Republican Party," 74, 77; Walter H. Ryle, *Missouri: Union or Secession* (Nashville, Tenn., 1931), 174–75.

4. J. V. Huntington to James S. Green, May 6,1858, St. Louis History collection, MoHS; Bryan M. Clemens to Nelly Clemens, Apr. 3, 1859, Mary C. Clemens Papers, Special Collections, St. Louis University.

5. Gerteis, *Civil War St. Louis,* 74, 77; Walter D. Kamphoefner, *The Westfalians: From Germany to Missouri* (Princeton, N.J., 1987), 112, 118; Kamphoefner, "St. Louis Germans and the Republican Party," 85 (1st quotation); Richard Johnson diary, Nov. 11, 1859, MoHS.

6. Adler, *Yankee Merchants and the Making of the Urban West,* 150, 165; Gleeson, *The Irish in the South,* 138, 151; William B. Faherty, *The St. Louis Irish* (St. Louis, 2001), 70–73; Christopher Phillips, *Damned Yankee: The Life of General Nathaniel Lyon* (Columbia, Mo., 1990), 193.

7. Gerteis, *Civil War St. Louis,* 41, 73–74; Adler, *Yankee Merchants,* 156–57; Ryle, *Missouri,* 186; William E. Nester, *From Mountain Man to Millionaire: The "Bold and Dashing" Life of Robert Campbell* (Columbia, Mo., 1999), 202; Christopher Phillips, "The Radical Crusade: Blair, Lyon, and the Advent of the Civil War in Missouri," *Gateway Heritage* 10 (Spring 1990): 26–27.

8. William E. Parrish, *David Rice Atchison of Missouri: Border Politician* (Columbia, Mo., 1961), 138; Doris David Wallace, "The Political Campaign of 1860 in Missouri," *MoHR* 70 (Jan. 1976): 169; Christopher Phillips, *Missouri's Confederate: Claiborne Fox Jackson* (Columbia, Mo., 2000), 228 (Jackson quoted); Primm, *Lion of the Valley,* 232; William E. Parrish, *A History of Missouri,* vol. 3: *1860 to 1875* (Columbia, Mo., 1973), 2; Rowan, *Germans for a Free Missouri,* 103–4 (2nd quotation), 137 (1st quotation).

9. Thomas T. Gantt to Montgomery Blair, Oct. 29, 1860, correspondence to Montgomery Blair, reel 28.

10. Phillips, *Missouri's Confederate*, 236, 238–39; Gerteis, *Civil War St. Louis*, 81–82, 85, 88.

11. Parrish, *A History of Missouri*, 3–6; Galusha Anderson, *The Story of a Border City during the Civil War* (Boston, 1908), 43–44.

12. Primm, *Lion of the Valley*, 233; Gerteis, *Civil War St. Louis*, 88–90; Anderson, *Border City*, 71; Richard Johnson diary, Feb. 23, 1861, MoHS.

13. Gerteis, *Civil War St. Louis*, 94, 98, 107–8, 114; Parrish, *Frank Blair*, 102; Phillips, *Damned Yankee*, 192, 197.

14. Gerteis, *Civil War St. Louis*, 111–12, 132; Anderson, *Border City*, 116; Primm, *Lion of the Valley*, 242, 245.

15. Robert E. Miller, "'One of the Ruling Class': Thomas Caute Reynolds," *MoHR* 80, no. 4 (1986): 424–25; Robert E. Miller, "Proud Confederate: Thomas Lowndes Snead of Missouri," *MoHR* 79, no. 1 (1985): 169, 175.

16. Primm, *Lion of the Valley*, 233; Gerteis, *Civil War St. Louis*, 86; Joseph N. McDowell to editor, *Herald*, n.d. [1860], W. R. Babcock scrapbook, Missouri Militia Collection, MoHS.

17. Sarah Jane Full Hill, *Mrs. Hill's Journal: Civil War Reminiscences* (Chicago, 1980), 21; J. Crousher to unnamed friend, May 15, 1861, Camp Jackson Collection, MoHS; Anderson, *Border City*, 147.

18. Ochs, *A Black Patriot and a White Priest*, 107–8; *New Orleans Daily Crescent* Apr. 24, 1858.

19. Sacher, "'A Perfect War,'" vol. 2, 383–84; Thomas R. Landry, "The Political Career of Robert C. Wickliffe," *LHQ* 25, no. 3 (1942): 675; governor's message, Jan. 19, 1857, in Louisiana Legislature, *Official Journal of the House of Representatives of the State of Louisiana. Session of 1857* (Baton Rouge, La., 1857), 8; Thomas K. Wharton's private journal, June 6, 1858, LSU; Diket, *Senator John Slidell*, 179.

20. James K. Greer, "Louisiana Politics, 1845–1861, Chapter XIII," *LHQ* 13, no. 3 (1930): 447, 449 (Soule quoted); Sacher, "'A Perfect War,' vol. II," 406–8; Diket, *Senator John Slidell*, 113; Soule, *The Know-Nothing Party in New Orleans*, 108; New Orleans *Daily Crescent* Apr. 9, 1858; Works Progress Administration, *Administrations of the Mayors of New Orleans, 1803–1936* (New Orleans, 1940), 106, 111; Louisiana Legislature, *Official Journal of the House of Representatives of the State of Louisiana: Session of 1860* (Baton Rouge, La., 1860), 16.

21. Clark, "The New Orleans German Colony in the Civil War," 996; John F. Nau, *The German People of New Orleans: 1850–1890* (London, 1958), 32; New Orleans, *Daily Picayune* Nov. 7, 1859.

22. *Mayors of New Orleans*, 106–7; Soule, *The Know-Nothing Party in New Orleans*, 111–13; Wharton's journal, July 7, 1858, June 7, 1859, May 30, 1860 (quotation).

23. Mary Lilla McClure, "The Elections of 1860 in Louisiana," *LHQ* 9, no. 4 (1926): 648 (platform quoted), 691; Mary Lilla McClure, "Political Events of the Year 1860," in *Readings in Louisiana Politics*, ed. Mark T. Carleton, Perry H. Howard, and Joseph B. Parker (Baton Rouge, La., 1975), 208; Owen, "The Pres-

idential Elections of 1852, 1856, and 1860 in Louisiana," 95, 102, 125–26, 131; Greer, "Louisiana Politics, XIII," 479 (Slidell quoted).

24. Greer, "Louisiana Politics, XIII," 473; McClure, "The Elections of 1860," 661 (1st quotation), 664 (2nd quotation); Willie M. Caskey, *Secession and Restoration of Louisiana* (1938; rpt., New York, 1970), 6 (3rd quotation).

25. Greer, "Louisiana Politics, XIII," 477.

26. Owen "Elections of 1852, 1856, and 1860," 128; McClure, "Political Events of the Year 1860," 212 (1st quotation); McClure, "Elections of 1860," 668 (3rd quotation); Caskey, *Secession and Restoration*, 16, 20, 22, 23 (2nd quotation); Lane Carter Kendall, "The Interregnum in Louisiana . . . Ch. I," *LHQ* 16, no. 2 (1933): 184.

27. Caskey, *Secession and Restoration*, 22; Joseph G. Tregle Jr., "Thomas J. Durant, Utopian Socialism, and the Failure of Presidential Reconstruction in Louisiana," *Journal of Southern History* 45, no. 4 (1979): 493; Kendall, "Interregnum in Louisiana, I," 195 (*Picayune* quoted), 202–3; Charles B. Dew, "Who Won the Secession Election in Louisiana?" in *Readings in Louisiana Politics*, 214–26, 216–17.

28. Charles P. Roland, "Louisiana and Secession," *Louisiana History* 19 (Fall 1978): 389.

29. Charles B. Dew, "The Long Lost Returns: The Candidates and Their Totals in Louisiana's Secession Election," *Louisiana History* 10 (Winter 1959): 358–69. Figures for the citywide vote combined results for senate races in Orleans Parish, Left Bank and Right Bank; secessionists polled 4,413 votes, Cooperationists, 4,313; New Orleans *Bee*, Jan. 9, 1861, quoted in Kendall, "Interregnum in Louisiana, I," 208.

30. Lane C. Kendall, "The Interregnum in Louisiana in 1861 . . . Chapter II," *LHQ* 16, no. 3 (1933): 374, 398 (Moore quoted); John D. Winters, *The Civil War in Louisiana* (Baton Rouge, La., 1963), 10–12.

31. Dew, "Who Won Louisiana's Secession Election?" 220; McClure, "The Elections of 1860 in Louisiana," 696, 698–99; Kendall, "Interregnum in Louisiana, II," 397; Roger W. Shugg, "A Suppressed Co-Operationist Protest against Secession," *LHQ* 19, no. 1 (1936): 199–203; Ralph A. Wooster, *The Secession Conventions of the South* (Princeton, N.J., 1962), 110.

32. Rousey, *Policing the Southern City*, 103–4; Emily Hazen Reed, *The Life of A. P. Dostie: Or, the Conflict in New Orleans* (New York, 1868), 18, 24 (quotation); Peyton McCrary, *Abraham Lincoln and Reconstruction: The Louisiana Experiment* (Princeton, N.J., 1978), 76.

33. McCrary, *Abraham Lincoln and Reconstruction*, 96; Russell, *My Diary North and South*, 166.

34. Mrs. Edwin X. DeVerges, "Honorable John T. Monroe—the Confederate Mayor of New Orleans," *LHQ* 34, no. 1 (1951): 25; Neihaus, *The Irish in New Orleans*, 157; Reed, *Life of A. P. Dostie*, 37; State vs. Lucien V. Adams, July 5, 1856, case no. 12277, First District Court records, NOPL.

35. Thomas K. Wharton diary, Feb. 21 and Mar. 19, 1861.

36. Kendall, "Interregnum in Louisiana in 1861, II," 404–5.

37. *Correspondence between the Mayor and Federal Authorities Relative to the Occupation of the City of New Orleans, Together with the Proceedings of*

the Common Council (New Orleans, 1862), 7; Heald, "History of the New Orleans Typographical Union"; Billy H. Wyche, "The Union Defends the Confederacy: The Fighting Printers of New Orleans," *Louisiana History* 35 (Summer 1994): 282.

38. Feb. 4 (quotation), Mar. 3, Sept. 30, 1862, minute book, American Hook and Ladder Fire Co. No. 2, New Orleans Fire Companies Collection, TUL.

39. Russell, *My Diary North and South*, 171; Gerard M. Capers, *Occupied City: New Orleans under the Federals, 1862–1865* (Lexington, Ky., 1965), 80; Rousey, *Policing the Southern City*, 105; David G. Surdham, "Union Military Superiority and New Orleans's Economic Value to the Confederacy," *Louisiana History* 38 (Fall 1997): 396, 399.

40. William W. Chenault and Robert C. Reinders, "The Northern Born Community of New Orleans in the 1850s," *Journal of American History* 51 (Sept. 1964): 245; Ted Tunnell, *Crucible of Reconstruction: War, Radicalism, and Race in Louisiana, 1862–1877* (Baton Rouge, La., 1984), 69–70; Vaughan Baker, "Michael Hahn: Steady Patriot," *Louisiana History* 13 (Summer 1972): 231; Reed, *Life of A. P. Dostie*, 28; Tregle, "Thomas J. Durant," 493–94; James G. Hollandsworth Jr., *The Louisiana Native Guards: The Black Military Experienced during the Civil War* (Baton Rouge, La., 1995), 2, 6–7; Nau, *The German People of New Orleans*, 38; Clark, "The New Orleans German Colony in the Civil War," 998; Neihaus, *The Irish in New Orleans*, 162.

41. Winters, *The Civil War in Louisiana*, 84, 89, 97, 100; Chester G. Hearn, *The Capture of New Orleans, 1862* (Baton Rouge, La., 1995), 186, 252; Shugg, *Origins of Class Struggle in Louisiana*, 171.

42. McCrary, *Abraham Lincoln and Reconstruction*, 75; David G. Farragut to John T. Monroe, Apr. 26, 1862, in *Correspondence between the Mayor and Federal Authorities . . . of New Orleans*, 11; Richard N. Current, *Lincoln's Loyalists: Union Soldiers from the Confederacy* (Boston, 1992), 93; Tunnell, *Crucible of Reconstruction*, 9–10; Caskey, *Secession and Restoration*, 59, 61–62.

43. McCrary, *Abraham Lincoln and Reconstruction*, 95, 97–99; *Constitution of the Union League of Louisiana* (n.p., n.d.), 6–7, copy at TUL.

44. Caskey, *Secession and Restoration*, 46–47 (Butler quoted); Shugg, *Origins of Class Struggle in Louisiana*, 186; C. P. Weaver, ed., *Thank God My Regiment an African One: The Civil War Diary of Colonel Nathan W. Daniels* (Baton Rouge, La., 1998), 134; *Grand Mass Meeting of the Working Men's National Union League, Held in New Orleans . . . July 11th, 1863* (n.p., n.d. [1863]), copy at NOPL; Arnesen, *Waterfront Workers of New Orleans*, 4–5.

45. Tunnell, *Crucible of Reconstruction*, 20, 27, 56, 60–61.

46. McCrary, *Abraham Lincoln and Reconstruction*, 100–101; Joseph G. Dawson III, *Army Generals and Reconstruction: Louisiana, 1862–1877* (Baton Rouge, La., 1982), 15.

47. Haunton, "Savannah in the 1850s," 209, 211, 227, 232–33; Crowson, "Southern Port City Politics," 232, 240, 243; Shoemaker, "Strangers and Citizens, 360–61, 364; Carey, *Parties, Slavery, and the Union in Antebellum Georgia*, 230 (quotation).

48. Earl W. Fornell, "The Civil War Comes to Savannah," *Georgia Historical Quarterly* 43, no. 3 (1959): 257.

49. Amos, *Cotton City,* 229, 235–36, 238; J. Mills Thornton III, *Politics and Power in a Slave Society: Alabama, 1800–1860* (Baton Rouge, La., 1978), 420; Thompson, "Southern Rights and Nativism," 141.

50. Naragon, "Ballots, Bullets, and Blood," 179, 184–86, 201, 203–4, 260, 273, 275, 284; Gregg D. Kimball, *American City, Southern Place: A Cultural History of Antebellum Richmond* (Athens, Ga., 2000), 13–14, 223, 228.

51. Naragon, "Ballots, Bullets, and Blood," 258, 307; Kimball, *American City, Southern Place,* 232 (quotation); Crofts, *Reluctant Confederates,* 315; Emory M. Thomas, *The Confederate State of Richmond: A Biography of the Capital* (Austin, Tex., 1971), 9.

52. Crofts, "Late Antebellum Virginia Reconsidered," 274; Kimball, *American City, Southern Place,* 185, 229.

53. Naragon, "Bullets, Ballots, and Blood," 169–70, 190, 210, 220, 258, 273–74, 276.

54. Burckin, "The Formation and Growth of an Urban Middle Class," 432–33, 530–31, 533 (quotation).

55. Ibid., 507, 524.

56. Ibid., 537; John Alan Boyd, "Neutrality and Peace: Kentucky and the Secession Crisis of 1861" (Ph.D. diss., University of Kentucky, 1999); Lowell H. Harrison and James C. Klotter, *A New History of Kentucky* (Lexington, Ky., 1997), 124, 189–90; James E. Copeland, "Where Were the Kentucky Unionists and Secessionists?" *Register of the Kentucky Historical Society* 71 (Oct. 1973): 358; Charles K. Mesmer, "Louisville and the Confederate Invasion of 1862," *Register of the Kentucky Historical Society* 55 (Oct. 1957): 302–3.

57. Deusner, "The Know-Nothing Riots in Louisville," 147; William G. O'Toole Jr., and Charles E. Aebersold, "Louisville's Bloody Monday Riots from a German Perspective," *Filson Club Quarterly* 70 (Oct. 1996): 425.

58. Daniel E. Sutherland, "The Absence of Violence: Confederates and Unionists in Culpeper County, Virginia," in *Guerillas, Unionists, and Violence on the Confederate Homefront* ed. Daniel E. Sutherland (Fayetteville, Ark., 1999), 79–81, 87; Thomas G. Dyer, *Secret Yankees: The Union Circle in Confederate Atlanta* (Baltimore, 1999), 135; William Warren Rogers Jr., *Confederate Homefront: Montgomery during the Civil War* (Tuscaloosa, 1999), 104; William Blair, *Virginia's Private War: Feeding Body and Soul in the Confederacy, 1861–1865* (New York, 1998), 75, 80, 147; Current, *Lincoln's Loyalists,* 136.

59. Martin Crawford, "The Dynamics of Mountain Unionism: Federal Volunteers of Ashe County, North Carolina," in *The Civil War in Appalachia,* ed. Kenneth W. Noe and Shannon H. Wilson (Knoxville, Tenn., 1997), 63–64; Robert Tracy McKenzie, "Prudent Silence and Strict Neutrality: The Parameters of Unionism in Parson Brownlow's Knoxville, 1860–1863," in *Enemies of the Country: New Perspectives on Unionists in the Civil War South,* ed. John C. Inscoe and Robert C. Kenzer (Athens, Ga., 2001), 76; Jonathan D. Sarris, "'Shot for Being Bushwackers': Guerilla War and Extralegal Violence in a North Georgia Community, 1862–65," in *Guerillas, Unionists, and Violence,* 33–37; Stephen V. Ash, *When the Yankees Came: Conflict and Chaos in the Occupied South, 1861–1865* (Chapel Hill, N.C., 1995), 124–27; Wayne Durrill, *War of Another Kind: A Southern Community in the Great Rebellion* (New York, 1990); Michael Fellman,

Inside War: The Guerilla Conflict in Missouri during the Civil War (New York, 1989), chapter 2 and p. 232; Altina L. Waller *Feud: Hatfields, McCoys, and Social Change in Appalachia, 1860–1900* (Chapel Hill, N.C., 1988), 31; Phillip Shaw Paludan, *Victims: A True Story of the Civil War* (Knoxville, Tenn., 1981), 30; Richard O. Curry, *A House Divided: A Study of Statehood Politics and the Copperhead Movement in West Virginia* (Pittsburgh, 1964), 46, 50.

60. John C. Inscoe and Gordon B. McKinney, *The Heart of Confederate Appalachia: Western North Carolina in the Civil War* (Chapel Hill, N.C., 2000), 21–22, 57–59, 84 (quotation), 85; Martin Crawford, *Ashe County's Civil War: Community and Society in the Appalachian South* (Charlottesville, Va., 2001), 20–23.

61. Robert Tracy McKenzie, "Oh! Ours Is a Deplorable Condition: The Economic Impact of the Civil War in Upper East Tennessee," in *The Civil War in Appalachia*, 200, 202; Noel C. Fisher, *War at Every Door: Partisan Politics and Guerilla Violence in East Tennessee, 1860–1869* (Chapel Hill, N.C., 1997), 9–10, 18; Peter Wallenstein, "'Helping to Save the Union': The Social Origins, Wartime Experiences, and Military Impact of White Union Troops from East Tennessee," in *The Civil War in Appalachia*, 18; W. Todd Groce, "The Social Origins of East Tennessee's Confederate Leadership," in *The Civil War in Appalachia*, 34–35, 37–38, 41.

62. Fisher, *War at Every Door*, 11, 14, 16, 44; Crofts, *Reluctant Confederates*, 62–63, 182, 185–87; Crawford, *Ashe County's Civil War*, 22–24, 53; Inscoe and McKinney, *The Heart of Confederate Appalachia*, 87 (quotation).

63. Fisher, *War at Every Door*, 158–159; Fellman, *Inside War*, 232, 263; Carl H. Moneyhon, *The Impact of the Civil War and Reconstruction on Arkansas: Persistence in the Midst of Ruin* (Baton Rouge, La., 1994), 132.

64. Daniel W. Crofts, *Old Southampton: Politics and Society in a Virginia County, 1834–1869* (Charlottesville, Va., 1992), 126; Charles C. Bolton, *Poor Whites of the Antebellum South: Tenants and Laborers in Central North Carolina and Northeast Mississippi* (Durham, N.C., 1994), 113, 150, 156–57, 161, 164, 179; Victoria E. Bynum, *The Free State of Jones: Mississippi's Longest Civil War* (Chapel Hill, N.C., 2001), 98–101, 104; Samuel C. Hyde Jr., "Backcountry Justice in the Piney-Woods South," in *Plain Folk of the South Revisited*, ed. Samuel C. Hyde (Baton Rouge, La., 1997), 242–43. In a rare autobiography by a rural white laborer, brawling and tavern life have minimal connections to politics; see Charles C. Bolton and Scott P. Culclasure, eds., *The Confessions of Edward Isham: A Poor White Life of the Old South* (Athens, Ga., 1998), 6.

65. *Officers of the Corporation, 1858*; U.S. Secretary of State, *Register of the Officers and Agents . . . 1861*, 65; Wilmer, Jarrett, and Wilmer, *History and Roster of Maryland Volunteers*, 798; Scharf, *History of Baltimore City and County*, 179–80; *Sun*, Sept. 14, 1856, Jan 7, 1861, Oct. 8, 1864, Oct. 12, 1865; *Gazette*, Oct. 11, 1866; James Caulk, widow's applications, certificates nos. 323828c and 570493, and minor's application, certificate no. 767516, U.S. Army pension records, NARA.

Index